WE SHALL OVERCOME

is an eye-witness report of the racial troubles attending the integration of certain Southern universities during the fateful 1962-1963 period—a time that may go down in history as the crucial year of the civil rights revolution in the United States. Told with crisp urgency by an on-the-spot observer, the volume covers not only the happenings at the Universities of Mississippi and Alabama, but also such closely associated events as the death of a Freedom Walker, an interview with Attorney General Kennedy, and the riots in Jackson and Birmingham.

Michael Dorman was for five years with the Long Island **Newsday**. A seasoned reporter who has won numerous journalistic awards, he has also been associated with the Scripps-Howard chain, **The New York Times** and **The Wall Street Journal**.

WE SHALL OVERCOME

BY MICHAEL DORMAN

A REPORTER'S EYE-WITNESS
ACCOUNT OF THE YEAR OF
RACIAL STRIFE AND TRIUMPH

 A LAUREL EDITION

Published by
DELL PUBLISHING CO., INC.
750 Third Avenue
New York, N.Y. 10017

Copyright © 1964
by Michael Dorman
Laurel ® TM 674623,
Dell Publishing Co., Inc.

Reprinted by arrangement
with The Delacorte Press,
New York

DEDICATION: To Jeanne,
who epitomizes for me
the best that can
come out of the South.

First printing—
April, 1965

Printed in U.S.A.

CONTENTS

Foreword

This is the story of a crucial year in the United States' civil rights revolution of the 1960s. It was written in an attempt to give new depth and perspective to a chapter in history that has all too often been the victim of distortion—intentional and unintentional. In this era of push-button electronic journalism, there is a tendency to skim the surface of the news, condense it, oversimplify it. The result frequently is mass delusion and self-hypnosis, particularly on a subject as volatile as civil rights.

I chose to write this book because I spent a good part of the year between September, 1962, and August, 1963, covering the civil rights revolution in the South and North for *Newsday*, a Long Island newspaper. During certain periods, I had an unusual, even unique vantage point that permitted me to probe beneath the surface of the momentary crises.

The sights, sounds and sensations of a revolution are diverse, ranging from the spiritual to the violent and obscene. The civil rights revolution is no exception.

This crucial year began for me in Oxford, Mississippi, to the chants of University of Mississippi students:

> *"Hotty totty, gosh a'mighty*
> *Who in the hell are we?*
> *Hey!*
> *Flim, flam; bim, bam.*
> *Old Miss, by damn!"*

In the space of a few hours, the chants were replaced by the sound of Molotov cocktails being hurled at United

States marshals. Then came the whoomp-whoomp-whoomp of tear-gas guns, the splat-splat-splat of rifle fire, the crack-crack-crack of pistols. Through a long, bloody night, I watched the most serious conflict between the federal government and a state's people since the Civil War unfold on the green, velvet-like lawns of the Ole Miss campus.

Months later, the sights, sounds and sensations would be far different in Birmingham, Alabama. They would be symbolized by several thousand Negroes linking arms in a church, swaying from side to side and singing:

> *"We shall overcome; we shall overcome;*
> *We shall overcome—someday.*
> *Oh, deep in my heart, I do believe*
> *We shall overcome—someday."*

This would be followed by the boom of dynamite bombs, aimed at terrorizing a long-oppressed people who had finally decided the time had come for "freedom now."

In Jackson, Mississippi, the Negroes would sing:

> *"They say in Hinds County,*
> *'No neutrals have we met.*
> *You're either for the Freedom Ride*
> *Or you'll Tom for Ross Barnett.'*
> *Oh, which side are you on, boy?*
> *Which side are you on?*
> *Which side are you on, boy?*
> *Which side are you on?"*

This would be followed by the bark of an assassin's high-powered rifle. A single bullet would still the heart of Mississippi's most responsible civil rights leader. And his followers' voices would turn from songs to defiant screams: "We want the killer! We want the killer! We want the killer!"

In New York City, whites and Negroes would walk the picket lines on behalf of equal job opportunities. I would hear them sing:

> *"We shall not, we shall not be moved.*
> *We shall not, we shall not be moved.*

> *Just like a tree that's planted by the water,*
> *We shall not be moved."*

I would watch them fall deliberately in front of trucks to block deliveries of building supplies to projects where Negroes were being denied access to jobs. They would chain themselves to the tops of giant cranes. And, just as in the South, they would be carted off to jail.

The civil rights revolution, however, was more complicated than mere singing, violence and defiance. There was also statesmanship and demagoguery, hatred and love, despair and hope.

I have tried to capture the flavor of what may, a hundred years from now, be considered the most decisive year of our generation. The reader will find my opinions expressed frequently in this book. I make no pretense of being unbiased. But I do assert that these were not preconceived opinions. They were formed while watching this revolution unfold.

1 Riot at Ole Miss

1

Just as it was inevitable that Mississippi should be the scene of the most explosive clash between the federal government and a state since the Civil War, it was hardly surprising that the crisis should revolve around a slightly-built, soft-spoken Negro named James Howard Meredith.

Meredith seemed preordained for this role in the civil rights revolution of the 1960s. For, since boyhood, his temperament and experiences had led him inexorably into the struggle to crack Mississippi's segregation barriers.

Meredith was born on June 25, 1933, on an 84-acre cotton and corn farm near Kosciusko, in north central Mississippi's Attala County. The farm had been scratched out of the rocky bottom land by his father, Moses (Cap) Meredith, the son of a slave. The area around Kosciusko is not typical of Mississippi. Many Negroes, rather than working for whites, own their own farms. The area is considered more progressive than some other parts of the state. While Negroes elsewhere in Mississippi still are fighting for the ballot, Moses Meredith and other Attala County Negroes have been voting for years.

James Meredith, called "J. H." by his family, was one of ten children born to Moses Meredith and his wife, Roxie. "I was just a poor man and I never got beyond the fourth grade," says Moses Meredith. But he was bent on seeing that his children did better. All ten were graduated from high school and seven of them went on to college.

When James was a boy, he learned to plow and did chores in the fields before and after school. He also caught crickets and grasshoppers to sell as bait to white fishermen.

Every week day, he walked four miles each way to Tipton High School for Negroes. "He was one of the best students, always reading," his father recalls.

Meredith had strong feelings on racial questions, even as a small boy. In Kosciusko, one wealthy white man was fond of passing out nickels and dimes on the streets to Negro children. Meredith considered this degrading to the Negroes. He always refused the money.

When he was 12, Meredith paid a visit to the office of a white physician. On the office wall was a picture of the doctor, in his college days, wearing an Ole Miss football uniform. Meredith determined then and there that he would one day attend Ole Miss.

Constant exposure to Jim Crow restrictions merely spurred his ambition. At 15, he made a trip by car to Detroit with his family to visit relatives. When his father drove the remainder of the family back to Mississippi, Meredith and his brother stayed behind for a short period. They eventually traveled home by train. "The train wasn't segregated when we left Detroit," Meredith recalls. "But, when we got to Memphis, the conductor told my brother and me we had to go to another car. I cried all the way home. And, in a way, I have cried ever since."

A year after this experience, Meredith left Kosciusko to complete his last year of high school in St. Petersburg Florida. He had a sister and an uncle living in St. Petersburg, and felt he could get a better education there than in Mississippi. He was graduated from high school in June, 1951. He did not feel ready to begin college immediately, so he enlisted in the Air Force in July. He says it was well known among Negroes that they received better treatment in the Air Force than in other branches of service.

Meredith considers his Air Force days among the most significant in molding his future life. He served only in integrated outfits, and learned for the first time what it was like to live on relatively equal footing with whites. In 1953, while in service, he enrolled in the first of a series of college extension courses. He earned mostly Bs and a few As. Later, he was to receive 57 quarter-hours of credit toward a college degree for this work.

Meredith was scheduled to complete his first Air Force

hitch in 1955, but again decided that he was not ready to enter college on a full-time basis. He reenlisted. A year later, he married a girl he had met while stationed in Gary, Indiana. His wife, Mary June, had learned during their courtship of his long-range plan to try to enroll at Ole Miss. She concurred enthusiastically and encouraged him from the start.

Between 1957 and 1960, Meredith underwent an extensive maturing process. He was stationed in Japan during that period. And, like many another American Negro who has lived in Japan temporarily, he was able for the first time almost to forget the matter of his race. He and his wife, who accompanied him to Japan and worked as a civil service employee, were treated as the complete equals of whites and Orientals. It was a heady experience. And it made Meredith more determined than ever to try to improve the lot of the Negro back home in Mississippi.

In July, 1960, Meredith was discharged from the Air Force. He had risen to the rank of staff sergeant. By the end of July, he was back in Kosciusko. Much had happened in the field of race relations since his enlistment nine years earlier. In 1954, the Supreme Court had issued its historic decision declaring that racially segregated schools were unconstitutional. Most Southern states had moved, with varying degrees of reluctance, to begin desegregating their schools.

But not Mississippi. It had become the symbol of all-out defiance of the desegregation doctrine. It housed the national headquarters of the white-supremacist Citizens Councils, which had been given official sanction and operating funds by the state government. And it had been the site of the two most infamous racial lynchings of the decade—the 1955 "wolf whistle" murder of Emmet Till, a 14-year-old Negro boy, and the 1959 murder of Mack Charles Parker, a 23-year-old Negro who was dragged from a jail and shot after being accused of raping a white woman. In both cases, although the identity of the slayers was known, the lynchings went unpunished.

In this atmosphere, it took a rare brand of courage for a Negro to assert his right to an education at the segregated University of Mississippi. James Meredith has that brand of courage. He does not parade it. He is not a cocky man. But there is an air of calm determination about him. He seems to be guided by an almost mystical urge. From the start, he said that if he failed to accomplish his goal he might as well not have existed.

Meredith's surface appearance is not the kind that stands out in a crowd. He is a small man, only five feet six inches and 135 pounds. He has delicate features, a pencil-line mustache and large brown eyes. He dresses neatly, mostly in dark suits. His voice is soft. His laugh is barely audible. But when he speaks of the Negro's struggle for equal rights, his inner strength comes through. He gestures emphatically with his hands. A firm cast enters his eyes. A note of resolve enters his voice.

Along with this resolve, Meredith has a sense of restraint. He does not rush headlong into action without thinking through the consequences. Thus, he carefully mapped his campaign for entry to the University of Mississippi after his discharge from the Air Force. While doing so, he entered Jackson State College, a Negro school in Mississippi's capital city of Jackson. He quickly met other Negroes who shared his conviction that someone had to try to crack the racial barrier at Ole Miss. They encouraged him to be the one. As he neared the end of his first semester at Jackson State, he decided he was ready to make his historic move.

Meredith's assault on the Ole Miss segregation policy began officially with a seemingly routine exchange of correspondence. On January 25, 1961, he sent a typewritten request to the Ole Miss registrar's office: "Please send me an application for admission to your school. Also, I would like to have a copy of your catalogue and any other information that might be helpful to me. Thank you."

At this juncture Meredith carefully made no mention of the fact that he was a Negro. His return address—a Jackson apartment where he and his wife were living with their infant son, James, Jr.—gave no indication that he was a student at a Negro college.

Ole Miss received his letter on January 26. It was answered the same day by Registrar Robert B. Ellis. "We are very pleased to know of your interest in becoming a member of our student body," Ellis wrote. "The enclosed forms and instructions will enable you to file a formal application for admission. A copy of our general information bulletin, mailed separately, will provide you with detailed information. Should you desire additional information or if we can be of further help to you in making your enrollment plans, please let us know."

Meredith was not lulled by the apparent cordiality of Ellis' letter. He anticipated that difficulties would arise when Ole Miss officials learned that he was a Negro. And, having studied the history of similar cases in other Southern states, he expected that he would have to go to court to press his demand for admission. He was unable to finance a court fight on his own. So he went to see Medgar Evers, the Mississippi field secretary of the National Association for the Advancement of Colored People, to ask for legal aid. Evers suggested that Meredith write Thurgood Marshall, then chief counsel of the NAACP Legal Defense and Educational Fund in New York. (Marshall is now a judge of the United States Circuit Court of Appeals in New York.)

On January 29, Meredith wrote Marshall a long letter asking for legal help:

he various state agencies here in the state which are against my gaining entrance into the school. I have always been a 'conscientious objector' to my 'oppressed status' as long as I can remember. My long-preserved ambition has been to break the monopoly on rights and privileges held by the whites of Mississippi. . . . I am making this move in, what I consider, the interest of and for the benefit of: (1) my country, (2) my race, (3) my family, and (4) myself. I am familiar with the probable difficulties involved in such a move as I am undertaking and I am fully prepared to pursue it all the way to a degree from the University of Mississippi.

Marshall turned the matter over to the Legal Defense Fund's associate counsel, Mrs. Constance Baker Motley, like Marshall a brilliant civil rights lawyer. But, at this point, there was nothing for Mrs. Motley to do on the case.

Meredith had not yet formally submitted his application for admission to Ole Miss.

Meredith did so on January 31. At the same time, in a letter to Registrar Ellis, he disclosed that he was a Negro. Meredith wrote Ellis:

I am very pleased with your letter that accompanied the application forms you recently sent to me. I sincerely hope that your attitude toward me as a potential member of your student body reflects the attitude of the school, and that it will not change upon learning that I am not a white applicant.

I am an American-Mississippi-Negro citizen. With all of the occurring events regarding changes in our educational system taking place in our country in this new age, I feel certain that this application does not come as a surprise to you. I certainly hope that this matter will be handled in a manner that will be complimentary to the University and to the State of Mississippi. Of course, I am the one that will, no doubt, suffer the greatest consequences of this event. Therefore, I am very hopeful that the complications will be as few as possible.

Meredith noted in his letter that the application forms had called for character references from six Ole Miss alumni. "I will not be able to furnish you with the names of six university alumni because I am a Negro and all graduates of the school are white," he wrote. "Further, I do not know any graduate personally. However, as a substitute for this requirement, I am submitting certificates regarding my moral character from Negro citizens of my state." He asked Ellis for immediate action on his application, since registration for a new Ole Miss semester was to begin on February 6. Meredith signed his letter, "Very Hopefully Yours, J. H. Meredith, Applicant."

But, on February 4, Ellis wired Meredith that enrollment applications received after January 25 were not being considered by the university for the semester beginning February 6. On February 20, Meredith told Ellis in a letter that he would like his application considered a continuing one for the summer session beginning June 8. He asked Ellis to notify him whether the university had received all his transcripts necessary to make the application complete. He also requested immediate action on the application.

Meredith received no reply to his February 20 letter. He wrote several more letters to Ellis, inquiring about the status of his application, but again received no answers. Finally, on May 25, Ellis wrote him: "I regret to inform you, in answer to your recent letters, that your application for admission must be denied. The university cannot recognize the transfer of credits from the institution which you are now attending, since it is not a member of the Southern Association of Colleges and Secondary Schools. Our policy permits the transfer of credits only from member institutions of regional associations. Furthermore, students may not be accepted by the university from those institutions whose programs are not recognized. . . ."

The university thus was taking the position that it could not recognize the academic standing of one of its own sister schools. Jackson State College, like Ole Miss, is administered by the Mississippi Board of Trustees of State Institutions of Higher Learning. Ole Miss was contending, nonetheless, that Jackson State students could not qualify as transfer students. (Jackson State has since become an accredited member of the Southern Association of Colleges and Secondary Schools.)

But Ole Miss did not rely only on the issue of Jackson State's lack of accreditation in rejecting Meredith's application. Ellis' letter to Meredith also said: "As I am sure you realize, your application does not meet other requirements for admission. Your letters of recommendation are not sufficient for either a resident [of Mississippi] or a nonresident applicant. I see no need for mentioning any further deficiencies. . . ."

At this point, having been formally rejected by Ole Miss, Meredith asked the NAACP to follow up on his earlier request for legal aid. By this time, Mrs. Constance Motley had already interviewed Meredith during a visit to Jackson and been impressed by him. "I thought he was a good applicant," Mrs. Motley recalls. "He seemed very sincere. This was something he had pondered for a long time, and he was prepared for a long period of tension."

Mrs. Motley lost no time in taking action. On May 31, she filed suit on Meredith's behalf in U. S. District Court in Jackson, naming university officials and members of the Board of Trustees of State Institutions of Higher Learning as defendants. The suit charged that the reasons given by the university for rejecting Meredith were mere subterfuges, and that he actually was being refused admission "solely because of his race." It demanded a preliminary injunction, to be followed by a permanent injunction, each barring Ole Miss from refusing to admit Meredith on racial grounds.

James Meredith got a taste of the slowness with which the wheels of justice grind during the period immediately following filing of his suit. Six months dragged by as the opposing sides engaged in preliminary skirmishing. The defendants filed an answer to the suit, arguing that Meredith "was not seeking admission to the University of Mississippi in good faith for the purpose of securing an education and that . . . he did not have and would not have the proper respect for an education." Documents were subpoenaed. Depositions were taken from witnesses.

On December 12, 1961, after conducting a brief hearing, U. S. District Judge Sidney C. Mize rejected Meredith's request for a preliminary injunction. Exactly a month later, the U. S. Fifth Circuit Court of Appeals in New Orleans upheld Mize's ruling, but suggested a full trial of the case on its merits to decide whether a permanent injunction should be issued.

The full-scale trial began before Mize in Jackson on January 17, 1962. Representing Meredith were Mrs. Motley, Derrick A. Bell, Jr., also from the NAACP Legal Defense and Educational Fund in New York, and R. Jess Brown of Vicksburg, Mississippi. All three are Negroes. Representing the defendants were Mississippi Attorney General Joe T. Patterson, Assistant Attorneys General Dugas Shands and Edward L. Cates and Special Assistant Attorneys General Charles Clark and Peter M. Stockett, Jr.

The trial lasted 11 days. Meredith's attorneys contended that his race had been discussed at meetings of university officials and members of the Board of Trustees of State

Institutions of Higher Learning. They argued that this indicated Meredith had been denied admission because of his race. But a number of university officials and trustees testified that Meredith's race had never been discussed at official meetings. The defendants insisted that Meredith had been denied admission for reasons other than the fact that he was a Negro. Their attorneys made strong issue of an Air Force psychiatrist's report that said Meredith had suffered occasionally from a nervous stomach and that "his symptoms are intensified whenever there is a heightened tempo in the racial problems in the United States and Africa." They contended this ailment would make Meredith a poor candidate for admission to Ole Miss.

On February 5, nine days after the end of the trial, Judge Mize ruled that Meredith's attorneys had failed to prove he was denied admission because of his race. Mize dismissed Meredith's suit. An appeal was filed immediately with the Fifth Circuit Court of Appeals in New Orleans. The appeal was heard by Judges John Minor Wisdom and John R. Brown of the Fifth Circuit Court of Appeals and by U. S. District Judge Dozier DeVane. (It is common practice for a federal district judge to sit with appellate judges on a panel considering an appeal.)

On June 25, in a 2-1 decision, the court ordered the issuance of an injunction forcing Ole Miss to admit Meredith. The majority opinion, written by Judge Wisdom and concurred in by Judge Brown, held that Meredith's "application for transfer to the University of Mississippi was turned down solely because he was a Negro. We see no valid, nondiscriminatory reason for the university's not accepting Meredith." Referring to the trial evidence regarding the Air Force psychiatrist's report on Meredith's stomach ailment, the majority opinion said: "Meredith's record shows just about the type of Negro who might be expected to try to crack the racial barrier at the University of Mississippi—a man with a mission and a nervous stomach."

The appeals court ruled that Judge Mize should retain jurisdiction of the case. But it ordered him to issue the injunction forcing Ole Miss to accept Meredith. Mize did so. The legal battle, however, was far from over. The U. S.

Supreme Court, the only court with higher jurisdiction than the Fifth Circuit Court of Appeals, had gone into summer recess. But the Ole Miss officials and trustees appealed to Supreme Court Justice Hugo Black, who has responsibility for the Fifth Circuit, to issue an order preventing the injunction from taking effect. In early September, Black refused to do so, ordering Meredith admitted to Ole Miss for the fall semester.

At this point, a new character entered the drama and made a fateful decision. The character was Ross Robert Barnett, Governor of Mississippi. His decision was to declare an official state policy of defying federal court desegregation orders. Barnett went on a statewide telecast on the night of September 13 and directed state officials to go to jail rather than obey such court orders. In doing so, he invoked the controversial doctrine of interposition. This doctrine purports to declare void any federal law that a state determines is usurping the rights reserved to the states. Barnett contended that the operation of public schools, colleges and universities is vested in the states and, therefore, under state jurisdiction. The Supreme Court had previously ruled in a Louisiana case that interposition "is not constitutional and is illegal defiance of constitutional law."

Barnett chose to ignore that ruling. "We will not drink the cup of genocide," he said. "There is no case in history where the Caucasian race has survived social integration."

Holding up the signed interposition proclamation for the TV viewers to see, the governor said:

I hereby direct each official to uphold and enforce the [segregation] laws duly and legally enacted by the legislature of the State of Mississippi, regardless of this [the federal courts'] unwarranted, illegal and arbitrary usurpation of power, and to interpose the state sovereignty and themselves between the people of the state and any body politic seeking to usurp such power. If there be any official who is not prepared to suffer imprisonment for this righteous cause, I ask him now to submit his resignation and it will be accepted without prejudice. A man who is prepared to stand firm will be appointed in his place. If these measures should be considered extreme, they are invoked by extreme provocation, for which we are in no way responsible. There is no cause which is more moral and just than the protection of the integrity of our races.

There was a seeming inconsistency in Ross Barnett's assumption of his role as the South's most militant segregationist governor. Some observers in Mississippi said his public position on the racial issue was in conflict with his private behavior. Publicly, his oft-stated position was: "Mississippi must be kept segregated at all costs. . . . The Good Lord was the original segregationist. He made us white because He wanted us white, and He intended that we stay that way." But, privately, it was not uncommon for him to visit a Negro tenant farmer's home and toss a ball back and forth with the farmer's sons. Nor was it considered unusual for a poor Negro to be ushered into the governor's mansion late at night to tell his story to Barnett, then be handed some cash.

If Barnett was, indeed, a sincere white supremacist, he easily could have come by this philosophy naturally. It was the prevailing philosophy in Leake County in north central Mississippi, where he was born at the community of Carthage on January 22, 1898. Both his father and grandfather fought in the Confederate Army. The youngest of ten children, he plowed, picked cotton and sawed logs in his youth. "We were poor, poor," Barnett says. "I wasn't raised in a hothouse."

Barnett worked as a janitor and barber to pay his way through an agricultural high school at Lena, Mississippi, and Mississippi College at Clinton. He then taught and coached basketball at a high school before enrolling at the University of Mississippi Law School, where he also taught Sunday School for freshmen. After his graduation from law school with honors in 1926, he set up practice in the state capital at Jackson. Before long, he had become one of the most successful corporation and criminal lawyers in the state. He had a folksy manner that appealed to juries.

Without any previous political experience, Barnett ran for governor in 1951 and was defeated. He suffered the same fate in 1955. Then, in 1956, he became widely known throughout the South by going to Clinton, Tennessee, and volunteering to defend whites who had been arrested when violence erupted over school desegregation.

In 1959, with Governor J. P. Coleman ineligible to succeed himself, Barnett and Lieutenant Governor Carroll Gartin were the opponents in the Democratic gubernatorial primary runoff. Each man devoted his campaign primarily to trying to prove that he was a more rabid segregationist than his opponent. Barnett pledged: "I am going to put forth every effort to organize Southern governors, to create and crystallize public opinion throughout this nation with reference to our traditions and our Southern way of life."

The white-supremacist Citizens Councils, of which Barnett was an active member, rallied to his support. With their help, he defeated Gartin decisively in the runoff, which is equivalent to election in Mississippi.

After his election, Barnett's popularity waned. Somewhere along the line, he lost the speaking polish that had once captivated juries. He mumbled political speeches woodenly. And his classic ability to put his foot in his mouth became legend. Once, he referred to a Jewish audience as "a fine Christian gathering." Another time, a Mississippi convict with a history of previous escapes was taken to Arkansas by two prison guards to bring back a horse. The prisoner, a trusty, somehow persuaded the guards to let him pay an unescorted visit to a woman friend before making the return trip to Mississippi. As soon as he got out of the guards' sight, the convict fled. Barnett was asked at a press conference to account for the guards' action. His reply: "Well, if you can't trust a trusty, who can you trust?"

Later, a full-scale prison scandal erupted and put Barnett's administration under heavy fire. The criticism was heightened during a furore over the elaborate refurbishing of the governor's mansion—including installation of a new gold-plated bathroom at a cost of $10,000.

All in all, Barnett's popularity was perhaps at its lowest point since his election when he decided to intercede in the dispute over James Meredith's attempt to enter the University of Mississippi. Some observers believe Barnett seized on the Meredith case, with its opportunity for whipping up passionate support among Mississippians, as a means of turning the tide of voter popularity in his favor anew.

Whatever his reasons, Barnett had put himself in the middle of the Meredith affair. And his entry, with his interposition proclamation, set off 17 days of frantic activity by Mississippi and federal officials, Meredith and his lawyers, and state and federal judges.

Other Mississippi officials reacted with near-unanimous approval to defy federal court desegregation rulings. Former Governor J. P. Coleman, now a state representative from Choctaw County, told his cheering colleagues in the legislature: "It's going to take real men and women to stand up to them [federal authorities]."

The legislature responded by passing, with only two dissenting votes, a resolution to back Barnett to the hilt. The resolution praised Barnett for "his fearless and courageous stand against political aggression, abuses and misrepresentations designed to disrupt and destroy Southern institutions, traditions and way of living." From Washington came word that the Mississippi congressional delegation had pledged Barnett "unqualified support."

Justice Department officials in Washington had been watching the Mississippi situation with increasing concern. To this point, the dispute had been solely between James Meredith and the University of Mississippi. But now Mississippi officials were openly threatening to defy federal court orders. The Justice Department was bound by law to enforce those orders. It decided to enter the dispute.

The department's first act was to announce, on September 17, that United States marshals would be assigned to guard Meredith when he appeared at Ole Miss to try to register. The next day, Attorney General Robert F. Kennedy phoned Barnett to tell him personally of this decision. Kennedy told Barnett that Meredith would be accompanied to the Ole Miss campus by more than one, but fewer than five, marshals. The phone conversation was sufficiently cordial that James Symington, a special assistant to the Attorney General, confidently told newsmen he did not expect violence to erupt in Mississippi. "The state authorities don't want violence, either," Symington said. "Barnett is testing the issue in a legal sense. There is no indication he will support the use of force."

James Meredith himself emerged from several days of seclusion in Memphis, Tennessee, and waved aside questions about possible danger. "If I went around worrying about that, I'd be living a pretty miserable life," Meredith said. "I don't worry about me." He conceded, however, that "I don't expect anybody to send me a letter inviting me to join any fraternities."

Meanwhile, Justice Department attorneys went into federal court at Hattiesburg, Mississippi, and won permission to take part in any further legal proceedings arising from the Meredith case. The court order specifically granted the department permission to launch contempt of court proceedings if Ole Miss officials refused to admit Meredith.

Registration had already begun on the Ole Miss campus at Oxford, Mississippi. Students, fearing that Barnett might order the university closed to avoid desegregation, anxiously asked friends: "Where are you going to school tomorrow?" Anonymous inflammatory leaflets were circulated among the students. "Place yourself under the direction of Governor Barnett," the leaflets directed. "Do not engage yourself in force or violence unless he calls for it, and unless you are personally attacked. On the other hand, do not permit yourself to be intimidated by any leftist school administrators and officials."

In Jackson, state officials took a new tack to their campaign to keep Meredith out of Ole Miss. They had discovered that Meredith had listed Hinds County (Jackson) as his home in registering as a voter, but had testified during the desegregation trial that Attala County (Kosciusko) was his home. It was an apparently innocent discrepancy. Meredith was from Attala County, but was residing in Hinds County while attending Jackson State College. Nonetheless, state authorities filed charges accusing him of entering false information on his voter registration application.

On September 19, the legislature hurriedly passed a bill giving Ole Miss and all other state colleges and universities the right to bar any applicant convicted of a crime or with a criminal charge pending against him. The bill obviously was intended to apply to Meredith. Barnett stayed up until the predawn hours of September 20 to sign it into law.

That same day, Justice of the Peace Homer Edgeworth tried Meredith at Jackson on the false voter registration charge. Neither Meredith nor any of his attorneys was present. The trial lasted ten minutes, and Meredith was convicted. Edgeworth imposed the maximum sentence—a year in jail and a $100 fine. He ordered Meredith's immediate arrest. But Justice Department attorneys quickly went before the federal court at Meridian and got an order prohibiting Meredith's arrest.

The pulling and hauling between state and federal courts continued on other fronts as well. State Chancery Court Judge L. P. Porter, acting on a petition signed by 47 Mississippians who claimed Meredith's admission to Ole Miss would violate the state constitution, issued an injunction barring his enrollment. A number of federal officials were named as defendants in the injunction. Justice Department lawyers immediately asked the federal court at Meridian to overrule this injunction. They said the federal officials named as defendants were acting "under authority of the laws of the United States."

On the morning of September 20, Meredith's attorneys announced that he would try to enroll at Ole Miss that same day. There had been a rapid buildup of police officers on the campus in the previous day. About 200 state police had descended on the university. Oxford Police Chief J. D. Jones had deputized 30 firemen to augment the small city police force.

Meanwhile, Barnett had personally taken over the administration of the university. He had persuaded the university trustees to designate him as acting registrar and to give him other powers governing the university. He headed for Oxford to confront Meredith when the young Negro made his appearance on the campus.

Students had been gathering in clusters on the campus all day, with time on their hands and the urge for excitement. They were orderly for the most part, but occasionally broke into rowdy songs and yells.

Justice Department went before Judge Mize and demanded contempt of court citations against Old Miss Chancellor J. D. Williams, Dean Arthur B. Lewis and Registrar Ellis. All three had been among the defendants in the original suit, and the Justice Department contended they had violated court orders in failing to see that Meredith was enrolled.

Assistant U. S. Attorney General Burke Marshall, in charge of the Justice Department Civil Rights Division, personally appeared in Mize's court at Meridian to plead the government's case. About 200 spectators jammed into the small courtroom. Eleven were Negroes, four of whom sat in rows with whites. St. John Barrett was still a little unglued when called as a witness at the hearing. Describing the events of the preceding day, he several times referred to Governor Barnett as "Governor Patterson," bringing chuckles from the spectators. (He evidently had in mind John Patterson, then Governor of Alabama.)

Attorneys for the three Ole Miss officials argued that they had been unable to register Meredith because the university trustees had put the matter completely in Barnett's hands by appointing him acting registrar. Marshall argued that Williams, Lewis and Ellis had the power to enroll Meredith. "Efforts to remove that responsibility are ineffective as a matter of law," he said.

Mize upheld the position of the university officials. He refused to cite them for contempt, saying they had been trapped between "conflicting currents" when the university trustees turned over the registrar's powers temporarily to Barnett. Marshall immediately took the case to the U. S. Fifth Circuit Court of Appeals in New Orleans.

Meanwhile, repercussions of the Mississippi dispute were being felt far beyond the confines of the Deep South. On the other side of the world, Communist China seized on the affair as a propaganda weapon. It broadcast to color-conscious Asia a detailed report on the Meredith case. Radio Peiping declared: "Racialists headed by Governor Ross Barnett in the State of Mississippi, U. S. A., frantically blocked the Negro student from entering the university." The broadcast was entitled "School Integration in U. S. Still a Farce." In Washington, Barnett was the target of criticism from Northerners on the floor of Congress. Representative William Fitts Ryan, a New York Democrat, suggested that the government cut off all school funds to the University of Mississippi. He said the university was receiving $236,374 in federal funds.

September 24 was also the deadline set by Ole Miss for registration of students. But the feeling was that, if other obstacles could be overcome, the deadline would not keep Meredith out of the university. As attorney Constance Motley put it: "If we get a favorable decision [from the Fifth Circuit Court of Appeals], we expect to be able to get him registered. The university officials have tried to keep him out and they can't very well hold a deadline against him."

But, before the hearing could begin in New Orleans, Barnett took the offensive again. He obtained a state court order forbidding university officials to enroll Meredith and barring him from registering. And, perhaps more important, Barnett issued an executive order directing state police to arrest anyone who tried to arrest or fine a state official in connection with the Meredith case. The "anyone" clearly referred to federal officials. Thus, the possibility loomed for a test of physical force between federal and Mississippi authorities.

When the Fifth Circuit Court of Appeals convened to consider the contempt citations, Barnett was not present, but he was very much a part of the legal maneuvering. As defense attorneys put it in arguing against the contempt action: "The ultimate issue is whether the authority of this court is paramount to the authority of the governor."

Judge Richard Rives of Montgomery, Alabama, remarked: "I do not think the governor is above the prerogative of this court and I think this court may have to go further and cite the governor for contempt." Judge Joseph C. Hutcheson, Jr., of Houston, Texas, assailed Barnett's invoking of the doctrine of interposition. "Interposition was thrown out at Appomattox," Hutcheson said. "In our state, when a governor refuses to comply with a court order, we impeach him—not praise him."

It quickly became obvious to the university trustees that this court had little patience for further defiance of its orders. The trustees decided to bow to the court's authority. They agreed to enroll Meredith. In a statement issued after the hearing, they said they had made their decision because it "was apparent that fines and imprisonment in amounts unknown to us would not prevent Meredith's admission." They said they understood that the court would have appointed someone to register Meredith if they had not agreed to do so themselves.

Still, the tension continued to build. Deputy U. S. marshals had begun converging on Mississippi from other states to enforce the federal court orders in case of further defiance by Barnett and other state officials. Barnett, for his part, ordered the State Highway Patrol put on a 24-hour standby alert. More than 80 state police cars were moved into the area of the Ole Miss campus.

Amid all this deadly serious maneuvering, a lighter note suddenly was injected into the Meredith affair. In New York, a 35-year-old Negro revealed that he had spent an uneventful academic year at the University of Mississippi just after World War II. It was uneventful for the reason that he had been mistaken for a white student, chiefly because his skin is light and his last name is Murphy.

Ole Miss records confirmed that the Negro, Harry S. Murphy, Jr., had studied at the university for the full 1945-6 academic year as a Navy V-12 student. The V-12 program was a college training program leading to a Navy commission as an ensign. Murphy said he had volunteered for the Navy when he was 18 at an induction center in Washington, D. C.

"While I was going through the processing line with a lot of other fellows, some little Wave must have taken it for granted and marked my record 'W' [for white] or 'C' [for Caucasian] when she looked at me and saw my name," Murphy said. "They never asked me my race."

He said he had been anxious to get a college education and had not corrected the error, even when he had learned that he was being assigned to the segregated University of Mississippi. "But I must confess I was damned concerned," he said. However, he continued, the academic year "was as humdrum a freshman year as any student could find." Everyone assumed he was white, and he shared campus barracks and classes with the otherwise white student body.

Murphy chuckled when asked if he had any Irish blood to account for his last name. He replied, "Like all Americans who have been here for generations, my lineage is a mixture. I am part French, part Indian, one-quarter Jewish, as well as Negro—but no, no Irish. Oddly enough, my heritage includes people who owned slaves. I'd prefer not to go into how I got the name Murphy, which is certainly Irish-sounding, but it's not a matter of anybody changing his name or anything like that."

After his one year at Ole Miss, Murphy transferred to all-Negro Morehouse College in his native Atlanta, Georgia, where he was later graduated with a business administration degree. He is now a printing salesman in Manhattan.

The revelation that one Negro had once attended Ole Miss by mistake in no way diminished Ross Barnett's determination to see that another Negro would be barred from attending the university by design. The governor had not concurred in the university trustees' agreement to enroll James Meredith. Now, he set about thwarting that agreement.

By prearrangement with the university officials, Meredith was to appear for enrollment at the State Office Building in Jackson, where the university trustees normally meet, on Tuesday, September 25. Registrar Ellis appeared there, as agreed, to process Meredith's registration. But Barnett also appeared, with a group of state legislators and about 100 highway patrolmen and other out-of-town police, and ordered Ellis kept a virtual captive inside the trustees' office. A crowd of about 1,000 civilians was swarming outside the building.

Meredith arrived flanked by Justice Department Attorney John Doar and Chief U. S. Marshal James J. P. McShane. Boos and jeers arose from the crowd. Some spectators waved Confederate flags. Others shouted: "Go home, nigger," and "Communists!" Six highway patrolmen, marching two abreast, took up positions at the head of Meredith's party. Six more fell in behind the group. The police cleared a path through the crowd and led Meredith's party to the trustees' office.

There, Barnett stood in the doorway and blocked Meredith's entry. Politely but firmly, Doar told the Governor: "I call on you to permit us to go in and see Mr. Ellis and get this young man registered." Just as politely and firmly, Barnett refused. Twice more, Doar made the demand. Twice more, Barnett refused.

The Governor read a proclamation to Meredith. "I do hereby finally deny you admission to the University of Mississippi," he said. "I am complying with the Constitution of Mississippi, and certainly I am complying with the Constitution of the United States. My conscience is clear." He said he was denying Meredith's enrollment "to prevent violence and a breach of the peace, and in order to preserve the peace, dignity and tranquility of the State of Mississippi."

Doar heard Barnett out, then said: "All right, Governor. Thank you."

"I do that politely," Barnett replied.

"Thank you, and we leave politely," Doar said.

With that, Meredith's party turned and walked away. Highway patrolmen again cleared a path through the crowd, which surged toward Meredith, cursing and booing. Meredith, Doar and McShane drove away to a chorus of epithets.

Barnett left the trustees' offices with a crowd of legislative supporters. So many of them jammed into an elevator that it broke down under the excess weight and got stuck below the first floor. Barnett and his backers finally emerged from the building after about ten minutes, to be greeted by cheers and rebel yells.

Round Two was Barnett's.

2

President Kennedy and his brother, Attorney General Robert F. Kennedy, had been growing increasingly concerned over the events in Mississippi. They had been in constant touch all day September 25 as Governor Barnett was sending James Meredith away for the second time. They had decided it might be necessary to use federal troops, in addition to marshals, to enforce the court orders directing Meredith's enrollment.

No official statement was made on this point, but Justice Department officials were saying privately that the Ole Miss crisis was "heading right down the road" to the point where a show of force by federal troops might be necessary. Attorney General Kennedy phoned Meredith in Jackson and assured him that the Justice Department would pursue his case to whatever lengths necessary to get him enrolled.

Meanwhile, the nine judges of the Fifth Circuit Court of Appeals ran out of patience with Barnett. They directed the Justice Department to begin contempt proceedings against the Governor, and ordered Barnett to appear before them on Friday, September 28, to show cause why should not be cited for contempt. In addition, the judges issued a restraining order barring Barnett and virtually all of Mississippi's peace officers from interfering further with Meredith's attempts to register.

But the court's orders were to be defied again the very next day. On Wednesday, September 26, Meredith made a new attempt to enroll at the Ole Miss campus in Oxford. The campus was swarming with police, about 400 of them from all over the state—highway patrolmen, sheriff's officers and city police. More than 100 police cars were used to set up roadblocks at the university's five gates. Only the handful of Ole Miss campus police wore guns. The others, after arriving at the campus, unstrapped their sidearms and put them in their car trunks. The state police at the five gates wore steel helmet-liners and carried billy clubs and gas masks. About 200 yards inside the university's main gate, six police dogs were kept at the ready in police cars.

Barnett was on his way to Oxford by car. He had planned to fly, but bad weather in Jackson had prevented him from taking off. Lieutenant Governor Paul Johnson was in charge at the campus in his absence when Meredith arrived with Justice Department lawyer Doar, U. S. Marshal McShane and five carloads of deputy marshals. Johnson stood before a cordon of highway patrolmen at a university gate and barred the way to Meredith and the federal men. A large group of newsmen, including TV cameramen, looked on as Doar tried to walk through the line of grim state patrolmen.

"We want to take him in," Doar said.

"I am going to have to refuse on the same grounds the Governor did," Johnson replied. "I refuse because of imminent breach of the peace."

McShane and several of his deputy marshals tried to shove their way through the highway patrolmen. The state officers closed ranks and shoved back. This was the first physical contact in the federal-state struggle that was to flare four days later into violence and death.

Three times more, the marshals tried to push their way through the cordon. Each time they were pushed back. Johnson snapped angrily: "You are senseless in trying to show off in front of television cameras for the rest of the nation to see."

McShane replied: "I'm not showing off, but doing my duty."

The shoving stopped. The federal officials and Meredith turned, walked back to their cars and drove away.

Round Three was Mississippi's.

The federal government now began stepping up its massing of manpower for a showdown. From all over the country, hundreds of deputy U. S. marshals were converging on the Millington Naval Air Station at Memphis, Tennessee, 87 fast highway miles north of Oxford. Most of these men had been given special training in riot control. Some were not full-time deputy marshals, but specially deputized agents from such federal law enforcement agencies as the Border Patrol and the Bureau of Prisons. They, too, had been chosen for their special training in riot-control work.

In addition, the first contingent of army troops to be called on in the crisis got its orders to move. These were 110 army combat engineers from the 70th Engineer Battalion at Fort Campbell, Kentucky. They were ordered to the naval air station at Memphis to provide "logistical support" for the marshals. Both the army and the Justice Department said the engineers would not be used directly in attempts to get Meredith enrolled.

"They have with them the capacity to set up a tent city to furnish bedding, cooking and that type of service for the marshals," said Lieutenant Colonel T. A. Price, deputy commander of operations at Fort Campbell. Nonetheless, it did seem significant that the army had been called into the crisis.

At this point, an unusual behind-the-scenes drama began to unfold. Mississippi business and civic leaders, meeting privately and conferring by telephone, started expressing serious misgivings about the policy being followed by Barnett. Until then, they had seemed to be firmly behind him. Now, word reached the Governor that these influential men favored the principle he was trying to support, but were afraid that Ole Miss and the state might be damaged by the methods he was using.

Meanwhile, Attorney General Kennedy had been applying heavy pressure on Barnett in a series of phone calls to end his defiance. Barnett began looking for a face-saving way out of his dilemma. On Thursday, September 27, Barnett and Lieutenant Governor Johnson were stationed at the Ole Miss Alumni House in anticipation of a new registration attempt by Meredith. At 12:50 P.M., Barnett got a call from the Attorney General. A representative of Barnett's had suggested to Kennedy earlier in the day that there might be a solution to the crisis in the making. Barnett quickly made clear the solution he had in mind— a plan that would permit him to maintain an aura of defiance, but be overwhelmed by federal forces.

Under this bizarre plan, Barnett and Johnson were to stand before a column of unarmed state police at an Ole Miss gate. Chief Marshal McShane and about 25 marshals, all armed, would bring Meredith up to the gate. Barnett and Johnson would refuse to let them enter. McShane would then draw his gun. Under the original version of the plan, the other marshals would put their hands on their holsters. Barnett, literally under the gun, would have no choice but to move out of the way and permit Meredith to enter and be registered.

Later in the conversation, Barnett changed the plan. He felt the threat of only one drawn gun would not look sufficiently imposing to permit him to surrender. He insisted that all the marshals should draw their guns. Reluctantly, Kennedy concurred. He felt that, unusual as Barnett's plan was, it would accomplish the desired purpose of bringing about compliance with the court orders while avoiding bloodshed. Kennedy agreed to have McShane, Meredith and the marshals appear at the university gate at 5 P.M. that same day. He immediately sent word to the naval air station at Memphis, where Meredith and the others had been waiting.

But, only an hour after their first conversation, Barnett called Kennedy back. He said there was a large crowd gathered on the campus and he was not sure it could be kept under control. Johnson came on the line and told Kennedy he feared that sheriffs and deputies, not directly under the governor's control, might prove troublesome. They asked that the new attempt to register Meredith be postponed for two days, until Saturday.

At 2:20 P.M. however, the Attorney General received another call from Barnett. Everything had been worked out. Kennedy could revert to the original schedule and have Meredith show up at 5 P.M. that day. Barnett promised there would be no violence. The Attorney General immediately phoned the naval air base and gave McShane the order to move on to Oxford. A convoy of 13 green sedans owned by the Border Patrol swept out of the base and headed south on U. S. Highway 55.

In 12 of the cars were a total of 25 deputy marshals, all carefully chosen and rehearsed on the roles they would play in the staged surrender arranged with Barnett. At the wheel of the 13th car was Border Patrolman Charles Chamblee, a specially deputized marshal. Beside him sat McShane, his Irish lantern jaw set with determination. In the back seat were James Meredith, seeming entirely composed, and attorney John Doar.

Now it was 3:35. The convoy was well on the way to Oxford. Attorney General Kennedy phoned Barnett again to insist on detailed promises that order would be kept on the Ole Miss campus after Meredith's arrival. Barnett replied evasively. He talked generally about keeping order all over the state. "We always do that," he said.

What Kennedy did not know at the time was that Bar-

nett had gotten himself in over his head. The state policemen and sheriff's officers standing guard at Ole Miss knew
nothing of his negotiations with the Attorney General.
Many felt their duty was to block Meredith's entry, even if
it meant death. There was no clear agreement among the
state officers on how to react if the marshals tried to force
their way onto the campus. Barnett feared that some hot-
headed state officers might touch off a holocaust.

The crowd at the campus gates had grown to 2,000.
Judge Russell D. Moore III, put in command of the forces
at Oxford by Barnett, initially had ordered all the state
police and sheriff's officers to leave their weapons in their
car trunks. But now he received word that the federal
government was sending a "goon squad," armed with tear
gas and billy clubs, to the campus. He decided to let the
state police don helmets and bring out gas masks and night
sticks. He told the sheriff's officers they could carry black
jacks, bring police dogs and keep tear-gas guns ready.

At 4:35, only 25 minutes before the marshals were to
arrive at the campus with Meredith, Barnett called Kennedy again. He was extremely worried. He said he felt it
would be impossible to control the crowd. A hundred persons might get killed, he said. "That would ruin all of us,"
Barnett said. It would be embarrassing to him. "I don't
know if it would be embarrassing," Kennedy replied. "That
would not be the feeling."

Kennedy put in an urgent call ordering the convoy of
marshals to turn back to Memphis. The convoy was just
20 miles from Oxford when the message came. The Attorney General announced in a statement: "The marshals
escorting James Meredith to Oxford, Mississippi, have been
directed to return to Memphis without attempting to enter
the University of Mississippi. This action was taken after
receipt of information from Oxford that a large crowd had
gathered and that the force accompanying Mr. Meredith
might not be sufficient to accomplish its mission without
major violence and bloodshed for the citizens of Mississippi. Several hundred additional United States marshals
are proceeding to Memphis to augment the small force
which has been there since last week."

Round Four had ended in a stalemate.

But Attorney General Kennedy made it clear the federal government was determined to break that stalemate. "Mr. Meredith will be registered," he said firmly.

It was becoming increasingly apparent that a much larger force of marshals than any used in the previous attempts would be necessary to put James Meredith inside Ole Miss. Into the Millington Naval Air Station at Memphis swarmed 552 deputy marshals. Only 122 of these were full-time deputy marshals. Another 100 were federal prison guards and 330 were Border Patrol officers with riot-control training, all especially deputized for the Ole Miss assignment.

In charge was Chief Marshal McShane, 53, a battle-hardened officer with a reputation for heroism, straight shooting and hard punching. Danger had lived at McShane's elbow for 30 years. A onetime New York Golden Gloves welterweight champion, he had had a spectacular career on the New York police force. Within two years after joining the force, he had twice fought gun battles with burglars and holdup men. He wounded two, each in the gun hand, and killed a third who was firing at him. During one 30-month span alone, he had been involved in seven gun battles.

After retiring from the police force in 1957, McShane went to work as a staff investigator for the Senate Rackets Committee under Robert F. Kennedy. With the committee, he did an intensive job of investigating Teamster Union violence in Tennessee. When the Kennedy administration took office in 1961, McShane was appointed U. S. marshal for Washington, D. C. He figured he would settle into a routine paper-work job, but within a month he was handed a mission that provided invaluable experience for the Ole Miss assignment.

The Freedom Rides were at their zenith, and violence had flared in Alabama, with buses being bombed and burned and Negroes being attacked. President Kennedy had sent marshals into the state capital of Montgomery to preserve order. Placed in charge of the marshals was McShane. He frankly admits today that there were some mistakes made during subsequent riots in Montgomery, mistakes from which he and other federal officials had learned lessons that were to prove important at Ole Miss. For one thing, the Montgomery mission had not been organized with sufficient care. For another, the marshals lacked necessary training in riot-control techniques.

After being appointed chief U. S. marshal on June 20, 1961, McShane set about correcting these deficiencies. Deputy marshals from all over the country were sent in relays to the Greenville, South Carolina, air force base for special riot-control training under the direction of guerrilla-warfare experts. About 400 of the nation's 600 deputy marshals, as well as many Border Patrolmen, prison guards and other officers, had undergone the training by the time of the Ole Miss crisis.

The men who were to serve at Ole Miss were carefully chosen from the groups trained in riot-control methods. They were members of highly coordinated teams that had trained together, although they had come from diverse parts of the country. Unlike the deputy marshals who had suffered from a certain amount of poor organization at Montgomery, these men had a precise chain of command. In addition, McShane had taken great pains long in advance of the crisis to prepare for any eventuality. On September 15, more than two weeks before the Meredith affair reached its most crucial stage, he had made a secret visit to Oxford with about 25 marshals. In civilian clothes, apparently unnoticed by local residents and university students or officials, they had studied the layout of the town and the campus. Later, they had prepared detail maps for use if a showdown should come.

Now, on Friday, September 28, the showdown was fast approaching. With marshals streaming into the Memphis naval air station, the first army unit also made its appearance. This was the 110-man detachment of combat engineers from the 70th Engineer Battalion, which had been ordered to Memphis for use in setting up a tent city to house the marshals, if necessary.

The engineers rolled into Memphis at 3 P.M. Friday, after a 200-mile overnight ride. Their 49 vehicles included tractor trailers carrying heavy equipment, trailer-drawn vans, jeeps and trucks. Although the government had said these men would be used only for "logistical support," and not for trying to enroll Meredith, reporters noted that the soldiers were armed with M-1 rifles and pistols.

In Washington, the President and the Attorney General were in almost constant consultation. After completing a political speech in Wheeling, West Virginia, during which he was interrupted to take a call on the Mississippi crisis from his brother, the President had flown back to the capital Thursday night. Secretary of Defense Robert McNamara flew home from a trip to Germany to be available for discussions on the possible use of troops in enrolling Meredith. The White House let it be known that the President considered the situation so critical that he probably would cancel plans to join his family for a weekend at Newport, Rhode Island.

From various states in the South and elsewhere, Governor Ross Barnett was getting offers of physical and moral support in his fight against the federal government. In the forefront of those lining up beside the defiant Governor was former Major General Edwin Walker.

Walker had been in command of the federal troops sent into Little Rock, Arkansas, by President Eisenhower in 1957 to prevent violence from blocking school desegregation. But Walker's career had taken many a bizarre turn since then. First, he was disciplined by the army for indoctrinating troops with John Birch Society propaganda. Then he quit the army amid a sensational round of congressional hearings that saw the Pentagon accused of "muzzling" officers. Next, Walker had run for the Democratic nomination for governor of Texas, but finished last in a field of six.

Now, Walker broadcast a radio appeal for 10,000 volunteers from all 50 states to come to Barnett's aid. He was to fall far short of his goal of 10,000, but hundreds of troublemakers from diverse states were to heed his call.

Typical of them was Melvin Bruce, 36, of Decatur, Georgia. Bruce had once been a chauffeur for George Lincoln Rockwell, fanatic head of the American Nazi Party. More recently, he had become a John Birch Society adherent. After hearing of Walker's call for volunteers, Bruce sent off two telegrams, one to Barnett and the other to Admiral John Cromelin of Wetumpka, Alabama, a leader of right-wing groups. The existence of the telegrams has since been revealed by federal authorities, but they have so far refused to disclose the contents.

Bruce armed himself with ammunition and a heavy-caliber Mauser rifle, plastered with such John Birch Society slogans as: "This is a republic, not a democracy—let's keep it that way." Then he set out for the Ole Miss campus by car. More was to be heard from him later.

In Gulfport, Mississippi, Bill Simpson, a close associate of Barnett, said about 4,000 civilian volunteers all over the state were available for the Governor's use in defying federal authority. Simpson's brother Jim, also a political ally of the Governor, said Mississippi Highway Patrol Director T. B. Birdsong had issued a directive that any means necessary must be used to protect Barnett and prevent his arrest on contempt charges.

In Homer, Louisiana, William M. Rainach, former state senator and former chairman of the segregationist Citizens Councils of America, was getting calls from citizens who wanted to organize a march to Mississippi to "defend" Barnett. "Indications are that more than 10,000 Louisianans would join this march upon the proper call," Rainach said.

Barnett, for his part, had made his office a fortress against process servers. His staff locked the office doors against unauthorized visitors and refused to accept letters or telegrams. But the Justice Department insisted that Barnett had already been served with the papers ordering him to show cause why he should not be held in contempt of the New Orleans appeals court.

The Mississippi Legislature also was active in the campaign to protect Barnett. It passed a bill aimed at preventing federal courts from seizing the Governor's personal property for payment of fines if he should be convicted of contempt. Barnett was due in the New Orleans court at 11 A.M. Friday to answer the contempt action. He did not show up. But a formidable battery of Mississippi attorneys, headed by former American Bar Association President John C. Satterfield, appeared on his behalf.

Assistant United States Attorney General Burke Marshall represented the government. He argued that Barnett had been in contempt of court and should be punished, but only if he failed to halt his resistance to Meredith's enrollment by a deadline the following week. "The court can impose sanctions which we are prepared to enforce," Marshall told the court. Referring to the court's original desegregation ruling, he added: "The court order will be enforced whether the Governor purges himself of contempt or not."

Despite contrary arguments from Barnett's lawyers, the court followed Marshall's recommendations. The judges ruled that Barnett had committed civil contempt of court. They gave him until the morning of Tuesday, October 2, to purge himself of contempt by retracting his proclamations of resistance, withdrawing any force he had massed to prevent integration and removing himself from Meredith's path to enrollment. The judges said that, if Barnett ignored the deadline, they would impose a dual penalty. They would order the Governor arrested and held in jail until he agreed to comply with their ruling. And they would order him to pay a fine of $10,000 for each day he failed to obey the order.

In the state capital at Jackson, the legislature moved anew to protect Barnett and other state officials from punishment by the court. After shelving an absurd proposal that Mississippi seek to withdraw from the Union, the legislature passed and Barnett immediately signed a bill declaring that acts of public officials in seeking to bar school desegregation were "sovereign acts of the sovereign state of Mississippi" and not individual fancies. It was a desperate move, and one that legal observers considered of little or no value.

Meanwhile, H. C. Strider, chairman of the Mississippi Game and Fish Commission, announced that 250 of his supervisors and game wardens had been alerted to join the other peace officers already gathered at Ole Miss to take part in the defense of segregation, if needed. The federal government, marshaling its own forces, made clear its determination to use whatever manpower was needed. Defense Secretary McNamara, back from his trip to Germany, said: "We're prepared to respond to whatever emergencies may develop." Attorney General Kennedy repeated his earlier vow: "Mr. Meredith will be registered."

On Friday afternoon, the Attorney General met with General Maxwell Taylor, chairman of the Joint Chiefs of Staff, and four other military leaders. Most of them, including Taylor, had helped prepare the operation in which Eisenhower had sent paratroops into Little Rock in 1957. They tentatively agreed that, if troops were necessary at Ole Miss, they would use two battalions of military police, a battle group from the Second Infantry Division at Fort Benning, Georgia, and whatever logistical forces were needed for housekeeping chores. Although this meeting was kept secret at the time, hints that troops might be called upon were being leaked to the press. A source described as "close to the President" told reporters that Kennedy would exhaust every alternative before using troops, but that the military would be called out if Barnett resisted Meredith's enrollment strongly enough.

The behind-the-scenes activity was mirrored by public debate in Congress over the crisis. Seven Northern senators signed a resolution sponsored by Republican Kenneth B. Keating of New York and Democrat Paul H. Douglas of Illinois, declaring that Congress would support the President in efforts to enroll Meredith "by every appropriate means." This clearly included use of troops, if necessary. Seven Mississippi congressmen, however, wired the President: "The highest state of heat and tension prevails in Mississippi. . . . A holocaust is in the making." They urged the President to withdraw the army engineers' unit from the Memphis base and to "set at rest all reports and rumors that other troops are to follow."

But Kennedy drew support from his predecessor, Eisenhower, who told a news conference in Hershey, Pennsylvania, that the President had the right to use troops if needed to get Meredith admitted to the university. Eisenhower branded as "absolutely unconscionable and indefen-

sible" the defiance of federal court orders. "When the executive branch, the heart of government, does not support
the judiciary and the decisions it makes, then the America
we know will no longer exist," Eisenhower said.

Barnett, for his part, was drawing additional support of
his own. From Alabama came word from Governor
John Patterson that his state stood with Mississippi "in this
fight and will continue to resist all unlawful encroachments
by the federal government." Patterson said in a telegram to
Kennedy: "If troops are sent into Mississippi, I ask if you
are ready to invade Alabama as well?"

From Dallas came further word from General Walker.
"It is time to move," he told his followers. "We have
talked, listened and been pushed around far too much by
the anti-Christ Supreme Court. Now is the time to be
heard—10,000 strong from every state in the union."
Walker said his band's rallying cry should be: "Barnett *si*,
Castro *no*." Curiously, this ludicrous slogan was to take
hold. Segregationists by the thousands were to try to
equate the Mississippi and Cuba situations. Their constant
refrain was to be that the President should be using force
against Fidel Castro, not Ross Barnett.

Walker said thousands of Americans were ready to join
him in defense of Mississippi's sovereignty. He urged all
right-thinkers to oppose any soldiers sent into the state. "I
intend to go to Mississippi if and when they use federal
troops," he said. "Lots of people are not waiting for me.
They're already going to Mississippi, from California to
Carolina."

Meanwhile, other problems were descending on Ole
Miss as a result of the crisis. From Atlanta, the executive
council of the Southern College Accreditation Board,
which once before had lifted Ole Miss' accreditation because of political interference in the university's operations,
threatened to do so again. The council gave Ole Miss until
November to take corrective measures, eliminating political control, or again face removal of accreditation.

In addition, fears were becoming increasingly widespread
that Barnett would close the university before seeing it desegregated. Several businessmen from Oxford, which de-

pends chiefly on the university for its economic existence, had approached U. S. District Judge Claude Clayton of Tupelo and sought assurances that the university would be kept open by court order if Barnett closed it. Clayton assured them the university would be reopened within 48 hours if Barnett ordered it shut. But this assurance was kept secret. Students, knowing nothing about it, sat on the steps of the Ole Miss administration building, the Lyceum, and debated Friday afternoon which would be worse—integration or closing of the school.

One 19-year-old boy from Memphis, a sophomore, said: "I'd rather see Ole Miss closed than integrated. Integration would have social reverberations that would last 1,000 years. It would change the whole social structure of the South. There would probably be total social integration, mongrelization of the races. I don't want my children and grandchildren to be half-nigger."

A contrary view was taken by another sophomore, a 19-year-old blonde coed from Greenville. "I'd definitely rather see Meredith a student here than see the university close," she said. "I don't think there'll be any violence if he's admitted, although he'll probably have to listen to some pretty nasty names. I know this: I'm a lot more interested in whether I can finish my education than in whether he's admitted."

A Methodist minister from nearby Bruce, Mississippi, visited the campus Friday afternoon at the request of several parishioners concerned about their children's future at Ole Miss. "What bothers me," he told a reporter, "is that these parents are a lot more concerned about the possibility of the university being closed to their children than they are about the ethical implications of whether Meredith should be admitted."

By late Friday, students were leaving the campus in droves for Jackson to attend a Saturday night football game between Ole Miss and Kentucky. Most of the state police and other officers who had been guarding the campus also were leaving. By nightfall, the campus was virtually deserted. There were reports that Barnett and federal officials had agreed to a weekend truce.

The reports were false. Before the close of the weekend,

the tranquil campus would be turned into a bloody battle-field. But now, Friday night, a sense of calm hung over Ole Miss.

3

After watching the crisis build in Mississippi for several weeks, *Newsday*'s editors had decided in midweek to send me to Oxford. I had caught a plane late Thursday from New York to Memphis. I had been handling rewrite on the Ole Miss story most of the week, tying together stories from a part-time correspondent on the scene and from members of *Newsday*'s Washington bureau.

The flight to Memphis had been a long and arduous one. After spending about a half-hour in the air and almost reaching Philadelphia, we had been forced to turn back to New York when three of the airliner's four engines conked out. Waiting at the airport for another plane, I had been told by a stewardess that a number of federal men, destined for Mississippi, were aboard. They had declared, on boarding the plane, that they were carrying weapons.

When we finally were airborne again, I searched out the federal men, told them who I was and tried to find out precisely where they were going. Most of them would say nothing. But one, Joe Denson, a deputy U. S. marshal from Staten Island, pricked up his ears when I mentioned I worked for *Newsday*.

"You know Jim O'Rourke?" he asked me.

"Sure, he's one of our photographers," I said.

"Well, I work with his brother, Gene. He's a deputy marshal in our office."

I did not know Gene O'Rourke. But I did know Tom Dugan, the U. S. marshal who was Denson's superior.

Denson and I formed a friendship on the plane ride that was to last long after the Ole Miss crisis. But when we left the plane in Memphis, I had no idea whether I would see him again. He was taken, with a group of other marshals who boarded the plane at stops along the way, to the naval air station in Memphis. I rented a car and drove the remainder of the way to Oxford.

It was a pleasant ride through the section of Mississippi made famous by William Faulkner. Oxford and surrounding Lafayette County (pronounced Lu-FAY-et by local residents) had been the home of Faulkner and his family for generations. They had served as the models for his fictional town of Jefferson and his Yoknapatawpha County. After filing one story from Oxford on the prevailing mood at the campus, I had settled down, like most of the other reporters, for what appeared would be a weekend lull. Since I did not have a Sunday edition, I set about gathering as much information as possible about Faulkner, his family and their roles in the community. I planned to use the material in a story for Monday's paper, provided there were no major news breaks over the weekend.

Faulkner had died two months earlier. But the people, places and atmosphere he had immortalized in his fiction were all there, just as he had described them. Just outside Oxford were the farms, with Negro sharecroppers, whose cotton fields had only recently been picked. The bare stalks stood dark and bleak, rustling in the autumn breeze. Negro children ran barefoot in yards outside shabby, unpainted shacks.

In Oxford (population 5,300), just as Faulkner had described it in *Intruder in the Dust*, there was the town square: ". . . the amphitheatric lightless stores, the slender white pencil of the Confederate monument against the mass of the courthouse looming in columned upsoar to the dim quadruple face of the clock lighted each by a single faint bulb with a quality as intransigent against their four fixed mechanical shouts of adjuration and warning as the glow of a firefly."

Within three days, this square was to echo to the boots of soldiers brandishing bayonets. But now, Saturday, it was as it had been for almost 100 years. Two elderly Negroes, just as they had done every day for weeks, set up a watermelon stand on the courthouse lawn. A white sheet of paper nailed to a tree announced a repossession sale. Saturday shoppers drifted in and out of Shaw and Sneed's Hardware Store. A sign pasted in a window pledged: "You can

fence over this Meredith business if he were still alive," she said.

In the absence of William Faulkner, the man in Oxford best suited to speak for him was his brother John, also a writer. And John Faulkner was no fence-straddler. He had strong opinions, which he wo'd voice to a reporter he considered friendly.

I visited John Faulkner's home, just off the Ole Miss campus, after being told by several other Northern reporters that his wife had chased them off, fearing they would not be sympathetic to his views. To get to the house, I walked down a footpath between rows of towering evergreens. I had the feeling I was walking into one of William Faulkner's novels. The trees seemed to be closing in on me. At the house, John's wife answered my knock.

"Friend or foe?" she asked. I assured her I was a friend. She told me about chasing off some reporters from Chicago and St. Louis (she was referring to Ray Coffey of the *Chicago Daily News* and Tom Yarbrough of the *St. Louis Post-Dispatch*). I assured Mrs. Faulkner I was a Southerner at heart, and she agreed to let me see her husband.

I interviewed him in the antique-filled parlor of the rambling, two-story house. He dragged slowly on a cigaret as he spoke. "This is actually a fight on whether the states have any rights left," he told me. "The Supreme Court desegregation decision of 1954 is unconstitutional. It is based on social theory, not law. The court's findings came out of seven books. Three of those books were written by Communists and four by fellow travelers." He argued that white Southerners, if left alone, would work out a solution to social problems. "We get along all right with our Negro friends down here," he said. "We look after them and they look after us." He said that he and a majority of Mississippians were solidly behind Governor Barnett. "He is our first citizen," Faulkner said. "He speaks for us. He is supporting the Constitution of the State of Mississippi and the Constitution of the United States. We will do whatever he tells us to do."

John Faulkner, 61, four years younger than William,

was a wispy man with white hair and a neat mustache. He looked like a carbon copy of his brother. His own writings, while much less ambitious works than William's, had achieved a measure of acclaim and popularity. His books included *Dollar Cotton, Men Working* and *Chooky*. At the time of the Ole Miss crisis, he was working on a biography of his brother. He was to complete it prior to his death on March 28, 1963.

Before his death, however, John Faulkner was to experience sharp disillusionment. As he was interviewed on that Saturday afternoon in September, 1962, he was supremely confident that Mississippians would solve their racial crisis with dignity. "It's not going to come to violence," he predicted. "It's going to come to a courtroom fight." Little more than a day later, his own son would lead a unit of National Guardsmen through rioting Mississippians and other Southerners to try to bring order back to the rubble-strewn, tear-gas-choked Ole Miss campus.

In Washington, Saturday was a beautiful, sunny autumn day. Attorney General Robert F. Kennedy was at his desk by 10 A.M. With him were a handful of Justice Department officials who had unofficially become a special task force for the Mississippi crisis. Among them were Deputy Attorney General Nicholas Katzenbach, the number-two man in the department, a lanky, balding former University of Chicago law professor; Burke Marshall, a scholarly former antitrust lawyer; and Edwin O. Guthman, a Pulitzer Prize-winning newspaperman who now was the Attorney General's special assistant for public information.

At 11:50 Washington time (9:50 in Mississippi), Kennedy received a call from Governor Ross Barnett. The Governor offered no new proposal to resolve the stalemate. Kennedy hung up the phone, peered somberly at the others and said: "We'd better get moving with the military."

At 12:15, he reached his brother by phone. The President told him to come to the White House. As the Attorney General walked out of his office, he shook his head grimly and said, "Maybe we waited too long."

"No," Ed Guthman told him. "The result would have

been the same. And the record is clear that we've done everything possible to avoid this."

Marshall accompanied the Attorney General to the White House. There the two of them went to work with the President on a television address scheduled tentatively for Sunday night, on a proclamation federalizing the Mississippi National Guard and on plans for using regular army troops at Ole Miss, if necessary. While they were working, another call came in from Barnett. He proposed a new plan. On Monday morning, he would wait at Ole Miss with Lieutenant Governor Johnson, the state highway patrolmen and sheriff's officers. In the meantime, marshals would "sneak" Meredith into Jackson, where he would be registered. Barnett would feign surprise, complaining of federal trickery. But the next day, he would permit Meredith to enter Ole Miss. Barnett promised the President that the highway patrol would maintain order.

The President and Attorney General mulled over the proposal all afternoon. Then, in a 7-P.M.-phone conversation, the President and Barnett personally agreed upon the plan. Barnett pledged that Meredith would be on the campus, without hindrance, by Tuesday. Accordingly, the President did not issue his proclamation federalizing the National Guard. In addition, he canceled the TV time scheduled for his talk.

Meanwhile, in Mississippi, outsiders were beginning to arrive at the Ole Miss campus. Among the first was William M. Rainach, former Louisiana state senator. Rainach rolled up to the front of the Lyceum in a black Oldsmobile, accompanied by a friend, and conducted an impromptu press conference. "We're here today because we said we would come to Oxford to survey the situation," he said.

"I've been visited by and received communications from various individuals and groups who are anxious to organize a voluntary march to Oxford to join in the defense of Governor Barnett and the State of Mississippi. Indications are that more than 10,000 Louisianans would join this march upon the proper call. They would come as volunteers, provided they would be given enlisted status in the Mississippi National Guard and assured of proper command."

However, Rainach continued, he had just come from conferring with Barnett in Jackson and the Governor had not encouraged such a march. "Barnett said he was delighted to know of the support from people in Louisiana," he said. "But he said he would not invite volunteers into the state because large groups might prove undisciplined and prove disruptive of his prearranged plans. However, the Governor added that he would not tell the volunteers not to come."

His press conference over, Rainach climbed back in his Oldsmobile and drove away with his companion. Whether his volunteer march would take place was left unclear. But reports were already circulating that many outsiders, from Louisiana and elsewhere, were on their way to Oxford.

Undoubtedly, when Rainach had quoted Barnett as speaking of "prearranged plans," he assumed the Governor meant plans for preventing James Meredith's enrollment. There was no reason for him to suspect that Barnett actually was negotiating a face-saving deal with the President of the United States. For Barnett was letting very few of his closest advisers, much less visiting firemen from Louisiana, in on his secret negotiations with the White House.

Subject to intense pressure from all sides, Barnett was wavering like a sapling in a windstorm. Only three hours after concluding his agreement with the President for Meredith to be registered in Jackson on Monday, the governor was back on the line to Washington. Nick Katzenbach answered the phone in the Justice Department shortly after 10 P.M., Washington time. The Attorney General had just left the office for his home in McLean, Virginia. Ed Guthman, hearing Katzenbach tell the operator that Barnett could reach the Attorney General there, remembers thinking: Here we go again.

Guthman's fears were justified. When Barnett finally reached the Attorney General at home, he told him that he was calling off the agreed plan. Kennedy's Irish temper flared. He told Barnett that this amounted to breaking an agreement with the President of the United States. But, eventually, the conversation ended on a more amicable note. Instead of the previous plan, the Attorney General and Barnett agreed on a new one, in which marshals would arrive in force Monday morning with Meredith, at the Ole Miss campus, rather than Jackson. Barnett said he would call the Attorney General again at 11 the next morning, Washington time, to check on final details.

By now the federal officials had little confidence in Barnett's word. They decided to place regular army troops in position from which the soldiers could move swiftly into the campus area, if needed. They also decided to go through with the original plan to federalize the Mississippi National Guard, both to prevent its use by Barnett and to make it available for use, if necessary, by the federal government.

It was late Saturday night. President Kennedy sat at a long table in the White House Indian Treaty Room. With him was Norbert A. Schlei, head of the Justice Department's Office of Legal Counsel. The President, pen in hand, leaned over a proclamation federalizing the Guard. He signed his name.

Then, before writing the date, he asked: "Is it past midnight?"

Schlei looked at his watch. "It's just 20 seconds past 12," he replied.

The President wrote the date, "September 30, 1962," on the proclamation. It was a date that was to become engraved on the history of this country's race relations.

In Mississippi, it was still September 29. At the municipal stadium in Jackson, where Ole Miss was playing its football game against Kentucky, Ross Barnett was basking in the adoration of 41,000 cheering fans, many of them waving Confederate flags. At half-time, Ole Miss was in the lead, 7–0. Barnett stood on the field at a microphone, smiling. The crowd fell silent. Barnett raised his right fist in a gesture of defiance.

"I love Mississippi," he said. From the stands came a roar of approval.

"I love her people." Again came the roar.

"I love our customs." Now, the roar was deafening. All 41,000 spectators knew that "our customs" meant, primarily, segregation customs.

The crowd was in Barnett's palm. He had the opportunity here to strike a forceful blow, for either law and order or lawlessness. But he did neither. He had whipped the crowd into a frenzy. Now, he let that frenzy fizzle. He uttered not one word of advice on how to cope with the crisis. During the second half, a newspaperman entered Barnett's box and told him that President Kennedy had federalized the Mississippi National Guard. He asked the Governor to comment, but Barnett refused.

Events were moving swiftly.

In Fort Bragg, North Carolina, the 700 men of the 503rd Military Police Battalion—specialists in riot control—were loaded hurriedly into four-engine C-130 Hercules transports. They were told only that they were part of "Task Force Alpha," but did not immediately know where they were headed. Before takeoff, the battalion's officers were given unopened crates of riot shotguns. They began to suspect where they were going.

At Fort Dix, New Jersey, the 680 men of the 716th Military Police Battalion also were loaded aboard transports. They were under orders similar to those of the 503rd MP Battalion.

Shortly after midnight Mississippi time, the planes began setting down at the Millington Naval Air Station at Memphis. In the eerie darkness, 58 huge Hercules transports bumped down on the runways within two hours. Men and materials were disgorged rapidly from the bowels of the huge aircraft.

The soldiers were in full battle dress. They wore combat fatigues, highly polished boots and authoritative MP armbands. They were armed with pistols, M-1 rifles, carbines and bayonets. Immediately after landing at Memphis, they began pitching pup tents alongside the runways.

Almost as impressive as this array of manpower was the equipment massed at the naval air base. Unloaded from the transports were 250 jeeps, 30 two-and-a-half-ton trucks with trailers, 25 three-quarter-ton trucks, four truck cranes, four gasoline trucks and seven ambulances. Nearby stood 24 transport helicopters.

At 3:05 A.M., the 110-man detachment of the army engineers previously sent to Memphis from Fort Campbell, Kentucky, rolled out of the naval air base in a 49-vehicle convoy. Its destination was a secret, but newsmen trailed at a close distance. The convoy headed southeast on U. S. 78 into Mississippi. Reporters wondered why that route was being taken. U. S. 55, a new superhighway, was the shortest route to Oxford.

Deep in the woods of the Holly Springs National Forest, 15 miles northeast of Oxford, 41-year-old Cotton Tabor, his wife Mary, and two sons, Joe, 18, and Jerry, 15, were sound asleep in their four-room cabin. Tabor ran a fishing camp on an 18-acre site leased from the federal government. A few minutes after 4 A.M., Tabor was awakened by a loud pounding on his front door. Three miles from his nearest neighbor, he was astonished by the sound. "It scared the hell out of me," he recalls. He jumped out of bed and hurried to the door.

"Who's there?" he called.

"We're from the army," came the reply.

Tabor opened the door. To his amazement, several soldiers in full combat dress were standing outside, some with M-1 rifles slung over their shoulders, others with .45-caliber automatics strapped to their hips.

The detachment of engineers had reached its destination.

Commanding officer Major Ralph S. Christopherson, of Pittsfield, New Hampshire, explained to Tabor that the unit had been assigned to erect a tent city across the road from his cabin to house deputy marshals and army men assigned to enforce the court orders directing James Meredith's enrollment at Ole Miss.

The first military detachment ordered into Mississippi in the crisis swiftly got down to work. In a matter of hours, the tent city had risen in a clearing in the forest. In addition to tents for housing the army men and marshals, there were a communications headquarters, a medical tent, a mess tent and an administrative headquarters.

Tight security was clamped on the area. Except for myself and a few other newsmen who made their way to the tent city, only those on official business were permitted past army roadblocks set up on a narrow, deeply rutted back road leading to Tabor's camp. A number of Tabor's customers were turned away. Tabor himself was not permitted to cross the road separating his cabin from the tent city.

"This burns me up," Tabor told me. "They're ruining my Sunday business. I have 30 boats that I rent for $1.50 each. Usually, I can rent most of them at least twice during a Sunday. It's my busiest day. But they're stopping my customers and sending them away. I don't like it a damn bit. I was in the army and I know these fellows are just following orders. But it burns me up that they're doing all this for a nigger who doesn't really want an education in the first place."

The army engineers and MPs were not the only ones on the move during the night. On U. S. 51, between Jackson and Oxford, a white compact car raced north through the darkness. In the car was a lanky, erect man in a dark suit and a broad-brimmed white hat. In Jackson, he had been given a ticket to the football game. But, hearing that the crisis was coming to a boil in Oxford, he had given back the ticket and headed north with friends. Arriving at Oxford in the predawn hours, the white car pulled in at the Mansel Motel. The man in the broad-brimmed hat registered under an assumed name. His real name was General Edwin Walker.

At 6:12 A.M., Mississippi time, Secretary of the Army Cyrus Vance ordered all Mississippi Army and Air National Guardsmen to report to their armories and air bases. In a telegram to Governor Barnett, Vance said that the 11,450 Guardsmen were in federal service, as of midnight, and would remain so for an indefinite period. Among those who reported to an armory in Jackson was Lieutenant Ross Barnett, Jr., son of the Governor and a member of the 155th Infantry "Dixie" Division of the National Guard.

In Oxford, National Guard Captain Murry C. (Chooky) Falkner, son of John Faulkner and nephew of William Faulkner, was relaxing at home. (John and William were among the few members of the family to spell their names with a "u.") Captain Falkner's phone rang. He assumed it was a call from a local hospital, where his wife had just given birth. Instead, it was from the National Guard. He and the 63 men under his command in the 108th Armored Cavalry Squadron were ordered to report to their armory in combat dress by 8 A.M. and await further orders.

Most of the men were at the armory before 8. A guard

stood at the front door, barring entry to all but authorized personnel. In a fenced yard behind the armory stood two small tanks, three trucks and four jeeps. The Guardsmen were laughing and clowning inside the armory. It seemed like a lark to some of them. To a man, they were segregationists opposed to Meredith's enrollment at Ole Miss. But, in less than a day, they would be braving gunfire, tear gas, Molotov cocktails, bricks and rocks to help bring about his enrollment.

It was another beautiful autumn day in both Washington and Mississippi. Attorney General Kennedy and his task force on the Mississippi crisis were in the office by 9 A.M. Washington time.

James Meredith had spent the night at Dillard University in New Orleans. He was flown to Memphis in a Border Patrol plane, a Cessna 310. At Memphis, the marshals were awakened at dawn and told to be ready to load in C-47 planes by noon if necessary. Additional army troops were being flown into Memphis in C-130 transports as Meredith landed in the Border Patrol plane.

Chief Marshal McShane was in charge of the marshals at Memphis. By now, he had gotten to know his men, even those from other organizations such as the Border Patrol and the Federal Bureau of Prisons, sufficiently well to pick out the leaders and those with special talents. These veterans of both riot-control training and previous racial assignments were given key roles in the upcoming enrollment attempt at Ole Miss. Deputy Chief Marshal John W. (Jack) Cameron, a chunky blond with a crew cut, was second in command to McShane. The men were divided into three groups, each with a veteran marshal designated as group leader.

Many of these marshals had been top men in their home offices and, before becoming federal officers, had served with distinction in local or state police departments. Most came from Southern states. But there were Northerners, as well, some of whom were to leave Oxford with wounds suffered in the enforcement of Southern court orders. There was Gene Same, from Indianapolis, Indiana, who was to come closest of all the marshals to losing his life. And there was my new friend, Joe Denson, whose life was to be saved by a leather folder containing his marshal's credentials.

Besides such men as these, who were to serve with the frontline "troops" in the coming battle, McShane was to use to advantage the particular talents of a special corps of marshals. Typical of this special corps was the man who was to be Meredith's personal bodyguard, Deputy Marshal Cecil Miller of Miami, Florida. Miller, a 200-pound-plus judo expert, comes closest to being the "James Bond of the Marshals' Service." He is huge, lumbers on flat feet, but has catlike reflexes. As another member of the special corps of marshals, Group Leader Clarence Albert (Al) Butler, puts it: "Cecil can't run very fast, but he doesn't have to. He doesn't run; he stands and fights."

All these men had been called from their home offices on short notice to report to Memphis for possible use in the Mississippi crisis. McShane himself had first been ordered to Memphis while at his office in the Justice Department building in Washington on September 15. This was so that he could represent the government in the initial attempts to register Meredith. Even today, he recalls the events of that month with such clarity that he can recite the addresses and phone numbers of minor participants in the drama. "I was in my office when I got the word to go to Memphis," he says. "I flew down there, and stayed at the Holiday Inn. I met Meredith for the first time at about 9:30 that night at 588 Vance Street, the law office of A. W. Willis, a Negro attorney."

At their first meeting, McShane and Meredith discussed such routine matters as where and when the marshals would pick Meredith up for the initial registration attempt. But McShane also gave Meredith some instructions that were to hold for the duration of the crisis: "When we get out of our cars, stay close to me and those with me."

After the first enrollment attempt had been balked by Ross Barnett, McShane had returned to Washington. Then, on Wednesday, September 19, he got word at his office, to go back to Memphis for a new registration attempt. A niece of McShane's was visiting with him at the time. The niece had never seen the Robert E. Lee home in Arlington,

Virginia, not far from McShane's home in Alexandria. So McShane had driven his wife and niece to the Lee mansion, telling them he would pick them up at 3:15 P.M. But, after learning that he was to return to Memphis on short notice, McShane got tied up in a Justice Department strategy conference until 5:10. His plane was to leave Washington National Airport at 6.

When the conference ended, he raced to Arlington, picked up his wife and niece, then rushed home and hurriedly packed a suitcase.

"Make sure you have enough shirts," his wife called.

"Don't worry," he yelled. "I've got plenty of shirts."

He hopped in his car, headed toward the airport at a breakneck clip and arrived at 5:55, just in time to hear that there would be a half-hour delay on his flight. His suitcase was loaded aboard the plane while he waited to board. It contained not a single shirt. The only shirt McShane was to have to his name in Memphis and Mississippi was the one on his back. He made do with borrowed shirts from some of his men.

Now, on Sunday, September 30, McShane was wearing a borrowed shirt—as usual—while awaiting instructions at the Memphis naval air station. He and Justice Department attorney John Doar, who was to become a sort of high-level baby-sitter for Meredith during the crisis, were watching over the young Negro.

In Washington, Attorney General Kennedy received another phone call from Barnett shortly before Meredith's arrival in Memphis. The governor had a new plan, patterned after his Thursday suggestion, but on a much grander scale: on Monday morning, he proposed to wait for Meredith at an Ole Miss gate, backed by the state troopers, who in turn would be backed by local police and sheriff's officers from all over Mississippi, who in turn would be backed by citizens and students. Here would be a so-called wall of flesh that the Kennedys would be obliged to move out of the way in order to enroll Meredith. The potential for disaster was immense.

Under Barnett's plan, he would read a proclamation barring Meredith from Ole Miss. Then the federal men would draw their guns. Barnett then could step aside, claiming he was bowing only to the threat of armed attack by the federal men.

The Attorney General bristled. His voice was icy. He told Barnett that the Governor of Mississippi had an obligation to think of other matters besides his own political future: his state and his nation were dependent on him for responsible action. Barnett seemed unmoved, so Kennedy switched to a new tactic. He told Barnett that, unless he kept his word to the President to cooperate in maintaining order while Meredith was enrolled, the President would tell a nationwide TV audience that the Governor had reneged on his promise. And to prove his point, the President would spell out in detail all the behind-the-scenes negotiations.

"Oh, my God," Barnett said. "Don't do that! Don't do that!"

Barnett yielded. He would do whatever was necessary, he said, to maintain order. Several times, he appealed to the Attorney General to be sure the President would say nothing on television that would reveal the nature of the secret phone calls. The Attorney General proposed that Meredith be flown onto the campus on Monday by helicopter to register. Marshals and state officers would work together to control any crowd that gathered.

Barnett realized that his supporters planned some action on Monday to defy the desegregation attempt. He told Kennedy that Mississippians were in an ugly mood; that hundreds of racist agitators were heading toward Ole Miss from numerous states in the South and, in some cases, the North. Because of the possibility of a holocaust if the enrollment attempt were made on Monday, Barnett and the Attorney General agreed that Meredith should be brought on campus before dark that same day, Sunday.

Kennedy stipulated that Meredith should be safely placed on campus before the President's television speech, then set for 5:30 P.M. Mississippi time. Barnett was to send his highway patrol chief, pudgy Colonel T. B. Birdsong, to Oxford to take personal charge of the state's security measures. In two more phone calls during the next few hours, Barnett and Kennedy firmed up details of the plan. Barnett repeatedly assured the Attorney General that order would be maintained. The highway patrol would escort Meredith onto the campus.

At 2 P.M. Washington time, key members of Kennedy's Mississippi task force boarded a military Jetstar plane and headed toward Oxford. Aboard were Nicholas Katzenbach, who was to be in charge of the federal contingent at Ole Miss; Edwin Guthman, Kennedy's special assistant for public information; Norbert Schlei, who had drawn up the proclamation federalizing the Mississippi National Guard; Harold Reis, Schlei's chief assistant; and Dean Markham, a special assistant to the President.

Also in the air at the time, flying from Atlanta, Georgia, to Jackson, Mississippi, was a bulky man with a red beard and an untrimmed red mustache. His name was Paul Guihard, and he was a newspaperman. Born to French and British parents, he was covering the Mississippi crisis for the French news service, Agence France-Presse, and as a special correspondent for British newspapers. Traveling with the 31-year-old Guihard was chubby, dark-haired Sammy Schulman, chief United States photographer for Agence France-Presse. Guihard was hungry. A pretty stewardess brought him several small sandwiches and a soft drink. Amused by his appearance and his accent, she tried to guess his occupation. "Oh, I know—you're goin' down to the nigger thing," she drawled.

Guihard tried to smile. He said in French to Schulman: "These people. It will take them a hundred years to start forgetting." Later, he scribbled a note in his pad: "Hostess, 'about that nigger.'" It was to be one of the last notes of his career. Before the night was over, Paul Guihard would lie dead, a victim of an assassin's bullet on the Ole Miss campus.

James Meredith ate an uneventful lunch at the cafeteria of the naval air station at Memphis. Justice Department attorney Doar, his "baby-sitter," spent much of the lunch period on the phone to Washington. He was told to be ready to take off with Meredith in the light Border Patrol plane by 3:30 P.M. Mississippi time. Later, Doar got word to be over Oxford by 5:30 and to have the pilot circle until ordered to land. As Doar spoke to Washington, he could hear the roar of the engines of four transports preparing to take the first contingent of 170 marshals to Oxford. A convoy of 30 Border Patrol cars with two-way radios was preparing to take another 60 marshals to the campus from Memphis.

In Oxford, a half-dozen newspapermen were eating lunch at the Mansion restaurant when General Edwin Walker, wearing his broad-brim hat, strode in and took a seat at a booth across the aisle. Several of us moved over to ask Walker what he planned to do in Oxford, but he waved the questions aside. He said he might have a press conference later in the day.

At the Executive Mansion in Jackson, Ross Barnett designated four state officials to go to Oxford as his personal representatives. Placed in charge of the delegation was State Senator George M. Yarbrough, president pro tem of the Senate and third-ranking official in the state, behind only Barnett and Lieutenant Governor Johnson. The other three delegation members were County Judge Russell Moore, State Senator John C. McLaurin, and State Representative C. B. (Buddie) Newman.

Barnett gave Yarbrough a written order empowering him "to do all things necessary that the peace and security of the people of the State of Mississippi are fully protected." This delegation of authority—in effect an order getting the monkey of responsibility off Barnett's back—later was to play an important role in determining how Mississippi met its challenge to quell the Ole Miss riot.

The four men were apprehensive about the coming events. They feared they might be arrested by the marshals or even killed if violence erupted. (Barnett had not briefed his four delegates on his negotiations with the President or the Attorney General.) Newman's fear was so great that he hastily made out a will, and asked the other three members of the delegation to witness it. Upon leaving the mansion, however, Newman and the others felt they had an abundance of time before the crisis. They understood that the attempt to place Meredith on the campus would be made Monday, not Sunday. Their plan was to arrive in Oxford on Sunday to prepare a force of state officers similar to the one that had formed ranks at the university on Thursday.

Yarbrough notified the highway patrol to be on hand at Oxford by the time he arrived. Moore went on the highway patrol radio and directed 70 of the state's 82 sheriffs to meet him at the Lafayette County Courthouse at 10:30 Sunday night with some of their deputies. McLaurin ordered three fire trucks with high-pressure pumpers, capable of hosing a man to the ground at 200 feet, on standby duty for use at the campus.

Yarbrough flew in a light plane to his big cattle farm at Red Banks, a short distance from Oxford. The other three planned to join him at Oxford about 6:30. McLaurin drove to his home in suburban Brandon, outside Jackson, before making the flight to Oxford. He walked into the yard and said goodbye to his four-year-old son. It was a touching scene, pointing up the fears held by McLaurin and the others.

In Jackson on Sunday afternoon the Citizens' Councils were conducting a mass rally to stir support for the segregationist cause. The rally, symbolically, was taking place directly in front of the white stone Executive Mansion occupied by Ross Barnett. About 2,000 persons were whooping it up at the rally when reporter Paul Guihard arrived with photographer Sammy Schulman. They had rented a white you-drive-it car immediately after landing in Jackson and had driven directly to the rally from the airport.

There was a festive mood on the mansion grounds. Women doled out sandwiches and coffee. The Rebel Broadcasting Company station, WRBC, aired Mississippi fight songs. Hundreds of portable radios were turned in to the station. Periodically, an announcer called upon all listeners to toot car horns as a symbol of unity in defiance of integration.

The chairman of the Citizens' Council membership committee, undertaker John Wright, announced over a bullhorn microphone that marshals were en route to Jackson to arrest the governor. He said "reliable sources" had brought the report at dawn, and that intelligence reports from Oxford said the planes carrying the marshals were on the way. Actually, the planes were headed for Oxford. Wright urged the segregationists at the rally to form a "wall of flesh" to protect Barnett from the federals.

Paul Guihard, despite warnings from Schulman that racist crowds could be ferocious with newsmen, walked right into the middle of the rally. He had joked earlier that he was going to cover the Mississippi crisis like a Southern colonel, "with a mint julep in my hand." Now, he felt confident enough of his safety to wade right into the racist camp. And his confidence, at this point, was justified. He managed to persuade segregationist leader Louis W. Hollis to grant him a half-hour interview in the Citizens' Council office, even though the office was buzzing with activity. Hollis figured Guihard was on the segregationist side, since he could not conceive that anyone so urbane as Guihard could believe in the integration cause.

Hollis liked Guihard so well that he permitted the newsman to dictate his story to his home office in French over the Citizens' Council phone. It was to be his last story. And it was a prophetic one. "The crowd laughed and sang under the warm autumn sun," he wrote. "And it was apparent it hadn't the vaguest idea of the enormity of its actions."

4

At 4 P.M., Mississippi time, the military Jetstar plane carrying the Justice Department contingent from Washington set down at a small civilian airport just outside Oxford. Immediately after landing, Deputy Attorney General Katzenbach phoned Attorney General Kennedy in Washington. He was told the operation was still on, but there was one change in plans. Although James Meredith still would be brought on the campus Sunday, his registration would not take place until Monday.

About 170 of the deputy marshals from the Millington Naval Air Station at Memphis had landed at the Oxford airport in C-47s by the time the plane from Washington arrived. Chief Marshal James McShane was among them, and was in direct command of the men, under Katzenbach's supervision. Meredith, Justice Department attorney Doar and Deputy Marshal Cecil Miller were still back in Memphis. The deputy marshals were loaded in six army trucks brought to the airport from the tent city set up Sunday morning in the Holly Springs National Forest. With Katzenbach, McShane and other Justice Department officials leading the way in Border Patrol cars, the trucks headed in a convoy toward the Ole Miss campus.

On the road between the airport and the campus, the convoy was met under a prearranged plan by the head of the Mississippi Highway Patrol, Colonel T. B. Birdsong. Katzenbach and McShane emerged to exchange pleasantries with the short, chubby, amiable man upon whom much of the responsibility for maintaining order this day would depend. With a highway patrol escort, the convoy rolled again toward the campus. The marshals' Group Leader Al Butler, smiling broadly, was riding the running board of the third truck in the convoy. He had seen large crowds often before, and the crowd that was gathering along the roadway leading to the campus seemed little more menacing than many others.

The marshals were wearing orange riot vests, with pockets for tear-gas canisters, and white helmets marked with the stenciled letters "U. S. Marshal." The crowd instantly sensed what was happening. "Nigger lover," one young man shouted at Butler. The marshal just smiled back. "You'll be sorry," another bystander yelled. Butler smiled again. Some spectators applauded. It was hard to tell whether the applause was genuine or sarcastic.

Alongside the road, Butler spotted a boy of about five wearing an outsize cowboy hat. Sensing a look of fear in the boy's face and thinking of his own children back in Florida, Butler smiled some more, waved and shouted: "Hi, Cowboy!" The little boy laughed and waved a greeting in return.

About 4:30, the convoy wheeled onto the west limits of the campus. At a gate on Sorority Row, highway patrolmen standing guard opened a way for the trucks to pass. The trucks rolled past rows of white sorority houses, around a tree-lined area of the campus known as "the Grove" and finally up to the front of the white-columned Lyceum administration building.

Katzenbach conferred again with Birdsong at the Lyceum. Birdsong agreed to maintain law and order, to work in cooperation with the federal authorities and to seal off campus entrances and exits. At Katzenbach's request, he agreed that it would be all right for the marshals to dismount from their trucks.

The marshals dismounted shortly after 4:30. The group leaders split them into four groups, each guarding one of the four sides of the Lyceum. The first group of marshals to arrive on the scene formed a thin line surrounding the building, but with some rather wide holes. There just were not enough men to stand shoulder to shoulder around the entire building. So the marshals concentrated on the columned front side of the Lyceum, facing east. Al Butler, still smiling, placed his 48 men directly in front of the Lyceum's front steps.

In front of the men lay the tree-studded circle that had looked so calm a day earlier, and, indeed, still looked relatively calm. Squirrels nibbled at acorns under the giant oaks. Lovers still stole a kiss here and there as they strolled across the campus. But now, with the arrival of the marshals, there was intense curiosity. History was about to be made again on this lovely campus, famed for its football teams, its beauty queens and its education of some of Mississippi's finest men and women.

Colonel Birdsong stationed his highway patrolmen, sheriff's officers, city policemen and other state lawmen in a circle between the marshals and the crowd. The idea, presumably, was for the state officers to serve as a buffer between the citizenry and the federal "invaders."

Upon returning from lunch at the Mansion, where I had talked briefly with General Walker, I had gone back to my room at the Colonial Hotel in downtown Oxford to write what the newspaper fraternity calls an "overnight sidebar." What this amounts to is a feature story, rather than a spot news story, that is written early enough to make the first editions of the next day's afternoon papers and still be timeless enough to be newsworthy at the end of the next afternoon's press run. For my story, I was concentrating on the family of Cotton Tabor, the fishing-camp operator whose acreage had been taken over by the Army to erect the tent city.

About 4 P.M., I ran out of cigarets and walked around the corner to the drugstore frequented by many of Oxford's most prominent citizens, including the Faulkners. While there, I heard from a local tipster that the marshals were entering the campus. With my story almost completed and the Western Union office right in the Colonial Hotel, I debated momentarily whether to file as much as I had written with Western Union and then go to the campus or to go there immediately. I chose to go immediately. It was one of the luckiest decisions I have ever made, for it enabled me to be the first reporter on the campus, and the only one there for a long period during which the crisis built in intensity second by second.

I ran to my rented car and jumped in hurriedly. As I began backing out of the parking space, across the street from the hotel, I heard a sound that was unmistakable. It was the thump-thump-thump of a flat tire. "Son of a bitch," I remember saying aloud. Of all the times for a flat, this was the worst I could remember in my 11 years of newspapering.

Things didn't remain all that black. I met a man I knew vaguely—at this point I can't even remember his name—and persuaded him to give me a ride to the campus. "It's no use goin' up there in such a hurry," he said. "The police have set up roadblocks. They won't let any reporters in. They won't even let townspeople in, unless they're on business."

Nonetheless, I elected to go to the campus and take my chances on getting inside. I have found that one way for a reporter to get into places where he is unwanted is to play dumb. Just get in a crowd, blend with the scenery and walk in. It sometimes helps to hold a door open for a lady or an elderly man, particularly when trying to get into such spots as gambling houses.

When my benefactor dropped me off at the Illinois Central Railroad trestle adjoining the campus, I saw a group of reporters I knew standing disconsolately in a group, commiserating with one another over the fact that state police roadblocks prevented them from entering the campus. I immediately walked in the opposite direction from the group. I did not want the police to associate me with the other reporters.

There were only two state troopers manning the roadblock. They had all they could do to check students and faculty members for identification. They were cutting a few corners. If a group of students or adults with Ole Miss identification cards walked toward the roadblock, one ID card was sufficient to clear the entire group. So I took off my tie—a sure sign that I was a reporter—tucked my large steno notebook in the crook of my arm, under my jacket, and joined a group of students walking across the trestle. The students did not know me; I did not know them. But, for this occasion, I acted as though they were my longtime buddies. It was enough for me to con my way past the roadblock.

I walked again across the campus, past the Confederate monument, fully expecting to find some other enterprising reporters waiting for me in front of the Lyceum. But I didn't. Instead, I saw only the two rings of lawmen—first the marshals in their riot vests, with their billy clubs and teargas guns, closest to the building, and then the state officers, interspersed between the marshals and the crowd of about 500 standing along the curb opposite the Lyceum.

The crowd was mostly jovial. There was some vile razzing of the marshals by male students and several coeds, but there certainly was no indication of immediate danger. Several fathers carried children on their shoulders. It was more like a July Fourth parade than a budding riot. There were some ominous signs, though, including the attitude taken by the Mississippi law enforcement officers. They seemed to think it was all very amusing. Periodically, they would halfheartedly instruct the students to back up slightly. But they gave few solid indications that they meant business. Mostly, they snickered at the epithets hurled at the marshals.

Al Butler, pacing back and forth in front of his group of marshals before the Lyceum steps, quickly got tagged with the nickname "Smiley." It has stuck with him ever since.

"Smiley, where's your wife tonight—home with a nigger?" Butler smiled.

"You got a nigger mistress, Smiley. You got nigger children." Butler smiled some more.

Other marshals did not take it so well. They said nothing, merely stared back at their verbal tormentors. But their jaw muscles tightened. They clutched their billy clubs a little tighter. I wondered what the Mississippi cops would have done if subjected to that kind of merciless heckling.

The inside of the Lyceum, on the ground floor, is shaped like a cross. It is about a dozen long strides from the front door to a hallway running perpendicular to the one leading from the front door to the back door. If you make a left turn, you are headed straight toward the office of the registrar. If you make a right turn, you are headed toward a row of four phone booths and, beyond that, a ladies' rest room and a staircase. If you walk straight toward the back door, the offices of the chancellor and some of his aides are on the right and left.

When Nick Katzenbach arrived inside the Lyceum, he set up a command post in the registrar's office. Communications were established, by radio and phone, with various strategic points in the Oxford area and in Washington. Among them were the White House, the Justice Department, the tent city in the national forest, the post office building in Oxford (where Louis Oberdorfer, assistant attorney general in charge of the Justice Department Tax Division, was coordinating federal activities downtown), and the Millington Naval Air Station in Memphis.

Katzenbach and Dean Markham set up separate phone connections to the White House and Justice Department in the second-from-the-right phone booth and the extreme-left phone booth, respectively. (Federal men are wary of using phones other than toll phones in hostile territory, for those that go through a switchboard or are individually installed in homes or offices are more susceptible to eavesdropping and outright wiretapping.)

The Attorney General was still at the Justice Department during the early maneuvering. Later, he was to go to the White House and spend the taut hours of the crisis with his brother. But while at his office, he alternated between twisting a green velour sweater into knots as he sat in his red leather armchair and trying to relax by twirling a mahogany yo-yo he keeps on his desk or by tossing a football back and forth across the room with one of his aides.

Now, as the hands on the ornate clock in the Lyceum tower moved toward 5, Nick Katzenbach told Bob Kennedy (his aides call him "Bob," not "Bobby") that the campus appeared sufficiently safe for James Meredith to be brought onto the campus. Katzenbach advised bringing him to the Oxford airport in the Border Patrol plane, and then having him driven from the airport to the campus with a small but well-chosen group of marshals and state officers as a convoy.

At this point, the Lyceum was considered secured. There was a reasonable degree of cooperation among the Justice Department officials, university officials, Colonel Birdsong and, to a lesser degree, the state law enforcement officers. Those officers under Birdsong's direct control, the highway patrolmen, were expected to follow his orders. But there were large numbers of red-neck sheriffs, city policemen and political hacks with badges. How they would handle themselves remained to be seen.

At Memphis, Meredith, John Doar, Deputy Marshal Cecil Miller and a pilot climbed into a little light green Border Patrol plane. The takeoff was smooth. Meredith seemed calm and detached, but the nervous stomach he had developed in the Air Force was tightening a bit.

It is a short hop from Memphis to Oxford, but this flight was not to be all that short. For Meredith's plane was under instructions to circle until ordered to land. As it circled Oxford and got its landing instructions, it was joined by two others, almost identical in design and even in color. Which one was Meredith's?

Nick Katzenbach and Ed Guthman, who had driven with Birdsong to the airport shortly after 6, had no idea. The first plane landed. It was a light blue and white Cessna 310. Katzenbach and Guthman ran out to meet it. But they saw neither Meredith, Doar, nor Miller. Tensely, they walked back to the terminal to await the second plane. It swooped low over the field, set down gently and rolled toward the terminal. This was it.

Meredith, Doar and Miller alighted. On the way to the airport Katzenbach had noticed a fairly large crowd gathering alongside the road leading from the campus. He asked Birdsong to have the road cleared. Birdsong complied. He was cooperating with the federals in a manner that made ludicrous Ross Barnett's later claims that he had never negotiated a deal with the Kennedys. If his claims were true, then Birdsong must surely have been disobeying orders, which seems hardly likely in view of his continuation as director of the highway patrol.

It was now 6:15. Meredith climbed into the back seat of a green Border Patrol sedan. Katzenbach and Doar sat on either side of him. In the front seat, with a Border Patrol driver, were Miller and Guthman. Birdsong rode in a highway patrol car at the head of the convoy. Behind this car was a six-by-six Army truck carrying an additional 25 marshals. Directly behind the Army truck was the car containing Meredith and the federal officials.

There was considerable radio communication among the vehicles. Continually, Meredith heard himself called "the subject" in these conversations. Finally, he nudged Doar with an elbow and cracked: "How about that? The student has become the subject!"

The remark was as good an indication as any of Meredith's coolness under stress. He is an intense person. He has a tart tongue. He is capable, in the loneliness of his own room, of churning his insides to the point of physical illness over the frustration of the Negro's lot in America. But he also is disciplined. Under fire, he has an amazing ability to maintain his composure, until he can permit himself the luxury of blowing off steam.

The convoy rolled swiftly along the cleared roads from the airport to the campus. Only a few students and reporters were gathered at the west entrance as the convoy climbed a hill leading to the main buildings of the university. By this time, about 40 marshals had been sent to Baxter Hall, a dormitory where a two-room suite had been designated for use by Meredith and his guards. The dormitory had been secured, and two-way radio communication had been set up between Baxter and the Lyceum.

Without incident, Meredith was dropped off at the dorm, along with Doar and Miller. He was officially residing on the Ole Miss campus, even if he still had not been registered.

At 7, Guthman and Katzenbach were back at the Lyceum. By now, the crowd had grown to close to 2,000, and it was becoming increasingly mean. I had watched the crowd build from a small group of good-natured students and faculty members, many of them feeling sufficiently safe to carry small children, to its current state. In a little more than two hours, it had changed from a group to a crowd and was now in the process of becoming a mob.

The shouting of obscenities had increased at least tenfold. The crowd pressed in time and again on the marshals. At first, the state highway patrolmen and plainclothesmen had instructed the civilians to stay beyond the curb opposite the Lyceum. But the crowd had become so large and unruly that the state officers had virtually abandoned attempts to keep it back. The marshals held their original ground, neither budging an inch nor making any physical contact with the civilians.

Twice between 5 and 7 P.M., I had been called aside by state highway patrolmen and directed to identify myself. When I showed my press card, they had frowned, made it clear I was on the campus at my own risk, asked me if I had a camera (I didn't), frisked me (evidently for a camera, rather than a weapon) and sent me on my way.

It is a fact of history that cameras and tape recorders are often more dangerous than guns in the midst of race-baiting mobs. From Little Rock to the 1961 Freedom Rides, newsmen had taken their lumps whenever mobs had spotted them. And the easiest way to tell a newsman in a mob is by his camera, his lights (in the case of a newsreel man), a tape recorder (in the case of a radio-TV man) or his notebook and pencil. A newspaper reporter can put his notebook in a pocket, or, as I did, hide it under his jacket. But there is no way in the world to hide a Speed-Graphic camera or the massive equipment needed by the electronic media. Shortly, the antagonistic nature of electronic news-gathering equipment was to be demonstrated on the Ole Miss campus. But for the present, I remained one of the few reporters who had managed to enter the campus. I stood squarely in the middle of the crowd in front of the Lyceum, still holding my notebook between my arm and my body, under my jacket.

I was making mental notes for later entries in my notebook—about the snickering sheriff's officers in plainclothes, who seemed to be enjoying every epithet aimed at the marshals; about the seeming reluctance of the highway patrolmen to do anything to prevent the civilians from enjoying this demonstration against federal authority; about the knuckles of some marshals turning white as they gripped their billies ever tighter; about the apparent lack of leadership among the state officers; and about the contrasting chain-of-command leadership among the marshals.

As 7 o'clock approached, I spotted several reporter friends in the crowd, trying, as I was, to appear as inconspicuous as possible. The first one I noticed was Bob Carpenter, with whom I had been sharing a room at the Colonial Hotel. Bob and I had worked together more than six years earlier on Scripps-Howard's *Houston Press*. Now, he was a reporter-photographer for Hodding Carter's Pulitzer Prize-winning daily in Greenville, Mississippi.

I didn't see Bob walk up. He suddenly materialized in the crowd, just as I must have seemed to him to materialize. He had a small camera hanging around his neck, as did numerous students in the crowd. Occasionally, very unobtrusively, he would snap the shutter. At first Bob and I stayed apart, on the theory that two suspicious looking characters were more apt to be ejected from the campus or attacked than one. Later, however, it became clear that the highway patrolmen and sheriff's officers cared little about us, except if we were about to take their pictures doing something that might prove embarrassing. About a half-hour after I first saw Bob, I was to wish for once that I had a camera to record the shameful act of at least one state officer.

But much was to occur before that. Now, I spotted Ray Coffey of the *Chicago Daily News* in the crowd. Ray is short, slender and light-haired. He could easily have passed for a graduate student. He was wearing a dress shirt, open at the neck, and light summer trousers.

"How long you been here?" he asked me.

"Since a little after the marshals got here."

"How'd you get in?"

"I just walked in with a bunch of students. How about you?"

"I had to go down the hill and cross the railroad tracks," Coffey replied.

It amazed me that more reporters had not arrived by the same route. If the highway patrolmen were not guarding the ravine separating the campus from Oxford, through which the railroad tracks passed, almost anyone could have crossed the tracks and climbed the hill to the campus. As a matter of fact, many white agitators from Mississippi and elsewhere later were to use this very route to join the mob.

At about 6:40 P.M., Katzenbach, Guthman and Doar had begun a meeting with university officials to discuss Meredith's registration at 8 the following morning. The Justice Department was dealing chiefly with Hugh H. Clegg, a former FBI agent who is assistant to Chancellor J. D. Williams and also serves as the university's director of development. Earlier, Katzenbach had met with Clegg, Registrar Ellis and Dean of Students Leston L. Love in Clegg's office. They had made the arrangements for Meredith's dormitory suite. The key to the suite and directions on how to reach it had been provided Katzenbach by Clegg.

Now, with the second meeting in progress, Guthman reported by phone to Attorney General Kennedy at the White House. He then stepped outside the Lyceum to survey the crowd. He immediately sensed that it had grown larger and noisier. Rebel yells, football cheers and obscenities were being shouted at the marshals.

"Six-five-four-three, to hell with Kenn-e-dy."

"Barnett *sí*, Castro no."

The Mississippi officers still seemed to think it was all very funny. They smiled at the students and adults who were heckling the marshals. These were not the smiles of an Al Butler, who was doing his best to keep from antagonizing anyone. These were the snickering, dirty-joke smiles of men who failed to grasp the danger involved when immature minds—adolescent and adult—are whipped into a frenzy.

Suddenly, off to my right, I saw a bright light that could only be the kind used by a newsreel cameraman. The crowd surged toward the light. There was a crash that sounded like the breaking of glass. The light, belonging to an Ohio cameraman, had been broken by members of the crowd. The crowd became a mob.

Another newsreel cameraman, Gordon Yoder of Tele-news in Dallas, Texas, was spotted. Perhaps 100 persons, mostly of college age, swarmed around him as he advanced on foot toward the Lyceum with his television camera. Race-hating mobs were nothing new to Yoder. He had covered racial stories from Little Rock to the Autherine Lucy case at the University of Alabama. But Yoder and his pretty blonde wife were about to be subjected to the worst going-over of all. And, from this point on, it would become increasingly clear that James Meredith would not be registered at Ole Miss without a major outbreak of violence.

The mob that had surged toward the bright light earlier now swarmed about Yoder, beating him and trying to get his camera. I ran toward the mob, not realizing exactly what was happening. "What's going on?" I asked a student.

"That guy's a goddam reporter. Let's kill him," the student replied. He ran off, anxious to be among the campus "heroes" bludgeoning the cameraman.

For several seconds, I did not recognize the man in the middle of the mob. I was trying to get through to help him, no matter who he was, since he was a fellow newsman. At the same time, I was still trying to hold my notebook under my coat so that I wouldn't be spotted as a newsman until I could reach him. Then, as I got closer, I recognized Yoder, with whom I had covered several stories while working on *The Houston Press*.

I tried calling to him to move toward me, but he couldn't hear me above the shouts of the mob. He seemed to be holding his own. His camera was still in his hands. He was flailing his arms, trying to beat off his attackers. I tried shoving my way through the mob, but at least a dozen rioters stood between Yoder and me. I couldn't budge them.

"You nigger-lovin' sonuvabitch," someone yelled.

"Kill the bastard. He ain't gonna take our goddam pictures."

Just as it seemed that Yoder was about to be knocked

down, two highway patrolmen finally made their way to his side and freed him from his attackers. They led him to his station wagon, a short distance away on the circle leading to the Lyceum. Yoder's wife was at the wheel. They had been married only a few months. And, despite the dangerous nature of the Ole Miss assignment, she had accompanied him to Oxford and the campus "because I love him."

Now, the highway patrolmen opened the right front door of the station wagon and Yoder sat down beside his wife. The mob, if anything, had grown larger and more frenzied. The sight of Mrs. Yoder infuriated some rioters. She was a native Mississippian, but to the mob she was a "nigger-lovin' bitch." She was only there to be with her husband, but the mob considered her "a goddam Commie."

About 200 rioters, including students and adult rednecks, surrounded the station wagon. Some jumped on the hood, others on the top of the wagon. They kicked dents in the metal. Others threw rocks at the headlights, smashing them.

"Kill the nigger-lovin' bastards—Beat the shit outa them—We'll teach 'em to go back up Nawth, where they came from."

The windshield was smashed. So were all the windows. The door panels were kicked in. Several highway patrolmen stood nearby, doing nothing.

Rioters plunged halfway through the broken windows of the station wagon, flinging punches at Yoder and his wife. Then the rioters began using a favorite tactic of racial mobs —trying to turn the station wagon upside down. They rocked it back and forth from side to side, at first slowly but later with increasing speed. At one point, I saw a uniformed Mississippi police officer put his shoulder to the left rear side of the station wagon, trying to help the rioters overturn it. Seconds later, a siren could be heard and a flashing red light could be seen coming through the mob from the direction of the Lyceum. It was a highway patrol squad car, approaching slowly to keep from running over any of the rioters, who moved out of the way only reluctantly.

Two highway patrolmen emerged from the squad car

just as the station wagon seemed about to be overturned. It was at a 45-degree angle to the ground when the Yoders, with the officers' help, slid out and jumped hurriedly into the patrol car. The car made its way through the mob to safety. But somewhere along the way Yoder's camera and film, which he had clutched tightly throughout the mob attack, was pried from his grasp and disappeared.

It seemed significant that the highway patrol had come to the Yoders' rescue only when their lives were clearly endangered. This mob now gave strong indications that it was thirsty for blood. I wondered how the highway patrolmen and other state officers would react if the going got much rougher.

Cameraman Yoder had entered the university grounds when state highway patrolmen abandoned the roadblocks at Ole Miss gates at 6:30. Now, just as Yoder had entered, dozens of other newsmen flooded into the campus. And so did hundreds of citizens, some just curious, but many bent on causing trouble.

It was now past 7 P.M. In front of the Lyceum, a marshal returning to his post after being sent on a mission to James Meredith's dormitory was hit in the face with a large piece of concrete hurled by someone in the mob. The left side of his face and his left sinus were fractured. It required eight stitches to close the wound.

At 7:15, State Senators George Yarbrough and John McLaurin, two of Governor Barnett's four personal representatives during the Ole Miss crisis, materialized in front of the Lyceum. McLaurin, with State Representative C. B. Newman and County Judge Russell Moore, had arrived at the Oxford airport in the small plane that had landed just before Meredith's.

It was this plane that Ed Guthman and Nick Katzenbach, who did not know the state officials, had run to meet in the hope that Meredith was aboard. Barnett's representatives, who knew nothing of the Governor's negotiations with the Kennedys, had been shocked to find the airport swarming with military planes and equipment. "It's completely occupied," McLaurin said in astonishment. He remembers thinking: Bobby and Jack jumped the gun.

When Katzenbach peered into their plane window,

then turned away, the state officials contemplated taking off and leaving Oxford. They feared search and seizure of the plane. But, when nothing further happened after Katzenbach and Guthman departed, they decided to remain and make their way to the campus. "We got through the federal lines untouched," Moore recalled later.

McLaurin, Newman and Moore met Yarbrough at the Ole Miss Alumni House at 6:30. From there, they phoned Barnett to tell him about the premature "invasion" of the campus by the federals. They learned then that Barnett already knew about the "invasion." But Barnett still told them nothing about his deal with the Kennedys. He had other things on his mind. He was preparing a surrender statement. Shortly before 7, he had the statement read over the phone to Washington for Attorney General Kennedy's approval.

"My heart still says 'never,'" Barnett's statement read. "But my calm judgment abhors the bloodshed that would follow. . . . Mississippi will continue to fight the Meredith case and all similar cases through the courts."

The Attorney General approved the statement. Among others with him and the President were Burke Marshall and presidential aide Lawrence O'Brien. The President's office was jammed with television technicians, wires and equipment. The President, after delaying his TV address until Meredith was safely on the campus, was preparing to go on the air at 10 P.M. Washington time (8 o'clock in Mississippi).

The Attorney General, Marshall and several presidential aides met with the President in the Cabinet Room. There was unanimous agreement on the content and attitude of the address. At the Attorney General's suggestion, a passage appealing to Ole Miss students to maintain law and order was added to the text.

Robert Kennedy took over the open phone line to the Lyceum and asked Ed Guthman to find out what steps the university was taking to keep order. Guthman immediately phoned Chancellor Williams. The chancellor told Guthman he had recorded a statement to the student body, insisting on law and order. The statement was being broadcast every 30 minutes by the campus radio station.

Senators Yarbrough and McLaurin, after talking with Barnett from the Alumni House, made contact with Colonel Birdsong. With Birdsong, they approached John Doar in front of the Lyceum. They asked to see whoever was in charge, and were taken inside the Lyceum to the office of Hugh Clegg.

"Who's in charge?" Yarbrough demanded.

Katzenbach said that he was. Before the conversation could progress, Birdsong burst in to plead that Katzenbach tell Yarbrough he had not given the marshals police protection. "I've been telling these people that all I've done is escort you onto the campus," Birdsong told Katzenbach. "Will you please clarify this?"

Yarbrough cut Birdsong off. He stepped toward Katzenbach and said: "You've occupied it, and now you can have it. . . . I want to avoid bloodshed. To do so, we must withdraw the highway patrol."

Katzenbach, a husky man whose law professor's attitude masks an inner toughness, bristled. "I have the same interest—that is, to provide law and order," he said. "But while federal marshals are here, this in no way displaces the state authority. All law enforcement officers must cooperate to maintain law and order. I want to be very clear about the fact that I think the withdrawal of the state troopers will not avoid violence, but is the one decisive thing that will lead to violence."

Yarbrough said he disagreed. He insisted that he would withdraw the highway patrol. The only question was what time this would be done. The debate turned to whether the pullout should come at 8 P.M. or 9.

Katzenbach already had taken Birdsong to task for pulling the troopers away from the roadblocks at 6:30. He had insisted that the roadblocks be manned anew, but Birdsong had refused. He said he had only about 25 patrol cars, with two men each, and that his unarmed men could do little. (The highway patrolmen's guns were supposed to be locked in their car trunks.) Katzenbach suggested using the sheriff's officers and police from various cities who had converged on the campus. But Birdsong insisted he had no authority over these men. Birdsong finally had agreed to send some men to the roadblocks if Katzenbach would send a larger number of marshals to accompany them. Katzenbach said he could not spare any marshals.

During this debate, and the one that followed between Katzenbach and Yarbrough, outsiders by the hundreds were flooding past the unguarded roadblocks. Some were Mississippians. But many were white agitators who had come from as far off as California to heed the call of General Walker for 10,000 volunteers to support Mississippi's "holy cause." Many of them had figured the showdown would not come until Monday or Tuesday. When it became clear that the showdown was now in progress, they rushed to the campus.

At 7:25, FBI agents monitoring the state highway patrol frequency advised the Justice Department that the patrolmen had been ordered to withdraw from the campus. Nine minutes later, the FBI advised that the pullout had begun.

At 7:40, Attorney General Kennedy came on the open line to the Lyceum. He ordered Katzenbach to tell Yarbrough that, if the patrol left, the President would tell the nation in his TV address 20 minutes later that Barnett had made a deal and then reneged. Yarbrough knew nothing of any such deal. He was not impressed.

The Attorney General called Barnett on another line to insist that the highway patrol return to the campus. A few minutes later, Barnett phoned Yarbrough and told him to bring back the patrol. Sullenly, Yarbrough turned to Katzenbach and muttered that he would do so.

By now the crowd had grown in both size and fury. Rocks and chunks of concrete were being hurled in increasing numbers at the marshals. The six army trucks used to transport the marshals to the campus were standing in front of the Lyceum. The drivers, several of them Negroes, were getting a verbal going-over from the mob. Swiftly, it turned from verbal to physical. A rock was thrown at one of the Negro drivers. Someone seized a fire extinguisher and squirted chemical spray into another driver's face. Molotov cocktails, made by filling pop bottles with gasoline and igniting a paper or cloth wick stuffed into the bottle neck, came into play. They were tossed first at the marshals, then at the truck drivers, then at the tarpaulins covering the army trucks. Lighted cigarets and flaming paper airplanes soared into the trucks. One tarpaulin caught fire. A GI mounted the side of the truck and tried to snuff it out. He was pelted with rocks.

I was standing directly in front of the Lyceum, between two of the army trucks, with about a dozen other reporters. I recall Claude Sitton of *The New York Times*, Stan Opotowsky of the *New York Post*, Ray Coffey of the *Chicago Daily News*, Sterling Slappey of *U. S. News & World Report*, and several British newspapermen being in the group. Ed Guthman came down the Lyceum steps to tell us that he had tentatively scheduled a press conference for about 8 o'clock at the Ole Miss Motel.

"Ed, that's silly," I told him. "The Ole Miss is 'way downtown. We probably couldn't get through this mob to get there. And I, for one, wouldn't leave the campus for any press conference."

"I promised some of the boys I saw at the airport that I'd meet them at the Ole Miss," Guthman said. "I don't want to break my word."

"Hell, most of them are probably here by now," I said. "Maybe we can get them all together and have the press conference somewhere on the campus."

"If you can get them together, that will be OK," Guthman said.

I began rounding up as many reporters as I could find. I told them Guthman would meet with us on the campus if we would all stay in a group. The group of a dozen of us in front of the Lyceum grew to perhaps 40. Several of the newsmen, particularly those carrying cameras, told of being slugged and stoned by the mob.

It was fast approaching 8. The mob grew even more surly. Several rocks and bricks thrown at the marshals fell short and struck me on the legs. Deputy Marshal Butler, standing before his men in front of the Lyceum, also was hit on the leg, by a poorly-made Molotov cocktail. The fuse was snuffed out when the bottle hit the ground. A few minutes later, he was hit on the left arm by an empty bottle.

The mob had reached more than 2,000. Football cheers, "Dixie" and obscene jeers rained on the marshals. Al Butler was especially jolted by the vile words hurled at him and the other marshals by young girls in the mob. But he kept smiling, through the obscenities, through the jeers, even through the spit aimed at him. Some in the mob were throwing coins.

"Here, Marshal, pick these up—Smiley will pick 'em up."

The mob pushed forward. Some of the highway patrolmen had returned to their original positions, between the marshals and the mob, but were doing little. Pieces of pipe came flying through the air at the marshals. Butler took a three-foot length of pipe to Chief Marshal Jim McShane. "How much more of this are we going to have to take?" he asked.

Another group leader, Don Forsht of Miami, asked permission to use tear gas. "Hold it off for awhile and maybe things will ease up," McShane replied.

Katzenbach asked Yarbrough to go outside the Lyceum and appeal to the mob for order. Yarbrough agreed. But, when he made his way into the mob, he was mistaken for a marshal. Boos filled the air, drowning out some of his words.

"I don't like this any more than you do," Yarbrough said. "I'm Senator George Yarbrough, and I represent the Governor. I'm on your side. I live just 40 miles from here at Red Banks. We don't want any violence. Get back off the streets and, if you will, go back to your dormitories."

The mob paid no heed.

"We want Ross . . . We want Ross . . . We want Ross."

Yarbrough replied: "All right. If y'all get off this street, I'll go see if I can get the Governor to come up here."

The mob calmed slightly at this word. And, for a brief period, the highway patrolmen who had returned to the Lyceum area began moving the mob back across the gutter.

When Yarbrough walked back inside the Lyceum, he spotted Justice Department attorney Doar and told him he would phone Barnett and ask the Governor to come to Oxford to calm the mob. "But first I want assurances that the Governor will not be arrested," he said.

Doar got Attorney General Kennedy on the phone, then handed the receiver to Yarbrough. The Senator repeated his demand for an assurance that Barnett would not be arrested if he came to the campus. But Kennedy replied: "I don't think it's best for the Governor to come up there now." He said that Barnett's presence, while it might calm part of the mob, would also draw hundreds of additional outsiders to the scene.

In Jackson, a group of rabid segregationists had spent most of the day drawing up plans for what was believed would be a confrontation with the federal authorities on Monday. The group included some of Barnett's closest advisers—William Simmons, an urbane and articulate racist, who served as administrative head of the Citizens Councils and as Barnett's speech-writer; Fred Beard, a television station manager, who was arranging TV coverage for Monday; Citizens Council executive M. Ney Williams; and George Goodwin, a Jackson advertising man who handled the Governor's press relations during the crisis. But, as close as these men were to Barnett, he had not taken even them into his confidence about his deal with the Kennedys. Consequently, they had no advance knowledge that the confrontation would come Sunday, instead of Monday, and that Barnett would fail to turn back Meredith at the Ole Miss gate.

Beard had gone as far as to draft a statement he hoped Barnett would read Monday in sending away the Negro student and the federals. The statement said: "We do not submit to the illegality of your takeover. We are a peaceable people. We will not take up arms against the federal government. If you move over us, you will move over us by pushing us aside." Here again was the "wall of flesh" formula for resisting the federals. The "wall of flesh" would have to be moved aside if the federals wanted to get Meredith registered. And, given the explosive nature of the situation, this "wall of flesh" might rise up and fight, despite Beard's assurance that "we will not take up arms against the federal government."

But Beard's statement, of course, was never to be delivered. Instead, Barnett went on the radio Sunday night and read the surrender statement he had already submitted to Attorney General Kennedy for approval. The radio statement stunned many of Barnett's supporters. Citizens Council official Lou Hollis now ran across the street from the council's office to the Governor's Mansion and burst in on Barnett. He could not believe what he had heard on the radio. Tears were in his eyes. "Governor, everybody thinks you've surrendered," he cried. "Everybody in the office is crying. You've got to tell them you haven't surrendered."

Actually, of course, Barnett had surrendered. But the realization that he had done so did not make itself clear to most Mississippians at once. In fact, many of them insist to this day that there was no surrender. This can be described only as an advanced case of mass self-hypnosis.

If Barnett had surrendered, however, the mob on the Ole Miss campus had not. After falling back briefly, following Yarbrough's promise to try to get Barnett to come to Oxford, the mob grew impatient and again began pushing in on the marshals. Fred Deckard, a cameraman with KTAL-TV in Shreveport, Louisiana, was in the midst of the crowd. He was carrying a large light. Several rioters came up behind him, grabbed him around the shoulders and neck, beat him savagely and grabbed his light. He called to a Mississippi officer for help. "Forget it," the officer said.

Deckard freed himself, minus his $300 light, and made his way to the group of newsmen in front of the Lyceum, where I was standing. We heard of other beatings. Somehow, despite the rain of rocks, bricks and Molotov cocktails being fired in our direction, we felt safer in the group than we would have alone.

The mob became more boisterous than ever. Hundreds of rioters swarmed about the army trucks. The highway patrolmen did little to hold them back. The rioters were right behind us as we stood between the two trucks directly in front of the Lyceum steps. The rioters began letting the air out of the truck tires. Then they started rocking several of the trucks from side to side, as they had Gordon Yoder's station wagon, in attempts to overturn them.

A deputy marshal approached the group of newsmen. "Would you mind stepping over this way?" he asked. We wondered why we were being asked to move, but followed him to the south side of the Lyceum. It soon became clear why we were being moved.

"Gas!" Jim McShane shouted.

This was the signal for the marshals to don their gas masks, but not to fire their tear-gas grenades. The marshals pulled the masks over their faces, adding an eerie touch to an already weird scene.

As I stood with the other reporters, I spotted a familiar figure donning a gas mask. It belonged to Joe Denson, the deputy marshal I had met on the plane ride to Memphis. We had several mutual friends. His boss, then U. S. Marshal Tom Dugan, is a Long Islander I have known for some time. Dugan, a former federal narcotics agent, is a good friend of several agent friends of mine.

"Hi, Joe," I called. He waved a cheerful greeting. The next time I was to see him would be inside the Lyceum, sprawled on the floor, his chest penetrated by two shotgun pellets.

It was 7:50 P.M. As we stood on the south side of the Lyceum, the mob grew more and more enraged by the sight of the gas masks. Eggs flew at the marshals, along with rocks, bricks and chunks of cement. Suddenly, an eight-foot length of pipe with an ugly augur at its tip hurtled through the air. It struck a marshal's helmet, putting an inch-deep crease in it. (This helmet now sits in Attorney General Kennedy's office as a souvenir.)

Several of the reporters were becoming anxious for the press conference Guthman had promised us. Since the situation was becoming increasingly tense, they felt we should urge Guthman to start the press conference immediately.

I was designated as the press corps' emissary (without portfolio) to the federal contingent in the Lyceum. I was to try to persuade Guthman to meet with us before the situation became so serious that we would have to scatter. I walked through the line of marshals to the Lyceum. Guthman was standing on the steps. He had just ushered Colonel Birdsong inside the Lyceum to talk by phone with the Attorney General.

"Ed, the boys want to have the press conference right away," I told Guthman. "It's getting pretty rough, and they want to talk to you while we've got the chance. It looks like it's going to get a lot rougher pretty soon."

Guthman replied: "I can't do it right now. But you tell the boys to stick together. I'll get with them as soon as I can." He told me to come back to see him after I had passed the word to the other reporters.

I walked back through the line of marshals, gave the message to the reporters and then returned to the steps of the Lyceum. Just then, a bottle hit Al Butler on the arm. A white fluid splashed on his hand and ran down his arm. It was hours before Butler discovered that the fluid was acid.

It was 7:57.

"Fire!" Jim McShane shouted.

Whoomp . . . whoomp . . . whoomp . . . whoomp . . . whoomp.

Tear-gas cartridges went flying out of the guns of the marshals directly in front of the Lyceum. They skidded across the ground. Marshals who didn't have tear-gas guns heaved gas grenades into the mob. Several persons, including highway patrolmen, were struck by either grenades or the wax wadding in the cartridges. The mob began scattering to escape the gas.

Whoomp . . . whoomp . . . whoomp . . . whoomp . . . whoomp.

Another salvo was fired by the marshals on the north side of the Lyceum, still another by those on the south. Eerie clouds of gas drifted across the campus. Rioters, with tears streaming down their cheeks and their noses running, raced back and forth, shouting obscenities at the marshals. Then came new volleys of rocks, bricks and Molotov cocktails.

The Ole Miss riot was on now in dead earnest. And there would be no stopping it.

5

I was standing on the steps of the Lyceum with Ed Guthman when the tear gas was fired. Guthman told me, "Let's get inside for a minute, 'til it clears a little."

We walked in the front door to a scene of confusion, but relative order when compared with what was going on outside. Nick Katzenbach was on the line with Attorney General Kennedy when the gas went off. He did not know immediately what had happened. There was some fear that one of the marshals might have fired his gas gun prematurely.

But then Jim McShane came in the door, peeling off his gas mask. Despite the mask, tears were pouring down his face. "It's all right," he said. "I gave the order to fire. I had to do it. There was no choice."

Katzenbach said: "Bob, I'm very sorry to report that we've had to fire tear gas. I'm very unhappy about it, but we had no choice."

The President was about to begin his television address to the nation. Robert Kennedy, in the White House Cabinet Room, said to Katzenbach: "I think I should really go tell the President about it. He's just going on the air." The Attorney General rushed to his brother's office. But he was too late. The TV address had already begun.

John F. Kennedy wore a somber expression as he addressed his countrymen. He said:

The orders of the court in the case of Meredith vs. Fair are beginning to be carried out. Mr. James Meredith is now in residence on the campus of the University of Mississippi.

This has been accomplished thus far without the use of National Guard or other troops. And it is to be hoped that the law enforcement officers of the state of Mississippi and the federal marshals will continue to be sufficient in the future.

This is as it should be, for our nation is founded on the principle that observance of the law is the eternal safeguard of liberty and defiance of the law is the surest road to tyranny. The law which we obey includes the final rulings of the courts, as well as the enactment of our legislative bodies. Even among law-abiding men, few laws are universally loved, but they are uniformly respected and not resisted.

Americans are free, in short, to disagree with the law, but not to disobey it. For, in a government of laws and not of men, no man, however prominent or powerful, and no mob, however unruly or boisterous, is entitled to defy a court of law.

If this country should ever reach the point where any man or group of men by force or threat of force could long defy the commands of our court and our Constitution, then no law would stand free from doubt, no judge would be sure of his writ and no citizen would be safe from his neighbors.

The President then reviewed the legal history of the Meredith case. He pointed out the government's responsibility for seeing that court orders were enforced:

Even though this government had not originally been a party to the case, my responsibility as President was therefore inescapable.

I accept it. My obligation under the Constitution and statutes of the United States was and is to implement the orders of the court with whatever means are necessary, and with as little force and civil disorder as the circumstances permit.

It was for this reason that I federalized the Mississippi National Guard as the most appropriate instrument, should any be needed, to preserve law and order while United States marshals carried out the orders of the court, and prepared to back them up with whatever other civil or military enforcement might have been required.

I deeply regret the fact that any action by the executive branch was necessary in this case, but all other avenues and alternatives, including persuasion and conciliation, had been tried and exhausted.

Had the police powers of Mississippi been used to support the orders of the court, instead of deliberately and unlawfully blocking them; had the University of Mississippi fulfilled its standard of excellence by quietly admitting this applicant in conformity with what so many other Southern state universities have done for so many years, a peaceable and sensible solution would have been possible without any federal intervention.

The nation is proud of the many instances in which governors, educators and everyday citizens from the South have shown to the world the gains that can be made by persuasion and good will in a society ruled by law. Specifically, I would like to take this occasion to express the thanks of this nation to those Southerners who have contributed to the progress of our democratic development in the entrance of students, regardless of race, to such great institutions as the state-supported universities of Virginia, North Carolina, Georgia, Florida, Texas, Louisiana, Tennessee, Arkansas and Kentucky.

I recognize that the present period of transition and adjustment in our nation's southland is a hard one for many people. Neither Mississippi nor any other Southern state deserves to be charged with all the accumulated wrongs of the last 100 years of race relations. To the extent that there has been failure, the responsibility for that failure must be shared by us all, by every state, by every citizen.

Mississippi and her university, moreover, are noted for their courage, for their contribution of talent and thought to the affairs of this nation. This is the state of Lucius Lamar and many others who have placed the national good ahead of sectional interest. This is the state which had four Medal of Honor winners in the Korean War alone. In fact, the Guard unit federalized this morning, early, is part of the 155th infantry, one of the ten oldest regiments in the Union and one of the most decorated for sacrifice and bravery in six wars.

In 1945, a Mississippi sergeant, Jake Lindsey, was honored by an unusual joint session of the Congress. I close, therefore, with this appeal to the students of the university, the people who are most concerned:

You have a great tradition to uphold, a tradition of honor and courage, won on the field of battle and on the gridiron as well as the university campus. You have a new opportunity to show that you are men of patriotism and integrity.

For the most effective means of upholding the law is not the state policeman or the marshals or the National Guard. It is you. It lies in your courage to accept those laws with which you disagree, as well as those with which you agree. The eyes of the nation and all the world are upon you and upon all of us, and the honor of your university and state are in the balance. I am certain the great majority of the students will uphold that honor.

There is, in short, no reason why the books on this case cannot now be quickly and quietly closed in the manner directed by the court. Let us preserve both the law and the peace and then, healing those wounds that are within, we can turn to the greater crises that are without and stand united as one people in our pledge to man's freedom.

Thank you, and good night.

The President's speech was heard by many of the rioters at Ole Miss. In the midst of the riot, they alternated between hurling rocks and bottles at the marshals and listening to the President over transistor radios. For the most part, the speech fell on deaf ears. The riot, if anything, picked up intensity during and after the speech.

Meanwhile, the state highway patrolmen had begun withdrawing again from the campus. They claimed their gas masks were ineffective against the type of gas being fired by the marshals. Forty-three patrol cars, containing highway patrolmen, sheriff's officers and police from various Mississippi cities, lined up bumper to bumper in one convoy and pulled slowly off the campus. Now, it was the marshals and a handful of campus policemen standing alone against the mob.

Senators Yarbrough and McLaurin, Representative Newman and Judge Moore, still functioning as Governor Ross Barnett's representatives on the campus, set up headquarters in the Alumni House. This is about 100 yards north of the Lyceum. Yarbrough had resented keeping the highway patrolmen in the area filled with gas by marshals' guns. At one point, after Highway Patrolman Welby Brunt had been seriously wounded by a tear-gas canister fired by a marshal, some patrolmen appealed for permission to remove their own guns from car trunks. A few patrolmen actually got their guns without permission. Yarbrough ordered the weapons locked up again.

A rumor started circulating that Colonel Birdsong had been killed. Yarbrough quickly determined that the report was untrue, and squelched it. He felt that the riot had gotten so far out of hand that there was no sense in his staying on the campus with his three companions. Shortly after the highway patrolmen had pulled out, Yarbrough phoned Barnett and received permission to leave the campus with McLaurin, Newman and Moore. They headed back to Jackson.

The marshals surrounding the Lyceum moved out periodically into the grassy circle of trees in front of the building and fired volleys of tear gas to move the mob back. It was a hit-and-run type of action. The marshals advanced, fired, then fell back. The rioters retreated from the gas, reformed their ranks, then charged. Their eyes were tearing, their bodies sweating, their noses running. But they were in a rage. Many, particularly adult outsiders, had been drinking. They heaved anything they could get their hands on at the marshals. And their ranks were swelling, both with outsiders who had flocked to Oxford upon hearing of the riot and with Ole Miss students who came filtering back to the campus from their football weekend.

Inside the Lyceum, I had commandeered one of the four phone booths. I knew that, on a night like this, possession of a phone booth was more important to a reporter than a notebook. In the booth to my left, Nick Katzenbach was talking on an open line to the White House. In the booth to my right, Katzenbach's chief assistant, Joe Dolan, was talking to the Justice Department.

I phoned *Newsday* to tell my editors where I was and what I was doing. It was too early to start putting together a story. Since *Newsday* is an afternoon paper, its first edition does not go to press until 6:50 A.M. (4:50 in Mississippi). So I had more than eight hours of working time before the first edition. Even allowing for the time it takes to write a story and get it set in type, I was many hours away from deadline.

But my obligation was not to *Newsday* alone. Since I had entered the Lyceum with Ed Guthman only because I was representing the entire press corps, and since I remained for the time being the only reporter inside the Lyceum, I felt obliged to supply those newsmen on the outside with information on a "pool" basis. The term "pool," in newspaper parlance, represents an arrangement under which one or several reporters cover a story for all media. Usually, this is arranged by raffle in advance of a story that would be impractical for a large group of reporters to cover. The "pool" reporters witness the action, then brief other newsmen on what they have seen.

In this case, it was luck, and not any particular skill, that provided me my excellent vantage point inside the Lyceum. Many other reporters had been driven off campus by the tear gas. They had gone back to the Colonial Hotel and the Ole Miss Motel. I felt a responsibility to give them a fill-in on what was happening inside the Lyceum and on the campus.

I explained to Ed Guthman what I planned to do. He thought it was a good idea, since he now had no chance to keep his promise to conduct a press conference for the newsmen. I got him to give me a fill-in on all that had happened. Then I phoned the Colonial Hotel and got Stan Opotowsky of the *New York Post* on the line. I filled him in, and he promised to spread the information to the other reporters at the hotel. I next phoned the Ole Miss Motel. There, I could reach none of the reporters I knew. But I reached one reporter I did not know, explained the situation to him, extracted a pledge that he would brief the other reporters at the motel and then gave him a fill-in.

This process continued throughout the night. I would dash outside the Lyceum, get whatever information and "color" material was available, then go back inside the Lyceum to phone the other reporters. Later in the night, I was joined inside the Lyceum by Tom Joyce, an extremely capable reporter from the Washington bureau of the *Detroit News*. He alternated with me in phoning the other newsmen.

Some reporters had not been lucky enough to make it either to the Lyceum or back downtown. Fred Powledge of the *Atlanta Journal*, who worked part-time as a "stringer" (non-staff) correspondent for *Newsday*, was trapped in an automobile between the marshals and the mob. Earlier, he had been slugged by rioters. Crouching low in the car, Powledge was faced with a dilemma: If he ran out of the car and toward the rioters, he would be mobbed and beaten. But, if he ran toward the marshals, he could be mistaken for a rioter and drenched in tear gas. Suddenly, he heard a voice behind him: "Let's get that son of a bitch in the car." Now, he had no place to go. A group of rioters was bearing down on him. Just then, three marshals rushed up from the opposite direction. One leaped into the air and fired a tear-gas canister over the car roof. "A beautiful burst of smoke" swelled over his attackers, Powledge recalls. One of them yelled: "Kennedy is a son of a bitch." But the rioters dispersed.

On the road between Jackson and Oxford, French reporter Paul Guihard and photographer Sammy Schulman were approaching Ole Miss in their rented car. Upon hearing President Kennedy's speech, Guihard got the impression that they were about to witness only a mopping-up operation. "Oh, hell, the story's all over," he told Schulman. "But we might as well go and clean it up."

On the ride north, Guihard and Schulman had been passed by numerous cars bearing Confederate flags and bumper stickers expressing support of Ross Barnett. Neither of the newsmen realized that many of these cars contained returning students and outsiders bound for Oxford to join the riot.

Guihard was in an expansive mood. He talked about his past life, about his early desire to be an actor, then his beginning days as a reporter and his ambition to become a full-time playwright. When they reached Ole Miss, they discovered that the riot and the story were far from over. They parked near the Grove, the tree-studded area northeast of the circle facing the Lyceum. They could hardly hope to pass as either students or red-necks. Guihard's full red beard and his accent, and Schulman's cameras, clearly tagged them for what they were. Some students spotted them instantly, but turned out to be friendly.

"Hide your cameras," one student said. "Some bums up there [near the Lyceum] are smashing them."

Guihard told Schulman: "I'll see what's doing, and meet you back here at the car in an hour." At that point, the mob surged toward them. Guihard, still confident of his safety, waded straight into the mob. It was to be the last time Schulman would see him alive.

In the circle before the Lyceum, the rioters had somehow gotten their hands on a fire hose and had hooked it up to a source of water. They were using it to douse tear-gas canisters and to knock down marshals with the spray. A group of marshals, among the few carrying sidearms, charged the rioters with pistols drawn. A few well-placed bullets, fired into the hose, stopped the rush of water.

The rioters regrouped at the Confederate monument at the foot of the circle. They rushed the Lyceum again, heaving more bricks, rocks, chunks of cement and Molotov cocktails.

"You nigger lovers go to hell," they yelled.

"You goddam Communists go to hell."

One group, led by a student in a blood-smeared shirt, descended on Dan McCoy, a *Black Star* photographer, working on assignment for *Newsweek* magazine. McCoy was beaten savagely. McCoy recalls:

A big fellow—they said he was a football player—hit me with a right and knocked me down. I got up and he hit me and knocked me down again. There were four guys in a sheriff's car. I said, "For God's sake, get me out of here." They were just sitting there. The students knocked me down again and started hitting me and working on me with kicks with the side of their feet. I figured I had just about had it. Then I felt some hands on my shoulders: I figured they were picking me up to hit me some more. But they were other students who had pushed them back. The big guy tried to come in again, but they rushed me into a building.

The corridors of the Lyceum were jammed with wounded men, mostly marshals. I was walking down a corridor when I heard a muffled voice saying: "Mike, how ya doin'?" I looked around and saw a half-dozen marshals sprawled on the floor, still wearing their gas masks, for the tear gas was seeping into the Lyceum. I recognized no one behind a mask. Then one man raised his arm and said: "Hi, Mike. It's Joe."

Joe Denson stared up at me.

"What's the matter, Joe? You hurt?"

"I got hit," he replied.

"With what?"

"A couple of shotgun pellets."

"Where?"

Denson reached inside his jacket and pulled something from his inside right breast pocket. It was his set of marshal's credentials, inside a leather billfold. There were two holes, the size of shotgun pellets, in the billfold.

"They went right through there."

"Where are the pellets now?"

"They're still in my chest."

"Have you seen a doctor yet?"

"They're trying to get one in here now."

Denson said the credentials and billfold apparently had saved his life by slowing up the pellets. As it was, they were embedded just beneath the surface of his skin.

"Where were you when you got hit?"

"Right over there on the side of the building, where you were standing a little while ago with the other reporters."

I felt a little chill run up my back. It could just as easily have been me as Denson, I thought.

"Anybody else over there get shot?"

"One other marshal got it in the throat," Denson said. "He's bleeding pretty bad."

This marshal was Gene Same of Indianapolis, Indiana. He lay in the middle of the corridor leading from the front door to the back door of the Lyceum. Each time his heart beat, blood spurted crazily from his throat, sometimes as much as a foot high.

Tender hands tried to comfort him. Someone placed a makeshift bandage over his throat to stop the blood from spurting. A buddy of Same's was crying unashamedly. "Get him on a stretcher or he's gonna die," he said. "You're gonna lose him if you don't move him out of here."

But, for the time being at least, there was no easy way to move Same. An ambulance tried getting through the mob to the rear door of the Lyceum, but the rioters drove it back several times. And, even if the ambulance had succeeded in reaching the Lyceum, it was doubtful that the marshals would have been able to get Same through the rioters on a stretcher to the ambulance's back door.

While the battle raged all around the Lyceum, Same lay helpless on the floor, his life seeming to ebb as he lost blood. A Justice Department aide barked into a shortwave radio: "Are we getting medical capability here? Let's get a doctor before this man dies." Temporarily, however, the most that could be done for Same was to make him as comfortable as possible until a doctor could arrive or he could be moved to a hospital.

About 9 P.M., the marshals began running out of tear gas for the first time. They were to run out periodically all night. And at 9, just as he was to do several times later, Border Patrolman Charles Chamblee of New Orleans left the Lyceum unobtrusively, slipped into a light green sedan and drove at breakneck speed off the campus to the airport. There, additional supplies of tear gas, flown in from Memphis, were waiting. A rented van was filled with tear gas, and Chamblee led it back to the campus.

On the way back, some highway patrolmen who were parked a short distance from the campus tried to stop Chamblee. He beat them out of his way with his billy club, and raced on through the night. Roadblocks had been set up by the rioters. Chamblee and the van crashed through them. They headed around the circle leading to the Lyceum.

The rioters shouted: "Truck . . . truck . . . truck."

Stones and bricks rained on Chamblee's car and the van. But they made it. And they were to make it again and again. Each time the marshals appeared about to run out of gas, Chamblee would turn up with his van filled with fresh supplies.

Now, former Major General Walker marched onto the campus. His white broad-brimmed hat was cocked on his head. At the Confederate monument at the foot of the circle, rioters had been shouting: "We want a leader! We want a leader! We want a leader!" When Walker appeared, a tumultuous cheer went up. The rioters shouted: "We have a leader! We have a leader! We have a leader!"

The word spread swiftly across the campus: "General Walker's here." Rioters swarmed to the monument to rally behind the man who had led federal troops at Little Rock and now was prepared to lead this mob against federal authority.

Walker climbed up the base of the monument to address the rioters. A hush fell over the mob. "I want to compliment you all on the protest you make tonight," he began. He said the people of Mississippi had been betrayed by Governor Barnett and Highway Patrol Director Birdsong. "But don't let up now," he implored. "You may lose this battle, but you will have been heard. This is a dangerous situation. You must be prepared for possible death. If you are not, go home now."

A student asked: "What if we find the power plant and cut off their lights?"

Walker replied: "Do you know where it is? Fine."

Another student asked: "What can we use to make the tear-gas bombs ineffective? Do you know any way we can attack and do some damage to those damn marshals?" Walker suggested using sand to snuff out the tear-gas bombs. "That stuff works real well," he said. "But where can you get it?"

Some rioters thereupon went looking for sand. Others set out to find the power plant.

Father Duncan Gray, Jr., rector of St. Peter's Episcopal Church in Oxford, tried to climb up on the monument to argue against Walker. But he was pulled away and shoved into the mob. A sheriff's officer led him to safety.

Walker descended from the monument and started walking slowly toward the Lyceum. Rioters fell in alongside, behind and in front of him. "Charge!" someone yelled. Some witnesses claim it was Walker who did so. He denies it. At any rate, there was a charge on the Lyceum. And Walker was in the mob making the charge. Rioters raced at the line of marshals, heaving sticks, rocks and bottles. The marshals closed ranks, charged at the rioters and fired volleys of tear gas.

The rioters, choking from the fumes, retreated to the monument. There, Walker made a new speech. A second charge began from the monument. Again, the marshals waded in and fired volleys of gas. Again, the rioters retreated. But this time the marshals chased them and took their first prisoner. His name was Edward Joseph Horbatch, and he was an Ole Miss student. Horbatch was taken into the Lyceum for questioning. It was only then that federal authorities learned of Walker's role.

Horbatch told the marshals that he had not bargained for any shooting of firearms, did not approve of it and wanted no part of it. For that reason, he said, he was willing to talk freely to the federals. He told of Walker's presence at the monument and the speech to the rioters. "Everyone said, 'There's General Walker,'" Horbatch said. He quoted Walker as telling the mob: "They're ruining the Constitution. . . . Other people [demonstrators] are coming in."

The Justice Department immediately began gathering as much information as it could on Walker's role in the riot. At 9:32 P.M., Ramsey Clark, son of Supreme Court Justice Tom Clark and the assistant attorney general in charge of the Justice Department Lands Division, phoned the FBI from his Washington office and gave the order: "Arrest Walker if you can; maintain surveillance if you can't."

French reporter Paul Guihard had been confident of his safety even in the midst of the rioting mob. He was such a gregarious person, with such a zest for life, that fear was alien to him. But now he was being taken on a death march. Who accompanied him is a mystery to this day.

But how he died can be pieced together with relative clarity.

Guihard, with his red beard and French accent, had been picked out of the crowd as an outsider, an enemy who meant to blacken the name of the southland. Now, some self-proclaimed avenger was about to make him pay the price. The avenger pointed a .38-caliber pistol at Guihard and ordered him to march to a lonely area of the campus between the Ward women's dormitory and the Fine Arts Center. The riot was centered across the campus. There would be no witnesses. The avenger put the pistol flush against Guihard's back. He pulled the trigger once.

Guihard fell dead.

The avenger fled. He left only one clue—powder burns on Guihard's clothing indicating that the shot had been fired from immediate range. The bullet that ended Guihard's life was so mutilated that it could never be matched with the murder gun, even if one were found. And none has been found.

The time of Guihard's death has been estimated at about 9:15 P.M. But the area of the campus in which he was shot was so deserted that the body was not found until 10:35. Bulletins were flashed on the wires. Radio and TV stations across the country spread the word: "Newsman killed at Ole Miss."

In my home at Commack, Long Island, my wife Jeanne had stayed up late to hear the news from Mississippi. The bulletin panicked her. She phoned the *Newsday* city desk, her heart pounding and her hands trembling. "I just heard on TV that a reporter was killed at Ole Miss," she told John Van Doorn, working on the night desk at *Newsday*. "Do you know if Mike's all right?"

Van Doorn told her: "He must be. He's on the phone to the office right now. And he's one of the only reporters inside the Lyceum."

"I feel much better," Jeanne said. "Don't tell Mike I called."

Van Doorn didn't.

In Jackson, shortly after 9 P.M., Governor Ross Barnett's advisers saw in the riot a new possibility for advancing the cause of segregation. Perhaps the rioters could drive the marshals off the campus and prevent James Meredith's enrollment. Then, in the light of the bloody rioting, maybe Meredith's registration could be delayed further on the ground that it might provoke new violence. Reinforcements to back up the rioters already at Ole Miss might be all that was needed. Barnett could merely announce that he was on his way to Oxford. That would draw additional thousands to the campus. Or, better still, Barnett could issue a call to battle. Of the thousands who would turn out in support of the Governor, many might die. But they would die in a just cause. And their deaths would warn the nation, and the world, of the dangers of a "federal dictatorship." Some of the Governor's advisers said they were ready to move on Oxford and sacrifice their own lives for the cause.

Amid this hysterical clamor, one adviser argued heatedly for sanity. His name is Thomas Watkins. He is a red-haired, 53-year-old corporation lawyer who has been a friend of Barnett's for years. And he is respected as highly as any Mississippian by the power structure that rules the state.

As Barnett previously had shown in his dealings with the Kennedys, he is a wavering man. It has been said of him that his decisions last only as long as it takes for some new adviser to walk into his office. But now Tom Watkins argued passionately for a binding decision. He wanted a pledge from Barnett that he would not go to Oxford or otherwise encourage further violence. He won the pledge. Once more, the possibility of a wholesale slaughter at Ole Miss was avoided. But the violence was continuing to build.

At 9:25, the marshals were running out of tear gas again. Border Patrolman Chamblee, just back from one run through the mob to the airport, set out again in his sedan to pick up another load of gas supplies. A deputy marshal walked up to Nick Katzenbach. "Our men are being shot at with firearms," he said. "They request permission to return the fire."

It was a rugged decision for Katzenbach. The marshals were virtually down to fighting with their billy clubs against firearms, rocks, bricks and Molotov cocktails. But, with a furrowed brow, he called once again for patience. "If you can just hold your fire for a few minutes more," he told the marshal. "The President's on the telephone, talking to the Governor now."

The President, like Katzenbach, was trying to get the state highway patrolmen back to the Lyceum. But his talk with Barnett did little good.

In the Lyceum, Katzenbach appealed to Colonel Birdsong: "Get your men back." But Birdsong said that, since the patrolmen's gas masks had not protected them sufficiently from the tear gas, it was difficult to control them.

Katzenbach insisted: "If they want to get away from the gas, let them go down to the entrances and set up roadblocks."

Birdsong replied: "They can't do that. And, now that they've been gassed, I'm not sure that they are willing to."

Most of the patrol cars were gathered just off the campus. The patrolmen did little or nothing to prevent additional outsiders from pouring onto the campus. Even if they had not wanted to brave the tear gas, the patrolmen could have stopped cars on the road leading to the university and turned back those with no business there. But they did not. And now the cars, in increasing numbers, bore out-of-state license plates. Many contained toughs with greasy, ducktail haircuts. They had come from as far off as Florida, Georgia, Arkansas, Texas, Louisiana and Alabama. And they brought with them weapons of all kinds—high-powered rifles, squirrel guns, .22-caliber rifles, shotguns, pistols, knives and blackjacks.

One highway patrol car did temporarily intercept a convoy of 20 to 30 cars, each loaded with about four men, just outside Oxford. There was a brief debate among several highway patrolmen over whether the convoy should be stopped from entering the campus. But, in the end, it was not stopped.

Other patrol cars reported that a large number of civilians had entered the campus from cars abandoned on nearby roads, particularly State Highway 6. A chartered bus with about 50 armed men was reported headed for the college on Route 6.

But the federal forces were being beefed up slightly. At

9:28, 40 federal prison guards arrived from Memphis to back up the marshals. And, at 9:35, fresh supplies of tear gas arrived. President Kennedy again phoned Governor Barnett. The Governor agreed to get the highway patrolmen back at the Lyceum. But the patrolmen didn't come.

Assistant Attorney General Burke Marshall took over the phone from the President, and talked to Tom Watkins at Barnett's end of the line. He told Watkins the highway patrol had not returned.

"I can't believe it," said the man who had persuaded Barnett not to make a trip to Oxford this night.

"They're not there, Tom," Marshall reiterated.

"We'll get them back," Watkins pledged. His sincerity was unquestioned. But wanting to get the patrolmen back was not enough. Some simply were not about to return.

I was standing near Nick Katzenbach and Colonel Birdsong inside the Lyceum about this time. "What do you think, Colonel?" Katzenbach asked.

"Well, we've got those 60 men just sitting in the armory right downtown," Birdsong replied.

The 60 men Birdsong mentioned were members of Captain Murry Falkner's local National Guard unit. They had been at the armory all day, on call, but federal authorities had wanted to avoid using troops if at all possible. Now Katzenbach agreed with Birdsong's suggestion that the time had come to call upon the Guard. Rifle and shotgun fire could be heard by those inside the Lyceum. The riot was building with every passing minute. The mob had grown to at least 2,500. Some of the Ole Miss students, realizing the seriousness of the violence, had gone to their dorms and fraternity and sorority houses. But their places had been taken by older and meaner rioters.

Falkner had known little of what was going on at the campus until 6:30, when he had gotten a TV set brought to the armory. Now it was 9:50. The phone at the armory rang. It was Katzenbach calling. "I've just talked to the President," Katzenbach told Falkner. "He's ordered your unit to the campus immediately. How long will it take you to get to the Lyceum?"

"Ten minutes," Falkner said.

"OK."

Katzenbach gave Falkner no idea of what to expect at the campus. Nor did he suggest what entrance to use. He assumed Falkner was aware of exactly what the campus situation was. But Falkner had only sketchy information, provided by the TV set, and now says he wishes Katzenbach had given him more detailed instructions.

Falkner's men had only the most meager training in riot control. He had never believed his unit would be called into action. But now he had what he considered "this wild chain-of-command order" to proceed to the campus. Before leaving, he phoned his squadron commander in Ripley, Mississippi, for approval of Katzenbach's order. The squadron commander told him to move out. Falkner wondered whether to issue ammunition to his men. He was told not to issue any. At first, he was ordered to put a safe containing the ammunition on a truck and take it to the campus with him. Later, this order was countermanded. The safe, with the ammunition locked inside, was left behind at the armory. Falkner also left his five-man mess section at the armory to maintain security.

The other men were loaded into trucks and jeeps. Falkner was about to leave when the phone rang again. It was Katzenbach. "Are all your men going to follow you?" Katzenbach asked.

"Yes, sir," Falkner replied, taken aback by the question.

"Well, go out and see that they're all in the trucks."

Falkner was stunned. He had no doubt that his men would follow him. True, every one of them was opposed to the desegregation of Ole Miss. Some currently were Ole Miss students. Falkner himself had attended Ole Miss for two semesters. But they were now in federal service. It would be treason to disobey orders.

Falkner obeyed Katzenbach's directions, went outside and looked in the trucks. He returned to the phone. "They're all ready to go," he said.

"Well, move on out," Katzenbach replied.

Falkner told Katzenbach that his men knew virtually nothing about riot control, had taken only two hours of riot-control training in a year, and were equipped with only about 15 bayonets for the 60 men. But he said they would do their best to help.

The National Guard convoy formed on 18th Street. It consisted of three jeeps in the lead, then two two-and-a-half-ton trucks, one three-quarter-ton ammunition carrier and another jeep at the tail end. Falkner was in the lead jeep. Specialist fourth-class Harold Antwine, an Ole Miss senior from Jackson, was driving.

When the convoy reached a traffic light at University Avenue, Falkner passed the word for his men to don gas masks. There were some civilians on the street corners, who cursed at the Guardsmen but took no direct action to prevent them from moving through town.

As the convoy moved up University Avenue toward the campus, Falkner noticed large numbers of civilians walking toward the university. Near the Illinois Central Railroad trestle separating the town from the campus, the convoy was pelted with rocks. Most of them bounced off the truck tarpaulins without hitting the men.

When Falkner passed the Confederate monument, he noticed that all the lights on the campus were out. They had been broken by the rioters' rocks. At the monument, the convoy turned right and began moving around the circle leading to the Lyceum. Now it got rough. The mob bore down on the convoy, cursing and heaving anything it could find. A two-by-four was thrown at Falkner's jeep. It missed, but rocks and Molotov cocktails were finding the mark. "We had to keep moving to get people out of the way," Falkner recalls. "A rain of rocks and everything throwable was coming at us. There were lots of Molotov cocktails, but none of them went off. I found one of them behind me in the jeep."

Near the Fine Arts Center, someone heaved a brick at Falkner's jeep. He saw it coming and threw up his left arm to shield his face. The brick crashed through the windshield, sending glass showering over Falkner and Antwine. The brick hit Falkner in the wrist, breaking three bones. But he could not stop to consider the pain. If the convoy halted, it would be trapped and mobbed by the crowd.

Three concrete benches had been moved by the rioters from the Grove into the roadway. "Try to dodge them," Falkner shouted to Antwine. "If we had stopped for those benches," Falkner says, "the rioters would have ruined us. They would have killed us—and I mean that literally."

Antwine dodged the concrete benches. The other vehicles in the convoy followed suit. But it was still going to be a rugged trip for the 100 yards or so to the Lyceum. Bricks were raining down on the trucks and jeeps. Now shotgun blasts were aimed at the convoy. Luckily, the tarpaulins offered some protection to the Guardsmen in the trucks. The bricks and shotgun pellets bounced off the tarpaulins.

When the convoy reached a point about 30 yards from the Lyceum, the marshals charged out and fired a volley of gas. The mob retreated. The convoy then proceeded the rest of the way to the Lyceum under cover of gas. Falkner jumped out of his jeep, got his men down from the trucks, then conferred with Katzenbach.

This may have been an inexpert unit. It may have been only 60 men. It may have had only 15 bayonets to its name. But I can recall thinking at the time that I was never so glad to see some khaki uniforms in my life. And many others inside the Lyceum, and outside it, expressed similar sentiments.

Falkner came into the Lyceum to talk to Katzenbach. He was holding his broken wrist in between the buttons of his shirt, in makeshift sling fashion.

"You ought to see a doctor," someone said.

"I'll do that later," he said. "I want to get my men started first."

Lieutenant Robert Crowe, an Oxford resident and an Ole Miss student, took part of the Guard unit and fell in with the marshals in front of the Lyceum. Another group formed ranks on the north side and a third on the south side. These men had no ammunition, no tear-gas guns or grenades. But they were able to help the marshals push the mob back each time a volley of gas was fired. They also represented a great psychological weapon. Fighting with deputy marshals in civilian clothing is one thing. Fighting with men in military garb is quite another. Some rioters, particularly students from Ole Miss and nearby colleges, deserted the campus at the sight of the Guardsmen. But their places were quickly taken by the outsiders who were still flocking into Ole Miss from Mississippi and other states.

A dozen of Falkner's men had been wounded on the ride through the campus. Some were taken inside the Lyceum to await treatment. Others, despite the distasteful nature of their assignment on the campus, insisted that they wanted to stay on the battle lines.

Falkner began checking on the conditions of his wounded men. One had been struck by a rock that had broken the lens of his gas mask. Glass had shattered into his eyes. Another, a supply sergeant, had been hit in the chest by a stone and suffered a painful wound.

Falkner's wrist was bleeding profusely at the time. A marshal who was treating the supply sergeant said to the gaunt captain: "You've gotta have a bandage on that wrist." Falkner paused long enough for the marshal to put on the bandage. It was not until 12:30 A.M. that a doctor, who had finally arrived inside the Lyceum, looked at Falkner's wrist. He told him there was something wrong, probably a fracture, but that he did not have the facilities to set it. Only late the next morning was Falkner able to get the broken wrist set.

In the meantime, he continued working. Katzenbach thought it might be helpful for Falkner, as a member of an illustrious Oxford family and as the local National Guard commander, to try to reason with the mob. "Do you know how to use a bullhorn?" the deputy attorney general asked. Falkner did. One was provided. Falkner got eight volunteers, by the traditional "you, you and you" method, and headed for the mob at the southeast corner of the Lyceum.

Falkner planned to ask the mob to go home. But when he started speaking, he discovered that the bullhorn megaphone did not work. The mob charged. Falkner and his volunteers retreated as the marshals fired another volley of gas.

Falkner got a second bullhorn, tested it to be sure it worked and headed into the mob again. "I'm Captain Murry Falkner, commander of the local National Guard outfit," he said. "I want to ask y'all to go on home."

His words were drowned out by the shouts of the mob.

"Traitor . . . goddam Communist . . . Benedict Arnold."

Again the mob charged. Again the marshals fired a volley of tear gas. Again Falkner retreated. He reported to Katzenbach that his attempt had done no good. But now the battle came to a temporary halt.

Father Wofford Smith, Episcopal chaplain of the university, rushed out of the mob toward the marshals, waving a white handkerchief. He had heard a report that the marshals had wounded a student with a shotgun. Father Smith was taken inside the Lyceum. He discovered that the marshals had no shotguns.

The clergyman was stunned by the scene inside the Lyceum. Wounded marshals and Guardsmen lay on the floor, bleeding and groaning. He was dazed. Suddenly he heard a call to go outside. Some of the students were asking for a peace conference. A marshal led Father Smith out the front door and down the steps. The minister walked in front, waving the handkerchief again and shouting to the mob for quiet. The marshal was shining a flashlight on Father Smith's clerical collar.

Some rioters were throwing rocks and glass, and were cursing. Then the mob suddenly stopped shouting and hurling objects. It formed a line running north and south near the front of the circle, facing the Lyceum. Father Smith shouted: "You said you wanted to talk. I'm here to talk."

The marshal was yelling: "Here's your priest. He will talk to you."

The marshals also shouted for one student to come forward as a representative of the rioters. A young student with a shaved head—the sign of a freshman—stepped forward.

"Son, what is your name?" Father Smith asked.

"I'd rather not say."

"I don't blame you," the minister said. "You people said you wanted to talk. We must talk this situation out. This situation has reached proportions that I'm sure you don't wish as a student of this university."

The clergyman pleaded with the student and those he represented not to bring any more shame to Ole Miss. The student said he didn't want to shame the university, but that this was the only way the students had of displaying their disapproval of James Meredith's presence on the campus. He said he did not feel he had the power to negotiate, since he was only a freshman.

A marshal hollered: "Send us a senior!" An older youth walked forward. "I'm a senior," he said.

Father Smith thought he recognized the senior as one of the football players he had seen the previous night at the game in Jackson.

"Are you a football player?"

"Yes."

"Why are you out here?"

"We're here to demonstrate and protest."

"Will you cooperate and help break up this riot?"

"This is the only way we have to demonstrate."

"Well, why are you attacking these men at this point?"

"Because we want to get Meredith."

"To my knowledge," Father Smith said, "Meredith is not in this building. You have no right to attack these innocent marshals. They are policemen, just like policemen in any hometown."

The football player said he would talk to the mob. He spread his arms out. "Here's the deal," he yelled. "Here's the deal. The marshals will quit using the tear gas if we'll stop throwing rocks and bricks."

There was silence. Then, a deep-throated voice from the mob yelled: "Give us the nigger, and we'll quit."

The marshals were not about to give up James Meredith, as the mob must have known. Close to 40 marshals, under the command of Deputy Marshal Cecil Miller, were guarding Meredith in his Baxter Hall suite. Meredith was trying to sleep. He dozed fitfully. He could hear the shouts, the whoomps of the gas guns and the shotgun and rifle blasts. But he had little firsthand knowledge of the seriousness of the riot.

In front of the Lyceum, the temporary peace was shattered. A brick hurtled out of the mob at the marshals. Then came an assault with rocks, bricks and bottles.

Whoomp . . . whoomp . . . whoomp . . . whoomp . . . whoomp.

The riot erupted anew.

The marshals fired still another volley of tear gas. They were having poor luck with the gas. Some of the men were firing their gas guns in the wrong direction for taking advantage of wind conditions. Thus, the gas, after floating briefly above the rioters, was blowing back in the direction of the marshals. This was a difficulty that was to plague the marshals all night.

General Walker was one of the men who fled from the volley of tear gas that broke up the peace conference. Now, with his tie loosened, he stood at the rear of the mob, again near the Confederate monument. Rioters surged in his direction to ask for advice and encouragement. He answered firmly, staring straight ahead.

A rioter asked: "Sir, that minister with the marshals— he wasn't for us, was he?"

Walker replied: "No, he was against us. They all are. They're all selling us out."

Despite the failure of the peace conference, another football player attempted a short time later to bring about an end to the riot. The player, Buck Randall, had come to the front of the Lyceum and had been ushered inside. There he witnessed the same scene that had stunned Father Smith a short time earlier—the bleeding, moaning marshals lying on the floor and harried Justice Department officials working to improve the situation.

Randall saw Marshal Gene Same still lying on the floor in the corridor of the Lyceum, the blood spurting from his neck wound. Several attempts had been made by now to bring an ambulance to the back door of the Lyceum, in order to take Same and other wounded men to a hospital. Each time, the rioters had rushed the ambulance and prevented it from reaching the door.

Randall walked outside to address some of the rioters. He stood facing the circle, at the end opposite the monument. He raised his arms above his head to get the rioters' attention. "There's a marshal in there who's bleedin' to death," he said. "He's been shot through the throat and they can't stop the bleeding."

Someone in the mob shouted: "One of their own men shot him!"

But Randall continued arguing for peace. "I tell you, I

saw him. He's bleedin' to death, and they can't get the ambulance through. Why don't they do something? The guy's bleedin' to death."

The mob shouted Randall down. Being a football hero was not enough to guarantee that a young man could control this kind of mob.

The riot resumed.

Bullets began pounding against the Lyceum. Several snipers had zeroed in on the front door of the building, through which I had been running out periodically to get information. Now it became virtually impossible to go in or out the door. The splat-splat-splat of bullets against the white wood door and the surrounding red brick of the building was almost constant.

It was not even safe for us to walk past the windows of the building. Each time one of us did, a shot would be fired at the window. We took to crouching as we went past the windows or crawling on hands and knees, so we would be below the sills and could not be seen by the snipers.

Outside the Lyceum, the marshals crouched behind parked cars to escape the snipers' bullets. Again, the marshals requested permission to return the fire. The request was relayed to the White House. Permission was denied. Here, I think, is the answer to those critics of the federal authorities who charge that the Kennedys and their aides deliberately precipitated the riot and wanted a massacre. If that were so, why would the White House consistently deny permission for the marshals, who were under heavy fire, to use anything but tear gas and billy clubs?

At one point, I heard a marshal inside the Lyceum say to Nick Katzenbach: "We've got one of the snipers spotted on top of a building. We could pick him off with a rifle." But Katzenbach instead instructed the marshals to try to sneak around behind the sniper and capture him. Six men did come up behind the sniper. But he spotted them from on top of the building and escaped, leaving behind his high-powered rifle.

Baxter Hall, where James Meredith lay in his bed, was the only place where the marshals had permission, and it was secret permission, to use their guns as a last resort. But this never became necessary.

A small group of students, on learning that Meredith was in Baxter Hall, did try to rush the dorm. But the marshals drove them off with tear gas and were not forced to use their pistols. Curiously enough, these students did not spread the word to the great mass of rioters that Meredith was in Baxter Hall. If they had, the mob undoubtedly would have switched its attention from the Lyceum to Baxter. Most rioters seemed convinced that Meredith was inside the Lyceum.

It was 10:53. Marshal Group Leader Al Butler heard a motor start with a loud groan beyond the Grove. Then came the clank of treads. Captain Murry Falkner also heard it and thought with horror: They've gotten our tanks from the armory. But it was not the tanks. Instead, it was a bulldozer, bearing down on the Lyceum out of the haze left by the tear gas. It made a ghastly sight—a monstrous contraption being used as a battering ram. The mob was trying to crash into the Lyceum.

Butler waved a signal to his men. The bulldozer was bearing down on them. But, rather than retreat, they charged it, firing their gas guns all the way. A cloud of gas enveloped the bulldozer. At its controls was a husky, leering man in a navy uniform. Rioters were retreating from the gas, vomiting and cursing. Butler jumped on the bulldozer with Marshals Ed Bartholomew of Richmond, Virginia, and Albert Taylor of Chula Vista, California. The man at the controls, who turned out to be a sailor on leave from the naval air station being used by the marshals in Memphis, was roaring drunk. He fought viciously, but the marshals clubbed him into submission.

Butler started to disable the bulldozer, so it could be used no more. The rioters charged again on his right flank. Another rioter mounted the machine, headed it at the marshals, then jumped off. However, the bulldozer struck a tree. Marshal Carl Ryan of Indianapolis, Indiana, climbed aboard. He moved it up to the federal line, near the parked army trucks, and turned it about to face the rioters, with its lights on.

No sooner had Butler returned to his post in front of the Lyceum than he heard a wild rebel yell. A fire truck now was being used for the same purpose as the bulldozer. The rioters hoped to run it right up the steps and crash into the front door of the Lyceum. Then the mob would pour in behind it.

The fire truck swung around the circle, passed the Lyceum once and kept going. It made a second run around the circle. As it approached this time, Butler grabbed the handrail and swung aboard. The driver veered sharply to his left, and sent Butler rolling head over heels for 20 yards across the grass.

For a third time, the fire engine rounded the circle. As it approached the Lyceum this time, two marshals drew their pistols and shot holes in the truck's tires. They climbed on the truck and seized the driver, a thin young man.

The mob now took to burning cars parked on the campus. They looked for rented cars, which bore easily recognizable license plate numbers, knowing that most of the newsmen were driving such cars. Within an hour, more than a dozen cars would be in flames.

Orders had been given before 10 P.M. for regular army troops to leave the Memphis naval air station by plane, helicopter and truck for the campus. For some reason there was a long delay in getting these men moving.

At 10:13 a Justice Department official noted in his log of the night's events: "Men not in air yet. Afraid to tell the men holding out." At 10:21 he noted: "Memphis men still not airborne." At 11:02: "Helicopters not off yet. Road men have not left as yet. Asked what holdup was." Actually, it was to take hours to get the troops even out of the base, much less on the scene at Oxford. In the meantime, the embattled marshals and National Guardsmen would have to hold out by themselves.

A Justice Department attorney, Bill Geoghegan, phoned Major General Creighton W. Abrams, the army's assistant deputy chief of staff, who was the top military man on the scene in Mississippi. The Border Patrol had some C-54 planes in the area. "Would there be any advantage in flying them over the campus for psychological reasons?" Geoghegan asked. At 11:17 Abrams advised against doing so. That same minute, the Justice Department put out an urgent call for more medical help in the Lyceum. Thirteen wounded marshals had been brought inside the building by this time, in addition to the dozen wounded National Guardsmen.

At 11:27, Bill Crider, an Associated Press reporter from the Memphis bureau, was brought inside. He had been hit in the back by two shotgun pellets. The back of his shirt was soaked with blood. But he wasn't looking for a doctor. He was looking for a phone booth.

I ushered him to the far right booth in the row of four in the Lyceum corridor. I figured he deserved more than mere possession of that valuable commodity—a phone—so I gave him a fill-in on everything *Detroit News* reporter Tom Joyce and I had picked up. Crider maintained control of that phone booth virtually all night, alternating between gathering information along with Joyce and me and phoning the AP office in New Orleans, which was handling the story for the national news wire.

After awhile, Crider peeled off his shirt and got a bandage wrapped around his chest to help control the bleeding. But it would not be until after the riot was over that he would get the pellets removed from under his skin. Meantime, he continued working through the night.

The marshals were now taking prisoners. The seaman who had tried to crash through the Lyceum door with the bulldozer was so drunk he could not even give his name. He stood mute and incoherent as marshals tried to question him.

The prisoners, after being frisked in the Lyceum corridors, turned over their valuables to the marshals. These were placed in envelopes bearing their names, ages and addresses. Then they were taken into the registrar's office for questioning. From there, they went down the steps from the registrar's office to the basement, where a temporary jail was set up.

One teenager was brought in with a fire extinguisher strapped to his back. He had been running after the marshals' tear-gas grenades, dousing them with chemicals before they could gas the rioters. As he was led in the door of the Lyceum, he said: "I give up. I give up."

As it turned out, he was not quite ready to surrender. After he had walked past Marshal Gene Same, who was still bleeding from the throat as he lay sprawled on the floor, the youth decided he still wanted to fight. Border Patrolman Lou Galoppo of Union City, New Jersey, who was doing most of the initial questioning of prisoners, ordered him to remove the fire extinguisher. "Go to hell, you goddam Communist," the youth shouted. "Why aren't you in Cuba?"

Galoppo seized him roughly and removed the fire extinguisher himself. Then he ordered the youth to put his hands against a wall, so that he could be frisked.

"Fuck you!"

Galoppo seized him by the shoulders, spread the youth's hands out and put them against the wall, then pulled his legs away from the wall so that he would be in the classic position for frisking.

"Fuck you, you goddam Communist."

Galoppo lost his temper. "Listen, punk. We've got a buddy over there bleeding to death. Any more crap from you and I'm gonna knock you right through this fuckin' wall."

"Fuck you!"

Galoppo punched him, neither with full force nor with a mere tap, in the side. "I'm warning you, punk. We've got a buddy bleeding to death. One more word and you go right through this wall."

"Fuck you!"

Galoppo punched him again, this time a little harder.

"Fuck you, you bastard," the youth said.

Galoppo had been ordering previous prisoners to empty their pockets, so their valuables could be put in envelopes for future claiming. He could see that force was doing him no good with this prisoner. So he changed his tack. He put his hands in the side pockets of the youth's trousers. Then, with two swift jerks, he ripped the pockets open. The rips tore the trousers in half. The bottoms dropped around the youth's ankles. He stood self-consciously, facing the wall with his torn underwear hanging down.

There is nothing that takes the fight out of someone any more effectively than being reduced to standing around in his underwear. The youth quit cursing. He couldn't have been more polite in answering questions.

Galoppo's action had been a pure stroke of genius. It

not only took the fight out of a prisoner, but added a touch of comedy relief to a grim situation.

6

Governor Ross Barnett was distressed. As he sat nervously in the Governor's Mansion in Jackson, aides brought him message after message from supporters who were upset by his evident surrender to the federal authorities. Barnett felt that he must do something to combat this development. He decided on a radio message to the state. He went on the air at 11 P.M.

"Some reports are interpreting my statement [earlier] tonight as altering my stand," Barnett said. "This is positively untrue and wholly unfounded. My friends, I report to the people of Mississippi now: I will never yield an inch in my determination to win the fight we are engaged in. I call upon every Mississippian to keep his faith and his courage. We will never surrender."

The statement was an exercise in pure demagoguery. Barnett had already yielded much more than an inch. And, contrary to his statement, he had surrendered. But now, with the Old Miss campus a shambles and one man dead and many others wounded, he was bound and determined to make political capital out of a catastrophe that he himself might have prevented by judicious action earlier. There can be little doubt that Barnett's statement, self-serving as it was, stirred the Ole Miss rioters to further provocations against the federal forces.

At Oxford, the marshals and National Guardsmen were in another tight spot. Tear gas was running out again. The rioters seemed to sense what was going on. They became bolder. A Justice Department lawyer barked into a walkie-talkie: "Maybe these walkie-talkies aren't secure. Be careful what you say."

At 11:36 the marshals estimated they had enough gas to last perhaps 10 or 15 minutes. They were saving it for a severe emergency. All they had to protect themselves from the bullets, rocks, bricks, clubs and Molotov cocktails of the rioters were their billy clubs and their fists. A call went out: "Can't we get some more National Guard units in here?"

The National Guard outfits from two nearby towns, Water Valley and Pontotoc, were ordered to move toward Oxford. But it would take time for them to reach the campus. And where was the army? It had been ordered to move into Oxford by plane, helicopter and truck from Memphis, but it still had not arrived.

Second Lieutenant Donnie G. Bowman, one of 452 men of the 503rd Military Police Battalion ordered to Memphis from Fort Bragg, North Carolina, as part of "Task Force Alpha," had gone to sleep at the naval air station after watching President Kennedy's address on an officers' club TV set. Now he was awakened. His outfit was being rushed to Oxford by helicopter.

A lesson was about to be learned. It involved "the army way of doing things." Our military services are fond of boasting that we have the most mobile forces in the world. With helicopters and jet planes, we are supposed to be able to move GIs into such remote spots as Vietnam and Laos on incredibly short notice. Now, however, the Army was having all kinds of trouble moving even one GI out the gate—or off the ground—of the Millington Naval Air Station.

Lives hung in the balance. Yet the army was acting in its own methodical fashion, apparently as if it were carrying out some meaningless training exercise. It was little more than an hour's drive, and much less than an hour's flying time, from Memphis to Oxford. To those holding out in the Lyceum, it seemed like the distance between continents.

Ed Guthman, inside the Lyceum, took over the open line to the White House to talk to his boss, Attorney General Kennedy.

"What's it like?" Kennedy asked.

"Bob, it's sorta like the Alamo," Guthman replied in his flat, State-of-Washington voice.

Kennedy paused, then reached for a touch of gallows humor. "Well," he said, "you know what happened to those fellows."

Guthman chuckled. It was an exceedingly serious period

in American history. Perhaps it was an inappropriate time for humor. But a person who can keep his sense of humor in times of stress often is able to function more effectively than one who does not know how to relax for a moment and maintain his perspective.

Guthman and Kennedy a short time later were to break the tension again, at the expense of Chief Marshal Jim McShane. Before the Ole Miss assignment, McShane had last made major news in his attempts to bring back from Israel the fugitive Soviet spy, Robert Soblen. On a flight from Israel to London, McShane was aboard an airliner with Soblen, although the convicted spy would not reach American custody until the end of the journey. McShane was to keep an eye on Soblen, to be sure he did not somehow escape in London.

During the flight, McShane left his seat to go to the lavatory. Seizing upon the opportunity, Soblen slashed his wrists. He was rushed to a London hospital, recovered from the suicide attempt, but later died after taking an overdose of drugs while en route from the London hospital to another plane for the return flight to the United States. McShane had taken merciless ribbing for his failure to bring his prisoner back alive. Now Guthman called across a Lyceum corridor to him: "Jim, the Attorney General wants to talk to you."

McShane walked toward the phone. It took him a few seconds to peel off his gas mask. Guthman said nothing during this interval. But, just before he handed McShane the phone, he said: "Bob's got another prisoner he wants you to bring back from London!"

McShane's roaring laugh filled the room. He picked up the phone. What vital order did his superior have for him?

"Jim, you're staying out of the men's room, aren't you?"

McShane assured Kennedy that he was. But he had more serious matters on his mind. Where was that tear gas he needed? He had sent Border Patrolman Chamblee to the airport for another vanload, but Chamblee had not yet arrived. And where was the army? Kennedy assured him that everything possible was being done.

It was 11:39. There was a stirring at the back door of

the Lyceum. Chamblee was there, again just in time. He had 22 cases of tear gas.

A radio message crackled into the Lyceum from Baxter Hall, where James Meredith was trying to sleep. Deputy Marshal Cecil Miller and his contingent also were out of gas.

At 11:42, a driver left the Lyceum with fresh gas supplies for the Baxter Hall unit.

In Washington, President Kennedy was angry. Ross Barnett had made a deal, but now was trying to cover it up. His statement that "we will never surrender" was being interpreted by some as an invitation to continue the rebellion against federal authority. Kennedy called Barnett, as he was to do twice more before dawn, and insisted on help from the highway patrol. Barnett sent Lieutenant Governor Johnson to Oxford—the idea being that Barnett's own presence might be inflammatory. Johnson ordered the highway patrolmen back into action. He stationed them at roadblocks to halt cars and buses loaded with armed rednecks. By Johnson's own estimate, 600 to 800 vehicles loaded with armed riders were turned back by the patrolmen. "If we hadn't done that, there wouldn't have been a marshal left that night," he says.

It was 11:45. Ray Gunter, a juke box serviceman from nearby Abbeville, Mississippi, stood with two friends near several huge pipes that were to be installed in a new building under construction near the Confederate monument. Gunter and his friends were not rioters. They had merely been curious, like many of the Oxford area residents who had come to the campus this night.

Sniper fire had been coming from the general direction of the construction site, but now no gunfire could be heard. At least one sniper had been firing at the Lyceum with a high-powered rifle from a point behind where Gunter and his friend stood. Now, he apparently had changed his position.

Slap!

That's all it was. Not bang—the way the comic strips indicate the firing of a gun. Not boom. Just slap!

Ray Gunter slumped to the ground, a .38-caliber bullet

hole in his forehead. He died en route to the university hospital, an innocent bystander who paid with his life for curiosity. It clearly was a stray shot that killed him.

Still the riot raged, and still there was no sign of the regular army troops. Five cars were burning simultaneously to the north and south of the Lyceum. A television station's mobile unit truck was overturned and afire. The horn of one burning car blared as if in agony, its wiring short-circuited.

Nick Katzenbach, inside the Lyceum, shuttled back and forth among the various phones and communications points. I was on the phone to my office. Copy deadlines were beginning to be of concern to me. It was approaching 2 A.M. in New York. My editors decided, with my full agreement, that it was senseless for me to try to write a story from the scene. There were too many things happening in too many places—Washington, Jackson, Memphis and elsewhere—for it to be practical. A reporter sitting downtown in his hotel room could do it. I was cut off from the outside world, but at the same time had a bird's-eye view of the Ole Miss action.

It was decided that I would serve as legman on the story and John Cashman, a rewrite man (now working for the *New York Post),* would pull together a story from my information and that provided by the wire services. In some cases, the services were moving on the wires information initially provided by me on a "pool" basis. But how the information got to the *Newsday* office was academic. The important thing was to get it there, and communications were in a horrible tangle.

There were only 16 long-distance phone operators handling all the calls for the entire area surrounding Oxford. The lines were jammed. If you hung up the phone, you often could not get an operator back on the line for an hour. We took to holding the lines open, flashing the operator and then putting someone else on the line to place a new call. In some cases, calls to New York from Mississippi were being placed through switchboards of newspapers in Chicago and Detroit. Anything to get the story out.

At times, I would hold the phone to the White House or the Justice Department for Katzenbach, Ed Guthman, Joe Dolan and Dean Markham. It was that kind of situation.

We had no way of knowing when the rioters might storm through the door and tear us all apart.

From such crises are instant friendships made. I think I will always have a special kind of respect and admiration for men like these and others, like Jim McShane, "Chooky" Falkner, Tom Joyce and, in particular, Bill Crider of AP. This was not so much a case of North vs. South. It was Them vs. Us. At one point, a member of Captain Falkner's National Guard outfit—a Mississippian born and bred —seized a Confederate flag from a rioter, broke the staff and dropped the flag to the ground.

"How can you do that? You're from right here in Oxford," the rioter said.

The Guardsman drawled: "Listen, buddy. When you're out there throwing bricks and shooting at me, I forget I'm a Southerner. You're on one side and I'm on the other." It was as good an answer as I heard that night. The marshals, after all, were mostly Southerners themselves.

Katzenbach was getting edgy. "We can hold out another 15 or 20 minutes," he pleaded into a radio transmitter. "Just get in here."

It was past midnight, and still the army troops had not arrived. The sniper fire was picking up, particularly from the buildings edging the Grove.

At 12:08 A.M., General Abrams, commanding the army units in the area, reported that his helicopter unit had left Memphis with battle-ready MPs. Two minutes later, trucks bearing more MPs began rolling out the gate of the Millington Naval Air Station toward Oxford.

The snipers were banging away at the front door of the Lyceum. Someone opened the door and stood in silhouette in the doorway, a perfect target, with the lights behind him putting him in bold relief against the gassy murk outside. "Get away from that door," a marshal shouted. "They've got us zeroed in." The man in the doorway jumped back and slammed the door behind him. A short time later, Karl Fleming of Newsweek's Atlanta bureau dashed through the door. Three shots narrowly missed him.

I was to get to know Karl much better on future Southern assignments. He is a handsome, alert newsman with a pleasant Southern drawl. He was already a veteran of the

Albany, Georgia, protest demonstrations and other racial skirmishes. But this was the worst. "It was the first assignment I've ever had where I was actually afraid for my life," Karl said in *Newsweek*. "It hurt to realize these were people from your own culture doing this."

Despite Lieutenant Governor Johnson's orders, many Mississippi officers still were doing nothing to help the federals. The FBI reported around midnight that 150 state officers were just sitting around in their cars. At 12:25, the FBI suggested that this inaction might represent violation of the federal court orders regarding peace officers' roles in the Meredith case. The Justice Department went to work on the legal aspects of the question.

The helicopters from Memphis stole through the night sky. Lieutenant Donnie Bowman was aboard one of the first "choppers" to reach Oxford. There had been some discussion of having the helicopters set down right on the campus, for psychological and strategic reasons. But the campus was fogged with gas, and the battle lines were constantly changing. It was decided, instead, to send the helicopters to the airport.

It was after 1 A.M. by the time the last of the helicopters arrived. All but military air traffic into and out of the airport was barred. The airport was a jumble of activity and confusion. The "army way of doing things" again took precious time.

At 1:31, the Justice Department log of the night's activities records: "MPs are sitting at airport."

At 1:33: "MPs are expected on campus at 2."

Brigadier General Charles Billingslea, a lean, six-foot-four-inch paratrooper combat veteran, arrived from his post as commander of the Second Infantry Division at Fort Benning, Georgia. He was to take field command. President Kennedy reached Billingslea by phone at Oxford at 1:37 and gave the order: "Move in forthwith."

At 1:49 the troops were still at the airport. The President, the Attorney General and Burke Marshall were moving from telephone to telephone in the President's office and the Cabinet Room. They felt frustrated and angry. Why weren't the troops moving?

The Justice Department log records: "They're not moving. It's been over five hours since we told them to move [out of Memphis]. The President is on this other phone and he wants them to move immediately."

Finally, at 1:55: "They're rolling. They're on the way." Simultaneously, a call went from the White House to the Pentagon to arrange for additional medical help at the campus.

Four gray navy buses were at the airport to carry the MPs to the Ole Miss area. The men clambered aboard. They carried the new M-14 rifles, capable of firing several hundred rounds of ammunition a minute. The rifles were loaded.

At 2:04, the four navy buses pulled up to the campus and stopped just inside the Sorority Row entrance. In charge was Lieutenant Colonel John Flanagan, commanding officer of the 503rd MP Battalion.

Lieutenant Bowman's men were in the first and second buses. They were tight-lipped and businesslike. A group of marshals was waiting at the entrance for the MPs. One marshal told the army men the buses would never get through the mob. The MPs would have to march to the Lyceum. Some onlookers heckled the MPs, but made no move to obstruct them. "You'll get hurt up there," someone yelled sarcastically.

A state highway patrolman turned his flashlight into the face of one of Bowman's five Negro men. "What you doin' down here, nigger?" he asked. The Negro just stared back at him.

The MPs fixed bayonets. One out of every five men carried a loaded riot shotgun. Gas masks were slipped over the men's faces. Bowman's men formed a wedge and began marching silently toward the Lyceum, a half-mile away. They went past rows of stately sorority houses surrounded by trees. They could hear the sounds of the riot, could see the clouds of tear gas. They plodded stolidly ahead, grunting as they breathed through the gas masks.

As they neared the Lyceum, a storm of rocks and bricks seemed to come suddenly out of nowhere. It was an ambush. Molotov cocktails exploded. One broke against an MP's helmet, but failed to ignite. Gasoline dribbled down his face. Several men were knocked down by the missiles.

Others picked them up and carried or dragged them forward.

"Take it, men," Colonel Flanagan said, his face grim. "Just take it."

Bowman led his platoon around the flaming, toppled ruins of several cars. Still in formation, with bayonets held at the ready, they marched into sight of the Lyceum. A great cheer went up from the marshals.

But the riot was not over yet.

The mob's ranks were thinning, but its weapons were becoming more deadly. Now, increasingly, it was a case of trying to fight rifles and shotguns with tear gas. At 2:25, word came that four additional National Guard units were on the way. Tear gas was running dangerously low again.

Gene Same finally was evacuated from the Lyceum. But it took some doing. He was picked up on a stretcher, with a marshal at each of the four corners. An ambulance somehow had made it through the mob to the back door. A small group of marshals charged out the door, firing tear-gas guns. The marshals ran out behind them and hustled Same into the ambulance. The ambulance sped away to a hospital, where he immediately underwent surgery. His condition was critical.

Chief Marshal McShane requested permission to return the rifle fire with sidearms. Again Attorney General Kennedy said no—unless "absolutely necessary." Such decisions were being made by the Attorney General and the President alone.

There were only about 160 MPs on the campus now, plus the 60 National Guardsmen and the marshals, Border Patrolmen and federal prison guards. The mob was still numerically superior. Rioters choked off the lines to the Lyceum, overturning more cars and setting them afire. Huge stones and heavy planks were piled across University Avenue to block the main entrance to the campus, near the Confederate monument. As trucks, marshals' cars and jeeps reached the debris, they were forced to slow down. When they did, the rioters opened up with rocks, bricks, bottles and firearms. Outside the campus gates, some of the state officers were lounging again and watching the action from afar.

The army men were put under "load-and-lock" orders—meaning they were ready to fire their rifles and riot guns whenever they got the order. The word went out that, although martial law had not been declared, the military was empowered to use all powers authorized by military regulations—including a curfew and the right to search suspect automobiles. Prisoners were to be charged with participating in an insurrection against the federal government and assaulting federal officers.

At 2:46 A.M., General Abrams reported to Washington that 840 additional soldiers, mostly MPs, were on their way to Oxford. Their estimated time of arrival was 4:30 to 5 A.M. Mississippi time.

The riot waxed and waned. The MPs at first formed ranks in front of the Lyceum with the marshals and National Guardsmen. Then they began making forays into the mob, taking prisoners and pushing the rioters farther and farther back from the Lyceum. With bayonets pointed straight in front of them, they would charge into a group, grab the most aggressive rioters, then retreat.

I had begun dashing in and out of the Lyceum again during a lull in the sniper fire. I heard one of the marshals say, "We think we've got one of the snipers." I ran inside the Lyceum.

A short, balding, moon-faced man with a drawl was being questioned in the registrar's office by Lou Galoppo. "What's your name?" Galoppo asked.

"Melvin Bruce," the new prisoner replied. Bruce was to become one of the federal men's most important prisoners. He was the former chauffeur for American Nazi leader George Lincoln Rockwell—the man who had sent telegrams to Governor Ross Barnett and to the Alabama extremist leader, Admiral John Cromelin, before coming to Oxford from his home in Decatur, Georgia.

Bruce had been spotted by several marshals as they raced across the campus in pursuit of rioters. When they ordered him to halt, he fled. They chased him to a car. Inside, they found a .30-caliber Swedish Mauser rifle and some tracer bullets that did not fit the rifle. On the rifle butt was pasted a sticker with a John Birch Society slogan: "This is a republic, not a democracy. Let's keep it that way."

Bruce kept insisting that he had done nothing wrong. "The bullets don't even fit the gun," he said again and again.

"Why did you run from the marshals, if you hadn't done anything wrong?" Galoppo asked. Bruce had no answer.

"What were you doing down here?"

"I brought my gun down. There was other cars that were coming. We were going to report to Major Arch Roberts." Roberts was the information officer for Major General Walker in Europe during the furore over Walker's use of Birch Society material in a troop indoctrination program. There are no indications that he was in Oxford at the time of the riot.

Bruce seemed more bewildered than defiant. He seemed a meek little man. It later developed that he was a World War II veteran who had been in ill health, suffering from osteomyelitis and in danger of having a leg amputated. The marshals considered him one of their key prisoners. He was to be held in $25,000 bail—second highest of all prisoners taken during the riot.

Tension eased somewhat inside the Lyceum with the arrival of the first MPs. "It's a military problem now," someone said. The sight of those MPs, with their M-14 rifles, was comforting. But the danger was still present. A sniper was pounding away again at the Lyceum front door, apparently from the roof of the Science Building, across the circle and southeast of us.

Dr. Jerry Hopkins of Oxford had made it inside the Lyceum by 3 A.M. He had set up a first-aid station in the ladies' rest room on the ground floor, just down the hall from the phone booths the reporters and federal officials were using. In twos and threes, the wounded marshals and National Guardsmen streamed into the rest room to have their long-neglected injuries attended. Hopkins told Captain Murry Falkner he would have to leave the campus to have his broken wrist X-rayed and treated. Falkner caught a ride off campus with a university official who was evacuating other university personnel. Some university officials had been in the Lyceum all night with the federal men. Now they were going home, trying to avoid the mob by using back roads.

Falkner sent one of his officers, Lieutenant Robert Crowe, to the Sorority Row entrance to help General Billingslea lead the additional MPs to the Lyceum when they arrived.

By 3:30, a convoy of 161 trucks and jeeps, holding 320 more MPs, came rumbling down State Highway 6 from Memphis. Near an underpass at the approach to the campus, 200 rioters lay in ambush alongside the highway. Suddenly, a bombardment of railroad ties and spikes rained down on the convoy. All but 20 of the MPs were hit. The missiles smashed 128 windshields, but the convoy kept rolling.

At the Sorority Row entrance, Lieutenant Crowe waited to help lead the march to the Lyceum. He found Billingslea, told him what to expect on the campus and marched with the general at the head of the column. Falkner, riding off campus to get his arm treated, passed the column at 3:45.

Billingslea and his men arrived at the Lyceum about 4. The general, at 48, was an imposing man. He towered over almost everyone in the building. He looked tough, but he spoke softly and calmly. After conferring with Nick Katzenbach, he talked to the White House. His orders were direct: secure the campus.

The National Guard units from Water Valley and Pontotoc were now on the scene. They placed their men near Conner Hall, a classroom building just northwest of the Lyceum. This vicinity had been used as a staging area by the rioters. The National Guard units secured it, driving the rioters ever farther from the Lyceum.

The mob made an attempt to break into the Chemistry Building, in search of chemicals that could be used as explosives. The National Guardsmen, including Falkner's men, surrounded the building. Marshals, whose tear-gas supplies had been replenished, rushed in to disperse the mob with another volley of gas. Then they charged into the mob, coming out with more prisoners.

Shortly after 5 A.M., about 75 MPs and Guardsmen formed a long line and pushed across the campus with bayonets fixed. Behind them were marshals, ready to fire another salvo of tear gas. Many of the rioters retreated and fled from the campus to the downtown area. About 200 hard-core troublemakers remained. As the troops moved toward them, even these 200 turned tail and ran across the railroad trestle.

The first pink rays of sunlight were appearing. The horn of one of the flaming autos was sending a ghostly wail across the campus. The campus was a shambles. Tear-gas canisters were everywhere. Broken pop bottles and street lights littered the lawns. Concrete benches and street markers lay shattered. Scattered on the ground were cardboard signs reading: "Ross is right." The acrid smell of tear gas lingered in the air. From beyond the campus gates came the still-defiant chant: "Two-four-six-eight, we don't want to integrate."

The battleground shifted from the campus to the historic town of Oxford. And so did the character of what was left of the mob. Few Ole Miss students remained. The mob was made up almost entirely of outsiders who had streamed into Oxford during the night. A "preacher" with four revolvers and four high-powered rifles had arrived from St. Petersburg, Florida. "I'm an avowed segregationist," he said. An Alabaman in weathered work clothes led 30 men in six cars from Mobile to "fight for our Constitution." He carried a red cloth with the hand-lettered word: "Captain." On arrival, he had asked: "Where is that there school, anyhow?"

At 6 A.M., two other reporters and I toured the rubble-strewn campus on foot with Billingslea. At the end of the tour, Billingslea said with a trace of a smile: "Gentlemen, we declare the area secure."

I walked back inside the Lyceum, phoned my office, then ate my first food in close to a day. The marshals and troops had been fed, chow-line fashion, inside the Lyceum corridors. All that remained were a couple of hunks of bread and the juice from some stewed tomatoes. Ed Guthman and I stood over the food cans, hungrily eyeing the sad remains. "What the hell, Ed, it's better than nothing," I said. He nodded. We slopped some stewed tomato juice onto a slice of bread each and gorged ourselves.

Tears still streamed from our eyes. We were sweaty, unkempt, unshaven. We had bummed cigarets most of the night. The Coke and cigaret machines had long since run out of supplies. A package of Life Savers in my pocket, coated with pipe tobacco that had dropped out of a pouch, had provided me and several of my companions with our only nourishment. We had not slept, and there was no indication that we would be getting any sleep soon. But we felt, for the first time all night, that we were safe. The United States Army was taking over now.

At the Oxford airport, a tent city was sprouting alongside the runways and on nearby slopes. More soldiers were pouring in by plane, helicopter, truck and jeep. First-aid stations and field kitchens were erected. Military jets roared overhead.

In Washington, President Kennedy finally went to sleep. Attorney General Kennedy and Burke Marshall left the White House and returned to the Justice Department. The department log records: "Attorney General returns with a smile. Burke also."

But the riot was not entirely over yet.

Shortly after 6, in a light drizzle, a mob of toughs formed at the intersection of Lamar Street and University Avenue in Oxford. This is a busy intersection, for Oxford, since all four corners are occupied by service stations.

As jeeploads of MPs passed, the toughs heaved pop bottles at them. The jeeps kept rolling. Nearby, a group of state policemen leaned against squad cars and watched. A Negro civilian in a truck found his way blocked. The toughs swarmed around him. He backed his truck up, wheeled around and raced off in the opposite direction. Forty National Guard volunteers rolled up to the intersection and dispersed the group.

At 7:45 A.M., a platoon of MPs, wearing gas masks and marching with bayonets fixed, herded a group of toughs from Lamar Street toward the square. Outside the Lafayette County Courthouse, the rioters regrouped and opened a new barrage. Some tossed rocks from the balcony of a building facing the square. Others heaved a 55-gallon oil drum at jeep windshields, then retrieved it and heaved it again. The rioters were inflamed by the sight of

Negro MPs. They knocked one down with a bottle. "Why'd they have to put those niggers in there?" asked one Oxford man.

In the end, the MPs fired rifle shots over the heads of the rioters. The rioters surrendered. Thirty of them were led down University Avenue, onto the campus, then into the Lyceum with the other prisoners.

The riot was over at last.

7

At riot's end, the Lyceum was cluttered with prisoners, federal officials, marshals, army men and FBI agents. There were 93 prisoners—less than a third of them Ole Miss students—but more were being brought in all the time. They were being questioned by the FBI men and the marshals.

Two students from Memphis State University were caught with broken glass and rocks in their pockets.

"What were you doing down here?" a marshal asked.

"We were just sight-seeing," one of them replied.

A vast arsenal of weapons was confiscated from the rioters. There were pistols, rifles and shotguns of all kinds, blackjacks, knives, and lengths of hose and pipe. Invariably, when a gun-toter was asked what he was doing with the weapon, he would reply, "Squirrel hunting."

One youth had come from Vardaman, 60 miles away.

"Who asked you to come?" a marshal demanded.

"Nobody."

"Well, why'd you come?"

"Well, the whole town wanted to."

Even as the riot had been drawing to a close in downtown Oxford, James Meredith had been dressing in his dormitory room. He was about to take the historic step that had brought about the violence. At long last, he was going to register as an Ole Miss student.

At 7:25 A.M., Registrar Robert Ellis arrived at his office in the Lyceum, ready to accept Meredith's application. About five minutes later, a convoy of Border Patrol cars pulled up outside the back door. A heavy escort of marshals cleared a path through the dozens of newsmen who had converged on the building after the riot ended. Meredith emerged from one of the cars and entered the back door. He wore a dark blue-gray suit, a white shirt and a red tie. He carried a thin leather briefcase. His face was utterly devoid of emotion. But he dabbed at his eyes with a handkerchief, obviously bothered by the lingering tear gas.

Deputy Marshal Miller and Border Patrolman Chamblee entered Ellis' office with Meredith. They were joined by Deputy Attorney General Katzenbach, Justice Department attorney Doar, Chief Marshal McShane, information officer Ed Guthman and Ole Miss assistant registrar Freeman Gober.

Meredith sat down across a desk from Ellis. "I want to give you a late registration form, James," Ellis said, as if this were just a routine registration. Meredith accepted the form with a "thank you."

An hour later, Guthman poked his head out the door and said: "He's registered." It had taken 16 months of legal wrangling and an interminable night of bloodshed. But James Meredith was now an Ole Miss student. Guthman poked his head out again. "He's going to class now," he said.

Meredith walked out the door, brushing aside questions. The newsmen swarmed around him, and were pushed back by the marshals. Flashbulbs popped. Another mob scene appeared in the offing.

Guthman was annoyed. It had been a long, difficult fight and the strain was showing. "Either we're going to do this right and do it with dignity or we'll have to clear the campus," he warned the reporters. But few paid any attention.

Finally, the marshals pushed open a path. Meredith walked through briskly, swinging his arms freely. He fiddled with his eyeglasses several times.

Outside the building, Ole Miss students were waiting—and they were seething.

"Was it worth two lives, nigger?" one of them shouted. "You black bastard . . . Nigger, nigger . . . Two people died. How do you like blood on your hands?"

Meredith just stared straight ahead and kept walking. McShane, Doar and Guthman were alongside him. A student yelled: "You black son of a bitch." Meredith smiled. "Where are we going first?" he asked.

"The Peabody Building," Doar said. He had a campus map in his hand. After a few starts in wrong directions with the crowd swarming around, the group wheeled back to the Lyceum. Moments later, the party entered a car and drove off to the Peabody Building. As Meredith was about to enter, a reporter asked: "Are you pleased?"

Meredith replied: "No. This is not a happy occasion."

He began his first class, Colonial American history, at 9 A.M. Marshals waited outside the class. Inside, Meredith jotted lecture notes in a loose-leaf notebook. No one in the class spoke to him.

While Meredith was in his first class, Guthman announced that the Justice Department had filed charges against former General Walker and had issued orders for his arrest. The complaint against Walker charged:

On or about September 30, 1962, Edwin Walker did forcibly assault, resist, oppose, impede, intimidate and interfere with United States marshals and persons employed to assist such marshals . . . while they were engaged in performance of their official duties. . . . Edwin Walker and other persons unknown in the State of Mississippi did conspire to prevent by force, intimidation and threats U. S. marshals from discharging their duties and to injure them in their person while engaged in the lawful discharge of their duties. . . . Edwin Walker did incite, assist and engage in an insurrection against the authority of the United States and the laws thereof. . . . Edwin Walker and other persons unknown in the State of Mississippi did conspire to oppose by force the authority of the United States and by force to prevent, hinder and delay the execution of the laws of the United States.

The complaint, signed by United States Attorney H. M. Ray of Oxford, said that the charges were supported by information provided by Van H. Savell, an Associated Press reporter. The charges carried a maximum prison sentence of 39 years and a fine of $40,000. At the time the complaint was filed, Walker was still in Oxford. But he was making plans to leave town, and the federal authorities had no idea where to find him. Then he fell right into their lap.

Army roadblocks had been set up at all approaches to Oxford and the Ole Miss campus. Soldiers were searching all cars entering and leaving the area, in attempts to find weapons. About 11 A.M., just south of the Lafayette County Courthouse, Walker was spotted by a group of GIs from the Second Battle Group of the Second Infantry Division. Lieutenant Robert Clarke, who had been alerted about the complaint against Walker, recognized him from news photos. He detained Walker, who offered no resistance, until marshals could arrive to take the retired general to the Lyceum.

At 11:30, I spotted Walker in the registrar's office. He looked confused. When I asked him about the charges against him, he smiled wanly and replied: "No comment." Several other reporters edged into the office and began firing questions. Walker answered none of them. But, to no one in particular, he said: "I'm all right."

At 1 P.M., Walker was ushered into a courtroom at the Oxford Post Office Building for arraignment before U. S. Commissioner Omar D. Craig. He removed his white, broad-brimmed hat as he entered. A dark cowlick was sticking up at the back of his head. "Are you Edwin Walker?" Craig asked.

"Edwin A. Walker. Yes, sir," Walker replied, emphasizing his middle initial.

Craig explained that he was entitled to have a lawyer present and could ask for a preliminary hearing or waive his right to one. Walker said he wanted a Texas lawyer to represent him, but Craig would allow only two hours for the attorney to be summoned. "There are plenty of good lawyers in this state and in this county," he said.

Walker again seemed confused. He clenched his hands several times, first in front of his body and then behind his back. "Is it necessary that we go through this procedure?" he asked.

"No, you may waive a hearing," Craig reminded him. "If you do, I'll set bond and you're free to go as soon as you make bond."

After a delay of several minutes, Walker asked: "Is it proper that I waive under these circumstances—that I'm assured that the case would come back here to Mississippi?"

Craig assured him that the case would be decided in Mississippi. In doing so, he called Walker "Colonel," then corrected himself and said "General." Walker, referring to the fact that he had resigned from the army, snapped: "Mister, please. That's one of my problems already. All right, I'll waive this hearing."

Craig read the charges aloud. Walker listened attentively, but impassively. "Bail is set at $100,000," Craig said. Walker let out a long, low whistle. "You'll remain in custody until bail is made."

Walker, frequently so voluble on other occasions, had nothing to say to reporters after his arraignment. But one of his companions, 37-year-old Robert Surrey of Dallas, denied that Walker had participated in the rioting. He said the former general had urged "peaceable protest." Surrey said friends in Texas would try to raise the bail.

Marshals led Walker away to a cell. He was not to remain in Oxford long. Within hours, he was quietly removed from his cell by marshals and taken to the U. S. Medical Center for federal prisoners in Springfield, Missouri. U. S. District Judge Claude F. Clayton, on a motion by U. S. Attorney Ray, ordered Walker committed to the hospital for a psychiatric examination. Before issuing the order for Walker's mental examination, Clayton had studied a memorandum prepared for James V. Bennett, federal director of prisons, by Dr. Charles E. Smith, medical director and chief psychiatrist for the Federal Prison Bureau. The memorandum was a most unusual document, attempting to diagnose Walker's case in advance of the psychiatric exam.

Smith said in the memorandum that he had examined news reports on Walker's behavior. "Some of his described behavior reflects sensitivity and essentially unpredictable and seemingly bizarre outbursts of the types often observed in individuals suffering with paranoid mental disorders," the memorandum said.

"There are also indications in his medical history of functional and psychosomatic disorders which could be precursors of the more serious disorders which his present behavior suggests . . . may be indicative of an underlying mental disturbance."

In Springfield, Walker was interviewed for an hour upon his arrival by Dr. Russell Settle, the medical center's warden. He was then given a set of hospital clothes and put to bed. His case was already bringing ramifications in other parts of the country. In Texas and elsewhere in the South, there were complaints that Walker was being held illegally. And, in Washington, two senators suggested that Walker was mentally ill. Democratic Senator Wayne Morse of Oregon said: "Maybe he's a sick man. If he is, he ought to be committed. He ought not to be at large." Democrat Stephen M. Young of Ohio spoke of "psychopaths" in discussing Walker's case.

In Oxford, James Meredith was completing his first day as an Ole Miss student. After attending his 9 A.M. class in Colonial American history, he had returned to his dormitory until a 1 P.M. class in Spanish. Five marshals had accompanied him to each class, but waited in a corridor while the class was in progress. A late afternoon mathematics class, Meredith's last of the day, was called off because the classroom was still heavy with tear gas that had filtered in the previous night.

Meredith's classmates made a studied effort to ignore him. There were no incidents in the classes, but nobody greeted Meredith or made any clear effort to recognize his presence. He spent virtually all his time between classes in the Baxter Hall dormitory. Meals were brought to him there. Other students were in the same hall, and many of them shouted vile remarks toward the suite where Meredith and the marshals were housed. But the marshals seemed confident of their ability to maintain order in the dorm.

Now, after the worst part of the Ole Miss crisis was over, thousands more army and Mississippi National Guard troops were flooding into Oxford. The little university town looked like a military installation. By nightfall Monday, 13,000 troops were stationed in Oxford and the surrounding area. The number of troops far exceeded the permanent population of the town and the Ole Miss student body combined.

Tent cities sprouted on the campus and at the airports. In the circle directly in front of the Lyceum, where the riot had been centered Sunday night, soldiers were bivouacked in pup tents. The small civilian airport resembled an air force base. All kinds of military aircraft, from jet fighters and helicopters to Globemaster transports, overflowed the runways and hangar space.

A prisoner compound was set up in a garage at the airport. By late Monday, 300 persons had been taken into custody. Only about a third of them were students. All 300 were questioned by FBI agents. Except for 13, against whom charges were filed, all were to be released by Tuesday.

Meanwhile, doctors were tending to the hundreds of persons wounded during the riot. Almost half of the marshals sent to Ole Miss, 180 of them, had been wounded, 27 by gunfire. The most seriously wounded, Gene Same, made a remarkable recovery after being all but given up for dead.

Despite all the bloodshed, however, there were some diehard segregationists who were not yet ready to give up the fight against Meredith's admission. On Monday night, soldiers arrested two dozen more persons who were carrying weapons and looking for trouble. One man and his 14-year-old son had a collection that included a rifle, two shotguns, a saber, two hunting knives and a large supply of ammunition. Outside Baxter Hall, a group of students made a new assault on the marshals guarding Meredith. Without warning, they sent a barrage of bottles raining down on the marshals. The marshals fired a volley of tear gas, and the students fled.

Amid all this turmoil, a flurry of recriminations and attempts to fix blame for the riot began in Oxford, Jackson and Washington. Governor Barnett, still trying to shift the blame to the federals, appeared on a national television network Monday night. His version of what had happened at Oxford represented, to my mind, an interesting attempt at rewriting one-day-old history. Barnett said the Ole Miss students merely gathered and demonstrated. "They were noisy, they were boisterous, but not violent," he said. "This was a natural thing for students to do."

The Governor made a charge that was to be echoed numerous times by others—that the marshals had actually precipitated the riot by firing the tear gas. He took no cognizance of the fact that the campus situation had deteriorated to such a point that the marshals had no choice but to fire the gas. By Barnett's version the violence that had occurred before the firing of the tear gas actually resembled nothing more than a football-style pep rally. Barnett said:

The federal marshals were men who were inexperienced, nervous, you might say "trigger happy." Their instability and unwarranted brutality against unarmed youths will forever blacken the record of all federal officers. They were quick to fight American youths. But, to my way of thinking, they are extremely slow to fight Castro. The people of Mississippi are incensed, and rightly so. Free men do not submit weakly to this kind of treatment. . . . Our people have been inflamed deliberately in order that the resulting resistance can be cited as justification for military force against the people of a sovereign state, and the crushing of the rights of the states.

Barnett finally got around to giving his version of the negotiations with the President and the Attorney General. It differed markedly from the version to be given immediately afterward by the Attorney General. Barnett said:

From the time that it became apparent that the federal government intended to place Meredith in the University of Mississippi by armed forces, I have been called many, many times by the President and by the Attorney General of the United States, and I have called them many times in an effort to persuade them that their action should not be taken.

When it was made known to me that they would forcibly put Meredith in the university either Sunday or Monday, I realized that Oxford would be crowded Monday with thousands and thousands and thousands of people—not only from Mississippi, but from many other states. I knew there would be many deadly weapons there on Monday, and that hundreds of people would probably be killed.

Barnett conceded that he had suggested that Sunday would be a better time to bring Meredith on campus than Monday. "I believed then, and I believe now, that if he had gone into the campus of the university on Monday—today —there would have been probably 20,000 or more people there, many of them with guns, and hundreds of people would have been killed."

Barnett said the federal government had been the aggressor in the Meredith case and must bear the responsibility for the violence. "I understand from statements of Attorney General Kennedy, which I have not yet seen, that he has charged me with having withdrawn highway patrolmen from the campus Sunday night," Barnett said. "I emphatically and positively deny that statement."

A few minutes after Barnett had completed his TV address, Attorney General Kennedy made a reply on the same network. He paid tribute to the marshals' courage and restraint, saying that Mississippians and all Americans owed them a great debt of gratitude. Then he reviewed the events of the preceding day:

Governor Barnett had an understanding with us that was made at approximately 12:45 on Sunday morning that Mr. Meredith would be entered into the University of Mississippi, that he would be preceded by marshals, that Mr. Meredith would then come into the University of Mississippi and he would remain there.

It was Governor Barnett's responsibility, which he undertook at that time, to maintain law and order, to insure that no violence occurred and, if there were any disorders, to handle it with the state police, with the help and assistance of the marshals. When violence did occur, the state police were withdrawn.

I received notification of that at approximately 9:25 last evening. I got in touch with a representative of the Governor, protested, and said that this was a violation of the agreement that they had had, and the state police were returned approximately 10 minutes of 10—10 minutes before the President went on in his speech.

The situation became more difficult then, till, about a quarter of 11, the violence grew. And, at that time, the state police withdrew again—all of them—got in their automobiles and drove away and disappeared for approximately two hours and a half.

The Governor says he's not responsible for that. The fact is that the state police, when the violence became serious, withdrew and left this extremely precarious position to the United States marshals. We learned at approximately 1 o'clock last night that there were about 150 state police parked in approximately 80 automobiles about a quarter of a mile from the scene of all these disorders, and refusing to come back.

I think last night was the worst night I ever spent. We had these marshals who perhaps originally signed up thinking that they were just going to go from the jail to the judge's office, not realizing that they would be involved in things like this. . . . They were out there with instructions not to fire. They were fired on, they were hit, things were thrown at them. It was an extremely dangerous situation.

All they had, finally, was the tear gas. We received notification that the tear gas was running out, that they only had four or five minutes. The mob brought up a bulldozer and attacked the house in which they were staying.

And I think it was that close. If the tear gas hadn't arrived in that last five minutes, and if these men hadn't remained true to their orders and instructions, if they had lost their heads and started firing at the crowd, you would have had immense bloodshed, and I think it would have been a tragic situation.

So to hear these reports that were coming in to the President and to myself all last night—when the situation with the state police having deserted the situation, and these men standing up there with courage and ability and great bravery—that was a very moving period in my life.

The Mississippi Board of Trustees of Institutions of Higher Learning, whose members had been among the defendants in Meredith's suit for admission, issued a statement of its own. It accused the marshals of having poor leadership, of "amateurism," bad judgment and manhandling of prisoners.

But the University of Mississippi chapter of the American Association of University Professors took a contrary view. The chapter said in a resolution:

While it is obvious that errors in judgment were made by those in authority on the university campus Sunday, we have evidence that the attempt of men in prominent positions to place all the blame for the riot on the marshals is not only unfair and reprehensible, but is almost completely false.

Some news media in Mississippi have entertained irresponsible and secondhand stories in distortion of the facts and have thereby helped to provoke a general state of confusion, alarm and misdirected wrath. . . . We believe in the use of courts and ballot boxes to state our convictions. We oppose and deplore the useless employment of clubs and missiles against our fellow citizens in behalf of any conviction whatsoever. Riots, weapons and agitators have no place at a university.

These conflicting attitudes were mirrored on the Ole Miss campus. Some students were still defiant. They vowed they would never accept Meredith's presence on the campus, but would work through a "rebel underground" to drive him out. Others, however, were sorely shamed by the riot. "I just wish we could erase everything that happened at Ole Miss last night," a typical student said.

Many parents were keeping their youngsters home from the campus, for fear of further trouble. Attendance dropped from the normal 5,000 to 1,500. Some students said they planned to transfer to segregated colleges. Others expressed confidence that Meredith would not last it out to graduation from Ole Miss. But there seemed to be a sense of permanence attached to a one-sentence press release tacked on a Lyceum door by the university's news bureau. It said simply: "Pursuant to the mandate of the federal courts, the orders for the registration of Meredith have been followed."

The next day, Tuesday, October 2, was Meredith's first full day of classes at Ole Miss. McCandlish (John) Phillips of *The New York Times* and I were chosen to cover Meredith on a "pool" basis for the remainder of the newspapermen. We joined Chief Marshal McShane and three other marshals outside Baxter Hall. We would be able to accompany Meredith wherever he went, except inside classrooms, and talk to him both in between classes and after classes had ended for the day. Then we would report to a press conference, called by Ed Guthman, and brief the other reporters.

MPs with fixed bayonets were stationed all around Baxter Hall. McShane and two other marshals, after briefing us on what we would be permitted to do, went inside for Meredith. They emerged with him a few minutes later and climbed into a pale green Border Patrol car. The car proceeded slowly to Elma Meek Hall, where Meredith would take an English class. The car was followed by a jeep loaded with MPs.

At Meek Hall, a small group of students was waiting for Meredith. Someone yelled: "Shit, Meredith." Someone else hollered: "You black bastard." Meredith ignored the taunts and walked inside. There were 28 students in his class. Meredith sat alongside a wall, four rows from the front of the room. Another student was two seats away.

No one greeted Meredith as he entered the room, but there were no derogatory remarks either. The class was devoted to reading and analyzing two poems by Thomas Gray. One was "Ode on a Distant Prospect of Eton College." The other was "Ode on the Death of a Favorite Cat." Discussing the poems later with Phillips and me, Meredith would smile a bit, with a twinkle in his eyes, and say: "They were very interesting, to me."

After his English class, he was taken to the George Peabody Building for an algebra class. I walked up a flight of stairs with Meredith, to wait outside in a corridor with two marshals while the class was in progress. Meredith immediately walked inside the classroom. In the crowded corridor, no one had said a word to him. But, after he got inside, a group of students clustered at the door. Several of them tried to stop other students from entering Meredith's class. One of them said to a friend: "Hey, boy. Don't go in there. Meredith's in that class." The student walked in, anyway.

A short, pretty blonde walked up. The boys at the door started laughing. The girl sensed immediately what they were laughing about. "Oh, no, you're kidding," she said. "I guess I'll have to stay out of the class." Just then, Dr. T. A. Bickerstaff, the mathematics department chairman, strolled by on his way to another class. The girl appealed to him to give her an excuse for staying out of class. But he told her: "You'd be depriving yourself of the experience of seeing what it's like to be in a class with him." The girl reluctantly walked inside the classroom.

After his classes were over for the day, Meredith returned to Baxter Hall to unwind. It had been a long, tense day. But he consented to talk for awhile with Phillips and me.

His room was on the third floor, with a stairway leading to the street just outside the front door. Before getting to Meredith's room, we walked through the room serving as headquarters for the marshals guarding him. Meredith was sharing his own room with John Doar. The white-walled room was bare of pictures. It contained three metal cots, a desk and a dresser.

Meredith sat at the edge of one cot, dangling his legs lazily. Phillips and I tried to put him at ease, asking relatively innocuous questions at first. Meredith answered in a soft, high-pitched voice, choosing his words with great care. I asked him: "Do you have any message you'd like to communicate to the white students?"

He thought for a long while, swinging his legs absently back and forth a few inches above the floor. Finally, he replied: "I notice that a number of students look like they're mad. I don't know if they're mad at me or what. If they're mad at me, I'd like to know what about."

Meredith said the hooting and catcalling within Baxter Hall had died down somewhat since its height the night of the riot. As he talked, he riffled through a few of the hundred or more telegrams he had received since arriving at Ole Miss. "I'd like to express my appreciation for the support from these people," he said. "I've received only one telegram that I wouldn't consider of a favorable nature."

What did he think of the Ole Miss faculty? "From what I've seen," he said, "it is a more professional group than at any school I've been in before."

What did he plan to do after college? "What I do when I finish school depends a lot on the outcome of this situation. It is a fact that Negroes are looked on and treated as something other than first-class citizens in Mississippi. They are being denied many of the rights that are basic to American democracy. I'm most concerned with this problem and absolutely intent on seeing that every citizen is given a right to be something if he works hard enough. At this point, it's more for America than it is for me."

How did he feel about the riot? "I'm very sorry anyone had to get hurt. Change is never pleasant. But, if this stops me, then it's no different from being officially stopped. I hope the situation gets back to normal as soon as possible, so the students can get back to their studies normally. That's what I want more than anything right now."

Phillips and I shook hands with Meredith, wished him luck and left.

The next day, I flew home from Oxford. But I would be back, for the Ole Miss story was far from over. Meredith still faced a rugged year at the university. Former General Walker, who would leave the Springfield hospital a few days later on bail, still faced federal court charges. Others arrested in Oxford also faced court action. Governor Barnett had a contempt of court case on his hands. And two murders remained to be solved.

There would be charges and countercharges, action and reaction. Within a year, there would be another Negro student enrolled at Ole Miss.

And I would be there to cover the story.

2 Dignity at Clemson

By January of 1963, South Carolina remained the only state in the Union that had never admitted a Negro to a white public school at any level. Even Alabama had briefly enrolled Negro coed Autherine Lucy in its state university, though she was later expelled for criticizing officials over the handling of rioting that accompanied her admission.

In some ways it seemed natural that South Carolina should be the last holdout against desegregation. She had, after all, led the South out of the Union. And the first shot of the Civil War had been fired on her soil.

But now South Carolina was faced with the dilemma that had come to confront each of her Deep South neighbors. The federal courts had ordered the admission of Harvey Gantt, a 20-year-old Negro architectural student, to Clemson College, the state's land-grant college. How would South Carolina react? Would there be a repetition of the bloodshed that had marred James Meredith's enrollment at the University of Mississippi? Or would South Carolina, having learned from the tragic lesson of Ole Miss, handle Gantt's case with dignity?

Gantt's enrollment was scheduled for Monday, January 28. On Wednesday, January 23, my city editor, Bill McIlwain, asked me to make some preliminary checks on the prospects for covering the story. I phoned Joe Sherman, Clemson's director of public relations and alumni affairs. To my surprise, though he was a Clemson alumnus and spoke with a syrupy drawl, he formerly had lived in Uniondale, Long Island, just a short distance from the *Newsday* office.

"You're welcome to come down here, but there's not goin' to be any story," Sherman said. "We're not goin' to have any Ole Miss at Clemson. Gantt will be admitted and that will be that."

Justice Department and NAACP officials agreed with Sherman's prediction. To my mind, peaceful desegregation at Clemson, following the Ole Miss riot, in itself would be news. I do not hold with the theory that only violence makes news in the struggle for desegregation. Peaceful integration often can be more meaningful over the long haul than desegregation at the point of a bayonet.

"It looks like the South, for once, is going to do something with a little class," I told McIlwain. "Sherman and the others don't look for any trouble. Of course, they could be wrong. But, even if they're right, I think it would be a good idea to cover the story."

McIlwain, a Southerner, shared the view that Northern newspapers too often were inclined to cover only the racial stories that gave the South a bad name. "I think you ought to go down there," he told me. "We ought to be there to cover the story—whatever it is, whether there's violence or not."

I flew to Greenville, South Carolina, on Saturday, January 26. I rented a car there and drove the 32 miles to Clemson. The town, with a population of 1,650, is in the northwest part of the state, in the foothills of the Blue Ridge Mountains. Its hub is the college, founded in 1889 by Thomas Green Clemson, a mining engineer, farmer and scientific writer who was the son-in-law of John Calhoun. Fort Hill, a mansion built for Calhoun in 1803, is situated in the heart of the campus. The campus, now populated by a student body of about 4,200, was Indian territory for much of the 17th century. Nearby are "Treaty Oak," where General Andrew Pickens signed agreements with the Cherokees, and Fort Prince George, an English defense post against Indian raids.

Clemson has only one hotel, Clemson House, but it is a modern, well-kept establishment on a hill overlooking the campus. Soon after I had checked in, I was renewing acquaintances with a group of reporters who were regulars on the Southern racial beat. Claude Sitton of *The New*

York Times, Joe Cumming of *Newsweek,* Fred Powledge of the *Atlanta Journal,* Dudley Morris of *Time* and Herb Kaplow of NBC were among those already checked in at Clemson House. We spent a few hours touring the area, getting the feel of the place, then returned to the hotel for a beer-drinking and bull session. We were joined by George McMillan, a South Carolina free-lancer who was covering the story for the *Saturday Evening Post* and was a fountain of information about the state, the college and the political ramifications of the integration attempt. Joe Cumming, a good-natured Southerner who works out of Atlanta, regaled us with full-voiced renditions of South Carolina folk songs.

The atmosphere of the press corps, reflecting that on the campus, was much more relaxed at Clemson than it had been at Ole Miss. There were good reasons for feeling that there would be no repetition of the Ole Miss holocaust in South Carolina. The state had been preparing for months to meet its racial test with dignity and good sense. Unlike Mississippi, where there had been an almost total absence of responsible leadership, South Carolina had been blessed with some farsighted men at the top of its political, business and educational communities.

As far back as July 1, 1961, six months after Harvey Gantt originally applied unsuccessfully for admission to Clemson, South Carolina's best-known businessman had begun a drive to pave the way for integration with dignity. Charles Daniel, head of the biggest construction firm in the state, had told a watermelon festival in Hampton County:

The desegregation issue cannot continue to be hidden behind the door. The situation cannot satisfactorily be settled at the lunch counter and bus station. We have a definite obligation to increase the productivity of our Negro citizens, to provide them with good jobs at good wages and to continue to assure them of fair treatment. By raising their education and economic status, we would raise the whole economy of the state.

Daniel soon became a member of a small, informal group of leading South Carolinians that began working behind the scenes to prepare the state for the inevitable day when integration—court-ordered or otherwise—would come to pass. In addition to Daniel, the group included then-Governor Ernest Hollings; John Cauthen, executive vice-president of the South Carolina Textile Manufacturers Association; state senate president pro tem Edgar Brown, chairman of the Clemson Board of Trustees; Robert Edwards, Clemson president; and Wayne Freeman, editor of the *Greenville News*.

Members of the group sent feelers out unobtrusively to other segments of the political and economic power structures of the state. By the end of 1961, they had let it become generally known among South Carolina's leading figures that there was a significant movement afoot to see to it that law and order were preserved, even at the cost of permitting desegregation. This knowledge, however, initially remained solely with the power elite. The general public continued to feel that political leaders somehow would cast a magic spell and drive the integration problem away, or, at the very least, would go to jail to preserve the holy cause of segregation.

Governor Hollings was concerned about the failure of the public to face reality. Harvey Gantt, after having his first application to Clemson rejected in January, 1961, applied again in January, 1962. That same month, Hollings conducted his customary briefing for newsmen, just before the convening of the General Assembly. He chose the occasion to make clear his feelings on desegregation.

"Before 1962 has passed, South Carolina's legal defenses will fall like a house of cards," Hollings told the reporters. "You might as well start preparing your readers for the inevitable. We are not going to secede."

Soon a number of South Carolina newspapers began giving extensive coverage to Gantt's attempt to enter Clemson. The college never acted on his second application. On July 7, 1962, NAACP attorneys filed suit for him in United States District Court, seeking to compel Clemson to enroll him. With the Ole Miss crisis building up at the time, South Carolinians began to realize that their test soon would be coming.

Hollings sent Pete Strom, head of the South Carolina Law Enforcement Division (SLED), to Ole Miss during the crisis to study techniques used by Mississippi and federal lawmen. Strom then set to work with Hollings' counsel, Harry Walker, on laying out a security plan for Clemson. The Governor instructed them to be sure that the plan was sufficiently effective that there would be no need for federal marshals. He also specified that it should be able to prevent even the possibility of permitting a crowd to gather and should provide for carefully controlling the press' movements.

The suit filed by the NAACP was opposed by the state in a series of legal skirmishes through the fall. But, by November, it became clear that the state would have to submit to a court order directing Gantt's enrollment. So far the group working behind the scenes to ease the way for integration had made no public statement. But now a Charleston reporter called Clemson Board Chairman Edgar Brown and asked: "Now that it is pretty certain that the Clemson board is going to admit Harvey Gantt, what explanation would you give to the people who elected you, in the event of such a decision?"

Brown took down the reporter's question and promised to provide an answer later. Brown met with Clemson president Edwards and businessman Cauthen to draft a reply. He released it to both the Charleston newspaperman and the wire services. It said: "If the ultimate decision of the federal courts directs that Harvey Gantt should be admitted, my position is that the board of trustees and the administration at Clemson College will not tolerate violence on the Clemson campus."

With Brown now on the record, a number of the state's leading newspapers echoed his sentiments. It became clear also that the economic and political power structures, while some of their leaders were not making speeches on the subject, were committed to the same position as Brown. The public began getting the long-delayed message that South Carolina's leaders had no intention of seeing the state go the route that Mississippi had gone. At the same time, some Clemson student leaders started laying the groundwork for a smooth welcoming for Gantt, if and when he entered the college. Several of them visited Gantt, indicating to him that he would be treated decently as a

Clemson student and that they wanted to be his friends. They also spread the word on campus that any breach of discipline would be dealt severely with by the student government and the college administration.

Amid these hopeful signs, however, there were fears that some influential South Carolinians might move to prevent Gantt's admission and that this, in turn, might provoke racists to abandon law and order. The three public figures considered most likely to take some action to bar Gantt's enrollment were State Senator Marion Gressette, chairman of a legislative committee assigned to maintain segregation laws; State Representative A. W. (Red) Bethea, who was threatening to push through legislation to close Clemson, and James F. Byrnes, former Supreme Court Justice, Secretary of State and South Carolina governor, who was a Clemson trustee.

To counteract the possibility of action by ardent segregationists, the group seeking integration with dignity at Clemson moved to round up additional support. John Cauthen attended a meeting of 18 of South Carolina's leading textile executives in Columbia on January 3, 1963. Cauthen read a statement he had drafted. It said: "The major business and industrial interests of the state strongly approve the announced determination of the board of trustees and the administration of Clemson College to maintain law and order at all times."

Cauthen passed out file cards and asked the 18 executives to write "yes" or "no" on the cards, indicating whether they approved of the statement. All 18 voted "yes." A day later, the South Carolina Chamber of Commerce polled 52 of the state's top businessmen by phone on the subject. All 52 approved the statement. The state's broadcasting and banking associations registered their approval.

Governor Hollings was about to end his term, to be succeeded by Donald Russell, a Spartanburg lawyer. On January 9, Hollings made his farewell address to the legislature:

As we meet, South Carolina is running out of courts. This General Assembly must make clear South Carolina's choice, a government of laws, rather than a government of men. We must move on with dignity. It must be done with law and order. The state's institutions and all law enforcement agencies have been charged with their responsibilities.

A day later, Hollings phoned Attorney General Kennedy to assure him that federal marshals would not be needed at Clemson. He outlined the elaborate security precautions being taken by the state. The Attorney General pledged not to send marshals.

On January 12, Hollings met with key advisers and law enforcement officers to go over the security plan. Representing incoming Governor Russell was his son and adviser, Donald Russell, Jr. The written plan informed law enforcement officers:

The state of South Carolina has assumed responsibility of maintaining law and order as a state function, and the state is capable of carrying it out. . . . Tolerate verbal abuse or similar harassment but, when faced with violation of the law, perform duties with efficiency and dispatch. . . . If trouble occurs, remove troublemakers quickly to detention areas set aside for large numbers of persons.

The security plan called for sheriff's officers from counties surrounding Clemson to assist state police. A police plane would patrol the area. Officers would take movies and still pictures of the integration attempt. Fire-fighting and medical equipment would be on hand. Judges would be prepared to issue warrants, if necessary.

At Clemson, college officials arranged briefings for the student body and faculty. The student government would be in charge of discipline among the undergraduates. Students were told: "Gatherings which indicate unnecessary curiosity will be avoided. Counseling, advising and frank discussions should solve most problems. Situations requiring more forthright action will be dealt with firmly and effectively."

The critical test at Clemson was fast approaching. On January 22, in compliance with a ruling by a federal appeals court, United States District Judge C. C. Wyche signed an order directing that Gantt be admitted to Clemson. In the legislature, State Senator John Long immediate-

ly charged that it would be cowardly of Clemson to enroll
Gantt without a fight. "I would prefer that my children be
raised in ignorance—not knowing 'B' from Bullsfoot—than
to see them cringing and bowing before tyranny," Long
insisted.

State Senator H. H. Jessen supported Long's stand.
"South Carolina should not lie down and let itself be
walked over," he said.

Now Senator Gressette rose to speak. A hush fell over
the chamber, which had filled up rapidly when word of the
integration debate had spread around the capitol. As
chairman of the legislative committee charged with maintaining segregation, Gressette was considered an important spokesman. But his voice was to speak for moderation,
not defiance. "A lot of things happen in life," he said. "We
have disappointments. Sometimes, I feel like making a
speech like my two friends made. We have lost this battle,
but we are engaged in a war. But this war cannot be won
by violence or inflammatory speeches. I have preached
peace and order too long to change my thinking."

Gressette offered to resign if the legislature felt he had
failed in his duties. But, instead, those in the chamber gave
him a standing ovation. Senator Long then asked his colleagues to remain standing for a vote of confidence for
Gressette.

Later in the day, James F. Byrnes finally issued a statement on the Gantt case. "Gantt has succeeded in forcing
himself into Clemson," Byrnes said. But he added that the
young Negro would not be welcomed by the student body.
"Thank goodness, not even the Supreme Court has ordered
that be done—as yet," said the man who once had sat on
the highest court in the land.

Before the day was out, incoming Governor Russell, Senator Gressette and Clemson President Edwards conducted
separate press conferences to emphasize that Clemson
would be desegregated peacefully. Russell told newsmen:
"We shall meet and solve this problem peaceably, without
violence." Gressette said: "Peace and good order must be
maintained both on and off the college campus." Edwards
said the college trustees had approved complete good-faith
compliance with the court order directing Gantt's enroll-

ment. "Gantt will be admitted exactly as any other transfer student," he said.

Thus, six days before Gantt's scheduled enrollment, the prevailing climate in South Carolina seemed to assure that his arrival at Clemson would be in marked contrast to James Meredith's riot-scarred arrival at Ole Miss. But nobody could be sure of this. Who could say that swarms of red-necks would not descend on the campus, as they had at Ole Miss, to try to block Gantt's enrollment?

State Representatives A. W. Bethea and F. Mitchell Ott were continuing to insist that Clemson be closed to prevent desegregation. Bethea claimed that Clemson officials had "brainwashed students to do nothing" about trying to prevent Gantt's admission. He and Ott threatened to introduce a legislative resolution to set up a committee that would advise Clemson students of their rights to protest. "There is no reason why they can't have orderly demonstrations," Bethea said.

Amid such statements, no one could be certain in advance that Gantt's enrollment would be totally free from trouble. An air of uncertainty hung over Clemson when I arrived there. Certainly, the campus and the town seemed tranquil. But then so had Oxford, Mississippi, and Ole Miss on the eve of James Meredith's arrival.

Gantt was spending the days immediately prior to his scheduled enrollment at his home in Charleston. As was his habit, he was trying to remain out of the limelight as much as possible. Gantt's attitude varied markedly from Meredith's. While Meredith repeatedly emphasized that he was trying to accomplish a breakthrough for the Negro race, Gantt insisted: "I simply want to get an education in this state. I live in South Carolina; my folks live here. It's my home."

When pressed, Gantt would concede he felt that "it's time we Negroes stepped out to claim some of our rights." But he was far less militant on the subject than Meredith. One of his few shows of militancy had come when he had taken part in a sit-in at a Charleston lunch counter. He had been taken into custody on a trespassing charge, but released two hours later.

Gantt, whose father is a shipyard machinist, had been graduated as salutatorian from the all-Negro Burke High School in Charleston. Highly respected by his classmates, he was elected to the National Honor Society. At five feet ten inches and 185 pounds, he starred as quarterback on the school's football team for two years. He decided during high school that he wanted to study architecture. Clemson was the only college in the state that offered an architecture course. When his first application for enrollment at Clemson was rejected, he went instead to Iowa State University. He compiled a B average there, and was described by professors as "an outstanding and well-adjusted student." But Gantt was determined to get his education in South Carolina and kept pressing for admission to Clemson.

On Sunday, January 27, the day before his scheduled arrival at Clemson, Gantt arose early to attend services at the Morris Street Baptist Church in Charleston. His pastor, the Reverend A. R. Blake, made brief mention of the integration case during the service. "We're all aware that Harvey Gantt is going up to Clemson tomorrow," he said. "We wish him luck."

Gantt spent the remainder of the day lying around the house and watching television. I phoned him from Clemson during the afternoon. He seemed relaxed and jovial. I asked him if he were nervous. "No, I just have the normal amount of anxiety that you would have on your first day in any new school," he said. Did he expect any trouble? "I haven't been alerted to any. I haven't had any crank phone calls or letters." What might his case mean for his race? "It means an opportunity for an education for a lot more Negroes, if I'm successful."

Gantt planned to drive to Clemson the next day with his father, stopping in Columbia to pick up NAACP attorney Matthew Perry. I phoned Perry at his Columbia home. "The state government has been very convincing that it's going to maintain law and order," Perry said. "We're happy to know that. I'm going to call Clemson prior to our arrival. I'm sure that the broad policing plan includes some kind of observation that takes into account the safety of our party. I'm sure the police will pick us up somewhere outside Clemson and keep us under watch until we arrive."

Perry said he had heard some "rather vociferous talk" about the Gantt case on a local radio interview program. "While no one expects any buildup of active opposition, who knows what might happen?" he concluded.

Anxious to learn the attitude of the student body, I spent several hours buttonholing undergraduates on the campus. A 20-year-old junior from Abbeville summed up his feelings this way: "I think everybody feels about the same. They're not in favor of Gantt being here, but there's nothing that can be done about it. I kind of doubt he'll be accepted as just another student. I don't expect anyone will slap him on the back and say, 'Let's go down to the show together.' But there's no indication there'll be any harassment. Most people probably will just ignore him."

Doug Campbell, an 18-year-old freshman, said: "I don't think there's going to be any disturbance. The college is taking this quite seriously. I think most people feel he deserves an education, but I don't think anybody is going out of his way to be friendly."

Ed Treese, a 20-year-old junior from Charleston, said: "Clemson has always had a tradition of accepting students for what they are. If Gantt comes here to study, he can study. If he comes to goof off, he'll flunk out. I think he'll be welcomed. If I pass him on the campus, I'll say 'Hi' to him. If there's a card game on his hall, I think they'll ask him to play."

These comments were typical of those voiced by more than a dozen students I interviewed. Not a single student said he knew of any organized campus attempt to keep Gantt from registering.

Joe Sherman was providing the college's official assessment of the situation:

The prevailing mood of the student body and faculty is one of good citizenship. All of these people are here for the purpose of either providing or receiving an education. If any one of them has any resentment, other than those which are normal and natural to their lifetime environment, it is a resentment that their educational processes might be disrupted or even disturbed.

Sherman said, with apologies for sounding like a radio

commercial, that he thought 99 and ⁴⁴/₁₀₀ percent of all Americans were responsible citizens. "The remainder are irresponsible ones who go about their daily activities with a soapbox in their hands, looking for a spot to drop it, mount it and draw attention to themselves," he said. "There may be some of these people who find their way to the Clemson campus during Harvey Gantt's enrollment. We hope the press media will not afford them the stage and spotlight they're searching for. We do not believe there will be any violence. We have taken the necessary precautionary measures, however."

Sherman had set up elaborate ground rules to govern the conduct of the press during Gantt's enrollment. A pool of 20 newsmen was to cover Gantt for the remainder of the press corps during key parts of his day. The pool was to consist of one network reporter, six network cameramen and technicians, four wire-service reporters and photographers, four South Carolina broadcasters, two South Carolina newspaper reporters or photographers, one non-South Carolina newspaper reporter or photographer and two news magazine representatives. I was chosen to be the pool man representing all newspapers from outside South Carolina.

Early Monday morning, 150 state policemen fanned out around the Clemson campus and the surrounding area. They sealed off the campus. Only those with special Clemson identification cards—which students were calling "Harvey" cards in Gantt's honor—or with press credentials were permitted past police roadblocks at the campus entrances.

At 9 A.M., four and a half hours before Gantt was scheduled to arrive on the campus, Clemson President Edwards conducted a press conference. In a prepared statement, he reviewed the legal history of the Gantt case. "It is now my purpose to inform you that, in accordance with the instructions of the board of trustees, we are prepared to enroll Mr. Gantt upon his appearance on the campus," Edwards said. "We have requested that the Clemson students and faculty go about the business of being good students and teachers in a perfectly normal way."

He was asked whether he had received any indications

of organized opposition to Gantt's enrollment. "The volume of correspondence I've had has been relatively small," Edwards said. "Certainly the overwhelming opinion as expressed in communications to me has been that we should preserve law and order—that we in South Carolina are law-abiding citizens. There has been an absolute minimum of crackpot communications."

A reporter asked: "Do you consider this a great day?"

Edwards thought a moment, then replied: "Certainly, it's a historic day. Whether it's a great day or not, we'll let the historians record later."

For the next few hours, newsmen toured the campus and the roads leading into the town, looking for signs of impending trouble. But none was to be found. Shortly after 1 P.M., the newsmen began gathering along the driveway leading to Tillman Hall, a 72-year-old red-brick four-story administration building with an imposing clock tower. It was here that Gantt would arrive to register. By 1:30, there were more than 150 newsmen lining the driveway. Behind them stood about 150 students, mostly curious and jovial.

At 1:33, three minutes behind schedule, a black 1959 Buick rolled up the driveway. Gantt emerged, wearing a dark suit, a checked topcoat and a sporty hat. He walked slowly toward Tillman Hall. Dozens of flashbulbs seemed to pop simultaneously. "I never believed I could see so many cameras in my life," Gantt said with a smile.

Someone shouted: "Smile, you're on Candid Camera."

Gantt laughed heartily and replied: "Is that right?"

A few students shouted wisecracks. But the remarks were goodnatured, not venomous.

Gantt walked into the building. He was held in an anteroom while the pool reporters got set up on a balcony overlooking the registrar's office to witness his enrollment. Precisely at 1:45, Gantt entered the registrar's office. Nonchalantly, he said "Hi" to a student employe standing behind a counter. He filled out some registration cards, then went to another room to have his student identification picture snapped.

Gantt emerged from Tillman Hall to find a battery of microphones waiting for him on the front steps. He was now a Clemson student. He removed his gray hat, smiled shyly, then spoke into the microphones. "Of course, I'm very happy to have an opportunity to attend Clemson," he said. "However, I want to say that my main purpose here is to get an education. So I'd appreciate it if you [newsmen] wouldn't hinder me."

A reporter asked what he thought of his reception at the campus. "It's even more than I expected," Gantt said. "I was very much surprised to see such a jovial crowd. I thought the kidding was very nice."

How did he think he would be treated? "I'd hope to be accepted as just another student," he said. "However, I understand the situation and will understand if I'm not fully accepted at first."

Gantt then walked about 150 yards to his dormitory room, trailed by six state policemen and swarms of newsmen. His 10-by-15-foot room had beige walls, a double-decker bed, a six-foot worktable, two wooden arm chairs, a sink and three large closets. As he unpacked, photographers pestered him to pose this way and that for what seemed like an interminable period. Finally, Gantt snapped to a TV cameraman: "Buddy, I'm tired—and I'm nervous, too." That ended the picture-snapping.

A white student looked in Gantt's window at this point and shouted to a companion: "It's a zoo. You ought to see the coon." This was one of the few bitter remarks made all day.

Later in the day, Gantt conferred with Dean of Architecture Harlan McClure about his curriculum and was welcomed to the campus by President Edwards. He ate dinner in the college cafeteria. While nobody sat at his table with him, several white students did walk over and greet him cordially. Gantt slept unguarded that night in his dorm room.

It was quite a difference from James Meredith's riot-scarred enrollment at Ole Miss. Responsible leadership in South Carolina's business, political and academic communities had created a climate in which Clemson could be integrated with dignity and without violence.

3 Death on the Highway

William L. Moore was an idealist. A 35-year old white man, he had been born in Chattanooga, Tennessee, and spent a good part of his boyhood in Mississippi. Two of his great-grandfathers had fought in the Confederate Army. But Moore was a champion of equal rights for Negroes. In April, 1963, he would lose his life for the advocacy of this cause. He would be shot down by an assassin on an Alabama highway while making a "freedom walk" to protest racial segregation.

Moore had risked his life before. As a Marine in World War II, he had fought against the Japanese on Guam. After the war, he had studied at European universities and at Johns Hopkins University in Baltimore, Maryland. In January, 1953, he suffered a nervous breakdown and was committed to Binghamton (N.Y.) State Hospital for treatment of schizophrenia-paranoia. He kept a journal of his life in the hospital. In late 1954, after receiving insulin shock treatments, Moore was discharged from the hospital.

From his hospital journal, Moore wrote a book, *Mind in Chains—Autobiography of a Schizophrenic*. The book was published by Exposition Press, a writer-subsidized vanity publishing firm. Authorities considered the book a unique description of a man's struggle against madness. Edward Uhlan, head of Exposition Press, said of Moore: "He was never sensitive about being insane and always referred to his dreams for mankind as 'crazy' dreams and to himself as a 20th-century Don Quixote."

On the first page of his book, Moore wrote: "I would save the world. Therefore, I am locked up to save the world from me." In the book's final paragraph, he wrote: "Whether I go forward as Don Quixote chasing his windmill or as the pilgrim progressing must be left you [the reader] to decide. I can only give my life. And you must make it or break it for me."

Moore and his wife, Mary, and their three children were living in Binghamton in late 1962. He became involved in racial integration activities and decided he wanted to live closer to the center of the integration movement. So he moved to Baltimore in November, got a job as a postman and threw himself into desegregation activities. Although they were not legally separated, Moore's wife stayed behind in Binghamton with the children, saying she feared for the youngsters' safety in Baltimore because of her husband's work in the integration movement.

In April, 1963, Moore decided to make his "freedom walk" on behalf of desegregation. He was on vacation from his post office job. On April 20, he hiked the 45 miles from Baltimore to Washington. He tried to deliver a letter, pleading for action on civil rights, to President Kennedy. He was stopped by a White House guard and told to drop the letter in a mailbox.

Moore told the President in his letter of his intention to walk from Chattanooga, Tennessee, to Jackson, Mississippi, to try to deliver another letter to Mississippi Governor Ross Barnett. He told the President he expected Southern hospitality to manifest itself in "less desirable forms" on his trek. He said he was "not making this walk to demonstrate either federal rights or states' rights, but individual rights."

Moore had told friends before leaving on the walk: "It's about time we Southerners solve our own problems and get rid of the black eye when it comes to race relations." Now, he set out from Washington for the South to try to spread that message. He rode a bus from Washington to Chattanooga on April 21. He then started hiking toward Mississippi. He wore sandwich-board signs on his front and back. One read: "Eat at Joe's, Both Black and White." The other said: "Equal Rights for All (Mississippi or Bust)."

Moore pushed a small shopping cart containing clothing, an extra pair of shoes and civil rights literature. On the afternoon of April 23, he passed through Gadsden, Alabama. He was interviewed by newsman Charles Hicks of radio station WGAD. He told Hicks that his feet were badly blistered, but that he planned to keep walking until he reached the Governor's Mansion in Mississippi. Hicks asked whether Moore feared violence. Moore replied: "I don't believe the people in the South are that way." Yet Moore had already made several entries in a diary to the effect that epithets had been hurled at him and rocks had been thrown at him as he walked the highways.

While Moore was being interviewed by Hicks, a state investigator named Roy McDowell drove up. McDowell told Moore he was afraid someone might harm him during the walk. But Moore declined McDowell's offer of protection, and the investigator went on his way.

Moore's diary for April 23 included these entries:

Walking again. Traffic cop waved greeting. . . . Invited to chat with a few men who had heard about my walk on TV. They didn't think I'd finish my walk alive. . . . Sheriff's car stopped to ask how long I'd been walking. Took a leaflet, wondered if I'd make it to Mississippi.

A couple of men who had talked to me before drove up and questioned my religious and political beliefs. [Moore was an atheist.] And one was sure I'd be killed for them. . . . Feet sore all over. Shoes too painful, walking without them. Adopted by hungry, thirsty, road-foolish dog. Only kids adopt dogs.

Moore left the dog with some children at a crossroads store on U. S. Highway 11. He bought a can of corn and a small pie at the store for his supper. Sometime within the next four hours, he was shot to death. A motorist found his body about 8 P.M. in front of a roadside park near the crossroads hamlet of Keener, ten miles outside Gadsden. Moore had been shot in the forehead and neck with a .22-caliber rifle.

The slaying had nationwide repercussions. President Kennedy, at a press conference, called the killing an outrageous crime. Alabama Governor George Wallace called the slaying a dastardly act and offered a $1,000 reward for its solution. In Binghamton, Moore's widow said: "Oh,

God, I don't know why anyone would want to hurt him. He was so kind. He was a crusader for people's rights and freedoms."

In New York, Edward Uhlan said of him: "Moore knew he'd wind up bruised, beaten, battered—even dead. But for him the goal was the thing."

On April 25, two days after the slaying, sheriff's officers arrested Floyd L. Simpson, 40-year-old operator of a rural grocery-service station, for questioning. Officers said Moore had stopped at Simpson's store on his way through Fort Payne, Alabama, the day of the slaying. Later in the day, they said, Simpson and a neighbor, Gaddis Killian, had gotten into a car and caught up with Moore on the highway and talked to him again.

Officers questioned both Simpson and Killian. Killian was released. Chief Etowah County Deputy Sheriff Tony Reynolds explained: "He is well respected in his community and we are satisfied he had nothing to do with the slaying." But Simpson was held on a general charge of suspicion.

The sheriff's office asked the FBI to make ballistic tests on the bullets removed from Moore's body and on a .22-caliber rifle owned by Simpson. The results of the tests were never made public. But on April 28 Simpson was charged with first-degree murder. Sheriff Dewey Colvard said: "We don't know if anyone else was involved."

Simpson was a Korean War veteran. He had six children, ranging in age from one to 17. The Reverend Russ Porter, pastor of a Baptist church attended by the Simpson family, described the accused slayer as "a good, hardworking man." Simpson was freed in $5,000 bail to await grand jury action.

Feelings against outsiders were running high in Fort Payne and suburban Collbran, where Simpson lived. Residents, predominantly mill workers and farmers, showed strong hostility. A reporter for the *Gadsden Times*, M. L. Ray, went to Simpson's store to seek information about him. He was shoved outside by an unidentified man who warned: "You'd better get out. I'm not going to tell you a second time."

Meanwhile, movements were being organized by civil rights groups to resume the "freedom walk" begun by

Moore. On May 1, eight Negroes drove from Birmingham to Attalla, Alabama, where they planned to begin their hike. They carried signs reading: "Equal Rights for All Men." But within minutes after they had begun walking, they were arrested by sheriff's officers on breach-of-the-peace charges. Deputy Sheriff Felton Yates walked up to one of the marchers and said: "Gimme that sign, boy, and get in the car." With that, the hike ended.

But another group of marchers was on the way. This group, made up of five whites and five Negroes, had begun its trek at Moore's starting point, Chattanooga. The hikers crossed the foot of Lookout Mountain, then began a relatively short hike across a strip of Georgia toward Alabama.

Alabama authorities announced that the marchers would be arrested as soon they set foot across the state line. But the marchers kept on walking. Along the way, they were taunted with catcalls and cries of "nigger lovers." At one point, a handful of gravel was hurled at them from a passing car. When they stopped for lunch on a Georgia roadside on May 3, about a mile from the Alabama border, they were pelted with eggs. A short distance farther down the highway, they were attacked by a group of white thugs. One of the Negro marchers, Winston Lockett of New Haven, Connecticut, was knocked to the ground by a white man. Another Negro marcher, Robert Gore of New York City, was hit in the head with a rock. Neither was seriously injured. The marchers continued toward the state line.

There, a dozen Alabama highway patrolmen were waiting. Newsmen accompanying the marchers were barred by the patrolmen from crossing the state line. But the officers cleared a path for the marchers and allowed them to enter Alabama. Immediately after the marchers had crossed the line, they were told they were under arrest. The marchers sat down in the middle of the road. They were carried, in spread-eagle fashion, to waiting police cars.

Two weeks later, civil rights groups let it be known to selected newsmen that they planned a memorial service for Moore on the spot where he had been slain. The service was set for 2:30 P.M. on May 19, a Sunday. It would be followed by attempts by other marchers to resume the "freedom walk" begun by Moore.

I heard about the memorial service and decided to cover it. On May 19, I met Claude Sitton of *The New York Times* and Karl Fleming of *Newsweek* in Birmingham and we drove together the 60 miles to Gadsden, where the service had been organized.

Preparations for the service and the resumption of the march were made in the office of the Gadsden Christian Citizens Committee, a civil rights group, on the second floor of an old but neat building next to a service station. When Sitton, Fleming and I arrived, about a dozen whites and Negroes, most of them in their early twenties, were gathered in the committee's office. Some, who planned to take part in the march, wore knapsacks on their backs and canteens on their hips. Others were working on picket signs that the marchers would carry. As they worked, they sang some of the songs of the integration movement:

> I woke up this morning with my mind set on freedom.
> I woke up this morning with my mind set on freedom.
> Hallelu, Hallelu, Hallelujah.
> Oh, we'll walk, walk, walk, walk
> With our mind on freedom.
> Oh, talk, talk, talk, talk
> With our mind on freedom.
> Hallelu, Hallelu, Hallelujah.

Some of the songs had lyrics written in memory of Moore. For example:

> I'm goin' to sit at the welcome table.
> Oh, Lord, I'm goin' to sit at the welcome table.
> I'm goin' to sit at the welcome table, one of these days.
> I'm goin' to walk for William Moore.
> Goin' to walk the streets of Gadsden.
> I'm goin' to walk in Birmingham.
> I'm goin' to walk all over 'Bama.
> We will never turn back.
> We are marching on to freedom.
> Black and white together.

Sitting quietly in a corner of the office was a slender, unobtrusive man named James D. Peck. A close friend of Moore, Peck had come to Gadsden from his home in New York City to lead the eulogies at the memorial service. He was the editor of the Congress of Racial Equality (CORE) newsletter. He had been active in the civil rights movement since 1946. In 1961, he had been savagely beaten while making a Freedom Ride. Later, he had written a book entitled *Freedom Ride*. He had been arrested more than 30 times in civil rights protests.

At the other end of the room was a pretty ash-blonde, Madeleine Sherwood, a Broadway and Hollywood actress. She had appeared in such films as *Cat on a Hot Tin Roof*, *Baby Doll* and *Sweet Bird of Youth*. She had never before played an active role in the civil rights movement. But now she felt compelled to join the ranks of those demonstrating for equal opportunity. She would be one of those to resume Moore's march.

I asked her what had made her decide to leave New York and come to Gadsden for the march. "I could think of a million reasons not to come and so could my friends," she said. "My agents didn't approve. They felt this was not my fight. But I could think of a million and one reasons why I should come. I've come to the conclusion that this is the fight of every human being in this country. This is the first total commitment I've ever made."

Miss Sherwood was wearing a white blouse, gray plaid culottes, a straw sun hat with a white ribbon, white socks and white shoes. She wore a canteen on her hip. Pinned to her blouse was a button declaring: "I believe in human dignity." In her brassiere she had tucked a toothbrush and a dime, with which she planned to make a phone call if arrested. I asked her if she had any fear of what might happen during the memorial service or the march. "Yes, I'm afraid," she said. "I'm scared stiff."

A few minutes later, the demonstrators filed down the stairs to cars that would take them to the memorial service. Miss Sherwood carried a sign reading: "Human Rights for All Human Beings." Other signs read: "Peace, Love and Brotherhood" and "Eat at Joe's, Both Black and White."

The spot where Moore had been slain lay nestled in a picturesque green valley between Lookout and Sand Mountains. About 40 whites and Negroes gathered at the site for the memorial service. Across Highway 11, a herd of Holstein cattle grazed lazily in a pasture. Peck, standing beside a wreath containing 15 yellow chrysanthemums, told the gathering: "Bill was a genuine idealist. He worked for brotherhood all his life. Eighteen walkers have followed him. They have been arrested. Eleven more are ready to follow in his steps today."

The Reverend E. W. Jarrett, Negro pastor of the Galilee Baptist Church in Gadsden, said: "We are gathered on this spot of ground to commemorate the gallant stand taken by William Moore, who died—but not in vain. His death has shown to the world the ugliness of segregation and the so-called Southern way of life. They crucified Jesus. They shot William Moore. But his voice is still heard. It tells us and those yet unborn that we are determined to be free— not tomorrow, not yesterday, but now."

"Amen," someone shouted.

"That's right," someone else yelled.

The next speaker was Nelson T. Barr, Jr., a white man from Chattanooga. "I've come here to make amends for everything that's been going on down here for the last 200 years," he said. "In my home in Chattanooga, I grew up under segregation. This system has destroyed both races and made us look into our souls and see the sin and guilt in all of us. If Christ was on this earth today, I'm sure he would be killed just like William Moore. He would be crucified again."

"That's right," murmured a middle-aged Negro woman in a white cotton dress.

The service ended with the 40 whites and Negroes linking arms, swaying from side to side and singing the integration anthem, "We Shall Overcome":

We shall overcome, we shall overcome.
We shall overcome, some day.
Oh, deep in my heart I do believe
We shall overcome, some day . . .
Black and white together. Black and white together.

Black and white together, some day.
Oh, deep in my heart I do believe
Black and white together, some day.

Peck placed the chrysanthemum wreath on the ground alongside the highway. The crowd then observed a minute of silence.

Four state highway patrolmen and two deputy sheriffs had been standing by, directing traffic past the memorial service. The officers had made no effort to interfere with the service. But now, as the "freedom march" was to begin, they moved into action. Miss Sherwood and ten other marchers, five white and five Negro, lined up in single file alongside the highway. Highway Patrol Sergeant R. P. Hooks called to them: "If you walk on the highway, we'll have to arrest you. Don't get over that white line." (The line marked the outer edge of the highway.)

The marchers began singing "We Shall Overcome." They then walked a few steps down the highway—without ever crossing the white line. Just the same, Hooks told them: "You're under arrest for violating the law of the State of Alabama. Come right over here and get in these cars." Seven of the marchers followed his orders. The four others, including Miss Sherwood and two white men and one Negro man, lay down on the grass alongside the highway. Hooks, evidently referring to previous occasions when demonstrators had used the sit-down technique, snapped: "Oh, we got some more who can't walk. I don't know why you people want to be so stubborn."

Nelson Barr, one of the four on the grass, replied: "A man's got the right to walk the highways in peace and freedom."

Hooks apparently thought Barr was a spectator, rather than a marcher. "If you don't stop that, we'll take you in for interfering," he told Barr.

Barr replied: "Well, I want to go, if you have room."

Hooks said: "Oh, we've got room, all right."

With that, another state trooper told Hooks that Barr had been a marcher. Barr and the two other young men were hauled away by officers and dumped roughly into a patrol car. Two officers then grabbed Miss Sherwood under the arms and carried her to a car, where they deposited her in much more gentle fashion.

As the 11 prisoners were being driven away, to be held in the Etowah County Jail at Gadsden on breach-of-the-peace charges, they could again be heard singing: "We shall overcome. We shall overcome. We shall overcome, some day."

Almost four months later, on September 12, a grand jury finally got around to considering the case of Floyd L. Simpson, the grocer who had been charged with the murder of Moore. The grand jury, composed of 17 whites and one Negro, refused to indict Simpson. He went free.

4 Birmingham

Birmingham, Alabama, had often been called the most segregated big city in the South. The title had not been bestowed lightly. From 1957 to 1963, there had been no fewer than 18 racial bombings—leading Negroes to call the city "Bombingham." More than 50 cross-burning incidents had occurred during the same period.

Schools, restaurants, lunch counters, rest rooms, drinking fountains and department store fitting rooms all were rigidly segregated. Birmingham had abandoned its professional baseball team to prevent it from playing integrated teams in the International League. It had closed down its city parks rather than desegregate them in compliance with a federal court order. Because of the city's refusal to desegregate its municipal auditorium, the Metropolitan Opera Company had ceased visiting Birmingham. Most theatrical companies touring with Broadway hits had begun bypassing the city for the same reason.

One might assume that a city so fiercely determined to maintain the so-called "Southern way of life" would have tight bonds with the history and tradition of the old South. Not so. Birmingham did not even exist during the Civil War. The land upon which it now stands was then a prosperous farm. The city was not incorporated until 1871, six years after Lee's surrender to Grant.

Nor was Birmingham a typical Southern city. With its smoke-belching steel mills, it resembled an industrial metropolis of the North far more than it did its sister Southern cities. As late as 1941, the Works Progress Administration's guide book on Alabama—written by Alabamans

—had described Birmingham as "the most unsouthern of southern cities." It added: "Birmingham people are a new type of southerner. They are not so much concerned about where a person was born . . . as about his political opinions and how much money he has." The city had not changed appreciably over the years.

Yet Birmingham had failed to assume the progressive role in race relations that might have been expected from its background. Despite its industrial makeup, it had adopted the racial philosophy of the old Southern plantation. Year after year, it had helped elect segregationist state officials and a segregationist city government.

For 23 years, the best-known fixture of the city government had been Theophilus Eugene (Bull) Connor, the tough, gravel-throated commissioner of public safety. Ole Bull, as Connor was fond of calling himself, had been symbolic of Birmingham's unbending insistence on segregation. Connor's police had hauled Negroes off to jail any time they had attempted to demonstrate for equal rights. The police had once even arrested a United States senator who walked through a door marked "colored" while in Birmingham to make a speech. Connor himself had screamed defiance at the Supreme Court. He had offered to fight Attorney General Kennedy. And he had predicted that "blood would run in the streets" of Birmingham before it would be integrated.

Now, in the spring of 1963, Birmingham's segregation policy was about to be put to the stiffest test in the city's history. A task force of Negro civil rights leaders had descended on the city to lead the local Negro population in a drive for integration. The task force was headed by the Reverend Dr. Martin Luther King, Jr., of Atlanta, Georgia, president of the Southern Christian Leadership Conference (SCLC).

King had become the most symbolic leader of the Negro protest movement in the South and perhaps in the entire country. He had first won national attention with the 1956 Negro boycott of segregated buses in Montgomery, Alabama. From then on, he had endured jailings and physical attacks while leading sit-ins, Freedom Rides and other forms of protest throughout the South.

In Birmingham, King was taking on the most explosive assignment of his career. The potential for violence was immense. The chief demands of King and his task force were desegregation of lunch counters, rest rooms, fitting rooms and drinking fountains in major stores; upgrading and hiring of Negroes on a nondiscriminatory basis throughout the city's business and industrial community; and creation of a biracial citizens' committee to try to work out solutions to problems between the races. In some Southern cities, such demands could have been taken in stride by the white population. In Birmingham, many considered them revolutionary.

Three times, Attorney General Kennedy and other Justice Department officials persuaded King not to begin street demonstrations to support his demands. They, and some white leaders in Birmingham, felt the Negroes' aims might be accomplished without demonstrations if the city were given a little time. For Birmingham was undergoing a significant change in its municipal government. In November, 1962, voters had decided to change the city's form of government from its longtime commission system to a mayor-council system. This meant that Bull Connor and his two fellow commissioners would not get to serve their full terms, which were due to last until 1965.

The election to choose a new mayor and council was set for April 2, 1963. Connor sought the mayoralty. He was opposed by Albert Boutwell, a soft-spoken former lieutenant governor, known as a moderate on racial issues. Boutwell, with strong backing from Negro voters, won the election by a narrow margin. But Connor and his fellow members of the old commission government filed suit to keep Boutwell's administration from taking office. While the suit was in the courts, Birmingham was treated to the spectacle of both administrations serving in office simultaneously. Hope for a quick solution to racial problems was stalemated.

During the election campaign, Dr. King and his associates had decided against beginning their threatened civil rights demonstrations. They did not want the demonstrations to be used "to cloud the issues" of the campaign, King said. But as soon as the election was over, King refused to delay any longer. He arrived in Birmingham the day after the election, with his task force. "Birmingham is the most thoroughly segregated big city in the U. S. today," he declared. He said he would lead demonstrations in the city until "Pharaoh lets God's people go."

That same night, King sat on a platform at Birmingham's St. James African Methodist Church, listening to a talk by the Reverend Fred Lee Shuttlesworth, local Negro leader and head of the Alabama Christian Movement for Human Rights, an affiliate of King's SCLC. "We have been asked to wait," Shuttlesworth said. "We're tired of waiting. We've been waiting for 340 years for our rights. We want action. We want it now."

And so the demonstrations began.

At first, King and his aides encountered trouble in trying to round up sizable groups of demonstrators. When small groups of demonstrators did turn up at downtown stores, obviously intending to stage sit-ins at the segregated lunch counters, merchants quietly closed the counters. Some did not even bother to call the police. In other cases, police were called and made some routine arrests. Matters seemed relatively calm. But as the demonstrations continued day after day, tensions mounted. King's movement began attracting ever larger and more militant groups of Negroes. And Bull Connor, still running the police force during the dispute over which city administration was entitled to office, grew increasingly impatient with the demonstrators.

Connor ordered one march on the Birmingham City Hall broken up with mass arrests. "Call the wagons, sergeant, I'm hungry," he rasped to a subordinate. The next day, Connor ordered police dogs brought out to curb the demonstrators. One 19-year-old Negro boy took a poke at one of the dogs with a lead pipe. The dog leaped at the boy. A crowd of Negroes, one of them wielding a knife, swept toward the dog and police. It required about 15 officers and their dogs to quell the disturbance.

Connor and Police Chief Jamie Moore then went into State Circuit Court and got an injunction barring any further racial demonstrations in Birmingham. King announced that he would ignore the injunction, and led about 1,000 demonstrators on a march toward the business district. King and one of his chief aides, the Reverend Ralph Abernathy, were promptly jailed.

During the buildup of demonstrations, eight of Birmingham's top white religious leaders—Protestant, Catholic and Jewish—had issued a statement calling the demonstrations "unwise and untimely." From his jail cell, King wrote a lengthy reply to the clergymen. The letter, entitled "A Letter From the Birmingham Jail," received wide attention.

King wrote the white clergymen:

I think I should give the reason for my being in Birmingham, since you have been influenced by the argument of "outsiders coming in." . . . I am here, along with several members of my staff, because we were invited here. I have basic organizational ties here.

Beyond this, I am in Birmingham because injustice is here. Just as the eighth century prophets left their little villages and carried their "thus saith the Lord" far beyond the boundaries of their home towns; and just as the Apostle Paul left his little village of Tarsus and carried the gospel of Jesus Christ to practically every hamlet and city of the Graeco-Roman world, I, too, am compelled to carry the gospel of freedom beyond my particular home town. Like Paul, I must constantly respond to the Macedonian call for aid.

You deplore the demonstrations that are presently taking place in Birmingham. But I am sorry that your statement did not express a similar concern for the conditions that brought the demonstrations into being. . . . I would not hesitate to say that it is unfortunate that so-called demonstrations are taking place in Birmingham at this time, but I would say in more emphatic terms that it is even more unfortunate that the white power structure of this city left the Negro community with no other alternative. . . .

Oppressed people cannot remain oppressed forever. The urge for freedom will eventually come. This is what has happened to the American Negro. Something within has reminded him of his birthright of freedom; something without has reminded him that he can gain it. Consciously and unconsciously, he has been swept in by what the Germans called the *"Zeitgeist,"* and with his black brother of Africa, and his brown and yellow brothers of Asia, South America and the Caribbean, he is moving with a sense of cosmic urgency toward the promised land of racial justice. Recognizing this vital urge that has engulfed the Negro community, one should readily understand public demonstrations. The Negro has many pent up resentments and latent frustrations. He has to get them out. . . .

I have heard numerous religious leaders of the South call upon their worshippers to comply with a desegregation decision because it is the law, but I have longed to hear white ministers say, "Follow this decree because integration is morally right and the Negro is your brother."

In the midst of blatant injustices inflicted upon the Negro, I have watched white churches stand on the sideline and merely mouth pious irrelevancies and sanctimonious trivialities. In the midst of a mighty struggle to rid our nation of racial and economic injustice, I have heard so many ministers say, "Those are social issues with which the gospel has no real concern," and I have watched so many churches commit themselves to a completely other-worldly religion which made a strange distinction between body and soul, the sacred and the secular. . . .

I hope the church as a whole will meet the challenge of this decisive hour. But even if the church does not come to the aid of justice, I have no despair about the future. I have no fear about the outcome of our struggle in Birmingham, even if our motives are presently misunderstood. We will reach the goal of freedom in Birmingham and all over the nation, because the goal of America is freedom. . . . We will win our freedom because the sacred heritage of our nation and the eternal will of God are embodied in our echoing demands.

King and Abernathy, after serving five-day jail terms, were released. Meanwhile, day after day, the demonstrations continued. And day after day, there were large-scale arrests.

With the demonstrations growing in size and being joined by school children—some as young as 6 and 7 years— secret negotiations aimed at settling the dispute were begun on April 25 by Negro and white leaders.

A year earlier, the Birmingham Chamber of Commerce had organized what it called a "Senior Citizens Committee" to deal with desegregation and other matters. A subcommittee headed by Sidney M. Smyer, Sr., head of the city's largest real estate firm and a highly respected former president of the Chamber of Commerce, had conducted some talks with Negro leaders in the fall of 1962. The meetings had been prompted by sit-in campaigns and boycotts of white stores by Negro college students. These had resulted in a drop in business as large as 40 percent in some downtown stores.

Negro leaders contended that a number of promises about integration moves were made by the whites at these meetings. Some stores did take tentative integration steps, in spite of the fact that such measures were in conflict with local segregation ordinances. But, under intense pressure from segregationists, the stores later withdrew the integration moves. Contact between Negro and white leaders was broken off.

Now, in the spring of 1963, this contact was resumed under the auspices of Smyer's subcommittee. Smyer led the white negotiators in the new talks. He was assisted chiefly by two young lawyers, David Vann and Erskine Smith. Vann, a former law clerk for Associate Supreme Court Justice Hugo Black, had headed the movement the previous fall that resulted in the vote abolishing the old city commission form of government and brought about the election of Boutwell as mayor. Although the Smyer subcommittee had no official governmental standing and ostensibly was negotiating only on behalf of the white business community, Boutwell and his aides were being kept informed of progress in the talks. No such progress reports were being given to the rival commission form of government.

The chief negotiators on the Negro side were Dr. L. W. Pitts, president of Miles College, a Negro coeducational school in Birmingham; A. G. Gaston, a millionaire real estate man, insurance executive and funeral director; and John Drew, also a wealthy insurance man. Backing them up were Arthur D. Shores, a leading Negro attorney who had been directing the integration fight in the courts; Dr. James T. Montgomery, the only Negro member of the Jefferson County Medical Association; the Reverend Fred Shuttlesworth, and two ministerial aides to Dr. King. Eventually, King himself took a key role in the negotiations.

At first the talks were inconclusive. But pressure was mounting for a settlement. As the demonstrations continued, the atmosphere on the streets grew uglier and uglier. On May 3, violence erupted. The Negro demonstrators gathered in Kelly Ingram Park, a square block of grass and tall elms in the main Negro business section. Bull Connor, spreading his policemen and firemen throughout the park, looked on impatiently as the park filled with more and more Negroes. The demonstrators, mostly students, jeered and laughed at the policemen and firemen. Police dogs strained at their leashes. Firemen adjusted their hoses, setting them to apply high pressure. Suddenly, a Negro boy waved his arms and shouted: "Freedom. Get the white dogs."

Bull Connor rasped: "Let 'em have it."

The firemen turned on their hoses, and water roared from the nozzles with a sound like gunfire. One powerful stream ripped strips of thick black bark from the elm trees. Then it tore into a slender Negro girl in a white dress. She tried to brace herself against it, but was hurled to the ground. The hoses swung around and pinned a group of Negro girls against the wall of a building across the street from the park. Police dogs lunged at the demonstrators. Several of the Negroes, including three children, were bitten.

The demonstrators, for the most part, were orderly, following the nonviolence doctrine preached repeatedly by King and his aides. But other Negroes, untrained in nonviolent techniques and having little taste for them, had joined the crowd in the area of the park. One group of unruly, drunken Negroes began flailing their arms and heaving rocks at the policemen and firemen. From the roof of a nearby Negro business building, a rain of bricks and broken bottles came hurtling down at the officers. Several policemen and firemen and a newspaper photographer were injured.

Defiant shouts came from the crowd of Negroes. Rocks, bricks and bottles continued to clatter down on the lawmen. But gradually the fire hoses wore down the Negroes. They dispersed and left the area.

The next day was just as bad. The crowds of demonstrators were joined by tough Negro steelworkers who flocked out of bars. They almost broke through police lines separating the Negro and white sections of downtown

Birmingham. Realizing that the potential for serious violence was great, King's aides called off further demonstrations for the day and sent their followers home.

The nation and the world began to take notice of the mounting crisis in Birmingham. Sensational news pictures taken during these two days had brought the seriousness of the situation home. The pictures showing police dogs lunging at demonstrators and fire hoses knocking Negroes to the ground aroused protests from all over the globe. Attorney General Kennedy sent Burke Marshall, head of the Justice Department's Civil Rights Division, to Birmingham to try to bring about a settlement between the white and Negro negotiators. Marshall, a quiet, scholarly man who had built up a wealth of contacts among influential whites and Negroes in the South, shuttled between the two camps, helping to define the points in dispute and to narrow the differences between the two sides.

As the negotiations continued, so did the demonstrations. On May 5, a Sunday, several hundred Negroes conducted an orderly demonstration in a small park near the Southside Jail, where hundreds of arrested demonstrators were being held. The Negroes, after attending a two-hour prayer meeting at the New Pilgrim Baptist Church, started walking toward the jail, a half-mile away.

Police had set up a barricade two blocks from the jail. They had fire hoses ready to disperse the demonstrators. At the barricade, the marchers stopped and conducted an impromptu prayer meeting. Many of them knelt on the pavement. A local Negro leader, the Reverend Charles Phillips, called to the police: "Turn on your water. Turn loose your dogs. We will stand here till we die." Other Negroes began chanting the same words.

After a few minutes, the demonstrators crossed a street, scrupulously obeying traffic signals, and entered Julius Ellsberry Park, named for the first Negro to die at Pearl Harbor. Police made no effort to stop them. The Negroes knelt in the park and prayed for a half-hour. Then they marched back to the church, singing integration songs. Police made only a few arrests, involving those demonstrators who did not move along as quickly as officers thought they should have.

The next day Negroes staged their most massive demonstrations of the five-week crisis. The day started with distribution of handbills near Negro schools, urging students to join the demonstrations. "Fight for freedom first, then go to school," the handbills said. "Join the thousands in jail who are making their witness for freedom. Come to the Sixteenth Street Baptist Church now . . . and we'll soon be free. It's up to you to free our teachers, our parents, yourself and our country."

Hundreds of Negro students abandoned plans to attend school for the day, and headed for the Sixteenth Street church, a center of integration activities. One Negro educator reported that his school had only 87 students present and 1,339 absent.

A mass rally was in progress in the yellow brick church, across the street from Kelly Ingram Park, where many of the previous demonstrations had taken place. Negro comedian Dick Gregory, who had come to Birmingham to join the demonstrations, conferred in the church with King and his aides. He then walked along the street near the church, urging bystanders to follow King's nonviolence doctrine when the demonstrations began.

Police made repeated efforts to clear the sidewalks near the church. They brought up three fire engines with high-pressure hoses, but did not use them. About 1 P.M. Gregory led a group of 19 boys and girls out of the church. He carried a placard reading: "Everybody wants freedom." The marchers behind him chanted: "Don't mind walking, 'cause I want my freedom now."

Police Captain George Wall, a highly-respected peace officer, was waiting for the marchers in front of a union hall. Wall, who was wearing a white World-War-I-style helmet, asked Gregory: "You're leading this parade?" Gregory replied that he was. Wall advised Gregory and the other marchers that they were violating a city parade ordinance and the state court injunction against racial demonstrations. "Do you understand?" Wall asked.

"No, I don't," Gregory said.

Wall then explained the legal restrictions on such demonstrations again. He asked if the marchers would disperse. Gregory said they would not. "Dick Gregory says they will not disperse," Wall announced over an electric bullhorn. "Call the wagon." A paddy wagon was summoned, and Gregory and his companions were taken to jail.

For the next hour demonstrators poured out of the church in groups of 20 to 50. They were herded into paddy wagons and school buses for the ride to jail. Several groups walked away from the vehicles, circled the block in front of the church and then submitted to arrest. One group was arrested while kneeling in prayer a block from the church.

Bull Connor watched the proceedings with obvious amusement. As police loaded Negroes into the wagons and buses, he called: "All right, you-all send them on over there. I've got plenty of room in the jail." As some of the young demonstrators ran to the paddy wagons, he said, "Boy, if that's religion, I don't want any."

While the wagons rolled by on the way to the jail, the demonstrators chanted: "Freedom! Freedom! Freedom!" Connor snapped: "If you'd ask half of them what freedom means, they couldn't tell you."

One Negro woman resisted a policeman's attempt to move her off a sidewalk near the church. She was wrestled to the pavement by five officers, one of whom pinned her to the ground with a knee across her throat. News pictures of this incident were to bring outraged protests from all parts of the world. A Negro man tore a policeman's shirt and tried to wrench the officer's revolver away from him. Both he and the woman were taken to jail.

King and other ministers were standing on the steps of the church, waving prospective demonstrators inside. In the church, King repeatedly emphasized the necessity for nonviolence in the demonstrations. "The world is watching you," he said.

The demonstrators, chanting integration songs, marched toward a group of policemen waiting to arrest them. Older Negroes watched from porches along the line of march, applauding and singing a verse from the integration anthem, "We Shall Overcome." "Black and white together," they sang. "We shall overcome, some day."

A few minutes past 2 P.M., one of the Negro bystanders heaved a bottle. It crashed to the sidewalk a few feet from some policemen. A minister then emerged from the church and told those outside, "We want everybody in the church." The police had brought in heavy reinforcements, who now began clearing the streets. At 2:40, a man ran out of the church and shouted: "It's all over. It's all over for today." Those Negroes remaining in the area drifted slowly away.

By this time more than 1,000 demonstrators had been arrested. It was the highest arrest total for a single day in the five-week crisis. Police said about 40 percent of those arrested were juveniles.

The next day, Tuesday, May 7, tensions rose to their highest point since the start of demonstrations.

The day started routinely enough. Groups of marchers carrying integration placards left the Sixteenth Street Baptist Church in orderly fashion. Police, trying to confine the marchers to an eight-block area in the Negro section, turned the demonstrators back when they headed for the downtown section. At this point thousands of Negroes —some demonstrators, others former bystanders—surged through yards and back alleys leading to the business section. They formed ranks again in front of downtown department stores. For about a half-hour they turned the busy noon rush hour into a complete state of confusion on downtown streets. Some knelt to pray on the sidewalks. Others marched along the streets, singing freedom songs. Some crowded whites off the sidewalks. "We're marching for freedom!" they shouted. "The police can't stop us now. Even Bull Connor can't stop us now."

But the police, although seeming powerless at times to cope with the surging masses, finally did manage to clear the Negroes out of the downtown area. Many returned to the vicinity of the Sixteenth Street Baptist Church. There, the fire hoses were brought out and turned on the demonstrators. Near riot conditions ensued for another half-hour. Negroes, many of them flocking out of taverns in the area, hurled rocks and bricks at the police.

The Reverend Shuttlesworth, trying to help calm the crowd, was knocked to the ground by a heavy stream of water from a fire hose. Other Negro leaders pleaded with the crowd. "Go home," they said. "You are not helping our cause." But many of the Negroes—outsiders, rather than members of the demonstrating groups—would not heed the pleas. Police reinforcements from suburban cities surrounding Birmingham were rushed in to help local officers disperse the crowd.

In contrast to Monday, when mass arrests were made, only about 50 Negroes were arrested on Tuesday. Most of them were charged with throwing rocks. The arrests brought to more than 2,400 the total of demonstrators jailed since the beginning of the crisis.

Arthur J. Hanes, the mayor in the old commission form of government, called for help from the state police. "The crowds are becoming more belligerent and nasty," Hanes said. "The Negroes themselves must be expecting real trouble because they were pulling their children back from the area of the demonstrations today."

Governor George Wallace, a militant segregationist, announced that he was complying with Hanes' request and sending state troopers into Birmingham. By late Tuesday, about 575 troopers, virtually the entire manpower of the state police, were swarming into the city under the personal direction of State Public Safety Director Albert J. Lingo.

In Montgomery, the state capital, Wallace pledged in an address to the opening session of the 1963 legislature that he would carry out a program of "legal defiance" to all efforts to tear down segregation in the state. To the cheers of legislators, Wallace promised: "We shall fight agitators, meddlers and enemies of constitutional government." Such resistance, he said, was in the best interests of all the people and was "in reality a fight for liberty and freedom." In the event that the Birmingham demonstrations led to bloodshed, he vowed to hold Negroes responsible for the "highest of crimes."

2

Amid increasing signs that the crisis was deepening, efforts to settle the dispute by negotiation were intensified. The white and Negro negotiators began holding all-night sessions. And a certain amount of camaraderie seemed to be shaping up. The negotiators started calling one another by their first names. (While it is common for whites to call Negroes by their first names in the South, it is not customary for Negroes to call whites by their first names.)

Meanwhile, the Kennedy administration stepped up its own behind-the-scenes efforts to bring about a negotiated settlement. Attorney General Kennedy called upon other cabinet members to try to persuade Birmingham business leaders to yield ground. Treasury Secretary Douglas Dillon and Defense Secretary Robert McNamara phoned friends in Birmingham's industrial and banking community to seek their aid. A number of private citizens also offered to help the administration.

One of them was Eugene V. Rostow, dean of the Yale Law School. When he asked administration officials what he could do to help, it was suggested that he phone Roger Blough, board chairman of United States Steel. Blough was a Yale Law School alumnus and head of Yale's capital fund drive. And U. S. Steel's subsidiary in Birmingham, the Tennessee Coal and Iron Company, was a major force in the city's economic power structure.

Rostow phoned Blough and found him receptive to calling his subordinates in Birmingham and urging them to push for a solution to the crisis. Arthur Wiebel, head of Tennessee Iron and Coal and a member of the Senior Citizens Committee whose subcommittee had been negotiating with the Negro leaders, began taking a more vigorous interest in the negotiations. Other leaders of the Birmingham economic community followed suit.

Rostow also called in a member of his faculty, Professor Louis H. Pollack, who had done a great deal of work with the NAACP and was highly respected by Negro leaders. Rostow asked Pollack to try to persuade the Birmingham Negro leaders to moderate their demands. Pollack immediately flew to Birmingham.

Most of these attempts to bring about a settlement were kept secret at the time. To those of us covering the story in Birmingham, it seemed that the status of the negotiations was changing every hour on the hour. First, we would be told by insiders that substantial progress was being made. Next, we would be told that the talks were stalemated. This seemed to go on endlessly. Each reporter appeared to have an inside source with a different assessment of the situation. And swapping assessments was a favorite spare-time activity of most of the newsmen.

The press corps gathered in Birmingham included what was fast becoming a crew of regulars in racial crises. Many of the reporters were among those I had gotten to know while covering Ole Miss, Clemson and other Southern racial stories. These included Claude Sitton of *The New York Times,* Joe Cumming and Karl Fleming of *Newsweek,* Stan Opotowsky of the *New York Post,* Ray Coffey of the *Chicago Daily News,* Charlie Whiteford of the *Baltimore Sun* and Tom Yarbrough of the *St. Louis Post-Dispatch.*

As I have already mentioned, there is an unusual esprit de corps among out-of-town newsmen covering a story like a racial crisis. We are frequently considered outside troublemakers by local citizens and, in some cases, by local reporters. Under such conditions, it is only natural for us to feel a closer kinship than we might on some other assignment. One night over the dinner table at a Birmingham restaurant, some of us decided it was about time we formed a whimsical association of correspondents who had covered racial crises. We would issue special press cards bearing battle stars for every major racial trouble spot covered by each reporter. Some of the charter members of the organization could claim battle stars for crises as far back as Little Rock. Others, like me, had first gotten on the racial beat during the Freedom Ride riots. Sitton was elected president of the association. I was made vice-president. And Joe Cumming became recording secretary and all-around ramrod. Joe, it should be recorded for posterity, was the driving force behind the organization.

We decided we needed a name with a catchy abbreviation. After all, most of the civil rights organizations that were making news had such abbreviations. There was the Congress of Racial Equality (CORE), the Southern Christian Leadership Conference (SCLC or, as it was more commonly known, SLICK) and the Student Nonviolent Coordinating Committee (SNCC or SNICK). After much deliberation, we decided our group would be called Southern Correspondents on Racial Equality Wars. The abbreviation would be SCREW.

Lighter moments such as those involved in the formation of SCREW were few and far between in Birmingham. All of us realized that tension was rising day by day and the potential for serious violence was immense. The white and Negro leaders trying to negotiate a settlement also realized full well the danger of permitting the crisis to lengthen. Each side began to give a little. The whites became more receptive to a compromise. The Negroes agreed to scale down their demands.

Marathon negotiating sessions were conducted at the ranch-style home of John Drew. The sessions were frank and informal. Negotiators worked in their shirt-sleeves, with ties loosened. Some sat in chairs, others on the floor. A few even took off their shoes.

Assistant Attorney General Burke Marshall's part in the negotiations was described this way by one of the whites who participated: "It was like an orchestra tuning up. Burke was not leading it. He was kind of like the drums, the rhythm section. He kept up the beat and kept things going."

By Tuesday, May 7, the white negotiators felt that the Negroes' major demands would have to be met in at least a general way. Sidney Smyer, who headed the white negotiating team, called an emergency meeting of the Senior Citizens Committee. Among those present at the secret emergency meeting were Albert Boutwell, the mayor elected under the disputed new city government, and members of his city council. The meeting was told by Sheriff Melvin Bailey that local law enforcement agencies had been "strained to the utmost of capacity." Bailey said that unless the racial demonstrations were halted and order restored, martial law would have to be declared. Faced with this possibility, the Senior Citizens Committee authorized its subcommittee to come to terms with the Negro negotiators.

On Tuesday night, the negotiators met again at Drew's home. The atmosphere was warmer than at any previous session. At Drew's request, Smyer opened the meeting with a prayer. The Reverend Andrew Young, representing Dr. King's Southern Christian Leadership Conference, took the lead in proposing a settlement package upon which both sides could agree. A number of details remained to be worked out, but one white negotiator seemed sufficiently confident to remark: "I think we've got a deal. If we can get everyone to agree, perhaps the worst of this is over."

The first public indication that a settlement might be in the works came early on Wednesday. Jail officials began releasing arrested juvenile demonstrators in their parents' custody, instead of insisting upon the $500 cash bonds that had previously been required. Later in the day, Dr. King told a press conference on the patio of the Gaston Motel, where he was making his headquarters, that there would be a one-day suspension of demonstrations. He said he hoped a settlement could be announced within 24 hours.

In Washington, President Kennedy took note at a news conference of the apparent improvement in the Birmingham situation. He said:

I'm gratified to note the progress in the efforts by white and Negro citizens to end an ugly situation in Birmingham.

I've made it clear since assuming the presidency that I would use all available means to protect human rights and uphold the law of the land. . . . Assistant Attorney General Burke Marshall, representing the Attorney General and myself on the scene, has made every possible effort to halt a spectacle which was seriously damaging the reputation of both Birmingham and the country.

Today, as the result of responsible efforts on the part of both white and Negro leaders over the last 72 hours, the business community of Birmingham has responded in a constructive and commendable fashion, and pledged that substantial steps would begin to meet the justifiable needs of the Negro community. Negro leaders have announced suspension of their demonstrations.

And when the newly elected mayor, who has indicated his desire to resolve these problems, takes office, the city of Birmingham has committed itself wholeheartedly to continuing progress in this area. While much remains to be settled before the situation can be termed satisfactory, we can hope that tensions will ease and that this case history, which has so far only narrowly avoided widespread violence and fatalities, will remind every state, every community and every citizen how urgent it is that all bars to equal opportunity and treatment be removed as promptly as possible. I urge the local leaders of Birmingham, both white and Negro, to continue their constructive and cooperative efforts.

The brightening of the situation indicated at the Kennedy and King press conferences was, however, darkened within hours. In midafternoon, King and his key aide, the Reverend Abernathy, were tried in Birmingham Recorder's Court on old charges of parading without a permit during one of the demonstrations. They were convicted, fined $300 each and ordered jailed for 180 days. In previous cases judges had set appeal bonds at $300. In the cases of King and Abernathy, the appeal bonds were set at $2,500 each. When they were unable to post the bonds immediately, they were jailed. This touched off heated statements from other Negro leaders, and brought the possibility that demonstrations might be swiftly resumed.

"We can only interpret this as an act of bad faith," said the Reverend Wyatt Tee Walker, King's executive assistant. "If necessary, we will pull out all the stops tomorrow."

Another Negro leader, the Reverend Shuttlesworth, was not even willing to wait until the next day. He announced bitterly that the truce was off, then put on his "marching shoes" and started to leave his motel room to lead a demonstration. Joseph F. Dolan, the assistant deputy attorney general who had been working with Burke Marshall in Birmingham, headed Shuttlesworth off before he could leave the motel. Dolan kept the Negro minister in the motel room while he phoned Attorney General Kennedy. The Attorney General persuaded Shuttlesworth to delay further demonstrations at least until the next day, to give the white and Negro negotiators more time to try to iron out difficulties and arrive at a final settlement.

A short time later, Negro millionaire A. G. Gaston, who had been participating in the negotiations, posted the $2,500 bonds for King and Abernathy. Upon their release, negotiations were resumed.

While the negotiations were continuing Wednesday night, 2,300 Negroes jammed into the Sixth Avenue Baptist Church for a mass rally to pledge unswerving support for the integration movement. The thick, damp air hung like a dead weight in the run-down, 82-year-old church. The thermometer read 88, but it felt more like 110. The Negro women in their faded cotton dresses and the men in their overalls sat uncomfortably in the pews, waving cardboard fans provided by the Booker T. Washington Insurance Company. But the discomfort was soon forgotten as the fervor of an old-fashioned revival meeting swept over the rally. Letting the sweat run down their faces, the spectators nodded their heads approvingly as one speaker after another urged them to carry on the fight against racial discrimination.

"Amen, brother, amen," the spectators chorused again and again. "We hear you, brother."

They gave the most enthusiastic receptions not to their local leaders, but to white rabbis and ministers—many of them from the North—who had come to Birmingham to support the desegregation campaign. Nineteen rabbis from all over the country, who had come directly from a convention in Greenfield Park, New York, attended the rally. One of them, Rabbi Seymour Friedman of Spring Valley, New York, taught the Negroes a Hebrew song. Translated, its title, from the book of Psalms, was: "Behold how good and how pleasant it is for brethren to dwell together in unity."

It was quite a sight—2,300 Negroes in Birmingham, Alabama, singing a Hebrew song.

Another rabbi, Richard Rubenstein of Pittsburgh, Pennsylvania, told the throng: "In August, 1961, I made a visit to East Berlin and saw policemen using police dogs against the citizens. A Berliner said to me that I was lucky that I was an American and didn't have to see that kind of thing in America. I agreed with him. But I was wrong. I have now seen police using police dogs in Birmingham. But, despite that, I want to tell you that you should not hate these policemen—you should love them. You're not a man until you can look your enemy in the eye and call him 'brother.' "

From the spectators came: "Amen, brother, amen."

The Reverend William S. Coffin, Jr., Protestant chaplain of Yale University, who was appealing a two-month jail term given him as a Freedom Rider two years earlier in Montgomery, Alabama, told the crowd: "This will only be the land of the free if the people are brave, like you people of Birmingham. This wasn't the cradle of the Confederacy, so much as the cradle of human justice. These people in Birmingham rocked the cradle until the baby got up and walked. He is now walking into every segregated playground, lunch counter, waiting room and rest room in the city."

As the rally closed, everyone in the church rose, linked arms, swayed from side to side and sang "We Shall Overcome." The throng filed out singing the line: "Black and white together, we shall overcome, some day."

The next day, Thursday, May 9, Dr. King announced at a press conference at the Gaston Motel that demonstrations were being suspended for another day. He also disclosed that the white and Negro negotiators had agreed on terms for desegregation of lunch counters and other facilities in downtown stores and for upgrading of Negroes in employment. King said an acceptable offer had been made by the white negotiators on a third point, but he would not say what it was. It later developed that this point concerned creation of a biracial commission to work for solutions to outstanding problems between whites and Negroes.

King did not at the time disclose the terms of agreement on each of these points. He merely said that agreement had been reached. But one major point—arrangement for the release on bond of those arrested demonstrators still in jail—remained unresolved. And King warned that, unless agreement on an overall settlement were reached by Friday morning, mass demonstrations would be resumed.

At this critical juncture in the negotiations, Arthur J. Hanes, the commission mayor, issued a statement aimed at sabotaging the efforts to reach an agreement. Hanes said that segregationist forces had King "whipped" and "on the run." He said it "breaks my heart" to see whites negotiating with the Negro minister. "If they would stand firm, we would run King and that bunch of race agitators out of town," Hanes said. "If this committee is doing such a grand thing for the white people of Birmingham, why are they ashamed to release the names of those on the negotiating committee?" (Although the names of the white negotiators were known to newsmen and had been published, there had not been any official acknowledgment of their identities. Also, the membership of the full Senior Citizens Committee had never been disclosed.)

"Is it because they're ashamed of the fact that they are selling the white folks down the river?" Hanes asked. "They call themselves negotiators. I call them a bunch of quisling, gutless traitors!"

Despite Hanes' tirade, the white negotiators continued their efforts to wrap up a settlement. Erskine Smith, one of the white negotiators, was assigned to handle his team's side of the attempts to get the remaining jailed demonstrators freed on bond. The major stumbling block was the fact that the Negroes had depleted their immediate sources of cash in posting bonds for the demonstrators already released. A large amount of cash was needed quickly if the Negro leaders were to keep a promise to their followers to get the remaining prisoners released.

At this point Negro leaders decided to turn to an outside source—the organized labor movement—for help. They phoned Washington and reached Walter P. Reuther, president of the United Automobile Workers and of the AFL-CIO Industrial Union Department. They explained their dilemma: it would take at least $160,000 to free the remaining 849 prisoners. Reuther called Joseph L. Rauh, Jr., Washington counsel for the United Automobile Workers, and instructed him to work out a solution to the problem. Rauh phoned J. Albert Woll, AFL-CIO general counsel, and David Feller, general counsel for the United Steelworkers. Woll got clearance from AFL-CIO President George Meany for the labor federation to put up some of the money that was needed. Feller got similar clearance from David J. McDonald, president of the United Steelworkers.

It was agreed that the AFL-CIO itself, its Industrial Union Department, the United Automobile Workers and the United Steelworkers each would put up $40,000. Rauh decided it would be simplest to withdraw $160,000 from the Industrial Union Department's bank account and forward it to Birmingham, then have the three other labor organizations repay the Department. With Reuther's approval, he withdrew the money and wired it through banks to Erskine Smith in Birmingham.

Friday morning came and went without the demonstration that Dr. King had threatened would take place if a full settlement had not been reached. But there was no immediate word on the presence or absence of such a settlement. King's executive assistant, the Reverend Walker, announced that there would be a press conference at noon on the patio of the Gaston Motel. Scores of reporters gathered on the sun-drenched patio. But noon passed, and the conference did not begin. Then 1 P.M. and 1:30 went by.

Why the delay? Was there some hitch in the negotiations and possible settlement? No one could say. But some reporters pointed out that there had been similar delays in beginning previous press conferences called by Walker.

Finally, shortly before 2 P.M., Walker appeared with King, the Reverends Shuttlesworth and Abernathy. They sat down at a round metal table at one side of the patio. All looked extremely weary. Walker introduced Shuttlesworth, who said he would read a statement on behalf of himself, King and Abernathy. The statement read:

'The city of Birmingham has reached an accord with its conscience. The acceptance of responsibility by local white and Negro leadership offers an example of a free people uniting to meet and solve their problems. Birmingham may well offer for 20th-century America an example of progressive race relations, and for all mankind a dawn of a new day, a promise for all men, a day of opportunity and a new sense of freedom for all America.

Responsible leaders of both Negro and white communities of Birmingham, being desirous of promoting conditions which will insure sound moral, economic and political growth of their city, in the interest of all citizens of Birmingham, after mutual consideration and discussion of the issues relating to the recent demonstrations in their city, have agreed to the following:

1. The desegregation of lunch counters, rest rooms, fitting rooms and drinking fountains in planned stages within the next 90 days. Cooperative prayerful planning is necessary to insure smooth transition.

2. The upgrading and hiring of Negroes on a nondiscriminatory basis throughout the industrial community of Birmingham. This will include the hiring of Negroes as clerks and salesmen within the next 60 days, and the immediate appointment of a committee of business, industrial and professional leaders for the implementation of an area-wide program for acceleration of upgrading and the employment of Negroes in job categories previously denied to Negroes.

3. Our movement has made arrangements for the release of all persons [arrested in demonstrations] on bond or on their personal recognizance. Our legal department is working on further solutions to this problem.

4. Through the Senior Citizens Committee of the Chamber of Commerce, communications between Negro and white will be publicly reestablished within the next two weeks. We would hope that this channel of communications between the white and Negro communities will prevent the necessity of further protest action or demonstrations.

The statement read by Shuttlesworth had set out the terms of the settlement. Now Dr. King attempted to assess the significance of the agreement. In his deep rumbling voice, he read a statement of his own:

I am very happy to be able to announce that we have come today to the climax of a long struggle for justice, freedom and human dignity in the city of Birmingham. I say the climax, and not the end, for though we have come a long way there is still a strenuous path before us, and some of it is yet uncharted.

Nevertheless, it can now be said that after a great struggle this day is clearly the moment of a great victory. The greatness of the triumph is measured by this one fact: it is a victory that cannot possibly be confined to the limited area of one race. Indeed, the agreements which have been reached over the last few days are signal accomplishments which redound to the credit of all Birmingham's citizens. As a matter of fact, I believe sincerely that this victory cannot even be confined within the limits of this sprawling metropolis, for Birmingham now stands on the threshold of becoming a great, enlightened symbol, shedding the radiance of its example throughout the entire nation. . . .

Without a doubt, the world will never forget the thousands of children and adults who gave up their own physical safety and freedom and went to jail to secure the safety and freedom of all men. I must say this, too: In these recent days, I have been deeply impressed by the quality of the white persons of the community who worked so diligently for just solutions to our mutual problems. They are men of good will. . . .

We now enter into a new day for Birmingham's people, a day when men will no longer fear to speak the truth, when citizens will no longer cringe before the threats of misguided men. We look forward now to continued progress toward the establishment of a city in which equal job opportunities, equal access to public facilities and equal rights and responsibilities for all its people will be the order of the day.

However, even these needful things are not our final goals. The deepest hope that surges up within our hearts is this: That Birmingham is on its way to the creation of a new kind of community—not simply a new image, but a new reality. We are looking forward to that moment—so nearly upon us—when this metropolis will truly become a magic city again, this time filled with the beautiful magic of a new brotherhood where men are free to know, respect and love each other. We seek ultimately a magic city where color will no longer be the measure of a man's worth, where character will mean more than pigmentation.

I cannot close without saying that the Negro community must accept this achievement in the right spirit. We must not see the present development as a victory for the Negro: it is rather a victory for democracy and the whole citizenry of Birmingham—Negro and white. . . .

This is the time that we must evince calm dignity and wise restraint. Emotion must not run wild. Violence must not come from any of us, and if we become victimized with violent acts or intent, the pending daybreak of progress will be transformed into a gloomy midnight of retrogress.

As we stand on the verge of using public facilities heretofore closed to us, we must not be overbearing and haughty in spirit. We must be loving enough to turn an enemy into a friend. We must now move from protest to reconciliation.

This, too, is our hope for Birmingham. It is a hope that will cause us to look at the signs which say "It's nice to have you in Birmingham" in a new way. Now, we will know that these words are meant for all men, and we will know they are sincere. Then, and only then, will all the citizens of this community be able to say in joyful response: "Thank you! It's great to be in Birmingham—a city of honor, respect and brotherly love."

The announced agreement indicated the extent to which the Negro negotiators had scaled down their demands. They had settled for promises of desegregated facilities and upgrading of Negro employes during specified time periods, whereas they previously had demanded that such measures take effect immediately. And they had settled for release of arrested demonstrators on bond, whereas they previously had demanded dismissal of all charges against the demonstrators. But it seemed clear that, if the agreement were fulfilled, Birmingham would represent a major victory for the civil rights movement.

The announcement of the settlement brought differing expressions of opinion from various quarters. Sidney Smyer, who had headed the white negotiating team, said:

We are pleased and greatly relieved, of course, that peace and order have been restored to our city. Our task has not been pleasant or easy. It was undertaken only after thorough deliberation and under the pressure of growing crisis. It is important that the public understand the steps we have taken were necessary to avoid a dangerous and imminent explosion.

Our committee [the Senior Citizens Committee] is broadly representative of our city's leadership. It represents the employers of perhaps 80 percent of the working force of Birmingham—white and colored. We are proud to have been in a position to be of service to our city, though we share the bitterness which every citizen must feel about the demonstrations and their timing. But recriminations will gain us nothing. . . . We call upon all citizens, white and colored, to continue their calm attitude, to stop rumors and to thank God for a chance to reestablish racial peace. . . .

We could not and we can not now speak for any city official, nor could we commit the courts or the boards of education involved to anything. . . . But now that peace has returned to our community, it is up to all to help preserve it by doing nothing which would destroy it.

In Washington, Attorney General Kennedy hailed the settlement as "a tremendous step forward for Birmingham, for Alabama and for the South generally." He said the Birmingham crisis illustrated "the importance of getting a dialogue" between Negroes and whites. "The alternative is going to be great violence, and it is going to be turning these matters over to extremists on both sides," he said. "We really have to start having greater exchanges, so that a Southern senator can talk to Burke Marshall or the Attorney General to a Southern governor and not lose votes for him, and a [Northern] politician can say something nice about some Southern leader and not feel that that is going to lose him the next election."

Bull Connor's view of the settlement was terse and blunt: "They [the Negroes] didn't gain a thing."

Arthur Hanes said:

The only thing I'd say is capitulation by certain weak-kneed white people under threats of violence by the rabble-rousing Negro, King, has encouraged him greatly to move to another area and upset some other fine city. King is greatly encouraged by these easy victories and by the Attorney General's office, and is becoming so power mad that he feels that he is truly the king of the United States. He should be put out of circulation because if any group, organization or person can divide a country, then it is wrong and should be stopped.

These so-called community leaders who took it upon themselves not to negotiate but to surrender have laid the groundwork for endless troubles of this nature in the future. I certainly am not bound by the concessions granted to the terrorist, King, and have no intention of doing one thing to implement or facilitate these agreements. Quite on the contrary, I will oppose these integration efforts.

Mayor Boutwell issued a calmer statement, but one hardly reassuring to the Negroes:

I have made no commitment with reference to any of these matters. I regard it as an unwarranted presumption for anyone to infer or suggest that there has been a "truce" between the city of Birmingham and any who have violated the law. . . . My administration will soon have complete freedom to act in the solution of all the city's problems; and it will do so vigorously. I shall use the influence of the mayor's office to promote peace and good will and to encourage our citizens to reconcile any difference which may hurt our city.

Those close to Boutwell insisted that, despite the negative tone of the first part of his statement, he would take forceful action to implement the biracial agreement once his administration was in undisputed control of the city government. They pointed out that several of the key white negotiators who had helped draw up the agreement were close political allies of Boutwell.

The next day Bull Connor went on a local radio station to attack the biracial agreement, which he had insisted only a day earlier had not gained the Negroes a thing. Connor called for a boycott by white citizens of stores that agreed to desegregate their lunch counters and other facilities. "The white people and other people of this city should not go in these stores," Connor said. "That's the best way I know to beat down integration in Birmingham."

Aside from Connor's statement, the situation seemed to be calming down in Birmingham. True, a rally of Ku Klux Klansmen from Alabama and Georgia was scheduled that night in suburban Bessemer, but all in all, tensions appeared to be easing.

State troopers began leaving town, along with a force of "irregulars" composed of game wardens, liquor agents, civil defense workers, sheriff's deputies from neighboring counties, and specially deputized lawmen. The departure of these officers was seen as a heartening sign. Some Negroes had complained that they had been manhandled by the out-of-town officers, and had charged that the officers were trying to provoke trouble.

The city seemed to be getting back to normal. The downtown area, which had swarmed with demonstrators only days earlier, now buzzed with shoppers. Kelly Ingram Park, the scene of many of the demonstrations, was virtually deserted. A few elderly Negroes dozed on a bench that had been occupied a day earlier by state troopers. Nearby, a Negro lay on the grass, listening to a radio. A woman sat alongside him, eating peanuts. Pigeons strutted across the grass.

The situation seemed so serene that Martin Luther King flew home for the weekend to Atlanta, where he planned to preach Sunday at his church. Assistant Attorney General Marshall flew back to Washington.

The serenity was not to last very long.

At nightfall, about 1,000 robed Ku Klux Klansmen gathered in Bessemer's Moose Club Park for their rally. Two flaming crosses sent eerie shafts of light shimmering across the park. Racist speeches were shouted into the night. It was 10:15 before the Klansmen began drifting away.

The Reverend A. D. King was relaxing at his home in suburban Ensley with his wife. Their five children were asleep. King, younger brother of Dr. Martin Luther King, was pastor of a local Negro Baptist Church and one of the leaders of the Birmingham integration movement.

At 10:45, a car sped by King's ranch-style home. A dynamite bomb arced out. The bomb hit the front of the house and rocked the entire building. King and his wife rushed to their children's rooms and hustled them to the back door. As they were dashing out the door, a second explosion, more violent than the first, shook the house.

No one was hurt, but the house was a shambles. King immediately phoned his brother in Atlanta. "They just bombed the house," he said. "But, thank God, we are all safe."

As police and firemen began arriving, an angry crowd of Negroes gathered near the shattered home. While officers inspected the rubble, the spectators slashed tires on police cars and fire trucks. But this outbreak was nothing, compared with what was to come later in the night.

At 11:58, another dynamite bomb exploded, this one at the Gaston Motel, the integration movement's headquarters. The blast blew a hole in a downstairs motel room, just below the one Martin Luther King had occupied, and damaged the motel office, while shattering windows throughout the motel and a nearby grocery. Three house trailers parked on a nearby lot were wrecked. Four persons were injured, but not seriously enough to need hospitalization.

Waitresses and diners in the motel restaurant began screaming. Some ran into the street. Other Negroes began pouring out of pool halls, taverns, night clubs and small groceries in the area. Many of them were liquored up on a local moonshine, called "Joe Louis" because it packs an awesome punch. When police arrived, they were pelted by the crowd with rocks, bricks, bottles and other missiles. The officers did not try to wade into the crowd, but held their position in the middle of a street.

The Negroes screamed: "Kill 'em! Kill 'em!"

The police replied: "We're your friends." But the Negroes only jeered as more and more white squad cars rolled onto the scene. Officers then waded several times into the crowd, trying to drive back groups of rock-throwers. But still the rain of missiles continued.

Dr. King's executive assistant, the Reverend Walker, came out of the motel with a portable electric bullhorn megaphone. He wore a sport shirt and slacks, and had a white handkerchief tied around his left arm as a peace symbol. "Please do not throw any bricks any more," Walker pleaded over the bullhorn. "Ladies and gentlemen, will you cooperate by going to your homes. Please. Please go home."

A brick hit Walker on the ankle. But he limped down the street, continuing to voice his plea to the crowd. It had little effect, however. The rioters shouted at him: "They started it! They started it!"

A white teenager drove by in a car. Rocks crashed through his car windows. He fled, blood rushing down his face. Two policemen ran down an alley after a group of rioters. One of them was stabbed twice in the back. Other officers were forced to abandon their squad cars and paddy wagons, and to flee on foot from the torrent of rocks and bricks.

Police reinforcements kept swarming in, but so did additional rioters. The police department's white, six-wheeled armored riot car rumbled onto the scene about 12:45 A.M. Sunday and roared up and down the streets, half on and half off the sidewalks, pressing the mob back. A squad car arrived with three police dogs. The sight of the dogs, and the memory of their use in the protest demonstrations, further inflamed the mob. Handfuls of gravel were hurled at the dogs and their handlers. "You'd better get those dogs out of here," one rioter shouted.

Gradually the city police and several Negro ministers managed to calm the mob. The hurling of rocks, bricks and bottles was virtually halted. The Negroes merely milled about, muttering sullenly. Then Colonel Albert J. Lingo, state director of public safety, arrived with Sheriff Jim Clark of neighboring Dallas County. They were accompanied by squads of state troopers and Clark's sheriff's posse, a band of "irregulars" that had been used by Lingo during the demonstrations. The mob was enraged anew by the sight of Lingo and his forces, which previously had been accused of manhandling Negroes. The rage was heightened by the fact that Lingo and Clark were brandishing repeater shotguns.

Birmingham Police Chief Jamie Moore urged Lingo and Clark to withdraw. "If you'd leave, Mr. Lingo, I'd appreciate it," he said.

Lingo snapped: "I'm not going to leave. I've been sent here by the Governor, and I'm going to stay."

Moore appealed: "Those guns are not needed. Will you please put them up? Somebody's going to get killed."

"You're damned right it'll get somebody killed," Lingo boomed.

A Negro who was trying to calm the mob passed by. Lingo poked him with the shotgun. "Git!" he commanded. A short time later, he ordered away three Negro civil defense workers who had been summoned to the scene by city police to help maintain order.

Arthur Hanes drove up. Lingo barked at him: "We are not under Jamie Moore. Get that straight." Hanes nodded.

The mob was getting out of hand again, and Hanes somehow figured it was all the fault of Attorney General Kennedy. "I hope that every drop of blood that's spilled he tastes in his throat, and I hope he chokes to death," Hanes said.

A white cab driver rolled by the scene. The mob set upon his cab. Someone stabbed him with a knife, but he managed to flee on foot. The mob overturned the cab and set it on fire. Some rioters set fire to two corner grocery stores owned by whites. The flames spread to other buildings—mostly Negro homes—and within a short time nearly a whole block was ablaze. The flames attracted still more Negroes to the area. By now, the mob had swelled to about 2,500.

The Reverend A. D. King arrived at the Gaston Motel from his bombed home at about 1:30 A.M. and joined other Negro ministers in trying to disperse the mob. He managed to herd about 300 Negroes into the motel parking lot, where he climbed on top of a Cadillac and pleaded for nonviolence. "We're not mad at anyone," he said. "We're saying, 'Father, forgive them for they know not what they do.' Violence has always been the tactic of the white man. Let it not be said we are the ones to bring violence. I want us to sing, and as we sing 'We Shall Overcome,' will you go home for us?"

The Negroes sang the integration anthem. As they finished singing, some headed for home. But many more did not.

The fire department, after waiting for police protection from the rioters, finally sent two fire engines to fight the block-long blaze in the Negro section. Some of the Negroes muttered angrily at sight of the engines, whose high-pressure hoses had been used to disperse demonstrators earlier in the Birmingham crisis. Suddenly, a rock flew at the engines. Then came another. Then a torrent of rocks. One of them struck Birmingham's chief police inspector, W. J. Haley, and sent blood streaming down his face.

Al Lingo came up at this point to survey the situation, withdrew, then reappeared at the head of a column of 35 state troopers wielding shotguns, rifles and billy clubs. Haley shouted to the troopers: "Get back! Get back!" But the troopers kept coming. They charged up and down the streets, clubbing and pushing spectators, climbing up on porches to shove Negroes indoors, and swatting bystanders with gun butts and billies. One trooper rasped to a Negro on a porch: "Get inside, goddamit!" As several officers walloped him, the Negro shouted: "I can't. I can't. The door's locked." The troopers crashed the door open with their gun butts, and pushed him inside.

On the street, other Negroes continued heaving rocks. Under the barrage, firemen gave up their fire-fighting effort and withdrew. Mayor Hanes, looking on, remarked: "You can't go in there and fight a fire with people throwing rocks at you. Goddamit, let it burn."

Flames shot 100 feet into the air. The stone chimneys on burning buildings buckled and tumbled to the ground. Soon only hollow shells of seven buildings remained. Nearby, a telephone pole caught fire, giving the appearance of a flaming cross, symbol of the Ku Klux Klan.

All told, the riot raged for more than four hours. Then a group of about 60 city policemen, sheriff's deputies and state troopers charged a large crowd of Negroes gathered in the entrance to the Gaston Motel. The charge broke up the crowd and sent many of the Negroes scattering out of the immediate vicinity. For a time, small groups of Negroes darted out of alleys periodically to hurl rocks at the police. Finally, by 4:30 A.M., officers had sealed off the area and dispersed the last of the rioters.

By dawn, hospitals were treating more than 50 persons wounded in the rioting. The neighborhood in the vicinity of the Gaston Motel was a shambles. Police cruised around in prowl cars, ordering Negroes off the streets.

3

In the aftermath of the bombings and rioting, tension gripped Birmingham anew. And with it came nagging questions—the most important being whether the biracial agreement would be honored.

Dr. Martin Luther King flew back to Birmingham from Atlanta on Sunday and expressed confidence that the agreement would stand up. He said that no new demonstrations were planned because of the bombings. "I do not feel the events of last night nullified the agreement at all," King said. "I do not think the bombings were perpetrated or even sanctioned by the majority of the white people in Birmingham."

Nonetheless, there were strong doubts in some quarters

about the possible effects of the night of violence on the implementation of the agreement. In addition, there was widespread fear that more violence might be in the offing. This fear led to a flurry of activity among federal officials. Assistant Attorney General Marshall, resting up from his Birmingham assignment at his farm in Berkeley Springs, West Virginia, was awakened by a phone call at 2 A.M. Sunday and told of the Birmingham violence. Attorney General Kennedy got the word a little later at his home in McLean, Virginia. President Kennedy, spending the weekend at Camp David, Maryland, was briefed on the Birmingham situation when he woke up.

The Attorney General, Marshall and other government officials phoned Birmingham white and Negro leaders from their homes to get the facts on the violence and try to calm things down. At 1 P.M., a government helicopter was sent to Marshall's farm to take him to Washington. He met first with the Attorney General at McLean. They then went to the Justice Department for a meeting with other officials. The Attorney General had taken his large black Newfoundland dog, Brumus, to the office with him. While Kennedy conferred solemnly with his aides, Brumus romped around the office.

Meanwhile, President Kennedy flew back to Washington from Camp David by helicopter. He immediately went into conference at the White House with Defense Secretary McNamara, Army Secretary Vance, Army Chief of Staff General Wheeler, and Theodore C. Sorenson, the President's special counsel. The presence of the military officials at the meeting gave rise to speculation that the President was considering using troops in the Birmingham crisis. But there was no immediate word from the White House on the President's plans.

Just before 6 P.M., Attorney General Kennedy, Marshall and Deputy Attorney General Katzenbach arrived at the White House to join the meeting. The President and the Attorney General had conferred by phone throughout the afternoon.

At 8:48, the President strode into the "Fish Room" of the White House to appear before the press and television cameras. Gravely, he read a statement:

I am deeply concerned about the events which occurred in Birmingham, Alabama, last night. The home of Reverend A. D. King was bombed and badly damaged. Shortly thereafter, the A. G. Gaston Motel was also bombed.

These occurrences led to rioting, personal injuries, property damage and various reports of violence and brutality. This government will do whatever must be done to preserve order, to protect the lives of its citizens and to uphold the law of the land. I am certain that the vast majority of the citizens of Birmingham, both white and Negro—particularly those who labored so hard to achieve the peaceful constructive settlement of last week—can feel nothing but dismay at the efforts of those who would replace conciliation and good will with violence and hate.

The Birmingham agreement was and is a fair and just accord. It recognized the fundamental right of all citizens to be accorded equal treatment and opportunity. It was a tribute to the process of peaceful negotiation and to the good faith of both parties. The federal government will not permit it to be sabotaged by a few extremists on either side who think they can defy both the law and the wishes of responsible citizens by inciting or inviting violence.

I call upon all the citizens of Birmingham, both Negro and white, to live up to the standards their responsible leaders set in reaching the agreement of last week, to realize that violence only breeds more violence and that good will and good faith are most important now to restore the atmosphere in which last week's agreement can be carried out. There must be no repetition of last night's incidents by any group. To make certain that this government is prepared to carry out its statutory and constitutional obligations, I have ordered the following three initial steps:

1. I am sending Assistant Attorney General Burke Marshall to Birmingham this evening to consult with local citizens. He will join Assistant Deputy Attorney General Joseph F. Dolan and other Justice Department officials who were sent back to Birmingham this morning.

2. I have instructed Secretary of Defense McNamara to alert units of the armed forces trained in riot control and to dispatch selected units to military bases in the vicinity of Birmingham.

3. Finally, I have directed that the necessary preliminary steps to calling the Alabama National Guard into federal service be taken now so that units of the Guard will be promptly available should their services be required.

It is my hope, however, that the citizens of Birmingham

themselves maintain standards of responsible conduct that will make outside intervention unnecessary and permit the city, the state and the country to move ahead in protecting the lives and the interests of those citizens and the welfare of our country.

The President's action did not order federal troops into actual operations in Birmingham. It provided only that they be sent to bases near Birmingham, to be available in case of further violence. Three thousand GIs with riot-control training were dispatched to Maxwell Air Force Base at Montgomery and Fort McClellan at Anniston from other bases outside Alabama.

Similarly, the Alabama National Guard was not actually called into federal service, but the preliminary legal steps toward federalization of the Guard were taken, so that the actual federalization could be accomplished in a matter of minutes if it became necessary.

Alabama's segregationist Governor Wallace was incensed by Kennedy's action. He fired off a telegram to the President, questioning Kennedy's authority to send the troops into Alabama. Wallace insisted in the telegram that "we have sufficient state and local forces" to handle the Birmingham situation, and asked Kennedy to leave the entire matter to the state and local governments.

The U. S. Constitution, Wallace said, "states that the federal government may send troops to quell domestic violence upon application of the state legislature or the governor of a state. The legislature of this state has made no request, nor have I. May I ask by what authority you would send federal troops into this state?"

In Washington, federal officials replied that Kennedy had acted under a law giving the President power to quell civil disturbances. The law, dating to 1871 and last revised in 1956, is Section 133 of Title 10 of the United States Code. The section is headed "Interference with State and Federal Law." It provides:

The President, by using the militia or the armed forces, or both, or by any other means, shall take such measures as he considers necessary to suppress, in a state, any insurrection, domestic violence, unlawful combination or conspiracy if it—

1. So hinders the execution of the laws of that state, and of

the United States within that state, that any part or class of its people is deprived of a right, privilege, immunity or protection named in the Constitution and secured by law and the constituted authorities of that state are unable, fail or refuse to protect that right, privilege or immunity or to give that protection; or

2. Opposes or obstructs the execution of the laws of the United States or impedes the course of justice.

In any situation covered by Clause 1, the state shall be considered to have denied the equal protection of the laws secured by the Constitution.

Sunday night passed without resumption of violence. But a state of virtual martial law existed in Negro sections of Birmingham, where 1,200 helmeted peace officers kept close watch for the possibility of further trouble.

On Monday, May 13, Dr. Martin Luther King set about trying to prevent such trouble. Few of the Negroes who had participated in the Saturday night rioting had been members of the integration movement. Rather, most of them had been the habitués of pool halls, nightclubs and taverns. King felt these Negroes had been missing his nonviolence message by spending their time in such places, instead of at church. So, like a wandering minstrel in search of an audience, he set out with a group of his aides on a tour of pool halls aimed at putting the message across. I went along.

At the smoke-filled New Home Billiard Parlor, the staccato clickety-clack of the cue sticks and pool balls was mingling with the mournful moan of a rock 'n roll record when King arrived. On one green wall hung a sign reading: "No Gambling. No Drinking. No Minors Allowed." About 100 Negroes, ranging from teen-agers to elderly men, clustered about the tables. The talk was boisterous, the language far from the kind you hear in church. It seemed hardly the place for an impromptu revival meeting. But a revival meeting was exactly what came about once King strode into the unlikely setting.

The pool-shooters obviously were surprised to see the renowned minister in their midst. But they obeyed respectfully when the pool hall manager told them: "All right, fellas, put your sticks down and come over here for a few minutes." They clustered around King and the Reverend Abernathy, some leaning on their cues, others sitting on the edges of the pool tables.

Abernathy, a spell-binding preacher, began the session in classic revival-meeting style, whipping the crowd to a fever pitch. "Every group needs a leader," he boomed. "Governor Wallace is not our leader. Bull Connor is not our leader."

"Right!" the pool-shooters shouted.

"Do you know who our leader is?" Abernathy asked.

"King!" came the reply.

"That's right. God sent Martin Luther King to be our leader. Are you willing to do whatever Martin Luther King tells you to do?"

"Yes!"

"Let's hear the King," Abernathy said.

"King, King, King, King, King, King, King, King, King, King, King!" the pool-shooters chanted.

Then King began to preach, his soft, melodious voice a sharp contrast to the deep rumble of Abernathy's. "We are engaged in a mighty struggle for dignity and human freedom," he said. "On Saturday night, after my brother's home and the Gaston Motel were bombed, we had a temporary reign of terror. Rocks were thrown; policemen were beat up; knives were used; stores were burned. I can well understand how deep-seated resentments can rise to the surface. But this is not the way we ought to act. We must make it clear that we can stand up to all injustices without fighting back with violence."

"Amen," shouted an elderly pool-shooter.

King continued: "As difficult as it is, we must not meet force with force. We must say, 'We don't care how many bombs you throw. We're not going to return violence.' For I believe that violence is immoral. But, more than that, it is impractical. We can't win with violence. Bull Connor is happy when we use force. He can cope with force. But he doesn't know how to handle nonviolence."

From the pool-shooters came: "Amen, brother, amen."

King urged them to spread his message to all their friends. "We must get rid of our knives," he said. "We don't need any guns. Try to get the idea of nonviolence over to the entire Negro community. That way, we can win. That way, we will win. I'm convinced that we shall overcome."

The pool-shooters then linked arms, some of them a bit self-consciously, and sang "We Shall Overcome."

The procedure was repeated at a second pool hall. When King set out for a third, a large crowd of Negroes fell in behind to walk with him. Two state troopers, evidently thinking a protest march was in progress, halted the procession. "Reverse and go back the way you came," one of the troopers ordered brusquely, brandishing a carbine. King, fearing the possibility of violence, decided to cancel the stop at the third pool hall.

As he turned and walked away, most of the Negroes behind him dispersed. But a few bystanders stood still. The two troopers, and four others who joined them, roughly pushed several of the Negroes, including an elderly woman, and told them to clear the area. With that, a sullen-faced young Negro who had followed King out of one of the pool halls turned to me and said: "I don't care what King says. I don't give a damn about that nonviolence stuff."

How many other Birmingham Negroes shared this view was an open question. But it did not take long to learn that racial violence had not ended completely in the city. On Monday night scattered incidents were reported. A white youth was attacked by a group of Negroes and slashed on the arm with a knife. A Negro man was hospitalized after being struck in the face with a steel ball fired from a white youth's slingshot. Windshields of autos belonging to both whites and Negroes were smashed, as were windows in about a dozen buildings owned by members of both races. But this violence did not swell into any major conflagration, and no move was made by federal officials to send troops into the city.

Ed Guthman, Attorney General Kennedy's special assistant for public information, had now come to Birmingham to handle the federal government's public relations for the duration of the crisis. At a press conference he said: "We've been informed that the President's statement and the moving of troops has had a calming effect on the Negro community. Our information is that there's less tension."

Guthman said Burke Marshall had conferred with Negro and white leaders in Birmingham during the day. "He's very impressed by the courage of the responsible leaders," Guthman said. "He's optimistic that city and county authorities will be able to do the job here—that .they'll be able to maintain law and order without any need for the intervention of troops."

There had been continuing reports of manhandling of Negroes by state troopers. A reporter asked: "Is the Justice Department officially unhappy with the use of state troopers in Birmingham?"

Guthman replied: "It's our feeling that city and county officials can handle this. That includes city police and sheriff's people."

Tuesday, May 14, passed uneventfully. On Wednesday, hopes for bolstering the desegregation agreement reached the previous week got a shot in the arm. The Senior Citizens Committee publicly came out in support of the agreement.

The move was seen as significant for several reasons. For one, there had been considerable speculation that the full committee would not back the actions of its subcommittee. For another, there had been repeated criticism of the Senior Citizens Committee's failure to identify its members. It now made public its membership. The members included 60 of Birmingham's most influential citizens —among them a number of ardent segregationists, such as former Governor Frank Dixon and former Mayor James B. Morgan.

The committee said in a three-page statement that the decision to announce support of the agreement was reached unanimously at a meeting attended by the 60 men. It said that some members had disagreed with terms of the desegregation agreement, but had voted to urge public support of the settlement in the interest of racial harmony. The statement continued:

The members of this committee firmly believe that, if this is to be a peaceful and law-abiding community, our race relations problems must be worked out between the residents of this community. It cannot be done either by federal agencies or by outsiders. . . . The committee urges all citizens to appraise the cost to him or her of more thoughtless irresponsibility, violence or hate. We urge all citizens to join with us in making this a city where we all can live in peace and prosperity.

Among the most prominent of the executives signing the statement, in addition to Dixon and Morgan, were: Walter Bouldin, president of the Alabama Power Company; Frank W. Hulse, president of Southern Airways Inc.; John S. Jemison Jr., board chairman of the Birmingham Transit Company; Claude S. Lawson, board chairman of United States Pipe and Foundry Company; B. A. Monaghan, Jr., president of Balcan Materials Company; Clarence Hanson, publisher of the *Birmingham News;* and James Mills, editor of the *Birmingham Post-Herald.*

Only two hours after the committee's statement was released, its members were denounced as "weak-kneed quisling traitors" in a speech to a segregationist rally by Arthur Hanes. The rally, sponsored by a group called United Americans for Conservative Government, drew about 1,000 persons to the City Auditorium. Hanes urged them to fight the desegregation agreement "by all legal means," but to avoid violence.

His 90-minute speech was laced with such terms as "the witch doctor" (for Dr. Martin Luther King), "the Congolese mob" (for Birmingham Negroes) and "a bunch of left-wingers, fuzzy-minded liberals, pinkos and Reds" (for the members of the Senior Citizens Committee). He accused the committee members of "selling freedom for a profit."

"These traitors have sold their birthrights to negotiate with these niggers," Hanes said. He said members of the Senior Citizens Committee had come to him and told him they realized that 95 percent of Birmingham's white citizens were opposed to desegregation. "They wanted me to enlighten these bewildered citizens," Hanes stated. "They said they were looking for a Moses to lead these people out of the wilderness. I told them to go get a black Moses."

The members of United Americans for Conservative Government ate up Hanes' speech. "Pour it on," they shouted again and again.

And pour it on Hanes did. He urged the public to begin a letter-writing and phone campaign aimed at persuading merchants and governmental officials at all levels to keep the biracial agreement from taking effect. He asked his listeners to "stand firm" in opposing segregation, but to leave physical measures to the police.

Those attending the rally actually did not appear to be the type to resort to violence. Many of them were middle-aged or elderly men and women. They did not seem to be violent—ardent segregationists perhaps, but not fanatics.

I was curious about what attitudes would be taken by members of groups more extreme than United Americans for Conservative Government. From law enforcement officers and other sources, I obtained the names of a half-dozen men described as well-known members of the Ku Klux Klan. I talked with each of the men to try to learn what the Klan might try to do to prevent the desegregation agreement from taking effect. From each, I got approximately the same answer: "You must have been given some misinformation. I don't have anything to do with the Klan."

This really was not surprising. The Klan is basically a secret society. One of the few "Kluxers" who openly parades his Klan activities is Robert M. (Bobby) Shelton, Imperial Wizard of the United Klans of America, Inc. Shelton lives in Tuscaloosa, Alabama, but was out of town and unreachable when I tried to talk to him. A month later, under different circumstances, I would get to know Shelton rather well.

In the meantime, I concentrated on another extremist group—the National States' Rights Party. The party's national headquarters was in a two-story house in a residential area of Birmingham, with a Confederate flag flying out front. The man in charge was Dr. Edward R. Fields, a clean-cut, 30-year-old chiropractor with two blond children, a soft voice and a faculty for speaking articulately on such subjects as Freudian psychology and the historical views of Arnold Toynbee. Despite these attributes, Fields was leading one of the nation's most vociferous hate organizations.

Fields had given up practice as a chiropractor to devote full time to working for the party, an ultra right-wing organization that ran Arkansas Governor Orval Faubus as its presidential candidate in 1960. In spite of its political activities, which were considerable, the National States' Rights Party was not a political party in the traditional sense. It was more a movement of fanatics, built along the lines of the Nazi Party, complete with armbands bearing the organization's insignia, a thunderbolt. ("Perfect for meetings and demonstrations, $1.50," read an advertisement in a piece of party literature.)

Fields greeted me cordially at his headquarters. While the mimeograph machine in an adjoining room ground out racist propaganda, he explained the mission of his group. "We're fighting for the survival of the white race," he said. "The nonwhites are diluting the blood of the whites. If you marry a nigger, three out of four of your children will be black, because the black gene dominates the white. That's a biological fact. We're opposed to the Jews because they're foremost in the drive to mongrelize the white race, and every civilization that has allowed mongrelization has been destroyed. It's a proven fact that the white race is the superior race. The nigger brain is smaller and lighter than the white brain."

Talking with Fields, it quickly became clear that his party was anti-Negro, anti-Jew, anti-liberal, anti-moderate, anti-Kennedy and anti-sundry other things. The party's official platform called for deportation of all Negroes and Jews from the United States, giving small doles to those willing to leave voluntarily and arresting the others; allowing only white Christians to migrate to the country; outlawing racial and religious intermarriage; and impeaching any public official "who advocates race-mixing or mongrelization."

"We don't believe the niggers are citizens," Fields said. "We don't believe they have the right to vote. We believe that, when the Founding Fathers said all men were created equal, they meant white men. They were slaveholders. They considered niggers pieces of property."

I asked Fields what made him so adamant in his insistence on white supremacy. He pondered for a moment, then replied: "As the father of two blond children, I want to know that 100 years from now one of my descendants will bring into this world a blond Nordic child—not a mulatto nigger." What had convinced him of the superiority of the white race? "Arnold Toynbee states that the white race is responsible for 14 civilizations," he said. "Asiatic races are responsible for five civilizations. As of today, Negroidal races haven't contributed one civilization."

Though some observers were content to chalk off the National States' Rights Party as a crackpot group with little or no following, this seemed a mistake to me. While its membership figures were kept secret, it had gained enough followers to be permanently on the ballot in Alabama, Louisiana, Arkansas, Delaware and Tennessee. In 1962, an Alabama restaurateur running under the party's banner in an at-large, statewide election to fill eight congressional seats had drawn 65,000 votes, more than half of them in Birmingham. The eight winning candidates had polled from 165,000 to 195,000 votes each.

Thus far in the Birmingham crisis, the party had contented itself with picketing the federal building to protest the presence of the troops at nearby military bases. But whether it would remain content to limit its activities this way remained to be seen.

Fields handed me a copy of the latest issue of the party newspaper, *The Thunderbolt*. One prominent story was headlined: "What if Whites Had Rioted the Way Negroes Have?" The story said in part:

For the last four weeks, Negroes have been marching through the streets of Birmingham. They have stoned policemen and firemen. They have attacked law officers with knives and broken bottles. They have run berserk through the streets after they loaded all available jails with thousands of prisoners.

What if we held daily meetings advocating riot and disorder, plus outright defiance of state laws? There can be no doubt that white people would find themselves under arrest by federal forces and charged with insurrection, treason and what have you. . . .

Kennedy won in 1960 because he received 80 percent of the

black vote, which carried the key industrial states. What if we whites gathered such demonstrations demanding our rights? REMEMBER, KENNEDY, THE SEEDS YOU ARE SOWING WILL REAP YOU THE WHIRLWIND OF WHITE COUNTERACTION! White men, now is the time to stand up for your rights.

Fields was not saying what form the proposed white counteraction might take. But, no matter what its form, if it developed it could spell only trouble for hopes of carrying out the desegregation agreement.

Other trouble was developing as well. On Thursday, May 16, a disagreement arose between white and Negro leaders over terms of the desegregation pact. The disagreement led to fears that the city's shaky racial truce might be in danger of falling apart. The dispute arose when Sidney Smyer released his version of the desegregation agreement. It differed in several major respects with the version of the settlement previously announced by Dr. Martin Luther King and other Negro leaders.

King had said the agreement called for all major stores to hire Negro clerks and salesmen and for upgrading of Negroes in industrial jobs. Smyer said it called for hiring one Negro clerk at one downtown store and contained no provision about jobs in industry.

King had said the agreement called for seven major downtown department stores and additional stores in outlying areas to desegregate lunch counters and other facilities. Smyer said the agreement covered only five stores.

King had said the lunch-counter desegregation was to take place within 90 days of the time the agreement was announced. Smyer said it was to take place within 90 days of the time the Alabama Supreme Court ruled on which of the two rival city governments was entitled to hold office.

Both King and Smyer said new negotiations would be conducted to try to resolve the disagreement. And King emphasized: "We're not accusing the committee [of white businessmen] of bad faith—we have faith in the people with whom we are negotiating and we feel the agreements will be met." Still, it seemed clear that the racial truce, if not at the breaking point, was at least seriously endangered.

King also underscored the serious tensions remaining

in the city in discussing the failure of police and FBI agents to solve the Saturday night bombings. He accused the investigators of laxity in probing the bombings. And he warned: "If the perpetrators of these bombings are not brought to justice, Birmingham will be in for many more dark nights of terror."

On Saturday, May 18, President Kennedy made a long-planned trip to Alabama and Tennessee to participate in ceremonies marking the 30th anniversary of the Tennessee Valley Authority. Before arriving in Alabama, the President spoke on civil rights at a Vanderbilt University convocation in Nashville. "This nation is now engaged in a continuing debate about the rights of a portion of its citizens," he said. "That will go on and those rights will expand until the standard first forged by the nation's founders has been reached—and all Americans enjoy equal opportunity and liberty under law."

Alabama Governor Wallace, who had called Kennedy a "military dictator" for sending troops into the state, had debated most of the week over whether to greet the President on his visit. Wallace finally had agreed to, under urging from some of his associates. There was much speculation about whether the two would attempt during the day to thrash out their differences over Birmingham and other racial matters, including a forthcoming attempt to integrate the University of Alabama.

The meeting between Kennedy and Wallace came at Muscle Shoals, a TVA center in northern Alabama. The two greeted one another cordially when Kennedy stepped from his helicopter. "We're glad to have the President of the United States in Alabama," Wallace said. But, though amicable, the meeting was not noticeably warm. Kennedy and Wallace walked about 100 yards to a chemical engineering building, where the President spoke briefly. He emphasized in his talk the federal government's role in helping Southerners through the TVA. He said the government, in cooperation with the states, had helped farmers of the area "to stay ahead of the bugs, the boll weevils and the mortgage bankers."

Wallace later accompanied Kennedy on a half-hour helicopter flight to the missile center at Huntsville. During the flight, they did get down to a discussion of Birmingham and other racial matters. White House Press Secretary Pierre Salinger called it a "not unfriendly discussion." But other sources said each man had held to his previous position, and that there had been no meeting of the minds. Thus any hopes that the meeting might bring about some sudden solution of Alabama's racial problems were swiftly dashed.

Meanwhile, Birmingham was poised for a crucial Saturday night test of the staying power of its racial truce. All week long, lawmen and leaders of the white and Negro communities had been saying: "If we get past Saturday night without any more violence, we could be in pretty good shape."

The emphasis on getting through this one night was caused by several factors. For one, the bombings and riots had occurred the previous Saturday night. But, more important perhaps, was the fact that recent Southern history had indicated that racial violence was more likely to erupt on Saturday night than any other time during the week. Whites and Negroes alike were off from work, with time on their hands and, in many cases, drinks in their hands. Under cover of darkness, tensions could heighten and violence could explode.

Dr. Martin Luther King recognized the problem. "I think Saturday will be a crucial night," he said. He also complained about the continued presence of state troopers in Birmingham. "I very definitely feel that the troopers are here to harass and intimidate, and not to encourage a solution," King said. "We contend that the presence of the troopers can cause the situation to degenerate into real tensions and bitterness. It's very important that some step be taken to get them out."

There were more than 700 regular and deputized state troopers patrolling the streets Saturday night, along with beefed-up squads of city police. Small groups of unarmed Negroes were guarding churches and the homes of integration leaders.

I spent a good part of the night sitting in Kelly Ingram Park with a group of other reporters. The park was right in the middle of the area torn by rioting the previous Saturday night. We expected that, if any trouble developed, we would be within shouting distance at the park. In addition, the state troopers had their huge communications truck stationed at the park, so we figured we could keep tabs on police activity from there.

What a contrast there was between this night and the previous Saturday night. A week earlier, there had been tumult, violence, flames. Now, there was an air of tranquility in the park. True, no one could forget that tensions still gripped the city. But on the surface at least, all seemed calm.

We joked with the state troopers, some of whom we had first gotten to know during the Freedom Ride riots two years earlier. We lounged on the park benches. And we waited for something to happen. But nothing did.

Claude Sitton, of *The New York Times,* and I took a ride around sections of the city that had been trouble spots in the past. We saw nothing to indicate trouble was brewing. We stopped by a hospital, where a week earlier the doctors and nurses had been hard-pressed to treat victims of the rioting. Now they had on their hands only the usual complement of accident and cutting-scrape victims that any city hospital handles on a Saturday night.

The city remained calm all night. Birmingham had come through this crucial test without further violence. The situation seemed to be brightening.

On Sunday, it seemed even brighter to me after an interview with a close adviser to Albert Boutwell. Boutwell, although described as a moderate on racial issues, had been wary about making any public statements indicating that he would support the desegregation agreement.

But his adviser, who asked that I not identify him, told me that Boutwell was firmly committed to the agreement. He said Boutwell was willing to accept one major concession to Negro leaders that was not even covered in the agreement. This was the proposed dismissal of all outstanding charges against the Negroes arrested during the protest demonstrations. While the city attorney and several judges had primary authority over these cases, Boutwell's approval of the proposal to dismiss the charges was considered significant.

I asked Boutwell's adviser next about the provision in the agreement for desegregating lunch counters. There had been some speculation that, although merchants agreed to integrate the counters, the city might enforce a local ordinance barring such desegregation. The adviser said: "Albert won't let that ordinance be used. He was put in office by the same people who were behind the committee that made the agreement. The whole idea was for him to be the instrument through which the agreement would be carried out."

On Thursday, May 23, the Alabama Supreme Court ruled unanimously that the new administration headed by Boutwell was entitled to sole control of the city government. The old administration, led by Mayor Arthur Hanes and Bull Connor, was put out of office.

When word of the court ruling reached the Gaston Motel, Negroes eating in the dining room burst into whoops of joy. Dr. Martin Luther King said of the decision: "I think we are all very happy that Mr. Connor will no longer have the legal reins in Birmingham, Alabama. He has been an influence for evil for many years, and I think that this is good riddance for the cause of democracy—not only in Birmingham, but everywhere. I think Mr. Boutwell is responsible enough to see the futility of massive resistance to desegregation. I believe firmly that there will be less police brutality."

The Reverend Shuttlesworth said: "The Negro people look to the Boutwell administration for direct progress in the area of race relations. Justice and progress have triumphed. Birmingham's image has already improved."

At a news conference, Boutwell took a position that supported the appraisal given me the previous Sunday by his adviser. He said he would be sympathetic toward the desegregation agreement, and that he had not taken a strong position in favor of the pact earlier because the dual form of government had prevented him from acting with authority. "Our attitude will be sympathetic to the harmonious solution of all the problems with which the people of Birmingham are confronted and the portions [relating to implementation of the desegregation agreement] . . . are an important part of our problems," Boutwell said. "We are now free to enter, clothed with full authority, upon decisive action to provide a progressive government."

The Boutwell administration's assumption of office marked the beginning of a steady improvement in Birmingham's racial climate. Differences between white and Negro leaders over the terms of the desegregation agreement were resolved. The agreement's provisions were carried out. Store facilities were desegregated. Negroes were given jobs previously denied them. A biracial commission was created.

This was not to say that Birmingham's racial problems were over. In September, 1963, white extremists would clash with police during court-ordered desegregation of Birmingham schools. Four Negro girls would be killed in the bombing of a church. But the Birmingham crisis of the spring of 1963 would be remembered as a major turning point in the history of this country's race relations. It marked the beginning of a new fervor that swept over civil rights groups throughout the country.

Negroes all over the South and North were impressed by the victory the civil rights movement had won in Birmingham—so long a symbol of rigid segregation. Inspired by the Birmingham protests, these Negroes carried their movement for equality into the streets of scores of other cities. They picketed, sat down, sat in, filled the jails. And, with increasing frequency, they saw their demands satisfied.

The surge of militancy that spread across the country resulted eventually in the August 28 March on Washington by more than 200,000 Negroes and whites to advance the cause of the civil rights movement. It also led to the fight in Congress for passage of the most meaningful civil rights bill that had been seriously considered in 100 years.

Perhaps all this ultimately might have come about even if there had not been a Birmingham crisis. But, as things worked out, the Birmingham crisis clearly seemed to have been the catalyst that sent the tide of integration activities sweeping across the land.

5 Return to Ole Miss

From Birmingham, I returned to Oxford, Mississippi, to check on James Meredith's progress at Ole Miss.

Meredith was about to complete his first academic year at the university. Much had happened during that period, in the aftermath of the Ole Miss rioting. Of the 300 persons arrested by federal authorities during and after the rioting, criminal complaints were filed against only 18. One of these was against retired Major General Edwin A. Walker.

Walker had been released on bail from the federal prison hospital in Springfield, Missouri, with the understanding that he would consult a psychiatrist. In November, 1962, Federal District Judge Claude F. Clayton conducted hearings in Oxford to determine whether Walker was mentally competent to stand trial for his alleged role in the rioting. At the hearings, Clayton received a report from a Dallas psychiatrist, Dr. R. L. Stubblefield, who had examined Walker. The report said that Walker was "functioning currently at the superior level." It added: "All psychiatric and psychological tests indicate that Mr. Walker appears to be able to deal freely and accurately with his recollections of the incident leading up to his arrest and present charges."

Clayton ruled that Walker was mentally competent to stand trial. But the question soon became moot. A federal grand jury that considered the charges against Walker refused to indict him. It also refused to indict 13 others against whom complaints had been filed. The charges against Walker and the 13 others were dismissed.

The grand jury indicted only four of the 18 against whom charges had been filed. One of the four was Melvin Bruce of Decatur, Georgia, the former chauffeur for American Nazi leader George Lincoln Rockwell. Bruce had been caught on the Ole Miss campus with a rifle plastered with a John Birch Society slogan. The others indicted were Philip Lloyd Miles, Richard Hays Hinton and Kline Lamar May, all of Pritchard, Alabama. None of the four was an Ole Miss student. The indictments charged that the defendants "did knowingly, wilfully, feloniously and forcibly resist, oppose, impede and interfere with deputy U. S. marshals" while the marshals were enforcing court orders.

Meanwhile, a state court grand jury had conducted its own investigation of the Ole Miss rioting. It indicted none of the rioters. Instead, it somehow reached the conclusion that the riot was all the fault of Chief U. S. Marshal Jim McShane. It indicted him on grounds of "inciting" the riot. The indictment charged that McShane had ordered marshals to surround the Ole Miss Lyceum building for "no valid reason" and that this had provoked students because the "Lyceum is symbolic of the university and its most hallowed building." The indictment further said: "Such action was apparently done for the sole purpose of agitating and provoking violence."

It also charged that, when McShane ordered tear gas fired, "the situation did not warrant such drastic action." The indictment stated that state highway patrolmen had the situation in hand until "the gas was fired with no warning in the backs of the patrolmen and university police." It concluded that this "was done for the purpose of inciting a riot" and that "this illegal action on the part of Chief Marshal McShane set off the tragic violence which followed."

Recalling the night of the riot, the indictment against McShane seemed laughable to me. It was not laughable to him. On November 20, the country's chief marshal was forced to travel to Oxford and surrender to a warrant for his arrest. He was released immediately on a writ of habeas corpus issued by Federal Judge Clayton. But he still must face the charges.

If it was any comfort to McShane, he was not the only high official facing court action as a result of the Ole Miss crisis. Mississippi Governor Ross Barnett and Lieutenant Governor Paul Johnson (later to be elected Barnett's successor as governor) both faced criminal contempt of court charges for their defiance of injunctions during the crisis.

The U. S. Fifth Circuit Court of Appeals in New Orleans had directed the Justice Department to file the criminal contempt charges against Barnett and Johnson. The two state officials then demanded a jury trial on the charges. Ordinarily, contempt cases are tried without juries. But, when the Fifth Circuit Court was asked to rule on the jury trial question, its judges split 4–4. The Fifth Circuit Court then asked the Supreme Court to decide on the issue. The Supreme Court heard arguments in October, 1963. At this writing [April, 1964], it has not issued a ruling. For this reason, Barnett and Johnson have not been brought to trial.

Charges and countercharges regarding responsibility for the Ole Miss riot continued to fly months after the riot had taken place. A Mississippi legislative committee, headed by State Representative Russell L. Fox of Pattison, conducted an investigation of the riot. The committee charged in its final report that "the blundering of inexperienced federal personnel, hastily deputized as U. S. marshals, and the total disorganization of the entire federal operation" at Ole Miss incited the riot and permitted it to continue throughout the night.

The committee accused the Kennedy administration of exploiting the Meredith case to foster its own political ambitions. It claimed that federal marshals had fired tear gas into the backs of state highway patrolmen who were trying to push the mob back from the Lyceum building. And it accused the marshals and military units sent to Oxford of committing "hundreds of violations of civil rights of citizens."

In describing the purported civil rights violations, the committee said that between 100 and 150 prisoners taken by the federal forces were placed in a stockade set up in a garage the afternoon following the riot. The committee charged:

Some had been badly beaten, others were ill. All persons, regardless of age or physical condition, were forced to sit on a concrete slab for periods up to 20 hours, with their knees drawn up toward their chins, their hands clasped around their knees, their eyes to the front, without turning their heads or speaking to anyone. This was planned and executed as physical torture. . . . When a prisoner moved his head from a direct front angle or spoke to any other person and was observed by a marshal, he was either clubbed or kicked by the marshals.

If a captive fell asleep or became cramped and moved his hands from around his knees, or changed the position of his legs as he was seated upon the torture slab, and was seen by the marshals, he was struck with a club or kicked, and threatened with further beatings. Some prisoners who fell asleep or changed positions were forced to place their hands above their heads, leaning tiptoe with their faces to the wall; then they were beaten, jabbed in the back and their feet kicked out from under them. Others were jabbed in the kidney or the groin with the marshals' clubs.

The committee did not name any witnesses who had given them evidence to support the charges of alleged civil rights violations.

Immediately after the committee report was issued, it was denounced by the Justice Department. The Department said in a series of prepared statements:

The report of the . . . committee is so far from the truth that it hardly merits an answer. It is strange indeed that none of the so-called brutalities were reported by the several hundred newsmen, including many from Southern newspapers, radio and television stations, who witnessed the riot and its aftermath.

These newsmen were in the Lyceum building throughout the night. They were outside observing the mob. The newsmen were free to go where they wished. And, rather than criticize the marshals, the newsmen praised the marshals' courage and calmness under fire.

About 350 deputy U. S. marshals were on duty around the Lyceum building during the riot. Of these, 180 were injured and of that number 27 were wounded by gunfire. The discipline and training of the marshals was exemplified by the fact that they did not return this fire. . . .

The report of this committee contains no names or facts that could be checked by anyone. The report is an untruthful document. Worse, it is a grievous slander against a courageous group of deputy marshals, more than two-thirds of whom are Southerners. Far from deserving such distortions and falsifications of fact, they deserve the greatest credit for their courage and dedication to their orders and to the laws of the United States. Their conduct, in a time of great danger, was in the highest tradition of American law enforcement.

If right and justice are on the side of the committee, as it claims, then it is shocking to us that facts would be distorted or ignored and incidents manufactured. The fact that the committee did not interview any objective observers who were there, much less the federal officials involved, is an indication of the accuracy and fairness of this report. . . .

The major criticism seems to be the charge that the Attorney General sent the marshals to the University of Mississippi as a political move. This does not make much sense.

What the report fails to point out and what the members of the committee are aware of is that the arrangement to put Mr. Meredith on the campus was made by Governor Barnett. Not only was the presence of the marshals at the University of Mississippi arranged for by Governor Barnett, but the number of marshals also was approved by Governor Barnett. It was Governor Barnett also who said that he and the State of Mississippi would maintain law and order. The marshals went to the university to uphold final federal court orders for Mr. Meredith's immediate admission to the university. The necessity of federal intervention to enforce those orders is not questioned by the report. . . .

It appears to us that this committee might do some self-examination. There is going to be very little possibility for progress and understanding among all of us as a people in this difficult field if responsible local officials put their heads in the sand and manufacture, rather than face, the facts.

As for James Meredith, he had spent one of the most trying academic years ever to confront a college student. A contingent of 15 federal marshals and 100 soldiers had remained in Oxford throughout the year to protect him. Everywhere he went, he was trailed at a close distance by marshals.

A "rebel underground" organized by die-hard students had done everything possible to make life miserable for Meredith and any students or faculty members who befriended him. Vile names were shouted at Meredith constantly. He was hanged in effigy. Small bombs were set off near his dormitory. False rumors that he was flunking out of school were spread around the campus.

One white student who ate a meal with Meredith in a school cafeteria later was subjected to such harassment that he decided to leave Ole Miss. The harassment started with threatening and abusive phone calls. Then a group of students invaded his dormitory room. They broke his record player, strewed dirty laundry around his room and wrote "nigger lover" on a wall with shoe polish.

Through it all, Meredith stuck to his studies and maintained a remarkable degree of composure. His grades, while not spectacular, were good.

When I arrived in Oxford on May 21, 1963, Meredith was in the midst of his final exams for the semester. But he set aside several hours both that day and the following day to talk with me at length. I also accompanied him as he went about his daily routine—walking to classes, taking his clothing to the college laundry, eating at the cafeteria.

It took me only a few minutes to get a taste of the kind of life Meredith had been living. As we left his room in the Baxter Hall dormitory, on the way to the cafeteria for lunch, we passed through a room occupied by the federal marshals. Two marshals walked out the dormitory door right behind us and trailed us at a distance of perhaps 15 yards. We walked past one Army MP, marching sentry duty with an M-1 rifle in hand, and two others parked at the curb in a jeep.

At the curb, Meredith paused to take a look at his sports car. It had been pelted with eggs during the night. As we walked past another dormitory, a student leaned out a window and shouted: "You nigger son of a bitch." I winced. But Meredith, grinning broadly, waved his hand in greeting to the student and shouted back jovially: "Hey, buddy, how you doin'?"

A few moments later, another student poked his head out of a dormitory window and yelled: "Watch out, you black son of a bitch. I'm gonna drop a bottle on your head." I looked up angrily and glared at the student. But Meredith just kept walking, seemingly impassive.

In the two or three minutes more that it took to walk to the cafeteria, Meredith was called a "black bastard" three times and "snowball" twice. Several times, he ignored the name-calling. But, once more, he waved and called to his heckler: "How you doin', buddy?"

This seemed quite a change from the James Meredith I had seen immediately following his enrollment at Ole Miss. Then, he merely stared straight ahead when other students shouted obscenities. Had he learned to accept the harassment, or was his seeming good-naturedness just a façade?

I asked him about his feelings during such episodes. "Hell, I can't be bothered payin' attention to that kind of stuff," he replied. "I can't walk ten yards without someone spittin' on the ground or callin' me a black son of a bitch. Sure, it bothers me—just as much now as ever. But I've got more important things to think about."

At the cafeteria, Meredith was treated courteously by the employes dishing out food. But when we walked to a table and sat down, all the students in that corner of the cafeteria picked up their food and moved to other tables. Several sneered at me for sitting at the table with Meredith and muttered: "Disgusting. Disgusting."

After lunch, we walked by the campus laundry. A woman behind the counter asked us in a surly tone of voice: "You want something?"

Meredith replied politely: "I'd like to pick up my clothes, please."

The woman asked: "What's your name?" It was, of course, an absurd question. Since Meredith was not only the lone Negro student at Ole Miss, but a man whose face had become familiar to millions of persons throughout the country, she surely knew who he was. I wondered what possible purpose she thought the charade would serve. Meredith merely smiled and gave her his name. She brought his clothes and dumped them on the counter with a sneer. It was a petty incident, but one that was illustrative of the day-in, day-out indignities that Meredith was forced to endure.

We went back to his dormitory to talk. He had added a few homey touches to his room since I had interviewed him there shortly after the riot. A stereo phonograph sat against one wall. On the walls were hung a plaque awarded him by the NAACP, another given him by a group in Newark, New Jersey, and a third bearing a map of Mississippi and some Japanese characters (which he had picked up in Japan while in the service).

Meredith offered me an armchair and took a straight-backed chair for himself. He was wearing a print sport shirt and a pair of gray slacks. On someone else, the clothes might have been considered to look casual. But Meredith rarely looks casual. His small stature and his quick-moving mannerisms give him a nervous, catlike appearance. He is a hard person to interview. Answers must be pulled from him. Often he will respond to a question by saying "Heh, heh"—nothing more.

He was wrapped up at the time in a project to establish a scholarship fund for underprivileged Negroes. He had contributed the first $1,000 himself, and hoped to raise $1,000,000 eventually. I asked him why, with all the pressures on him at the time, he had decided to get involved with the scholarship fund. "I've got quite a concern with death," he said. "I've never known anyone to live forever. Everyone's got just so much time on earth. You should always use your time for the best possible purpose."

We talked again about his harassment by other students. "What these other students do doesn't concern me at all," Meredith said. "What does concern me is why they do it. It's the whole system that's wrong. I don't have any idea of trying to change the students' attitude toward me. But I don't think I've ever tried to make any other point than that I want to help change the whole Southern system— social, political and economic."

I brought up the case of Dewey Greene, Jr., another Negro who was seeking admission to Ole Miss, but whose grades at a Negro college had been quite low. I questioned the wisdom of NAACP lawyers fighting a prolonged court battle for the admission of a Negro student who might flunk out of Ole Miss and thereby bolster the argument of segregationists that Negroes were not able to study on the same level with whites.

"Hell, any white boy with his grades could have gotten into Ole Miss," Meredith said. "A Negro should have the same right to get an F as a white. I don't see that it makes any difference, for example, whether I pass or fail. What's important is that I—and other Negroes—have the right to go to the best school in the state."

Meredith said one of his main goals was to open the way for greater progress by the average Negro. "Many attempts have been made to get the superior Negro the right to certain benefits," he said. "This is a dangerous position. There can be only token progress if opportunities are opened only for superior Negroes. But, if opportunities can be opened for average Negroes, the superior Negro will find his place."

Meredith had to do some studying for an exam, so I left him at this point. I returned the next day to continue the interview. I asked him about his relations with other students and members of the faculty. He said several faculty members, notably James Silver and William Strickland, had befriended him. (Silver later was to receive national attention for a speech in which he described Mississippi as a totalitarian society enslaved by "obedience to an official orthodoxy almost identical with the pro-slavery philosophy.") Meredith said he played golf frequently with Strickland.

"Where do you play?" I asked.

He replied with a chirping laugh: "At the university golf course. I doubt if I'd play at the country club. I doubt if they'd take my green fees down there."

As for relations with fellow students, Meredith said: "The most a student has done is be civil and maybe eat with me." He described a number of petty practices indulged in even by students who were not of the name-calling breed. In one classroom, he said, he habitually turned on the light if it were off. Other students, just to be rude, insisted on turning it off. When walking into a school building, he would hold the door open for the student behind him. The other student often would stop and not come in. Or, if another student were holding a door open, he would let it swing shut when he noticed that Meredith was about to enter.

Such incidents were hardly the kind that would cause traumatic shock in Meredith. But they were illustrative again of the everyday nuisances to which he was subjected.

I asked Meredith what he thought of the mass protest techniques being used by Negroes to try to achieve desegregation. He gave an oblique answer: "You know, once I was walking down a street and was going in the right direction. But I walked and walked and walked and never did get where I was going. I was on the wrong street."

I asked whether he agreed with other Negroes that, in the words of the integration anthem, "we shall overcome." He thought a moment, then replied: "Maybe so. But not by singin' about it. They've got to do something else besides sing."

I shook hands with Meredith, wished him luck and left him to his studies.

My next stop was at the headquarters of the army contingent assigned to protect Meredith. The headquarters was in a bivouac area a short distance down a dusty road from the Ole Miss campus. The commanding officer was Colonel William Lynch, a handsome, 30-year army man who had fought on battlefields from Anzio to Inchon. In typical military fashion, Lynch's mission was named USA-FOX (U. S. Armed Forces, Oxford).

In his headquarters tent, Lynch sat behind a desk, with three phones at his elbow. One was labeled "War Room." This was a semi-secured direct phone line to the Pentagon war room. Another was a console-model semi-secured phone with a set of push buttons that could connect Lynch instantly with any U. S. military installation in the world. The third was an ordinary phone.

Lynch described his operation as "the most unusual military command in the history of the United States." It was obvious that Lynch's mission had a number of distinctions about it. This was far from routine military duty. But his characterization still seemed an overstatement. "What makes your mission all that unusual?" I asked.

"I don't know of any precedent anywhere for a unit as

small as ours to be reporting directly to the army chief of staff," he replied. In other words, there were no other officers standing in the chain of command between Lynch and General Earle Wheeler, army chief of staff. If Lynch had a problem, he just picked up the phone and called Wheeler directly.

The bivouac area looked much like any other bivouac area, on a battlefield or an army training base. But, inside the headquarters tent, it was strictly a battlefield operation. Several Signal Corps radiomen were in constant touch with marshals and MPs on the campus, in helicopters above Oxford, at the post office building downtown and at other sites. There were code names for various places and persons. Meredith at first had been called "the package." When marshals escorted him to a campus building, they would talk on the shortwave radio about "delivering the package."

Other students took to monitoring the broadcasts and teasing the federal men about the code. So they changed the code words frequently. Since Meredith was the target of much attention, the code name for him in use during my visit was "magnet." Lynch was called "happy tiger." Chester Smith of Chattanooga, Tennessee, the deputy marshal in charge of the Oxford contingent, was "mate four."

Inside the communications tent was a huge map of the Oxford area. Numerous light bulbs on the map would light up to show the positions of Meredith and various federal units at any given time.

One of Lynch's main jobs had been to try to break down resentment by students, faculty members and townspeople over the army contingent's presence. He had invited student leaders, university personnel, Oxford officials, law enforcement officers and influential citizens to visit the bivouac area. Gradually, the resentment had lessened. "There has been a 180-degree change in relations between the local people and our people in the last few months," Lynch said.

To avoid morale problems and incidents, virtually all military personnel except Lynch were assigned to Oxford for only 30 days and were taken to Memphis on weekends for recreation. They did not fraternize with Ole Miss coeds or Oxford residents. The town and campus were off-limits to those on passes. Otherwise, USAFOX was largely like most military bases—with volley ball and ping-pong tournaments and a mimeographed newspaper called "USAFOX TALE." A major who submitted the name "USAFOX" for the mission won a transistor radio in a contest.

I talked with a number of Ole Miss students and officials and Oxford residents about the presence of the troops. Most were agreed that, although they would have preferred not to have the troops in Oxford, the soldiers had been well-behaved and had made the best of a difficult situation.

I left Oxford the night of May 22. Within a month, I would be back to watch a second Negro student's attempt to enroll at Ole Miss.

6 A Talk with the Attorney General

Ed Guthman, special assistant for public information to Attorney General Kennedy, had suggested while we were in Birmingham that it would be a good idea for me to interview the Attorney General.

Kennedy was going to be in New York on Friday, May 24. Ed arranged for me to interview him in the Kennedy family apartment at 24 Central Park South.

When I rang the doorbell at the appointed time, 9:30 A.M., the Attorney General himself answered the door. He was wearing a pair of blue slacks, a blue shirt, with the sleeves rolled up above the elbows, and a blue tie. He had a glass of fruit juice in his hand. Kennedy invited me into the living room. He asked me to speak softly, because one of his sisters was asleep in an adjoining bedroom.

We started by discussing the Justice Department's general techniques for coping with civil rights problems. Kennedy said the technique of sending members of the department's civil rights division into racial trouble spots to try to bring white and Negro leaders together in negotiations was a new practice that had not been employed by previous administrations.

I asked what had made the department decide to use this method. "The reason we do it is that civil rights is a sensitive area and there is a good deal of misunderstanding, mistrust and ill feeling," Kennedy said. "We would not take legal steps until we had permitted local officials to try to work out a solution to their racial problems. We have never brought suit without going to the local people, explaining our responsibility and giving them time to work something out. If we find a situation is going to get out of hand, we know a lot of Southern mayors and city and state officials, and we communicate with them. If we feel that the timing of protest demonstrations is bad, we communicate that to Negro leaders. We have communication with groups across the South. Frequently, we're the only ones available who'll talk to both sides."

On the timing of protest demonstrations, I mentioned that some observers had thought the Birmingham demonstrations had come at a poor time, since the city administration was about to change hands. The Attorney General nodded his head in agreement. "We stopped Dr. [Martin Luther] King three times from beginning demonstrations in Birmingham by telling him we thought the timing was bad," Kennedy said. "We tried a fourth time and couldn't persuade him. He was adamant. He said the Negroes had been waiting for 200 years and didn't want to wait any more."

In the days immediately preceding my interview with the Attorney General, events had begun to indicate that there would be a showdown the following month between the federal government and Alabama Governor Wallace over desegregation of the University of Alabama. The university had been ordered by a federal judge to admit three Negro students. But Wallace, who had vowed in his election campaign to "stand in the doorway" of any school threatened with integration, announced he intended to do just this at the university.

Now I asked Kennedy what kind of preparations the government was making for the showdown. He said the decision had already been made to send only a handful of marshals to the University of Alabama—in contrast with the hundreds who had been sent to Ole Miss. If additional federal forces were needed, Kennedy said, either federalized National Guard troops or army units would be sent in immediately. He said government officials felt there were not enough deputy marshals—only 600 in the entire country—to handle an Alabama crisis and still be able to attend to normal duties.

Kennedy implied that the government had learned from the Ole Miss riot that troops were more effective than marshals in handling racial mobs—if only for the psychological value gained from their military uniforms.

I asked whether any military units had already been alerted for the Alabama integration attempt. "No, we're still trying to determine what numbers of men would be needed and what the Governor's going to do," the Attorney General said. "He's said he's going to have state troopers surrounding the campus. If he's going to maintain law and order, we might need only a handful of men. If the crowd is large and disorderly, and the state troopers can't or don't maintain order, we'd need more. What made the situation difficult in Oxford was the withdrawal of the state troopers."

I asked about the behind-the-scenes negotiations between Mississippi Governor Ross Barnett, and the President and Attorney General during the Ole Miss crisis. "Barnett was always reasonably agreeable," Kennedy said. "Various agreements were made and ultimately were not brought to fruition. The last day, Barnett was recalcitrant —but then became more agreeable."

At this point, Kennedy's administrative assistant, John Nolan, and Burke Marshall arrived at the apartment. They sat down with us and listened, but took no part in the conversation.

I asked whether Kennedy thought sufficient progress was being made generally in the civil rights field. "We're making progress," he said. "But I don't know whether it's sufficiently rapid. I think the executive branch is doing all that can be done. Further legislation is needed. Unless it is passed, I don't think we can do any more than is now being done. A lot of steps need to be taken in local communities. Over the last two years, we've had considerable effect in trying to get the local people to take action themselves." He said the administration would seek new civil rights measures in education, public accommodations and other fields, but he would not go into detail on what the measures would provide.

What did he see immediately ahead in the civil rights area? "We're going to have a lot of problems in Mississippi and certain other states," Kennedy said. "A lot depends on the actions of business, labor and people like hotel managers, restaurant owners and theater owners."

Kennedy said he had another appointment in a few minutes and would have time for only one more question. I brought up a matter that had been causing some concern among Southern businessmen. If Justice Department officials were going to take active roles in racial negotiations, wasn't there the danger that some business leaders would feel there was an element of government coercion involved? If the business leaders refused to go along with terms suggested by the Justice Department, might they not fear retaliation in the form of investigations in fields over which the Justice Department has authority, such as antitrust and income tax prosecutions? "I don't see much danger of that," Kennedy said. "Somebody's going to have to do it [promote biracial negotiations]. In the long run, I think the effects will be beneficial."

With that, we shook hands and I left.

7 Violence in Jackson

I was back in New York for only ten days before I began another trip to the South. Trouble was brewing in Jackson, Mississippi.

Like many other cities in the North and South, Jackson was caught up in the wave of Negro protest activities touched off by the Birmingham crisis. But in Jackson, unlike some of the other cities, white citizens were resisting the integration movement with force. Day by day, the potential for serious violence was growing.

Jackson, the state capital, had long stood side by side with Birmingham as a hard-nosed bastion of rigid segregation. It was the national headquarters for the white-supremacist Citizens Councils, and many of its leading citizens, including Governor Ross Barnett and Mayor Allen Thompson, were council members. In Jackson, belonging to the council was virtually equivalent to belonging to the country club in another town. It was the "in" thing to do.

For a number of complex reasons, the possibility of reaching a peaceful solution to racial differences seemed far more remote in Jackson than it had in Birmingham. One of the reasons lay in the basic differences between the two cities.

Birmingham is a husky, smoke-belching steel town. Many of its biggest industries have headquarters in the North. During the city's racial crisis, some of the Northern executives of these industries had intervened behind the scenes to help persuade local business leaders to reach a settlement with Negro negotiators. In addition, many of Birmingham's leading citizens and its two daily newspapers, although all favored segregation, had taken responsible action to try to resolve the crisis.

But in Jackson it was a different story. Jackson, although Mississippi's largest city, is like a country town on a large scale. Its residents, unlike those of Birmingham, originally came mostly from rural areas. It is a light-industry town. Most of its businesses are owned by local residents, except for chain stores and plants operated by General Electric Company and American Cyanamid Company. So the businessleaders in Jackson did not have to answer to superiors in Northern home offices. Largely for that reason, there was an almost total absence of responsible leadership in the white community.

The Jackson newspapers, unlike those in Birmingham, seemed determined to avoid even token integration at any price. Almost every day, *Jackson Daily News* editor Jimmy Ward filled his front-page signed column with invective against Negroes. On the day I arrived in Jackson, for example, Ward told his readers: "It is rumored Dick Gregory is coming to Jackson. We understand the comedian has a new act. He'll parade up Capitol Street barefooted. Throw him peanuts and he catches them between his toes."

It was little wonder, in such an atmosphere, that Jackson's white leadership had turned a deaf ear to Negroes' demands for breaking down segregation barriers. The Negro integration campaign was being led by Medgar W. Evers, Mississippi field secretary for the NAACP.

On May 12, the Mississippi State NAACP organization had met in Jackson and drawn up a set of desegregation demands. The demands called for integration of rest rooms, restaurants, lunch rooms, theaters, schools, parks, playgrounds, libraries, and other public facilities; equal employment opportunities for Negroes; elimination of discriminatory business practices; and creation of a biracial committee to help achieve these goals.

The following day, Mayor Thompson rejected the demands. Supported by a group of 75 local business leaders, Thompson refused to deal with Evers and other Negro leaders. "The only thing that can come of such an arrangement is compliance with the demands of racial agitators from outside," Thompson said.

Thompson went on local radio and television the night of May 13 and assured the citizens of Jackson that, despite "terrible trouble in some of our neighboring states . . . we are going to continue our way of doing things." He added: "Although we are going to have turbulent times, when all of the agitation is over . . . Jackson will still be prosperous, people will still be happy and the races will live side by side in peace and harmony."

Thompson's theme was a familiar one in the South. Time and again I had heard it voiced by Southern politicians and businessmen. "Our niggers are happy," they would invariably say. "We've gotten along with one another for years. It's just the outside agitators stirring them up."

It was not total hypocrisy, but rather a measure of head-in-the-sandism, that accounted for such statements. A white politician or businessman would ask his Negro maid or porter his feelings about the desegregation question. The Negro, fearful of losing his job, would say he was perfectly happy. The white man, hearing what he wanted to hear, would let it go at that. What he did not take the trouble to find out was that this same Negro employe often could be found attending integration rallies and singing lustily "We Shall Overcome" after he got off from work.

On May 20, Medgar Evers received equal time from radio and television stations to reply to Thompson. He reviewed the long history of abuses against Negroes in Mississippi. Then he asked the white population: "If you suffered these deprivations, were often called by your first name, 'boy,' 'girl,' 'auntie' and 'uncle,' would you not be discontent?" Evers added:

The NAACP believes that Jackson can change if it wills to do so. If there should be resistance, how much better to have turbulence to effect improvement, rather than turbulence to maintain a stand-pat policy. We believe there are white Mississippians who want to go forward on the race question. Their religion tells them there is something wrong with the old system. Their sense of justice and fair play sends them the same message.

But, whether Jackson and the state choose change or not,

the years of change are upon us. In the racial picture, things will never be as they once were. History has reached a turning point, here and over the world. Here in Jackson, we can recognize the situation and make an honest effort to bring fresh ideas and new methods to bear or we can have what Mayor Thompson called "turbulent times."

As it turned out, "turbulent times" were to prevail.

After several exchanges of recriminations between Thompson and Negro leaders, the Mayor eventually agreed to meet May 27 with a Negro delegation. At the meeting, Thompson promised to appoint Negroes as policemen and school-crossing guards in Negro areas if the policies of "agitators" were rejected by local Negroes. But the Mayor firmly stuck to his earlier rejection of other Negro demands. He said the creation of a biracial committee under "threat of intimidation from pressure groups would result in the city being run by such pressure groups." When the Negroes threatened to take their integration fight into the streets with protest demonstrations, Thompson replied that such demonstrations would likely lead to "more misunderstandings, more ill will and eventually to disorder and possibly violence." On this point, he was to be proved correct.

Angered by Thompson's refusal to negotiate on their major demands, 13 of the 17 Negro leaders walked out of the meeting. Evers said the Mayor had left them no alternative but to begin demonstrations.

The demonstrations began the next day—and so did the "turbulent times" predicted by Thompson.

The trouble started shortly after 11 A.M. Memphis Norman, a 21-year-old Negro student at the predominantly Negro Tougaloo Southern Christian College, entered the F. W. Woolworth store in downtown Jackson with two Negro women students. They went to the lunch counter set aside for whites. A waitress referred them to the counter for Negroes. When they picked up menus and tried to place orders at the white counter, store employes immediately closed the counter.

Norman and his companions refused to leave the counter. Their sit-in remained peaceful for about an hour. Then, as increasing numbers of whites crowded around them and a city detective inside the store made no effort to break up the crowd, violence erupted.

Benny G. Oliver, a 26-year-old former Jackson police-man, knocked Norman from his counter stool and admin-istered a savage beating to the Negro student. As Norman lay sprawled on the floor, Oliver kicked him repeatedly in the face, to the cheers of the white crowd. Only after watching Oliver administer the beating did Detective J. L. Black take any action. He arrested Oliver.

The situation inside the store grew uglier. A contingent of uniformed police sent to the scene remained outside the store, making no effort to disperse the crowd. John R. Sal-ter, a white professor from Tougaloo, joined the sit-in. An unidentified young white tough smashed Salter in the cheek with his fist. Other whites poured salt, pepper, catsup and mustard from the lunch counter over his bruised face. Someone knocked Salter to the floor. With the help of an-other white man, he returned to his stool and continued the sit-in. The demonstration was joined by Walter Wil-liams, another Negro student. He was wrestled to the floor and beaten by a group of white toughs.

A white girl who joined the sit-in, Joan Trunpauer, was seized by a tall, blond white youth, James Glenn Spark-man, Jr. He pushed her to the front door and outside the store. Police arrested Sparkman on a charge of simple as-sault. They also arrested Memphis Norman and two other demonstrators.

By this time the crowd had grown to several hundred persons. It was becoming increasingly surly. Store em-ployes locked the doors and ordered everyone outside.

A short time later, a group of five whites and Negroes tried to begin a protest march with picket signs on Capitol Street, Jackson's main thoroughfare, about a block from the Woolworth store. Police immediately arrested the marchers.

Thus did Jackson's first day of demonstrations end. There had been the feared violence and the anticipated arrests. News pictures of Benny Oliver kicking Memphis Norman in the face, while white toughs shouted encouragement, were transmitted around the world and made the front pages of many leading newspapers. The pictures aroused expressions of disgust from all parts of the United States and from many foreign countries.

Shortly after the demonstrations began, a group of prominent white clergymen prevailed upon Mayor Thompson to meet again with Negro leaders. A meeting was arranged in Thompson's office.

That night about 550 Negroes gathered at an NAACP rally to hear the results of the afternoon meeting. One of the Negro leaders, the Reverend G. R. Haughton, announced that the mayor had agreed to meet several of the integration demands. Thompson, upon hearing of Haughton's announcement, said that he had agreed to only two concessions—the hiring of Negro policemen and of school-crossing guards. And, because of what he termed misrepresentation of his statements, Thompson said that he now would not even honor those concessions.

Medgar Evers, who had called a halt to protest demonstrations as a result of the meeting with Thompson, then announced that the demonstrations would be resumed. "We are not going to accept the Mayor's reneging," Evers said. "There will be further demonstrations. In fact, we are going to intensify them."

It was now midnight. Evers was still at the NAACP headquarters in a Negro Masonic temple. At his neat, green-paneled and brick ranch-style home on Guynes Street, his wife, Myrlie, was waiting up for him. Their three children were asleep. Mrs. Evers heard an automobile pass by the house. Suddenly, there was an ear-piercing boom. A Molotov cocktail had been hurled at the Evers home. Luckily, it fell short of its mark, landing in the carport. The family station wagon was damaged, but nothing caught fire and no one was hurt.

Police shrugged off the bombing as the work of mere pranksters. Perhaps they were right, but future events were to show that a more serious approach to the question of protecting the Evers family might have been in order.

In fairness, this must be said: I had seen the Jackson police in operation two years earlier during the Freedom

Ride crisis and again during the current demonstrations. For the most part, they went about their duties with dispatch and fairness. While many of them may have had strong feelings against Negro demonstrators, they seemed to use a minimum of force in making arrests. True, the arrests they made often appeared unfair and were later deemed illegal by the courts. But the officers were only carrying out orders from the city administration. By comparison with some other city police departments and state law enforcement agencies I had seen in the South, the Jackson department seemed a model of efficiency and impartiality.

Following the bombing, I wrote a profile of Medgar Evers. It was to be tragically prophetic. The profile said, in part:

When Medgar Evers was a young Negro boy in Decatur, Mississippi, a friend of his family was lynched by white terrorists. Although he did not witness the lynching, it left an indelible mark on him. "The man's clothing remained in the field where it occurred," Evers recalls today.

"For a long time, there were still shreds of cloth lying about. I used to see them when I went hunting, and I always remembered." That lynching helped decide Evers' choice of a career. He determined at an early age that he would try to do something to gain equal rights for Negroes. . . . His efforts resulted in an attempt to bring him the same fate as the lynching victim. A Molotov cocktail was hurled at his home, but damaged only a station wagon parked in the driveway and injured no one. It was not the first time violence had been attempted against Evers, and it probably will not be the last. He is taking extra precautions these days, such as calling his wife at intervals and locking doors he previously left open. But he is growing accustomed to living with danger.

In a matter of days, violence would indeed be directed again at Evers. His name would become a national byword. But, for the time being, he remained little known outside his own state and the civil rights movement.

I had first gotten to know Medgar during the Freedom Rides. I had found him an intelligent, articulate, reasonable man. I formed a healthy respect for him. I found that many others, including some of the white segregationists who opposed him vehemently, shared this respect. Although they might disagree with his aims and methods, they admired him as a man.

Medgar had his detractors, even in the Negro community. Percy Greene, the editor of a weekly Negro newspaper in Jackson, considered him "a fanatic and a fool." Greene once had charged that Evers planned to organize Mississippi Negroes into a Mau Mau society similar to the African terrorist group. Medgar denied the charge. "I do not believe in violence either by whites or Negroes," he said. "That is why I am working tirelessly with the NAACP in a peaceful legal struggle for justice." However, the oldest of his three children, ten-year-old Darrel Kenyatta Evers, had been named after the former Mau Mau leader, Jomo Kenyatta.

Medgar would often concede: "At one time, I was really violent." But then he would always add with a smile, "In thought, in thought."

The criticism from Negroes like Greene was generally discounted by those who knew Medgar. They contended that Greene, and some of Medgar's other critics, were "Uncle Toms."

It amused Medgar to hear segregationists, some of them originally from other states, speak of him as an "outside agitator." He was Mississippi-born and -bred, and he planned to spend his life there. He chided Negro and white demonstrators who spoke of staying in Mississippi "as long as I can." Medgar would say instead: "I may be going to heaven or hell, but I'll be going from Jackson. We're going to get Negroes registered and voting, despite the literacy test. With that basic political power, we'll continue working toward economic strength. When my sons are grown, they're going to find Jackson even better than New York City."

Born on July 2, 1925, Medgar went through school in Newton County, Mississippi, then entered the army in 1943. After World War II, he became the first Negro to apply for admission to Ole Miss. He was rejected, of course, but later achieved great satisfaction out of playing a secondary role in James Meredith's successful legal fight to enter the university. Rebuffed in his attempt to enter Ole Miss, Medgar enrolled at the all-Negro Alcorn A&M University in southwest Mississippi. Tall and husky, he played four years of varsity football. (He sometimes expressed amusement at a joke current on the Ole Miss campus during Meredith's time as a student. The football-mad Ole Miss students were fond of saying, "If we had to take a nigger, why couldn't it be Jimmy Brown or Big Daddy Lipscomb?")

His days at Alcorn A&M left him with a sour taste in his mouth on racial matters. "The president of Alcorn, a Negro, had discouraged us from trying to register to vote," Medgar once recalled. "He said we had no contribution to make to the community. I couldn't forget that."

After his college graduation, he went to work as an insurance salesman. He and his brother, Charles, were already members of the NAACP. They spent much of their spare time organizing racial-protest drives. They distributed auto bumper stickers throughout Mississippi to spread the message: "Don't buy gas where you can't use the rest room."

On his own initiative, Medgar began organizing NAACP chapters in various parts of the state. In 1954, he became a paid investigator for the NAACP and later was given the job of Mississippi field secretary.

Medgar had married his college sweetheart, Myrlie Beasley, on December 24, 1951. As soon as he went to work for the NAACP, he and his wife began getting abusive and threatening phone calls. Sometimes, during periods of racial tension, the phone would ring all night long. Often, Mrs. Evers would be left alone with the children at home while Medgar was on the road. And he took to the road virtually every time he learned of a Mississippi Negro being killed, beaten or otherwise deprived of his civil rights. In the Emmett Till and Mack Charles Parker lynching case, as in many others, he disguised himself as a field hand and went into the boondocks to gather evidence and witnesses. It was illustrative of Mississippi justice that, though the killers were known in both cases, lily-white juries and grand juries saw to it that they went unpunished.

Still, Medgar kept trying. On his out-of-town trips, he took extra precautions. Sometimes, he was followed out of small crossroads towns by hostile whites. He formed the habit of leaving such towns at rapid speeds, keeping an eye cocked in his rearview mirror. Once he was forced to flee at speeds up to 100 miles an hour when a group of whites tailed him out of town.

At home, Medgar taught his wife and children to stay away from lighted windows at night. He also trained them to drop to the floor if they heard an unusual noise. His precautions may have seemed slightly paranoid to others, but Medgar had ample reason for his fears. In 1961, for example, he had attended a trial growing out of Jackson's first sit-in demonstrations. During the trial, he had applauded the defendants. A peace officer had lunged at him and beaten him over the head with a revolver.

Now, in 1963, following the attempted bombing of his home, Medgar became obsessed with the possibility of death. He began working 20 hours a day, as if afraid he had only a short time left to accomplish his self-imposed mission. He began discussing death with his wife frequently, saying he did not mind dying if it were necessary, except for the tragedy it would bring his family.

The demonstrations in Jackson continued. They seemed rather ineffectual to me and to other reporters who had covered the crises in Birmingham and other Southern cities. Medgar, for all his talents, was not the kind of semimystical leader that Dr. Martin Luther King was. Medgar was an organizer. He was a fighter. He was a moralist. But he was not the kind of spellbinding orator that King was. He could not take the platform at a mass rally and hold thousands of Negroes in the palm of his hand. Also, he was relatively new to the mass-protest fill-the-jail technique developed by King. The NAACP, unlike King's Southern Christian Leadership Conference and other recently formed Southern protest groups, had long favored the court-of-law technique over the direct-action campaign.

Medgar could adapt fairly quickly to the necessities of a changing period in American race relations. But his followers, too long forced to endure indignities in silence, were slower to change their ways of thinking and behaving.

On some days the demonstrations consisted merely of pitiful little marches on Capitol Street by groups of four or five Negro school children, some as young as seven and eight. The children, wearing NAACP T-shirts provided by Medgar, would walk along the street carrying small American flags. A police officer would quietly halt them. "You can't parade on the street," the officer would say. "You're gonna have to leave. You don't have a permit to parade."

One of the children would pipe up with: "Arrest us, then." The officer would give the children several more chances to disperse. They would refuse. Reluctantly the officer would have them arrested and taken in squad cars to juvenile detention facilities.

This kind of protest, coming as it did so shortly after the mass demonstrations in Birmingham, gave the impression that the Jackson Negro community was not entirely behind Medgar. To some extent, this may have been true. But to a greater extent, it was an indication not of the Negroes' lack of faith in Medgar, but of their reluctance to risk arrest and jeopardize their jobs.

Sporadically, the demonstrations would spark some excitement—an outburst of violence or the arrest of some prominent person. But more often they were on the dull side. There was no clear indication that they were attracting the same kind of steady attention that the Birmingham protests had drawn. Consequently, they were not having the effect that the Birmingham demonstrations had produced.

Not until May 31 was there anything approaching the mass demonstrations of Birmingham. On that night about 600 Negro children, some of grade-school age, were arrested and taken to jail in trucks.

The students, singing freedom songs, and waving American flags and picket signs, had marched through the city toward the downtown shopping area. City policemen, state highway patrolmen and sheriff's deputies, many of them carrying riot guns, had formed a double line and headed off the students. The children refused to disperse. They waited in orderly lines to be arrested. The officers confiscated the students' flags and signs, then herded them into patrol wagons, garbage trucks and canvas-covered trucks for the ride to jail. En route to the jail, the students pounded on the walls of the trucks, continued their singing and shouted integration slogans. "We want freedom, yea! We want freedom, yea!" the children chanted.

Medgar Evers, standing on a street corner watching peace officers march away from the area in military drill fashion, remarked: "It's just like Nazi Germany. Look at those storm troopers."

Later, a Negro church on Farish Street was surrounded by police as junior and senior high school students made arrangements for a march the following day through the city's business district. The students were advised by their leaders to "bring your toothbrushes, because you're going right to jail." Police made no effort to break up the students' rally, but their presence outside was taken as an attempt at intimidation.

The students, however, were not about to be intimidated. Cleveland Donald, a junior at Brinkley High, told the other youngsters: "We'll march to freedom tomorrow. To our parents, we say, 'We wish you'd come along with us. But, if you won't, at least don't try to stop us.' " His statement exemplified the atmosphere in Jackson's Negro community, and the problems this atmosphere posed for Medgar and other civil rights leaders. It was not uncommon in the Deep South for youngsters to lead the way in the protest movement. But, without more cooperation than the civil rights leaders so far had been getting from the Negro adult population, the Jackson demonstrations seemed doomed to failure.

While the youngsters had the necessary spirit, they did not have the necessary buying power to make their protest felt in the cash registers of Jackson's merchants. And it was in the cash registers that the battle likely would be won or lost. It was only because they had been hard-hit by a Negro buying boycott and had feared demonstrations would damage the city's economy still more that Birmingham's merchants had agreed to negotiate with civil rights leaders.

Evers and other Jackson Negro leaders shortly were to take steps to bring the adult population more vigorously into the protest movement. But, for the time being, backing from the adults was conspicuously lacking.

Meanwhile, the movement got a taste of the brand of justice for which Mississippi had become notorious. In Municipal Court, a judge tried five Negro girls and one white girl arrested earlier in the week in sit-in demonstrations. The charge against them: trespassing. They had injured no one. Their offense had been to challenge the legality of segregated eating facilities. The verdict: guilty. The sentence: six months in jail and fines of $500 each.

Later, in the same court, Benny Oliver came to trial for his brutal attack earlier in the week on Memphis Norman. In this case, there had been physical injury. Norman had been kicked in the face repeatedly by Oliver. The verdict: guilty of assault and battery. The sentence: thirty days in jail and a $100 fine. What's more, Oliver came out of the case with a new job. In an example of the kind of racist cynicism that had long tarnished Southern politics, a candidate for lieutenant governor, David L. Perkins, announced that he was appointing Oliver as one of his campaign workers. Oliver, who was free on bail pending an appeal of his conviction, was lauded by Perkins as a man who "knows how to handle the racial problem." Perkins, a chiropractor, said Oliver "has shown without a shadow of doubt that he believes in states' rights, segregation of the races and maintaining the Southern way of life."

I was in the press room of the state capitol when Perkins' announcement was made. I laughed about it, along with some of the veteran Mississippi newsmen in the room. But it somehow didn't seem so funny when one of the Mississippians remarked: "It may seem funny to us, but I'll bet it gets Perkins plenty of votes from the red-necks." We had to agree that he was probably right.

Shortly after the mass arrests downtown, Roy Wilkins, executive secretary of the NAACP, arrived in Jackson, evidently to try to bolster the protest forces. At a press conference, he picked up Medgar Evers' theme that the police were employing Nazi techniques. "This is pure Nazism and Hitlerism," Wilkins said. "The only thing missing, gentlemen, is the ovens."

Someone asked Wilkins if he were willing to risk arrest while in Jackson. "If I weren't prepared to go to jail, I wouldn't be here," Wilkins replied.

This seemed to represent quite a departure for the head man of the NAACP. Few doubted Wilkins' courage, after his many years of fighting for civil liberties. But the NAACP historically, as I have noted earlier, had advocated the test-case approach to laws it considered unconstitutional, rather than the fill-the-jails approach of Dr. Martin Luther King and some other protest leaders. Nobody would have batted an eye if King had made the statement just uttered by Wilkins. Coming from Wilkins, however, it seemed novel. And it led to much speculation among newsmen that the Jackson Negro leaders were getting "desperate" for an attention-drawing device because their demonstrations so far had laid an egg.

The next day Wilkins, true to his word, was arrested with Medgar Evers and a Negro woman, Mrs. Helen Wilcher, while picketing outside the Woolworth store where the violence had erupted earlier in the week. They were charged with an unusual felony offense—conspiring to combine to restrain trade or hinder competition. The offense carried a maximum fine of $10,000, but no jail time, on conviction.

Two hours after the arrests, about 100 Negro children began a march through the Negro district toward the downtown area. Police were unprepared for the march. They chased the children up and down the unpaved streets of the Negro quarter. Finally, the police blocked all exits from the section. At that point, the children submitted willingly to arrest, were put into patrol wagons and driven to temporary jail facilities at the State Fairgrounds. As they were driven away, they could be heard singing happily: "Come on down to the Fairgrounds; we will still be there."

Also arrested during the day was Thelton Henderson, a Negro investigator for the U. S. Justice Department. Henderson had been standing near his car, watching some of the demonstrators. He held a notebook in one hand. A policeman stalked up and demanded: "Open up that notebook."

Henderson replied: "Let me show you my identification."

"Did you hear what I said?" answered the policeman, evidently unaccustomed to having a Negro question his commands.

Henderson pulled out his Justice Department credentials. The officer appeared incredulous at the sight of them. A Negro Justice Department official assigned to Jackson, Mississippi? Impossible. Four other policemen came up, took Henderson into custody and marched him to their superiors. A police captain asked: "You weren't passing out handbills, were you?"

"That's not part of my job," Henderson replied.

The police, with some embarrassment, released him. It was, perhaps, a trifling incident. But it was indicative of the kind of conditioned thinking that prevents so many Southerners—and Northerners, as well—from dealing rationally with racial matters. A Negro is standing on a street corner with a notebook in his hand. *Per se,* he must be considered up to no good. If he does not bow and scrape to a policeman's orders, he must be considered a disturber of the peace and arrested.

Roy Wilkins' direct participation in the Jackson protest seemed to be having some effect. Shortly after Wilkins, Medgar Evers and Mrs. Helen Wilcher had been arrested, Mayor Thompson conferred again with a group of Negro clergymen. He agreed once more to hire Negro policemen and school-crossing guards. And he accepted another Negro demand—to upgrade Negro city employes. Thompson again rejected the demands for creation of a biracial commission, but he agreed to further negotiation on some of the Negro demands. On the demand for school integration, Thompson said the city would abide by court decisions in cases already pending.

The situation seemed to be improving. Evers, Wilkins and Mrs. Wilcher were freed on bail, pending appeal. Evers said that for the time being there would be no more mass demonstrations. Token groups of Negro children, however, continued to appear on downtown streets with flags and picket signs. They invariably were arrested immediately, and hustled off to the Fairgrounds stockade before any crowd could gather.

Students of Southern racial history had already learned that it was foolhardy to assume that possibilities for violence were necessarily decreased by the slackening of demonstrations. Quite the contrary often was true. For the easing of demonstrations might result from partial agreements between white and Negro leaders. These agreements could inflame extremists even more than the demonstrations themselves. In Birmingham, for example, the bombings had come not at the height of the demonstrations, but after demonstrations had been halted with the announcement of the biracial agreement. In Jackson, a similar pattern seemed to be emerging. Threats on Medgar Evers' life increased after he had called off mass demonstrations on Mayor Thompson's agreement to make some concessions to the Negroes.

I talked to Evers about the threats, in his office at the Negro Masonic temple on Lynch Street. "Oh, I'm getting plenty of calls," he said. "They say I'm going to be dead soon, that they're going to blow up my house, that they're going to blow my head off. One man who called was obviously holding a pistol. He spun the cylinder, so I could hear it was a revolver. Then he said, 'This is for you.' I told him, 'Well, whenever my time comes, I'm ready.' And I am. If I die, it will be in a good cause. I'm fighting for America just as much as the soldiers in Vietnam."

That was Monday, June 3. That night, there was a mass rally in the Masonic Temple. Medgar was on the platform, together with Mrs. Ruby Hurley of Atlanta, Georgia, southeast regional secretary for the NAACP. Roy Wilkins had gone back to New York.

The hall was filled with Negroes, most of them students, but also a smattering of adults. Mrs. Hurley was the chief speaker. And she was livid with rage. "I feel sicker tonight than I've felt in a long time," she said. "I've been in and out of most of the trouble spots in the South for the last 12 years, and I can't recall ever feeling this way before. Why? Because nothing makes me feel worse than seeing the time come when children are being sent to do men's work. This shouldn't have to be."

There was some uncomfortable stirring among the adults in the hall. Mrs. Hurley's talk was contrived to make them still more uncomfortable:

You've been behind the Cotton Curtain too long. Emancipation Day is celebrated in June in Mississippi, instead of January 1, when the proclamation took effect. That's because Mississippi didn't get the news until June. And the way Governor Barnett, Mayor Thompson, the Jackson newspapers and others are acting, I wonder whether they still haven't gotten the news.

I can't carry this fight for you. They talk about outsiders. Every Negro in the United States is an outsider. We're outside freedom. I don't think these young people ought to have to go downtown and wind up in the stockade. The time has come for every one of you to stand up and say you want freedom yesterday—not tomorrow. To be satisfied with Negro policemen and crossing guards in 1963 is just like saying you were glad to have the shackles off you in 1863.

Call up your friends and tell them to make up their minds that they want to be free. Stop thinking like colored people. Make up your minds that there's going to be some suffering. For 54 years, the NAACP has been fighting your battles for you. Now it's time for you to fight your own battles.

I had been sitting near the back of the hall with several other newspapermen. Unaware that smoking was prohibited in the hall, I had been puffing constantly on a pipe. A Negro student was sent back by Evers to tell me I'd have to put the pipe away.

Six nights later, there would be another rally in the same hall. Again, Evers would be on the stage with Mrs. Hurley, together with singer Lena Horne. Again, a white man at the back of the hall would be smoking. Again, he would be asked to stop. But, instead, he would get up and leave the hall with two companions.

This incident meant little at the time. But later it was to take on great meaning. Mrs. Hurley would recall Evers handing her a note, asking her to request that the white man and his companions quit smoking. She would recall walking back and making the request. She would recall the men leaving. And she would identify one of the men as Byron De La Beckwith, a fanatic segregationist whose name would forever after be connected with that of Medgar Evers.

Mrs. Hurley was not the only person in Jackson on June 7 to take note of Beckwith. Two white taxi drivers, H. R. Speight and W. S. Swillow, would also recall him well. They would remember waiting near their cabs outside the Trailways bus terminal in Jackson and seeing Beckwith emerge. They would recall Beckwith asking them if they knew where Medgar Evers lived. They would recall replying they did not know, and then watching Beckwith walk back into the terminal to consult a telephone book. They would recall Beckwith asking them where Livingston Drive was, and telling him that could not be Medgar's address since it was in an all-white neighborhood. They would recall watching Beckwith return to the phone book twice more, only to return each time and ask about streets in white neighborhoods. And, most important of all, they would recall Beckwith saying: "I've got to find where he lives in a couple of days."

Now, it was four days later, Tuesday, June 11. The basic situation in the Jackson racial crisis was about the same. Only token demonstrations were taking place. But no further concessions had been made by Mayor Thompson. Tensions were high in both the Negro and white communities. Evers was still in fear of his life. He cautioned me several times to be careful what I said to him on the phone, even when talking over a line with his unlisted number, for he was certain all his phones were tapped.

Before leaving home for work Tuesday morning, Evers kissed each of his children. He held his wife in his arms for a long period before departing. Subsequently, he called home three times during the day to be sure his family was all right. Mrs. Evers kidded him about it, asking how he found time to make the calls. Evers told her he loved her and the children very much. "I'll see you tonight," he said.

Now it was 9 P.M. Martha Jean O'Brien was at her post as

a carhop at Joe's Drive-in restaurant on U. S. 49, just behind the Negro residential area where Evers' home was situated. Another white girl, Barbara Ann Holder, was standing outside the drive-in with a friend.

Both Miss O'Brien and Miss Holder saw a man drive up to the restaurant in a white Valiant automobile with a shortwave radio antenna. They watched the man leave his car, walk into the men's room, then return to the car and park it in a darkened corner of the drive-in parking lot, facing Evers' home. They did not see him emerge from the car. But, when both of them left the drive-in about 11:45 P.M., they noticed that the car was still there. They later recalled varying descriptions of the man. But each description fitted generally that of Byron De La Beckwith. And their recollection of the car fitted Beckwith's auto down to the last detail—the shortwave radio antenna.

Now, it was after midnight. Evers had attended a rally at the New Jerusalem Baptist Church. He dropped off another NAACP official, Gloster Current, before going home. Evers confessed to Current that he was worried. "Everywhere I go, somebody has been following me," he said. "I'm tired. I want to get home to my family." They said good night. But, instead of driving right off, Evers shook Current's hand and held it for a long time before leaving.

It was 12:40 A.M. when Evers wheeled his powder-blue 1962 Olds into the carport. Mrs. Evers had let the children stay up late. They were watching a movie on television. The children heard the car and shouted: "Mama, there's Daddy." They rushed to the door to meet him.

Nearby, a white woman, Mrs. Ann Coley, was walking with a boyfriend of her daughter's, Kenneth Adcock. They were passing by a clump of sweet gum trees and honeysuckle vines.

In that thicket, 150 feet away from Evers' carport, an assassin lay in wait. He propped his .30-.06 Enfield rifle on a steel fence. Peering through a telescopic sight, he could see Evers park his car, then get out. Evers was carrying a batch of NAACP T-shirts to be distributed to children. He had his house keys in his hand.

The assassin had Evers firmly fixed in his telescopic sight. With the technique of a skilled marksman, he squeezed the trigger gently.

Crack!

There was just one shot. The bullet tore into Evers' back. It ripped through his body, came out through the chest and crashed through the kitchen window. It landed on the kitchen table.

Evers staggered from the carport toward the door, trying to get into the house. His wife and children, as he had taught them, hurled themselves to the floor at the sound of the shot. Then, after a moment's pause, they rushed to the door.

"Oh, my God, my God," Myrlie Evers screamed as she jerked the door open. The children were all crying: "Daddy! Daddy!"

Mrs. Evers had sensed immediately that Evers had been hit. She prayed as she opened the door that he was still alive. He was, but just barely. He had sprawled face down on the steps. Blood seemed to be everywhere. Mrs. Evers dropped to her knees, cradled his head in her hands and screamed again and again at the monstrosity of the crime.

The children ran out of the house and bent over their father. "Daddy, get up," they said. "Please get up."

But Evers could not get up. He could barely speak.

The assassin, after firing the shot, had been startled by Mrs. Coley and young Adcock. They had nearly walked right into the line of fire. But they had not seen him. He hid the rifle in the honeysuckle thicket, where he had previously cleared enough space to give him a sniper's nest. Then he started running toward the parking lot of the drive-in, where two witnesses previously had seen a man answering Byron De La Beckwith's description leaving his car. Mrs. Coley and Adcock, although they could not see the assassin, could tell from the sound of his footsteps which way he was running.

On the steps of his home, someone put a blanket over Evers. His next-door neighbor, Houston Wells, had heard the shot. He grabbed his own pistol, fired a warning shot in hopes of scaring off the assassin and then ran outside. He reached Evers shortly after Mrs. Evers did. Another neighbor, Thomas Young, who lived across the street, was awakened by his wife. She also had heard the shot. Young then heard Evers' children screaming. He ran to the carport right behind Wells.

Wells went back into his own home and phoned the police. Wells and Young put Evers on a mattress, loaded him into Wells' station wagon and drove him to the University of Mississippi Medical Center in Jackson. During the ride, Evers mumbled incoherently at times. "Sit me up," he said at one point. "Turn me loose," he moaned at another.

At 1:14 A.M., about 15 minutes after being carried into the hospital, Evers died.

So now, as he had feared, Medgar Evers had been martyred for the cause that had been the consuming passion of his life. Would his death, though, serve the cause for which he frequently had said he would not mind dying? Or would it remain just a senseless, monstrous, unthinkable crime?

It was impossible at the time to say.

But this much was clear: the crime was so ghastly that even white Mississippians who had long resented Evers were thoroughly shocked. Mayor Thompson, on a trip to Florida, flew home immediately after hearing of the slaying. He announced that the city was offering a $5,000 reward for information leading to the slayer.

"Along with all of the citizens of Jackson, the commissioners and I are dreadfully shocked, humiliated and sick at heart that such a terrible tragedy should happen in our city," Thompson said. "We will not stop working night or day until we find the person or persons who are responsible for such a cowardly act, and we urge the cooperation of everyone in this search."

The Jackson newspapers offered an additional $1,000 reward. Jimmy Ward, editor of the *Jackson Daily News*, wrote in his signed column a piece that stood in stark contrast with his usual brand of Negro-baiting:

Despite numerous, most earnest appeals for law and order at

all times and most especially during the recent racial friction in Jackson, some conscienceless individual has stooped to violence and has greatly harmed the good relations that have existed in Jackson. [The reference to "good relations" apparently was another use of the myth of the "happy Negro."] All Mississippians and especially this shocked community are saddened by the dastardly act of inhuman behavior last night.

This expression of shock seemed, to me, curious from a man who had referred to the Congress of Racial Equality as "the Congress of Riot Encouragement" and had described the integration of a bus terminal's rest rooms as coming on "VD Day in Mississippi."

Ward and Thompson were far from alone among ardent segregationists in deploring the slaying. Even Governor Barnett said of the killing: "Apparently, it was a dastardly act and, as governor of the State of Mississippi, I shall cooperate in every way to apprehend the guilty party." (Perhaps significantly, Barnett spoke of "apprehending" the killer—not punishing him. Later, he was to appear gratuitously at the trial of Evers' accused slayer, who was defended by one of Barnett's law partners, and to chat warmly with the defendant in the courtroom.)

2

If white Mississippians were sincerely shocked by the killing, their shock was nothing compared to that of the Negroes. They were more than shocked. They were enraged. Within hours, the streets of Jackson were filled again with demonstrators. At 11:25 A.M., slightly more than ten hours after Evers' death, 13 ministers left the Pearl Street African Methodist Episcopal Church and walked silently toward the City Hall.

Police halted the ministers, who included some of Evers' co-workers in the civil rights movement, and ordered them to disperse. The ministers refused. They were swiftly arrested and loaded into a paddy wagon.

Ninety minutes later, about 200 Negro teen-agers marched out of the Masonic Temple building that had housed Evers' office and headed down Lynch Street toward the downtown area. They carried American flags and wore NAACP T-shirts, one of which bore the crudely lettered slogan: "WHITE MAN, YOU MAY KILL THE BODY BUT NOT THE SOUL."

A block from the temple, the marchers were halted by a contingent of 200 club-swinging policemen, sheriff's officers and state highway patrolmen. The officers, armed with riot guns and automatic rifles, drove the marchers back, then arrested 145 of them. Seventy-four of those arrested were younger than 17. One girl was hit in the face by an officer's club. A middle-aged woman spectator was wrestled to the sidewalk. Others were manhandled.

As the Negroes were hauled away in four large trucks, hundreds of Negroes jeered the policemen from nearby streets and yards. When a platoon of about 75 policemen marched down one street, with a sergeant shouting military cadence, the spectators joined sarcastically in the chant. One Negro boy hurled a rock at the platoon. The officers ignored it.

That night, about 900 persons gathered for a memorial service for Evers. With tears streaming down her face, his widow addressed the gathering:

I am left without the comfort of a husband. I am left with three children to rear, but I am also left with a determination to take up where he left off. I have his strength and I hope by his death that all of us will be able to draw some of his strength, courage and determination to finish this fight. I don't want his death to be in vain. That would be as big a blow as his death. I ask for united action in this effort in memory of my husband and for all mankind.

Mrs. Evers told how Medgar had often spoken to her of death, but had said that "he had rather go this way than to sleep away." She said his fight had been not only for Negroes, but for whites as well. "Sunday, he talked of death and was ready to go," she said. "Nothing can bring Medgar back, but the cause can live on."

Jackson Negroes, already prepared to throw themselves

into the fight with more vigor than they had ever shown when Evers was alive, now had a ringing call to action from his widow. They would answer it.

In the meantime, an intensive hunt was launched for Evers' killer. This was no perfunctory, *pro forma* investigation, like those so typical of Mississippi investigations of previous racial murders. This was an earnest, methodical, professional manhunt.

The Jackson Police Department, as I noted earlier, is quite a cut above the average Southern police department. Its chief of detectives, M. B. Pierce, whom I had first gotten to know and respect during the Freedom Rides, is a capable, genial law enforcement officer. He knows his job; he carries it out with a minimum of fanfare and a maximum of efficiency. And he commands a surprising amount of respect, even among Negroes whom he has ordered arrested for protest activities.

(It perhaps should be noted here that there are many Southern lawmen of Pierce's stripe, who are tagged with a racist brand because they are compelled to carry out the orders of superiors, often politically elected or appointed superiors. In Birmingham, for example, Police Chief Jamie Moore and some of his top assistants were highly respected, and so was the city police force, but the entire force got a bad name because of the antics of Police Commissioner Bull Connor. In Jackson during the Freedom Rides and the 1963 protest demonstrations, hundreds of civil rights advocates were arrested, but there was rarely any police brutality, as there had been in many other Southern cities.)

In addition to local police, FBI agents were sent into the hunt for Evers' killer at the express orders of Attorney General Kennedy. Normally, there is a great rivalry and considerable resentment between FBI agents and local policemen, particularly in the South. This results from the FBI role, first, as the chief investigative arm of the often-despised (by Southerners) federal government and, second, as the investigator of alleged civil rights violations committed by local officers. But in the Evers case there was relatively good cooperation between federal and local officers. The FBI men, realizing that even if they cracked the case they would probably turn their prisoner over to local authorities, traded information with police.

The investigation began with an exhaustive search of the area around Medgar's home.

City Detective John Chamblee placed himself in the spot where Evers had been shot. He looked off in the direction from which the fatal bullet apparently had been fired. His eyes focused on the small clump of sweet gum trees and honeysuckle vines where the assassin had hidden. Chamblee walked across the street toward the thicket.

About 200 feet from Medgar's home, Chamblee noticed a broken limb and some bruised vines. It looked as if someone had cleared a space. He called to another detective, O. M. Luke, to help him search the area. Luke pushed back the honeysuckle vines in numerous places, looking for evidence. His search was rewarded. He pulled back a section of vine and found the .30-.06 Enfield rifle hidden by the assassin.

A police department identification expert, Ralph Hargrove, dusted the rifle and its telescopic sight for fingerprints. He picked up one perfect print—that from a right index finger. This might help in pinning a case on the killer once his identity had been established by other means. But it could not help find the killer. For contrary to the popular notion, investigators cannot take just any fingerprint and trace it to a particular person, even if the person's fingerprints are on file. Only thumbprints are cross indexed in such a way as to make this possible. So in the case of an index fingerprint, for example, experts can use the print to verify a person's apparent guilt, but not to find him in the first place.

The police and FBI did, however, have two major clues —the rifle itself and its telescopic sight. The investigators determined that the rifle had been manufactured by the International Firearms Company of Montreal, Canada. The company's serial-number records showed that the weapon had been sold by mail order for $29.50 on February 2, 1959. The purchaser: Innis Thorner McIntyre, a young farmer and gun collector from Greenwood, Mississippi.

The officers did not have to go looking for McIntyre.

He came to them, the day after Evers' murder. McIntyre had seen a newspaper picture of the murder weapon. It looked familiar to him, so he phoned the Jackson Police Department and talked to Ralph Hargrove, the identification expert who had lifted the perfect fingerprint from the death weapon. McIntyre said he thought the gun might have belonged to him at one time. He asked for more information about the rifle. The next day, Hargrove got in touch with McIntyre and provided the information.

Yes, McIntyre said, that was his old gun, all right. He had traded it in January, 1960, to one of his Greenwood neighbors—and, incidentally, felt that he had gotten the short end of the trade. He suggested officers go see his neighbor. The neighbor: Byron De La Beckwith, the rabid segregationist who had been reported seen at the NAACP rally attended by Evers on June 7; who had requested information from the two Jackson cab drivers on how to find Medgar's home; and who had apparently driven his white Valiant automobile, with its distinctive shortwave radio antenna, into the parking lot of the drive-in near Evers' home on the night of the slaying.

At this point, investigators knew nothing about the events at the rally, nor about the two cab drivers, nor about the automobile parked in the drive-in lot. Beckwith was merely another link in the chain tracing the murder weapon from the Canadian factory to the sweet gum and honeysuckle thicket where it had been hidden.

Under questioning by officers, Beckwith conceded that he had been the owner of a gun such as the one found in the thicket. But he claimed his gun had been stolen from him two days before Evers was killed. A print of Beckwith's right index finger was compared with the one lifted from the murder weapon. Experts said the prints were identical.

Beckwith thought he had an answer to that. Why shouldn't his fingerprint be on his own gun? After all, he had handled it frequently in the period before it was stolen from him. What was wrong with this claim was that fingerprint men said the print found on the murder weapon was less than 12 hours old when the gun was discovered in the thicket.

Now officers had a good suspect in the murder. They needed more evidence, much more, to make a murder case, particularly in trying to convict a white man of the murder of a Negro "agitator" in Mississippi. But they had a start. Basically, they lacked two items if they were to be able to prove a circumstantial case—a motive, and evidence placing Beckwith near the murder scene at the time of the slaying. Beckwith insisted that he had been in Greenwood, a 90-minute drive from Jackson, at the time Evers was shot.

Motivation was not too difficult to provide. All one had to do was to look even superficially into the background of Beckwith and he could come up with a prima facie case that this man was fully capable of committing a crime such as Evers' murder.

Just who was this bizarre little man, Byron De La Beckwith?

"Delay" Beckwith, as acquaintances called him, was one of those self-appointed defenders of the "Southern way of life." He also was an ardent collector of guns and a man who knew how to use them.

Medgar Evers, had he known Beckwith, would have been amused by the fact that this fanatic advocate of the "Southern way of life" was actually an "outsider," compared with Evers. Evers had been born and reared in Mississippi. Beckwith, although part of his family had lived in Mississippi for generations, was actually a native of Colusa, California. His father, who was also a gun fancier, had died when Beckwith was a boy. His mother took him back to her home town of Greenwood, Mississippi. She died when Beckwith was 11, and he was reared by an uncle in Greenwood, William G. Yerger. Beckwith, only an average student, made it through high school but completed only one semester at Mississippi State University.

During World War II, Beckwith served with distinction in the Marine Corps for four years. He was in the first wave of Marines to storm the beach at Tarawa. Japanese machine-gun fire caught him in the leg and chest. But he swam and waded a half-mile to shore. Many times in later years, he would regale listeners with his account of this episode. In January, 1946, Beckwith was discharged from the Marines and returned to Greenwood.

He became a tobacco salesman, a good one, noted for his gift of gab. He also became a joiner of organizations such as the Sons of the American Revolution and fraternal orders. A small man—five feet seven inches and 160 pounds—he apparently felt bigger with a gun in his hand. He collected them by the dozens, trading them frequently with other collectors.

People generally liked Beckwith. He was genial enough, except for one subject. "Mention Negroes and he would fly into a rage," said his onetime employer, Vincent Cascio. Beckwith had many times demonstrated his willingness to take personal charge of efforts to "keep the niggers in their place." When a rumor spread through Greenwood in 1961 that Negroes were planning a "kneel-in" at white churches, Beckwith stood on the steps of an Episcopal church and assured Sunday morning worshipers that he would personally handle things. In a holster beneath his blue suit he bore a loaded pistol. Beckwith did not use his gun on that occasion. He was berated by the church's pastor, and left. But he continued to make clear his determination to use weapons, if necessary, to prevent desegregation.

Beckwith had been a prolific writer of letters to newspapers and organizations that he thought could help fight integration. Some samples:

I believe in segregation, just like I believe in God. I shall oppose any person, place or thing that opposes segregation.

I shall combat the evils of integration and shall bend every effort to rid the U.S.A. of the integrationists. And further when I die I will be buried in a segregated cemetery. When you get to heaven, you will find me in the part that has a sign saying "for white only" and if I go to Hades I'm going to raise hell all over Hades until I get to the white section.

For the next 15 years we here in Mississippi are going to have to do a lot of shooting to protect our wives, children and ourselves from bad niggers.

Beckwith passed out racist pamphlets around Greenwood and other areas where his tobacco-selling took him. He became known as a man obsessed, even by Mississippi standards, about the racial issue. At the Episcopal church, as one fellow parishioner put it, "If you talked about Noah and the ark, he'd want to know if there were any Negroes in the ark." Though Beckwith himself was a native Californian, he cherished mementoes of the Confederacy, such as a letter to his grandmother from Jefferson Davis. It went without saying that Beckwith would·be a member of the local Citizens Council. But he was such an aggressive recruiter for the white-supremacist organization that its officers finally asked him to stop.

After the war, Beckwith had married a Navy WAVE, Mary Louise Williams, a descendant of Rhode Island founding father Roger Williams. The Beckwiths had an erratic married life. They were divorced, reconciled, remarried and then separated again. Their one son, a teen-ager, was living with his mother in 1963. Beckwith was living alone in the ramshackle house left to him by his family. He had given up selling tobacco and was selling fertilizer.

Given Beckwith's background, with its clear indications of erratic, emotional behavior on the racial issue, investigators felt they had the right man in Evers' murder. But they still lacked the evidence that would put Beckwith at the murder scene. While they were pursuing this evidence, Jackson's Negroes were growing impatient. Enraged by Evers' slaying, they were further embittered by the seeming inability of the police and FBI to crack the case immediately. The Negroes had no way of knowing that Beckwith was under suspicion.

There were sporadic demonstrations and outbreaks of violence for several days following the murder. Arrest totals mounted. Police clubs, restrained as long as possible, were loosed on demonstrators when they refused to disperse. Tempers grew shorter and shorter.

On Saturday, June 15, prominent leaders of the civil rights movement descended on Jackson for Evers' funeral. The services were conducted in the steamy Negro Masonic Temple where Evers had made his headquarters. Mrs.

Evers sat in a front row, near the casket, which was draped with an American flag. Next to her sat the children, Darrell Kenyatta, Rena Denise and James Van Dyke.

Shortly before arriving for the service, Mrs. Evers had received a letter of condolence from President Kennedy:

I extend to you and your children my sincerest condolences on the tragic death of your husband. Although comforting thoughts are difficult at a time like this, surely there can be some solace in realization of the justice of the cause for which your husband gave his life. Achievement of the goals he did so much to promote will enable his children and the generations to follow to share fully and equally in the benefits and advantages our nation has to offer. Mrs. Kennedy joins me in tendering her deepest sympathy.

Today, in retrospect, the letter seems to carry a more moving message than it did at the time of Evers' death, for it would be only five months before John F. Kennedy himself would be the victim of an assassin's bullet and his wife would be the recipient of thousands of just such condolence letters.

At Evers' funeral, Dr. Ralph Bunche, Under Secretary of the United Nations, sat on the stage of the Masonic Temple, together with such other prominent Negroes as Dr. Martin Luther King, Roy Wilkins, Representative Charles C. Diggs, Jr., of Michigan and Clarence Mitchell, Washington representative of the NAACP.

Wilkins delivered the eulogy. It was not so much a tribute to Evers as a frontal assault on those Wilkins felt had been responsible—directly and indirectly—for his murder. He accused Southern politicians of being just as much responsible as the man who had actually pulled the trigger. He stated:

Southern white office-holders are not content with mere disenfranchisement of Negroes, but have used unbridled political power to fabricate a maze of laws, customs and economic practices which has imprisoned the Negro.

In far-away Washington, the Southern system has its outpost in the Congress of the United States, and by their deals and maneuvers they helped to put the man behind that deadly rifle on Guynes Street this week. The killer must have felt that he had, if not an immunity, then certainly a protection for whatever he chose to do—no matter how dastardly it might be.

Wilkins went on to accuse the Southern congressional bloc of raising "the familiar and sickening chorus of negations" to Kennedy's proposed civil rights legislation:

With surgery required, they talk of ointments and pills. With speed the essence, they cite their rituals of procedure. Man may die and children may be stunted. Ah, but the seniority system and the filibuster rule must remain inviolate. There appears to be a very real question as to whether the white man, so long an exemplar of bold and venturesome ingenuity in many fields, is not committing spiritual suicide here in the land fashioned as the home of free man.

He described Evers as "the symbol of our victory" and the defeat of white racists. He said:

Medgar was more than just an opponent. In life, he was a constant threat to the system, the system that murdered him, particularly in his great voter registration work. In the manner of his death, he was the victor over that system. The bullet that tore away his life four days ago tore away at the system and helped to signal its end. Oh, they can fiddle and they can throw a few more victims to the lions of repression and persecution, but Rome is burning and a new day is just over yonder.

Again, Wilkins turned his fire on the Southern politicians he considered responsible in part for the murder:

The lurking assassin at midnight June 11—12 pulled the trigger. But in all wars the men who do the shooting are trained and indoctrinated and keyed to action. And I say to you that the Southern political system put that man behind the rifle.

There were 2,800 persons in the Masonic Temple during the funeral service. After the service, most of them, accompanied by thousands of others who could not get inside the temple, began a mile-and-a-half march through the city behind a hearse carrying Evers' body to the Collins Funeral Home.

Mayor Thompson had temporarily lifted a ban on parades to permit the funeral procession. He had even arranged an eight-man police motorcycle escort. About 200 other policemen sealed off the line of march. The parade permit stipulated that the march be a silent one. The rule was obeyed by most of the adults in the procession, which included four block-long groups of marchers, but a group of younger Negroes—many of whom wanted leadership in the Jackson integration movement taken over from the NAACP by more militant action groups—refused to abide by the silence rule. As they crossed Jackson's main thoroughfare, Capitol Street, they began singing "We Shall Overcome."

Later, after each of the four groups of mourners had reached the funeral home, the younger Negroes decided to try to demonstrate in the business district in protest of Evers' murder. They started singing: "Before I'd be a slave, I'd be buried in my grave, and go home to my Lord and be free." At a signal from one of their leaders, about 250 of the youngsters suddenly surged toward Capitol Street. Other Negroes emerged from small stores, restaurants and taverns, and joined the group. Four policemen permitted the demonstrators to cross one intersection. But, as they approached Capitol Street, Deputy Police Chief J. L. Ray and 20 other officers headed them off.

Ray shouted over a bullhorn megaphone: "Your leaders said you wanted to have a private, mournful march. And we agreed under those circumstances." He ordered the group, which had swelled to about 1,000, to disperse. The crowd refused to obey. Ray was a familiar figure to the demonstrators. For several years he had been the police officer assigned to lead the breaking up of racial demonstrations. He had done so, for the most part, with calm dispatch. But just the same, the demonstrators now resented his presence.

"We want the killer!" they chanted. "We want the killer! We want the killer! We want the killer! We want the killer!"

Then: "We want freedom! We want freedom! We want freedom! We want freedom!"

And: "We want equality! We want equality! We want

equality! We want equality! We want equality!"

At the rear of the crowd, demonstrators began stamping their feet in cadence and shouting: "Freedom! Freedom! Freedom!"

Police dogs were brought to the scene, and officers used them to drive the Negroes back. One demonstrator after another was seized and hustled into a waiting paddy wagon. Those remaining grew more and more surly. White and Negro merchants in the area, sensing there might be serious violence, began bolting their doors.

Reinforcements from the Hinds County sheriff's office and the state highway patrol rushed to the area. Mayor Thompson, notified by police of the possibility of violence, asked Governor Barnett to alert units of the Mississippi National Guard. At Barnett's direction, two National Guard MP units were put on alert. In addition, state highway patrolmen from surrounding towns were ordered into Jackson.

The beefed-up contingents of lawmen now swarmed into the crowd in an effort to break the back of the demonstration. Billy clubs were swung fiercely. One deputy sheriff struck a Negro man in the face with a shotgun butt when he did not move quickly enough. A Negro woman was clubbed by another officer, fled to a car, but was dragged out and clubbed again. These tactics succeeded in pressing the remaining demonstrators into a one-block area. There the feared outbreak of violence took place.

The Negroes began throwing bricks, bottles, rocks and other missiles at the officers.

"We want the killer!" they chanted.

"We want freedom! We want equality! We want the killer!"

Some of the officers drew their pistols from their holsters.

"Shoot! Shoot! Shoot!" the demonstrators taunted.

The policemen held their fire. More bricks, rocks and bottles were heaved at them. Most of them fell short of the mark.

At this point an unexpected figure loomed on the scene— John Doar, of the Justice Department. He had been Burke

Marshall's key troubleshooter in racial crises. Tall, slender, soft-spoken, John was known and respected by many integrationists and segregationists alike. During his three years as an assistant attorney general, he had built up a wealth of contacts in both races in the South.

Now, his shirt sleeves rolled up and his jacket behind in the 103-degree heat, John walked through the ranks of the police officers and directly into the barrage of rocks and bottles. He held his arms out in front of him, signaling for the demonstrators to halt their bombardment while he spoke to them. But some of the young demonstrators did not know who John was. For all they knew, he was just another policeman. They continued hurling rocks, but John kept walking toward them. Gradually, perhaps admiring his courage in walking alone into their midst, they held their fire.

"Medgar Evers wouldn't want it this way," John told them. "Rocks and bottles won't solve anything. . . . There are a lot of people in the United States pulling for you. But you can't do it with rocks. . . . Hold hands with me and help us move these people along."

Some of the Negroes were hostile. But others, sensing they were dealing with a man who was genuinely on their side, joined hands with John and some of the other demonstrators and began clearing the area. Slowly, the crowd dispersed. The police, astonished to see one man accomplish what they had been unable to do with several hundred, drifted away along with the demonstrators. All told, they had arrested only 27 of the hundreds of demonstrators who had been attacking them.

It is perhaps unwise to attach great emphasis in a racial crisis to one incident. But, in retrospect, it seems clear that John Doar's act of courage and persuasiveness brought about a turning point in Jackson. From that time on, the situation began to improve. At the request of the President and Attorney General Kennedy, negotiations between Negro and white leaders were reopened.

On Tuesday, June 18, three days after Evers' funeral and the subsequent riot, Mayor Thompson and the Negro leaders hammered out a preliminary agreement to end the racial crisis. As a beginning, the city would hire Negroes as policemen and school-crossing guards and would upgrade Negroes already working in the sanitation department. The Negroes, in return, would bar future demonstrations. And further attempts would be made to win agreement on other demands previously made by the Negroes.

On Wednesday, Evers was laid to rest in Arlington National Cemetery. And so, to all intents and purposes, was Jackson's racial crisis. In death, Evers had been able to accomplish what had seemed impossible in life. To this extent, his murder had satisfied both his desire and that of his widow. His death had not been in vain.

On Thursday, Mayor Thompson swore in Jackson's first Negro policeman, Joe Lewis Land, 27-year-old caddy master at a local golf course. The mayor, smiling and cordial, shook hands all around with Negro leaders at the swearing-in ceremony. In Mississippi, where it is considered a breach of etiquette for a white man to shake hands with a Negro, even this seemed significant.

Only one major piece of business now remained—the solving of Evers' murder and the prosecution of the killer. The FBI and police had methodically been building a case against Byron De La Beckwith. By this time, they had established that the murder weapon had belonged to him; that his fingerprint on the death weapon was less than 12 hours old when the gun was found (seeming to rule out his alibi that the gun was stolen from him two days before the murder); and that he was a fanatic racist who previously had shown little hesitation about using violence to prevent integration. They now set about the task of placing him at or near the murder scene at the time of the slaying.

Piece by piece, the evidence was put together: The cab drivers who remembered Beckwith's attempts to find Evers' address came forward; the two girls who had seen a car identical to Beckwith's in the drive-in near Evers' home on the murder night were questioned; the woman and teen-aged boy who had been walking near Evers' home when the fatal shot was fired told about hearing someone running toward the drive-in lot immediately afterward.

On Saturday, June 22, FBI agents swore out a complaint against Beckwith. It did not charge him with murder, for there was no federal jurisdiction in the murder case itself, but with violations of the 1957 civil rights act. "Beckwith and others unknown conspired to injure, oppress and intimidate Medgar Evers in the free exercise and enjoyment of rights and privileges secured to him by the Constitution," the complaint charged. The "others unknown," if they actually existed, have never been identified.

That night, the FBI made arrangements with a cousin of Beckwith, Greenwood attorney Yerger Moorhead, to meet with Beckwith. At the meeting, they placed him under arrest. Beckwith, handcuffed, was taken to the Jackson police station from Greenwood by five FBI men. There he was fingerprinted. His right index fingerprint again was found to match that on the murder weapon. City detectives questioned Beckwith Saturday night. As he was led to a cell, he appeared supremely confident, joking with photographers as they snapped his picture. Perhaps he had reason to be so confident. This was, after all, still Mississippi. And who really expected a white Anglo-Saxon racist to be convicted in a case involving the murder of one of those "nigger agitators"?

On Sunday, city detectives filed their own charge against Beckwith—for murder. Since this case obviously took precedence over the federal civil rights violation, federal authorities turned Beckwith over to the local court's jurisdiction. The next day, District Attorney William Waller, a lifelong Mississippian and a segregationist, announced that he would seek the death penalty if, and when, Beckwith were indicted and tried on the murder charge.

Now Mississippi justice would be put to the test. First, would a grand jury composed chiefly of white segregationists indict Beckwith? Second, would the district attorney's office present a vigorous prosecution? Third, would there be a fair trial? And fourth, would a jury of Mississippians ever vote to convict a white man of the murder of a Negro, particularly an integration leader?

The first three tests were met. Beckwith was indicted, prosecuted vigorously and given a fair trial.

The trial began on January 27, 1964. Presiding was Circuit Court Judge Leon F. Hendrick, a native Mississippian, considered one of the most erudite judges in the state. Hendrick took great pains during the trial to show equal politeness to Negro and white witnesses, and to pronounce the word "Negro," rather than "nigger" or "nigra."

Waller was the chief prosecutor. Defending Beckwith were Hugh Cunningham of Jackson, a law partner of Governor Barnett, and two Greenwood attorneys, Hardy Lott, former president of the Greenwood Citizens Council, and Lott's partner, Stanny Sanders, a former district attorney. Funds for the defense had been raised by the Greenwood Citizens Council.

The jury panel consisted of 193 whites and seven Negroes. It quickly became clear that neither the prosecution nor the defense particularly wanted a Negro on the jury. It also became clear that the district attorney, even while prosecuting Beckwith for the murder of a Negro, felt it necessary to use a sort of reverse prejudice in picking the jury. He repeatedly cast his questions in such a manner as to suggest that perhaps Evers needed some kind of punishment, but that murder was too severe.

"The deceased, this Medgar Evers, was head of the NAACP," Waller said to one prospective juror after another. "He led demonstrations and did many things repugnant to you and to me. Can you put this out of your mind if you sit on this case?"

To other prospective jurors, he said: "Look back there in the courtroom today. It's only the beginning. Day after day, you may sit here and see this room jammed with nothing but niggers. Would that influence you in your deliberations?"

Or: "Did you hear that the niggers might want Mr. Beckwith acquitted, so they can go North and raise more money? That they could use his acquittal to get that pending civil rights bill passed?"

Or: "Do you hold with the theory that the killing of one man by another is murder? Are you strong enough to stand up to somebody on this jury who might try to change your honest opinion by asking if you'd convict that white man for killing that nigger? Would you hesitate to reach a just verdict just because you felt it would be unpopular with your friends or customers?"

Or: "Assume the worst thing you can about this Evers —and I don't care if it is true or not—admit he has done things that are repulsive to me as to you. But remember this: The law, regardless of who the victim is and who did the killing, says that it is murder when one human kills another. So tell me now if you can put these things out of your mind about Evers and still convict Mr. Beckwith."

For the defense, Stanny Sanders made clear in the questioning of the prospective jurors that Beckwith's counsel would seek to ignore the racial aspects so fundamental in the case. He did not use the word "nigger" at all. He used the word "colored" sparingly.

"Here in Mississippi, we live with our consciences in what we have to do," Sanders told the members of the panel. "The state is required to prove Mr. Beckwith's guilt beyond a reasonable doubt. Don't hold this indictment against him. Grand juries don't try cases. They only hear the evidence —often only one side. The fact that an indictment is returned may have no bearing on a defendant's guilt."

The defense was trying to make just another murder case out of the Beckwith trial. It was not, if the defense attorneys could help it, going to be a trial of Mississippi's conscience. It was going to be just what the docket sheet called it—the State of Mississippi *versus* Byron De La Beckwith.

On January 30, the jury was completed. As expected, it consisted of 12 white men.

Testimony began the next day. Evers' widow was among the first witnesses. She told of the events the night of the slaying—of hearing Medgar's car pull up at their house, the door slam and Medgar get out. "There was this loud blast," she said. "Then there was silence. When we got to the door, I saw my husband lying face down and a trail of blood behind him. He had keys in his hand. That is what I found."

Most of the prosecution's case was predictable. Waller and his assistant, Jack Fox, established that the murder weapon was the same gun traded to Beckwith, the one Beckwith claimed had been stolen. They established that Beckwith's fingerprint was on the gun, and an expert testified that the print was less than 12 hours old when the weapon was found.

They presented the testimony of the cab drivers who said Beckwith had sought their help in trying to find Evers' home. Mrs. Ruby Hurley, the NAACP official from Atlanta, testified that Beckwith had been one of the three white men she had asked to stop smoking at the rally five nights before Evers' murder. The two young women who had been outside Joe's Drive-in the night of the slaying told of seeing the car described as identical to Beckwith's. They gave descriptions of the driver, but said they had not seen him closely enough to identify him for certain. The woman who had been walking with her daughter's boy friend testified, as did the young boy, that they had heard the fatal shot and heard someone running toward the drive-in parking lot.

Other witnesses testified that when he was arrested, Beckwith had a scar over his right eye that could have been made by a telescopic sight in the recoiling of a high powered rifle. There was one ever-so-slight hole in the prosecution's case, but it seemed inconsequential in view of the mass of other evidence.

The prosecutors had shown that Beckwith was the owner of the gun found in the honeysuckle and sweet gum thicket. They had shown his fingerprint was on the gun. They had built a virtually airtight case that this gun was the murder weapon. But they were unable to prove beyond a shadow of a doubt that the bullet that killed Evers was fired by the Beckwith gun—or any other specific gun. For the bullet had been so mutilated as to make such identification impossible.

The law does not provide that every piece of proof must be airtight. It provides that the defendant must be proved guilty beyond a reasonable doubt, a doubt literally based on reason. The doubt created by the failure to prove the bullet had been fired by Beckwith's gun did not seem reasonably sufficient to bring his acquittal. But, for a juror who wanted an excuse to turn Beckwith loose, it could prove very convenient.

On February 5, after the prosecution had completed presenting its case, Beckwith took the stand. After leading his client through the circumstantial evidence presented by the state, defense attorney Lott asked: "Did you shoot Medgar Evers?"

"No, suh," Beckwith replied.

About his gun collection: "I've been collecting firearms all my life. . . . My interest runs to every phase of firearms. Anything that shoots, I like. . . . I trade guns the way you might trade dogs or stamps."

Beckwith conceded that the scar over his right eye had been made by the telescopic sight of the rifle during its recoil. But he said this happened the Sunday before the murder, not the night of the murder. "I shoot every Sunday," he said, referring to target shooting.

Waller took Beckwith over on cross-examination. These exchanges highlighted the cross-examination:

Q.: Mr. Beckwith, I will ask you whether or not, sir, if you have been rather public in your pronouncement of your ideas on segregation and what forces should be used to maintain segregation?

A.: I have been very pronounced in my ideas in regard to racial segregation and constitutional government and states' rights. Yes, suh, very pronounced. In fact, I have written many articles to many newspapers and a lot of them have published the articles. And I don't write under a pen name.

Waller then questioned Beckwith about numerous such articles and the letter to the National Rifle Association, in which Beckwith had written: "For the next 15 years, we here in Mississippi are going to have to do a lot of shooting to protect our wives, children and ourselves from bad niggers."

Q.: After you talk about killing bad niggers, I ask you whether or not you asked for advice on setting up a shooting range at Greenwood where white folks could train to shoot weapons?

A.: Mr. Waller, I've been interested for years in setting up a shooting range for white folks to use, a rifle and pistol range and run an arsenal range along with it as a way to make a living because I am interested in those things and I think the people should know how to use—have arms and use them.

Q.: Mr. Beckwith, let me read you this part of the letter, sir. "I have just finished an article on garfish hunting at' night"—which you underscored—"which is sure to be of interest to the reader along with several ideas I have on shooting at night in the summertime for varmints." Those are your words. . . .

A.: Do you know what a varmint is?

Q.: What is it?

A.: A varmint is game, disagreeable game, game that does no good, for instance a crow or a hawk. Well, a hawk may do some good, but—well, you might even call a squirrel a varmint, but we don't refer to squirrels as varmints, but down in the Natchez area you might call an armadillo a varmint. Or it's—it's wildlife that contributes nothing to the welfare of other animals and it's a—it's a great sport to varmint-hunt.

Q.: Are you talking about—would you say an integration leader is a varmint?

A.: Oh, that's a human being. But we're talking about varmints. I'm talking about crows and things like that. People go on the city dumps and shoot rats with .22 rifles. That's called varmint hunting.

Q.: Mr. Beckwith, could I refresh your memory and give you one title to your book [a book Beckwith was writing about the Evers case] that you have used in your correspondence to various editors and people in reference to your book?

A.: You certainly may, suh.

Q.: Is it "My Ass, Your Goat and the Republic?"

A.: [no reply]

Q.: Is that the title you have used frequently and the only title I have seen in any of your correspondence?

A.: You say that's the only title you have seen?

Q.: Well, other than "Varmint Hunters."

A.: Oh, that's not a title to a book or to anything. That's just a matter of expression.

Q.: That's another subject, but I want to talk about your book now.

A.: That is one of the 10 titles, now, "My Ass, Your Goat and the Republic."

Q.: Would you explain that to us?

A.: It is thus explained, by the left-wing forces riding my donkey. They intend to aggravate the public and continue on with their method of destroying states' rights, constitutional government and racial integrity.

Beckwith was asked where he was at the time of the murder. He claimed he was back in Greenwood, 90 miles from Jackson, and had witnesses to prove it.

Three witnesses took the stand to back Beckwith's alibi. All three were either full-time or auxiliary members of the Greenwood police department, whose members had contributed funds for Beckwith's defense.

The witnesses—Roy Jones, Hollis Cresswell, and James Holly—all told of seeing Beckwith on the night of the murder in Greenwood. They did not provide an alibi for the exact time of the murder, but for periods close enough that Beckwith would not have had time to drive to Jackson.

Why hadn't they come forward earlier? They said the defense attorneys did not want them to talk to "unauthorized persons" and only lawmen were "authorized."

Under cross-examination, Waller established that none of the three men could pinpoint a single day—much less a single hour—when he had ever seen Beckwith, except for the night of the murder. Yet each witness claimed he was able to pinpoint with great accuracy the time and place he had seen Beckwith the night Evers was shot.

The two sides rested their cases. All that remained were final arguments, the judge's charge to the jury and the deliberation.

John Fox, Waller's assistant, led off the arguments for the prosecution. He referred to Beckwith's self-assured, almost arrogant attitude on the witness stand:

Does this man come in and say humbly, "I'm innocent"? Does he have an air of innocence? He sat upon his throne of glory and reveled in it and his attitude was almost beyond comprehension. He is a fanatic, pure and simple.

Waller was even more scathing in his denunciation of Beckwith:

He did not come to Jackson just to kill Medgar Evers. He came to kill evil and get the number one man. He has gotten a real big kick out of being a martyr. Mr. Beckwith has written his true confessions, and he is trying to sell it. What worries me is that two or three months from now I will pick up a *Saturday Evening Post* and read "My True Story." He's already written it.

Without mentioning it, Waller evidently was recalling for the jurors the Emmett Till "wolf whistle" lynching in 1955. In that case, although the killers were known, they were acquitted by a Mississippi jury. A short time later, William Bradford Huie wrote an account for *Look* magazine in which he described the murder in such detail that it was obvious he had gotten his information from the killers themselves. It later developed that Huie had paid the killers several thousand dollars to tell him their story and sign a release assuring him of immunity from libel suits in publishing what amounted to their confessions.

Hardy Lott, arguing for the defense, contended: "The state has failed to put on a single witness who could place Mr. Beckwith in Jackson at the time of the crime."

Stanny Sanders took a more emotional tack. "I do not believe you will return a verdict of guilty against Mr. Beckwith to satisfy the Attorney General of the United States and the liberal national press," he said.

Sanders contended Beckwith's innocence had been established by the three witnesses who provided him an alibi for the night of the murder. He suggested that someone who knew Beckwith's strong views on the racial question might have framed him by stealing his gun and killing Medgar. "Every day all of us in this country say we are dedicated to fighting communism," Sanders said, referring to the evidence that Beckwith frequently had boasted of his fight against integration. "That doesn't mean I am going to take a high-powered rifle and shoot a Communist."

Judge Hendrick then charged the jury. His instructions were for them to return one of four verdicts—guilty as charged, carrying the automatic death penalty; guilty as charged, with a recommendation of life imprisonment; guilty, with no agreement on the punishment, which would also bring a life sentence; or not guilty.

The case went to the jury at 12:30 P.M. on February 6. Beckwith, who had appeared self-assured throughout the trial, had paled and looked somewhat down-in-the-mouth during the prosecution's summation. But now he brightened. For who should enter the courtroom to pay him a personal visit, shake hands and chat animatedly with him but Ross Barnett.

This was the same Ross Barnett who, immediately following Evers' murder, had called it "a dastardly act" and pledged his cooperation in apprehending the killer. It was not the first, nor the last time, that Barnett would show the political traits of a chameleon.

What happened in the jury room is, of course, supposed to be secret. But accounts of the deliberations have been pieced together through interviews with a number of jurors.

On the first ballot, the jury stood 10–2 for turning Beckwith loose. But the two jurors holding out for conviction refused to budge. And, as one ballot followed another, they began winning converts to their side. One of the jurors brought up Jack Fox's jury argument, in which Fox had said that whites as well as Negroes would have to live in fear if a man of Beckwith's stripe were set free. Some of the jurors began to examine their consciences in the light of 1964 thinking—not the Civil War philosophy that had so dominated Mississippi for a century. They decided it was time for a jury to decide that, even in Mississippi, a Negro's life could not be taken with immunity.

By the 17th ballot, the jury stood deadlocked 6–6. The vote was the same after the 20th ballot. There seemed no hope of breaking the impasse. On February 7, after 11 hours of deliberation, the jury reported it was hopelessly deadlocked. A mistrial was declared, and Judge Hendrick said he would later set a date for a new trial.

To Jackson Negroes, the hung jury represented, if not a total victory, at least a partial one. Evers' widow, who was so sure Beckwith would be turned loose that she had prepared a statement to be issued on his acquittal, said of the mistrial: "The fact that they could not agree signifies something."

It seemed clear again that in death Evers had accomplished what he could not accomplish alive. It was a ghastly way to win his point, but those who knew him felt he would have wanted it that way. Since his death, Negroes had made substantial progress in Jackson. Six had been hired as policemen, eight as school-crossing guards. Retail stores had begun hiring Negro clerks and stock boys. Several federal agencies had hired Negroes in jobs previously given only to whites. Negotiations were under way for hiring Negro bus drivers and for removal of segregation signs in public buildings.

Evers' job with the NAACP had been taken over by his brother, Charles. His work was being carried on. Charles Evers saw the death of his brother as a possible turning point in Mississippi race relations.

"When has it ever taken four days to choose a jury to try a white man convicted of killing a Negro?" he asked. "When has the Jackson detective branch made such an exhaustive investigation? When has a district attorney put up such a fight?"

Mrs. Evers was left to deliver what might have been her husband's epitaph: "Maybe people will soon realize that they keep themselves down when they keep others down. That you can't be free if others can't be free."

8 Ole Miss Once More

1

While I was covering the Jackson racial strife in June, 1963, the possibility of a new crisis developed at the University of Mississippi.

The new problem had been building slowly for months. It revolved around the attempt of a second Negro to enroll at Ole Miss. The Negro, Cleve McDowell, had been a fellow student of James Meredith at Jackson State College and had been encouraged by Meredith's admission to Ole Miss. After his graduation from Jackson State, where he was an excellent student, McDowell had applied for admission to the Ole Miss Law School.

The case had followed closely the pattern in the Meredith case. McDowell had been denied admission and, using the same NAACP attorneys who represented Meredith, had fought this denial through the courts. On May 28, 1963, Federal District Judge Sidney Mize had ordered the university to admit McDowell to the law school for the summer term beginning June 5.

Governor Ross Barnett, in trying to block McDowell's admission through the courts, unsuccessfully attempted to file an affidavit predicting new bloodshed if Ole Miss were compelled to accept the second Negro student. "I am convinced that [McDowell's enrollment] may well lead to discord, disorder, strife and bloodshed," Barnett said in the affidavit. But Mize refused to accept the affidavit, and rejected all pleas by the state that he lift an injunction ordering McDowell's enrollment.

Barnett had given no hint whether he might try to block McDowell physically from entering the Ole Miss campus, as he and Lieutenant Governor Johnson had done several times in Meredith's case. The federal government, while alert to all possibilities, expected no major crisis such as the one that had been precipitated by Meredith's enrollment.

There was no need for the kind of drastic military preparations made the previous September. The 300 Army MPs assigned to protect Meredith were still stationed at Oxford, where Meredith was attending summer school. So were the 16 deputy U. S. marshals assigned to guard Meredith. The only special arrangements being made by the government for McDowell's enrollment involved sending Jack Cameron, first assistant to Chief Marshal James McShane, to Oxford with four other hand-picked marshals and John Doar. (Because the state court indictment against him was still pending, McShane himself had decided to stay in Washington and leave matters in the care of Cameron, who had been second-in-command during the Ole Miss riots.)

On Tuesday, June 4, the day before McDowell's scheduled admission, I covered the racial demonstration in Jackson during the morning. About noon, I went to Barnett's office in the State Capitol, where his secretary had promised to get me an interview with the Governor for this book.

When I arrived at Barnett's office, I was told he was in an important conference and there was no telling when he would be able to see me. But I was invited to wait in his outer office. Various aides to the Governor tried to make me feel at home, even if I was a Yankee newspaperman. They plied me with various pieces of segregationist literature that tried to explain away Barnett's role in the Ole Miss riots and somehow place all the blame on the Kennedys and the communists (if, indeed, the two were not synonymous in the eyes of the authors of the literature).

After about a half-hour, Bill Simmons walked into the office. Simmons was the head man in the Citizens Councils, and Barnett's chief strategist and speech-writer on racial matters. Simmons and I had known one another since the Freedom Rides two years earlier. He had been most gracious to me during the Freedom Rides, taking me to lunch at his private club and spending a long period, at a time when he was quite busy, explaining the Citizens Councils' policies.

Although I disagreed wholeheartedly with his racist views, I liked Simmons personally and respected his intelligence. He was no red-neck backwoods politician. He was an erudite, soft-spoken man who, although he held strong views, respected the rights of others to disagree with him. He was, if you will, the Madison Avenue racist personified.

Ken Toler, Jackson correspondent for the *Memphis Commercial Appeal*, had picked up a rumor earlier in the day that Barnett might be considering making an appearance at Ole Miss the following day. Toler had mentioned it to me and to several other reporters. We were trying to check it out, but were having no success. The consensus seemed to be that Barnett, already facing one contempt-of-court charge, would not be so foolhardy as to make another attempt to defy a court order. But nobody could be sure.

After exchanging amenities with Simmons, I put the question to him bluntly: "Bill, is the Governor going up to the university tomorrow?"

Simmons smiled, seemingly surprised that word of this possibility had leaked out. "That's what we're going to try to decide in there right now," Simmons said. He told me the Governor was waiting and that he had no idea how long the meeting would last.

Within a short period, several other influential advisers to Barnett, including legislative leaders who had been at Ole Miss during the previous crisis, appeared at the office. The meeting clearly was taking shape as a major strategy session.

Although I knew some of the Mississippi politicians involved, I figured it would be wise to get one of the permanent Jackson correspondents to help identify those entering the Governor's office. I called Claude Sitton, *The New York Times'* chief Southern correspondent, who had done me numerous favors in the past, and told him what was happening. Claude arranged for Bill Minor, Jackson correspondent for the *New Orleans Times-Picayune*, to meet me at Barnett's office. Minor, who also worked part-time for *The New York Times* and did occasional stories for

Newsday, has a broad knowledge of Mississippi politics and invaluable contacts among key politicians.

When he arrived, he shortly sized up the situation, recognized several of the politicians inside Barnett's office who were unknown to me and agreed with my assessment that a new crisis appeared to be building. "They're all in there," he said. "All the segs [segregationists] who were involved the last time. Here we go again."

While Minor held the fort in Barnett's office, I slipped out to a phone booth to call Ed Guthman, the Attorney General's special information assistant. I owed Ed a favor or two. And besides tipping him off about what was brewing, I wanted to know whether the Justice Department had any information to indicate there might be trouble the next day. Also, since I planned to leave that night for Oxford, I wanted to make arrangements to get last-minute information from Ed in Washington about the department's plans for the following day.

When I told Ed what was happening, his immediate reaction was the same as Minor's: "Oh, boy, here we go again." He said I was the first one to give the department any information about the meeting in Barnett's office, and that he would try to get some confirmation from confidential sources in Jackson. He asked me to call him back in a little while to keep him posted on whatever I could learn around the state capitol. Just before I hung up, Ed said: "Be sure to call from a pay phone, Mike. Don't use any of those other phones."

He did not have to explain; the implication was clear. Eavesdropping on one of the lines going through the state capitol switchboard would be a simple matter for someone who suspected I was talking with the Justice Department. Moreover, it had been learned in previous racial difficulties that private lines, even those not going through switchboards, sometimes were tapped, presumably by individual segregationists in most cases but by official state and local agencies in others.

Barnett's conference with the segregationist leaders seemed to go on interminably. One man would leave, only to be replaced by another and another. It amazed me that none of the reporters besides Minor and me seemed aware of the procession into and out of Barnett's office. The list read like a who's who of Mississippi segregationists.

Minor left Barnett's office after awhile to attend to other matters. I sat for several hours on an overstuffed couch in the outer office, waiting to see Barnett. Also waiting for him, to get him to sign some certificates naming political cronies honorary Mississippi colonels, was a genial legislative candidate named W. E. (Bill) Gupton.

Gupton was a business representative of a number of small newspapers. We turned out to have several mutual acquaintances on papers in Texas, where I had previously worked. To while away the time, Gupton and I batted back and forth the racial question and the matter of who was to blame for the Ole Miss riots.

A piece of campaign literature he had handed me earlier made clear his stand on racial matters. It said: "I, Bill Gupton, pledge my time and energies to promote good government and service to the people of Jackson, Hinds County and Mississippi. I stand for . . . local self-government . . . state rights and segregation. . . . [I am] active in Jackson Citizens Council. . . ."

We were able to discuss the question in a cordial manner, even if our differences were marked. On the question of who was to blame for the Ole Miss riots, I was intrigued by the amount of misinformation he had been fed. He made many of the arguments against the federal marshals and the Justice Department that had been included in the state legislative committee's highly inaccurate report on the riots. But some of his arguments went far beyond the committee's report to detail absurd allegations against the federal men.

If an intelligent man like Gupton could be so easily hoodwinked, I shuddered to think of what some of Mississippi's less bright citizens might have been mesmerized into thinking. Of course, there had been, as I have discussed earlier, an element of mass self-hypnosis involved, in which Mississippians by the thousands talked themselves into believing what they wanted to believe.

Finally the meeting in Barnett's office broke up. Gupton got his honorary colonels' certificates signed. And Barnett suddenly appeared in the outer office. We had met during the Freedom Rides, but he obviously did not remember me. I introduced myself again, told him about the book I was writing and asked if I could talk with him for a few minutes. He cordially invited me inside his office, and sat down behind a modest-sized desk.

We talked generally about race relations at first, with Barnett giving the expected assurances that Mississippi's Negroes were genuinely happy with their lot. When I tried to question him about the Ole Miss riots, he begged off on the ground that his contempt case was still to be tried. We did discuss briefly, however, his deal with President Kennedy and the Attorney General, on which he had later reneged. Barnett tried to deny there had been any such deal, finally conceding that he had numerous phone conversations with the President and Attorney General. He said that most of these phone calls had been placed from the Washington end, not his end, as though that explained it all away.

Finally I asked: "Governor, are you going up to the university tomorrow?"

Barnett looked coldly at me and replied: "It's a beautiful day we're having, isn't it?"

We fenced for a few minutes. Then I asked the question again. "Let me tell you about all the industry we're attracting to Mississippi," Barnett said. And he proceeded to do just that.

Again and again, I returned to the same question—Would Barnett go to Old Miss to try to block McDowell's enrollment? It was like pulling teeth. But, in dribs and drabs, the governor conceded that Simmons and the other segregationist leaders had been advising him to do just that and that he was giving serious consideration to appearing at Ole Miss the next day.

"Why won't you come right out and say what you plan to do?" I asked.

"I don't want to make my plans known in advance," he replied. "If I said I planned to go up to the university, another crowd might collect. I don't want that."

"What about the possibility of sending emissaries in your place, the way you did last September 30?"

"What's the sense of sending someone else? If I'm going

to do that, I might as well go up there myself." He seemed to be saying that sending such emissaries might be construed by the courts as new evidence of contempt, just as much as if he made a personal appearance at the university.

We talked for about ten minutes more about racial matters in general. I found most of what Barnett said extremely boring. It sounded like a broken record I had heard many times before in Mississippi and other Southern states. It reminded me of an hour-long press conference I had covered during the Freedom Rides, in which everything Barnett said was so predictable that I had not taken a single note. Then, as during this later interview, Barnett sounded like a caricature of a Southern politician.

"Ninety-five percent of the Negroes in Mississippi are opposed to do-gooders and agitators coming in here from outside with their sit-ins and their Freedom Rides," Barnett said. "They say they're opposed to the agitation, because the white folks are good to the Nigras in Mississippi." There it was again—the myth of the "happy nigger," although Barnett alternated between calling them "Negroes" and "Nigras."

I asked whether Barnett felt there would be a time during our generation when Mississippians would accept desegregation. "No, I don't believe so," he replied. "I hope it won't happen. We here in Mississippi believe in the integrity of the races. Every civilization that has been integrated has been ruined. We don't want that."

And so on. And so on. And so on.

Barnett invited me, as I was about to leave, to come back to see him and talk about all the fine industry he was bringing to the state. I assured him it would be a pleasure, but first I had to get up to Oxford to see what happened when Cleve McDowell tried to enroll the next day. "Maybe I'll see you up there," I said.

Barnett did not reply. He still was keeping his own counsel about whether he planned to appear at the university to try to block McDowell's admission.

When I left Barnett's office, I went to a pay phone and again called Ed Guthman at the Justice Department. Ed is sometimes a hard man to reach on the phone. But this time his secretary was waiting for my call. "He's in with the Attorney General," she said. "But he told me to have your call switched in to the Attorney General's office. Ed's anxious to talk to you."

I ribbed the secretary, whom I had gotten to know during several visits to Washington. "It's amazing how easy it is for me to reach Ed when I have some information for him—and how hard it can be when I want some information from him," I said. She laughed, then switched the call into Kennedy's office.

Ed came on the line. "It looks like your information is correct, Mike," he said. "We're getting the same information now from our own sources down there."

"Just what is it they're saying, Ed?"

"About what you had—that the segs are pressing Barnett to go up to Ole Miss and that it looks like Barnett is going."

I told Ed what Barnett had told me—that he was seriously considering making an appearance at the university and saw no sense in sending someone in his place. Ed said that was the firmest indication the Justice Department had received on Barnett's intentions.

"What are you going to do about it, Ed?"

"Just what we originally planned, for the time being. We've got those troops already on the campus. John Doar will be there tomorrow. Jack Cameron will be there. We're sending a few more marshals—but just the number we orginally planned. We'll just have to see what Barnett does, and play it by ear from there."

"What can I say about the department's position right now?"

"You can say that the department expressed serious concern about persistent reports that state officials might be considering further acts in defiance of court orders."

I arranged to check later with Ed, before driving from Jackson to Oxford. I went back to the Sun and Sand Motel, where many of the out-of-state newsmen were staying, and found that most of them had no inkling of the meeting in Barnett's office or the possibility that the Governor might make an appearance at Ole Miss the following day.

Claude Sitton, as usual digging up information from

longtime sources in the South, fitted together a few of the bits and pieces on just who had taken the lead in suggesting that Barnett show up at Oxford. It seemed that Fred Beard, the TV executive who had been among those pressuring Barnett to defy the federal government during the previous Ole Miss crisis, had again been the leader in the new attempt to persuade the Governor to try to prevent McDowell's enrollment. Among the others were Bill Simmons and John Satterfield, Barnett's chief legal adviser and a former president of the American Bar Association.

At the motel, Dick Valeriani of NBC gave me an interesting tip. One of Barnett's closest advisers, he said, was predicting a holocaust at Ole Miss the next day if the federals insisted on going through with the plans for McDowell's admission. Dick wouldn't say who gave him the information or which one of Barnett's advisers was making the prediction, but it was a relatively simple matter to check out the logical segregationist advisers to Barnett and find the man. Within a short time, I had him on the phone. He repeated his prediction: "A holocaust is in the making." He said he did not know yet what Barnett planned to do the next day. But clearly, he said, a new crisis was building.

So now I had it from Barnett, from one of his key advisers and from the Justice Department that there was the possibility of the Governor's appearing at Ole Miss the next day, with all the attendant problems such an appearance could create. I wrote a story saying that a new crisis was looming and that Barnett was giving strong indications that he would go to Oxford to try to bar McDowell.

I recounted some of the possibilities—what Barnett might do if he appeared at Ole Miss, how the federal government might respond, and the chances of new violence. Then I added: "There was also speculation that Barnett might be stringing along the segregationists, holding out the hope that he would appear at Ole Miss, only to tell them at the last minute that he had decided against it. This strategy would serve the purpose of preventing the segregationists from coming to Oxford on their own to try to block McDowell's enrollment in Barnett's absence."

I filed my story at the Western Union office in Jackson

about 8 P.M. Then I headed for Oxford in my rented car with John Mashek, a Washington correspondent for the *Dallas Morning News*. John and I had met for the first time in the Birmingham airport, on our way to Jackson. By coincidence, I had been on the same plane from New York to Birmingham as the Reverend A. D. King, Dr. Martin Luther King's brother. At Birmingham, where I had to change to another plane for the flight to Jackson, I had stood in the terminal for several minutes with King, discussing what progress had been made in Birmingham since I had last seen him. When we parted, we shook hands. As I have previously discussed, it is uncommon for whites and Negroes to shake hands in the South. This was some kind of tip-off to Mashek, who also was changing planes in Birmingham en route to Jackson. He walked up to me blithely and asked: "Say, are you a newspaperman?" I confessed that I was. We introduced ourselves and sat together on the flight to Jackson.

It developed that John and I had a number of mutual friends both in Texas and in Washington. Since John was on his first Southern racial assignment, I gave him a fill-in on some of the people and problems we were likely to encounter—first in Jackson and later at Ole Miss. It had not been very long ago that I had been new to the Southern racial beat and had relied on such old hands as Claude Sitton and Joe Cumming *(Newsweek)* for such information.

Mashek and I spent a good part of the next two weeks together, sharing information, driving chores and (during one hotel-room shortage) a double bed. Now, as we headed north on U. S. 55 from Jackson toward Oxford, John took over the driving and I tried to catch a catnap. The roads were only lightly traveled, and John had a heavy foot on the accelerator.

Suddenly a siren sounded behind us and a state highway patrol car with its red light flashing came roaring up to cut us off. I had visions of John spending the day of Cleve McDowell's attempted enrollment in jail, waiting to be sprung on bond. In a number of Southern states out-of-town drivers are held under bail even for traffic violations until they can be tried. But the highway patrolman, after pulling us to the side of the road, proved quite cordial and understanding.

We explained who we were and where we were going. I casually dropped into the conversation the name of Colonel T. B. Birdsong, the head of the highway patrol. Mashek explained that we had gone a long stretch without seeing a speed-limit sign, and said he did not know the limit. The patrolman let us go with a warning to take it easy, both on the highways and at Ole Miss.

It was after 11 when we rolled into Oxford. By then, I felt like a part-time resident. Before going to the Ole Miss Motel, where I had reserved a room, we drove by Baxter Hall, the dormitory where James Meredith roomed. Meredith was out of town during the period between semesters, but the marshals and GIs were still very much in evidence. At Baxter Hall, we ran into John Martin, an attorney with the Justice Department. He needed a lift to the Ole Miss Motel, so we drove him there. Martin said everything seemed calm, at least on the surface. A tour of the campus and Oxford confirmed this assessment. Only a small complement of highway patrolmen was in the area.

There were a number of reasons that Oxford should be more calm now than it had been the previous September. For one, the horror of the September riot had sobered some Mississippians. For another, this was a summer school period, when smaller numbers of students were on campus. For another, Ross Barnett had not been acting nearly so belligerent, at least on the surface. For yet another, McDowell was applying for admission to the law school, whose students presumably were more mature and better able to accept his enrollment than undergraduates. Perhaps most important, there was not the same intensity of animosity toward McDowell that there had been toward Meredith. This was due in part to the fact that Meredith had paved the way. It was also due in part to the personality differences between Meredith and McDowell, and their stated reasons for wanting to attend Ole Miss.

McDowell was shy, where Meredith was outgoing and outspoken. McDowell was not nearly so vocal on racial questions as Meredith. McDowell shunned interviews; Meredith seemed to welcome them. McDowell said his main purpose was to get a law degree. Meredith made it clear that his degree was of secondary importance to asserting his right to attend the previously segregated university. But there were some similarities between the two. Like Meredith, McDowell was a native Mississippian. Like Meredith, he had grown up on a farm and worked long hours in the fields.

McDowell was eight years younger than Meredith. He was born on August 6, 1941, the sixth of ten children of Fudge McDowell, a tenant farmer at Drew, in the flat delta land 125 miles north of Jackson. A slender six-footer, McDowell had played basketball and football at Hunter High School and had been offered several athletic scholarships at Negro colleges outside Mississippi. But he decided instead on Jackson State because he considered it a better school than the others. He earned a several small academic scholarships that enabled him to enroll at Jackson State, and he took a campus job to pay living expenses.

In college, he gave up athletics when he found they interfered with his studies. At Jackson State, McDowell compiled a B-plus average, majoring in history and political science. He developed a minor complaint about one of the subjects. "Maybe I'm hostile, maybe I'm prejudiced," he said. "But I think we should let the Civil War die away. Of course, it has to be studied, but in a different perspective—as history. This continual reliving of the war doesn't help anyone."

Cleve was the only McDowell child to get a college education. Three younger sisters and a younger brother still were working the family farm. His older brothers and sisters had other jobs in the Drew area. As the family's only college graduate, McDowell felt an obligation to carry his studies to their logical conclusion—a law degree.

While not nearly so eloquent or outspoken as Meredith on racial matters, McDowell had firm opinions. "If you think along the line: 'I've been oppressed,' then that begins taking over your mind and you're as guilty of having a narrow outlook as the people on the other side," McDowell once said. An admirer of James Baldwin's essays on the Negro, McDowell could not accept some of Baldwin's more angry conclusions. "But I guess if Baldwin is saying that the Negro is just not going to wait any longer, that's what most Negroes believe," McDowell said. During the period when he was awaiting admission to the Ole Miss Law School, McDowell lived quietly in a small Negro hotel in Jackson, trying to avoid publicity.

2

At Oxford, John Mashek and I shared a double bed in the Ole Miss Motel because Mashek could not get a room or even a cot for himself. The motel was occupied chiefly by federal marshals and Justice Department lawyers. But also staying there were the attorneys for the alleged Ole Miss rioters, whose trials were about to start in federal district court at Oxford's post office building.

Wednesday, June 5, dawned clear and bright. I was up at 7 to start checking the atmosphere around Oxford and the campus. All still seemed calm. In the driveway of the motel, I encountered John Doar. "How's it look, John?" I asked.

"All quiet, so far."

"Heard anything about whether Barnett's coming?"

"Not a word."

On the campus, newsmen began gathering about 9 at the Lyceum. It was like old home week again for those of us on the racial beat. Claude Sitton was there, of course, as were Karl Fleming of *Newsweek,* Bill Street of the *Memphis Commercial Appeal,* Dudley Morris of *Time* and Paul Hope of the *Washington Star,* among others.

Press arrangements were being handled in a vastly different manner this time than they had been in September. Pat Smith, the head man in the Ole Miss News Bureau, had studied the pool coverage system used at Clemson College during Harvey Gantt's enrollment and had adopted it almost identically. The "Joe Sherman" plan used at Clemson (named for the college publicity director) had been bitterly assailed by the national correspondents because it gave a decided advantage to the South Carolina press in selection of the pool. The pool plan now being used by

Pat Smith at Ole Miss was equally unsatisfactory to us, for it gave us only a small percentage of the membership in the "pool."

At Clemson, and every other major racial-story place I had been at which a pool was used, I had been lucky enough to be chosen for the pool. I had tried diligently to get the information all my colleagues would need, and had made myself available for as long as they needed me after the event to fill them in.

But at best a pool arrangement is a poor substitute for having all the reporters cover the event on an equal basis. At Clemson, at least, Sherman had formulated a strict set of ground rules for the press, which were printed and distributed to correspondents well in advance of the Gantt registration. At Ole Miss, Pat Smith orally set down the ground rules at a noisy meeting in which some of us could not hear what was being said and others who planned to cover McDowell's registration were not even present.

Later, there would be confusion about the rules. As it developed, the entire national newspaper press—that is, newspapermen from outside Mississippi, excluding wire-service reporters—got one place in the Ole Miss pool. We drew lots for this place. For the first time in such a drawing, I lost. As it turned out, however, I wound up getting more information than I would have in the pool.

The pool reporters were instructed to report to the law school in the early afternoon to cover the actual registration. The remainder of us were to stay out of the law school, but had freedom to roam anywhere else we wanted. This gave us a freedom of movement that the pool men did not have. And, if violence erupted, this freedom might prove important in covering it.

At 9:15 A.M., Cleve McDowell left Jackson in a red and white Chevrolet hardtop with Deputy Marshals Chester Smith and John Gerland and Justice Department attorney Arvid Sather. Their trip was uneventful. The only excitement occurred when an army plane and a helicopter watching over the car from the air spotted another auto trying to catch up with the hardtop. The army pilots radioed a warning to the ground that racist troublemakers might be trying to overtake the car carrying McDowell. But the pursuing car turned out to contain additional deputy marshals assigned to escort McDowell to the campus. The incident was good for a laugh that helped break the tension.

When the marshals reached Oxford, they took McDowell unobtrusively to James Meredith's room in Baxter Hall. His arrival went virtually unnoticed among students and newsmen. Most of us were waiting in the vicinity of the law school. Claude Sitton, Bill Street and I had been sitting in the Alumni House lunch room, near the law school, trying to spot Highway Patrol Director Birdsong and some of the university trustees and alumni officials. We understood they were meeting in the Alumni House, and thought we might learn from them whether Barnett was coming.

Shortly after noon, about an hour before McDowell's scheduled registration, the suspense regarding Barnett's plans ended. The Governor went on a statewide television hookup to describe and explain his position:

The people of Mississippi, America and the world will recall the tragic events that followed the entry of a Negro into the University of Mississippi as a student on September 30, 1962, and on many occasions thereafter. Under an executive order of the President of the United States, as issued on September 30, 1962, the University of Mississippi has been under military control. Cleve McDowell, a Negro, is now attempting to register as a student at the university's school of law. The State of Mississippi cannot cope with the U. S. Army or the federal armed forces. It would be unwise and futile for the State of Mississippi to enter into a physical or shooting combat with the U. S. Army. Such would undoubtedly result in death or injury to many of our people.

Cleve McDowell's attempt to enter the campus and register in the school of law at the university meets with our positive and determined protest, and our sovereign state proclaims to all of our sister states that these acts are in violation and utter contempt of the rights of our people, as guaranteed by the federal Constitution. His entry is being procured by the armed might of the federal government—in fact, several hundred federal troops, armed with guns and bayonets, now surround the campus of the University of Mississippi. The federal authorities must, therefore, accept the responsibility for his presence and entry upon the grounds at the university. I do not recognize any validity in this unconstitutional act, and I shall not lend any assistance to its accomplishment. . . .

I have always believed in segregation of the races because I believe in the purity and integrity of both the white and Negro races. I know this—that everywhere integration has been practiced long enough and extensively enough, it has ruined every civilization.

My position now is stronger than ever before and my devotion to the fine Mississippi University students continues to grow with each passing hour. Students at Ole Miss have shown great courage and restraint and yet a complete unwillingness to surrender to force, threat or intimidation. I want to now commend those students and their parents for their wonderful attitude and conduct. Americans everywhere must realize that integration is the primary facet of the conspiracy to socialize and communize America.

This racial situation will most certainly inflict dreadful retribution and retaliation upon those who are aiding and promoting this deplorable condition. These pressure groups, like a brute and inhuman monster, will, when given the first opportunity, turn upon and devour their benefactors.

I am asking the people of Mississippi to keep faith, have courage and stand firm. I am confident that, as more good, sound-thinking people in other areas of the nation become confronted with similar problems that we are facing, their reaction, with ours, will cause the pendulum to swing back and we can all surge forward to a complete and honorable victory.

It is my most fervent prayer that God . . . in His infinite wisdom will lead the people of Mississippi through every dark period that we are called upon to pass.

Barnett had thus pulled a turnabout and, despite all his strong words about "standing firm," had agreed to keep hands off the McDowell enrollment attempt. The main question was: Why?

The answer came in "don't-quote-me" remarks from various Barnett advisers, members of the university board of trustees and alumni. They said that Barnett, as late as midnight, had been promising staunch segregationists that he would come to Ole Miss and try to bar McDowell. But then, in the early hours of the morning, trustees and alumni had put pressure on the Governor to stay away from Oxford. They feared that further interference by Barnett would lead to additional accreditation troubles for Ole Miss, which was already on probation with the Southern Association of Colleges and Secondary Schools because of the political machinations involved in the Meredith case.

The university board of trustees was split between Barnett appointees and appointees of his predecessor, J. P. Coleman. During the Meredith case, some of the Coleman appointees had shown reluctance or halfheartedness about backing Barnett's defiant stand against the federal government. But, in the McDowell case, it had been some of Barnett's own appointees who had threatened to break with him if he came to Oxford to try to bar the Negro student. Under pressure from them and influential Ole Miss alumni, Barnett agreed to stay away. Yet, as in the Meredith case, he kept some of his closest advisers in the dark about his plans until shortly before McDowell arrived on the campus. With Barnett now out of the picture, the main question was whether there would be any red-neck attempt this time, as there had been in Meredith's case, to thwart the enrollment.

Bill Street, Claude Sitton and I were strolling around the section of the campus between the law school and Alumni House, waiting for McDowell to arrive and watching for signs of trouble. A half-hour, then an hour dragged by. Still McDowell did not appear. It was now approaching 3 P.M. I went to a phone and called a contact with the army contingent at Ole Miss, which I knew would be keeping tabs on McDowell's car as it approached Oxford. "Any word yet when McDowell gets here?" I asked.

"He's already on the campus," my contact said.

"Where?"

"I'd better not tell you that. I think you can figure that out."

It was not hard to figure. Where had James Meredith been taken when he first arrived on campus in September? The dormitory, Baxter Hall. It stood to reason that was where we would find McDowell.

I told Sitton and Street what I'd learned. Claude agreed to protect Bill and me on whatever happened at the law school, while we went to Baxter Hall to try to find McDowell. Sure enough, just as we rode up to Baxter Hall, Pat

Smith of the university news bureau was leaving. It was obvious that McDowell must be inside.

Karl Fleming of *Newsweek* arrived at Baxter Hall about the same time. As we waited for McDowell to come outside, Karl asked: "What do you call these trees over here?"

A veteran of a brief stint with *Newsweek* myself, I ribbed Karl: "Boy, isn't that just like you magazine guys. You don't care what the hell the hard news is. All you want to know is what kind of trees are outside McDowell's dorm and whether he eats scrambled or fried eggs in the morning."

Karl, feigning insult, replied: "What the hell else is left for us? We don't come out every day, like you guys."

Arvid Sather, the Justice Department lawyer who had accompanied McDowell on the ride from Jackson, came out of the dorm and briefed Street, Fleming and me on their trip and what McDowell was doing. "He's just filling out some registration forms," Sather said. "Then he'll go directly to the law school."

A few minutes later, McDowell walked down the steps with marshals in front and back of him. He was wearing a green plaid sport jacket, brown trousers, a light shirt and a tan tie. He had his left hand in his trouser pocket. He was wearing dark glasses in the bright sunshine. He looked composed and self-assured. We tried to question him, but he said he was in a hurry and had to get to the law school.

McDowell climbed into the back seat of a white sedan with John Doar. In front, with another marshal at the wheel, was Deputy Marshal John Gerland. Their car was preceded away from Baxter Hall by another auto carrying five marshals, and a car carrying members of the campus police force. The second marshals' car and the car carrying the campus police took a different route down a steep hill to the law school from the one taken by the car bearing McDowell. I wheeled into position right behind the McDowell car and followed it all the way to the law school. Bill Street, beside me in the car, was taking notes for both of us. There was virtually nothing to take notes about. All seemed calm.

When we reached the law school, Doar and McDowell

got out of their car with several marshals flanking them. They walked toward the law school's front steps. Just before reaching the steps, Doar and the marshals pulled away. McDowell walked alone up the steps and into the building.

To someone who had not been at Ole Miss in September, this might have seemed a commonplace occurrence. But, compared with Meredith's registration, when he had been accompanied constantly by marshals and in some cases by MPs, McDowell's walking alone into the law school seemed almost startling. Not a catcall was heard from the several dozen students in the vicinity. Not a word, much less a rock, brick or Molotov cocktail, was hurled at the few marshals waiting outside the law school.

At 3:20 P.M., McDowell walked out of the office of Dean of Students L. L. Love with Campus Police Chief Burns Tatum. The young student had conferred briefly with Love and had been welcomed by him to the university. McDowell and Tatum then walked to the library, where McDowell filled out some forms, and then went to nearby Conner Hall to register.

At Conner Hall, McDowell sat at a desk with a few other students, filling out more applications. About a dozen persons were in the room in which he was registering. Among them, seated on a window ledge, was Registrar Robert Ellis. In Meredith's case, Ellis had personally registered the Negro student in a private session in his office. But McDowell was being processed like just another student. When he inadvertently skipped one step in the registration process, a student employe of the university told him courteously: "We don't take that. You pay that [tuition] further back."

McDowell calmly retraced his steps to the point where he was supposed to pay his tuition. He presented a $500 check, from a scholarship fund for Southern Negro students established by the Utilities Club of New York. His fee for the summer semester came to $179, leaving him $321 in change. McDowell inquired about depositing the $321 in an account or safety deposit box, so he would not have to carry it around. He was told there would be some complications in depositing the money that day, but he could do it easily the next day. "I'll keep it," he said. "It's OK. I'll bring it tomorrow."

Then he sat at a table with three coeds, filling out still more forms. The girls remained seated at the table, making no effort to leave, the way many students had done whenever Meredith sat near them. A male student walked into the room and sat beside McDowell. A few minutes later, McDowell dropped his last application cards in front of an employe and was officially an Ole Miss student.

He went directly from Conner Hall to the Lyceum for a press conference arranged by Pat Smith. McDowell sat behind a desk, seemingly at ease. We were clustered all around him. Before we got a shot at asking questions, McDowell said he wanted to make a statement:

I'm sure that many persons want to know why I wanted to come to the University of Mississippi. I'll clear this up, so there will be no question now or in the future. This is my answer. I came to get an education in law. I solicit the aid of everyone concerned in letting me do this without constantly being pursued for interviews and other information. I think that this registration was carried out quite well. There was evidence that someone had put in a lot of work on it in advance. I haven't heard even one rude remark.

In answer to questions, McDowell said: "This is in my estimation the best school in the state. This law school is the most desirable if you want to get a law degree."

He was asked about statements by Ross Barnett that he had sent emissaries to McDowell to try to persuade him not to try to enroll at Ole Miss. "Several persons talked to me," he said. "But no one brought himself to me as a representative of the Governor."

How did his reception at Ole Miss stack up with what he had anticipated? "I must admit this is just about what I expected," he said.

McDowell clearly did not relish answering the questions. He tried to be obliging, but it was evident that the press conference represented an unpleasant chore. Finally, he asked to be excused, saying once again: "I came to get a law degree, and will pursue this until I get my degree."

With that, he went back to Meredith's room at Baxter

Hall. Again, as he went, there were no catcalls, no boos, no rock-throwing.

Outside the law school, a few of us spotted John Doar. We walked up and shook his hand in congratulations. John seemed delighted. He didn't put it into words, but the grin on his face seemed to be saying: It could have been this way last September, if demagoguery and hate-mongering had not invaded this beautiful, now serene, campus.

All of a sudden, Karl Fleming walked up to our group. "John, I just found a gun up near Baxter Hall," he said to Doar. "I figured I'd better give it to you."

The grin left John's face. He turned pale.

Karl brought his hand out from behind his back. In the hand was a gun he had found on the campus, all right, but it was a small toy cannon.

John roared with laughter, and we joined in. What little tension had been left in our group was now broken. From this point on, it was all downhill on our latest trip to Ole Miss.

3

The next morning, most of the national correspondents left Oxford. John Mashek and I were among the few who remained. We wanted to cover McDowell's first day of classes prior to leaving.

Before we went up to the campus, we ate breakfast at a small restaurant in Oxford. There we ran into Hugh Cunningham, Ross Barnett's law partner, who was defending several of the alleged rioters arrested after the Meredith holocaust. (Cunningham was also one of the defense attorneys for Byron De La Beckwith, Medgar Evers' accused slayer.)

After breakfast, Mashek and I drove up to the campus. What little excitement had been engendered by the enrollment the previous day was now gone. The green velvet of the circle in front of the Lyceum again was filled with strolling students, seemingly as calm as if Cleve McDowell and James Meredith had never set foot on the campus. John and I split up for a short period, and during this time, while I was merely making a casual check of the atmosphere on the campus, McDowell unexpectedly appeared near the Lyceum. He was being tailed at a distance of about 30 yards by two deputy marshals. I walked up to him and, because of his plea the previous day that newsmen not hound him for interviews, I asked: "Do you mind if I walk along with you and ask a few questions?" To my surprise, he was receptive to the idea.

Just before I had spoken to him, he had stopped a white student and sought directions on how to find the campus bookstore. The white student, in a thick Mississippi drawl, replied courteously: "Sure. It's right over that way. Right behind the library."

McDowell thanked him and headed in that direction. "You know," I said to him, "that may not have seemed very significant to you, but that student was a whole lot more courteous to you than most of them have been to Jim Meredith." McDowell said: "Well, he [Meredith] was the first. Maybe it will be easier for me."

As we walked, I said: "I'm curious about what seems to be a difference between your attitude and Jim's. He says that it's immaterial whether he gets a degree from Ole Miss, that what's important is that he and other Negroes have the right to attend. His attitude seems to be that he is here primarily to advance a cause, and only secondarily to get a degree. What's your feeling?"

Without hesitation, McDowell replied: "I'm here just to get a law degree, period."

When we reached the bookstore, a student clerk behind the counter—obviously trying to show that he was treating McDowell routinely—looked straight at him and asked: "Can I help anyone?"

McDowell replied softly: "I'm looking for a law dictionary." The clerk went off to find one, eventually coming back to say that they were out of stock, but were expected in within a day or so. In the meantime, a coed who had walked unnoticed into the store behind McDowell and me turned to her friend and remarked sarcastically: "Why, he's not even a gentleman. He didn't let a lady be waited on first."

Outside the bookstore, a Negro porter walked up to us.

"Mr. McDowell, I'm Henry Jackson," he said. "I hope to see a lot of you. Good luck." McDowell thanked Jackson shyly. We walked on.

I ribbed McDowell about the fact that, after fighting a long court battle for the right to enter an Ole Miss classroom, he had showed up five minutes late that morning for his first class, legal history. He grinned and replied: "I wasn't the only one late. There were a lot of people confused about what time we were supposed to start."

I asked: "How'd you get treated?"

"They treated me just like another student," he said. "Several students said 'hello' to me, but there wasn't time or occasion to have any real conversation."

I shook hands with him, wished him luck and left him to attend his next class. For the next hour, I buttonholed white students and asked them their attitudes on McDowell's admission. Many of them replied that they were far more willing to accept McDowell as a schoolmate than Meredith. As several of them put it: "We wish McDowell weren't here, but at least he says he's here for an education. Meredith has been a troublemaker ever since he got here, and doesn't really want an education in the first place."

In various ways, many students made it seem clear that McDowell was likely to have an easier time at Ole Miss than Meredith. Part of this was only natural—Meredith had broken the ground; he had been an undergraduate and McDowell was a graduate student; and the circumstances of McDowell's admission were much less explosive than those in Meredith's case. But it could not all be explained away that simply. Undoubtedly, another factor to be reckoned with was the difference in attitude between the two men. Meredith, upon returning to the campus that day to resume classes, recognized at once the different attitudes shown by white students toward him on the one hand and toward McDowell on the other. He continued to be the object of catcalls. But none came McDowell's way. Marshals continued to stick close to Meredith. They gave McDowell more freedom of movement.

Questioned about it, Meredith said with a shrug: "Maybe it's just me the white students don't like." To some extent, he was correct.

I returned to my hotel room after talking with Mc-Dowell, the white students and Meredith. I planned to write an overnight story, file it from Oxford and then drive with John Mashek to Tuscaloosa, Alabama, where a crisis was building at the University of Alabama. But my writing was interrupted by a knock on the door.

I opened the door to find a short, squat man with a furtive look on his face waiting outside.

"Mr. Dorman?" he asked. I nodded.

"I'm J. B. Stoner, from Atlanta. I'm the attorney representing Melvin Bruce. May I come in? A couple of FBI men have been tailing me."

I let him in and shut the door behind him. Melvin Bruce was one of the alleged Ole Miss rioters who was due to stand trial that week in federal district court at Oxford. He was the former chauffeur for American Nazi leader George Lincoln Rockwell, and was the man who had been caught with a high-powered rifle by marshals the night of the riot. His lawyer, Stoner, was well known to me by reputation. He represented many Southern extremist groups, including the National States' Rights Party and various Ku Klux Klan units. His statement that the FBI had been tailing him did not surprise me, for Stoner was considered in some circles to be active in extremist groups, as well as attorney for them. I did not let on that I knew Stoner's reputation. I wanted to know why he had come to see me.

"Hugh Cunningham suggested I talk to you," Stoner said. "He said you had been in the Lyceum the night of the riot, when Bruce was arrested. I thought I might want to call you as a witness."

I laughed. "Mr. Stoner, I don't think I'd make much of a witness for your side. As a matter of fact, Mr. Ray [U. S. Attorney H. M. Ray] has been talking about possibly calling me as a prosecution witness."

"Why is that?"

"Well, I was there in the Lyceum when Bruce was arrested, all right. But what I would testify to would hang him. I heard him admit that he was carrying that big Mauser rifle and those tracer bullets. His only excuse was that the bullets the marshals caught him with didn't fit the rifle. I saw the rifle. It was plastered with John Birch Society propaganda. And I heard Bruce say that he had come to Oxford to answer some kind of call from Major Arch Roberts, the man who'd been General Walker's aide."

"Were you there when Bruce was beaten?"

"Beaten! Hell, no. Does he claim he was beaten?"

"Yes, sir. He says the marshals beat him right after he was arrested."

"Well, I saw him right after he was arrested. He looked wild as hell, but he didn't look as though anybody had laid a hand on him. And he didn't mention a word about being beaten, either. I'm sure he realized I was a newspaperman. Why wouldn't he have told me he had been beaten, if he actually had?"

Stoner did not reply. He seemed to have lost interest in calling me as a defense witness, having heard what I would testify. After a few moments, we got to jawing about the riots and the trials generally. "Hell, you're not worried about this case, are you?" I asked. "You could rest your case without putting on a witness and Bruce would never be convicted by a jury of white Mississippians."

Stoner laughed. "You may be right," he said. "But, don't forget, Bruce isn't from Mississippi. A jury may feel differently about a defendant from Georgia than it does about one from Mississippi."

"I don't think there's much chance of that," I said. "I'd pass out if any of these defendants was convicted. I was surprised as hell to find that any of them had been indicted. You noticed, didn't you, that not one of those indicted was from Mississippi?"

Still pretending I knew nothing about Stoner, I then asked him: "What kind of practice do you have—primarily criminal?"

He shook his head, smiled and replied: "No, I guess you'd call it a segregationist practice."

"Oh, really? Is that because of your beliefs, or is it just profitable?"

"Well, my practice coincides with my beliefs. But I must say it's pretty damned profitable."

We both laughed. A few minutes later, Stoner left, saying perhaps he would see me in court. But I never heard from him again. Later in the day, as John Mashek and I rode out of Oxford, we passed Stoner. He was driving in the opposite direction. Tailing him at a discreet distance was a car carrying two men who looked very much like FBI agents.

Because I had been delayed writing my story, I decided to finish it during the ride to Tuscaloosa. Mashek drove. I balanced my portable typewriter on my knees and wrote the remainder of the story on the road, then filed it at a Western Union office in Columbus, Mississippi.

The next day, two of the four alleged rioters who had been indicted—both represented by Hugh Cunningham— were found innocent by a jury that deliberated for 70 minutes. A third defendant named in the indictment with them had previously had his case dismissed. This left only Stoner's client, Melvin Bruce, to be tried. He, too, was found innocent. The verdicts surprised practically no one.

James Meredith commented a short time later on the acquittals, saying that "nothing happened to the guilty parties in the University of Mississippi riots." The comment, in a statement issued to the press, led Governor Barnett to try to get Meredith expelled from Ole Miss.

The grounds for the expulsion attempt lay in a directive issued previously by the university's chancellor, J. D. Williams. The directive advised the faculty, staff and students:

Under existing conditions, public statements and press, radio and television interviews which appear likely to create disorder or impair the effectiveness of the educational program at the university must be regarded as unacceptable behavior. Disregard of this request may render the individual concerned subject to appropriate action under the pertinent provisions of the university's policies.

In addition to criticizing the acquittal of the alleged rioters, Meredith's statement had attacked Southern politicians for creating the climate that had led to the riots and to the murder of Medgar Evers. The statement said:

> The blame clearly rests with the governors of the Southern states and their defiant and provocative actions; it rests with the blind courts and prejudiced juries; it is known by both blacks and whites that no white man will be punished for any crime against a Negro.

At Barnett's request, the university trustees considered asking federal court permission to expel Meredith. Dean of Students Love severely reprimanded Meredith, and obtained from him an apology and a promise not to issue any more statements without clearing them with university officials. Love also reprimanded and got an apology from a white student who wrote derogatory statements about Negroes on the campus newspaper. Neither Barnett nor any university trustee made any attempt to expel the white student.

Despite Barnett's efforts, the attempts to expel Meredith were unsuccessful. On August 18, 1963, only 100 yards from the spot where the riots had centered nearly a year earlier, Meredith was awarded his degree by Ole Miss. He thus became the first Negro graduate in the university's 115-year history. Like the other 439 graduates, Meredith walked through the Lyceum and the grove of trees that had been filled with clouds of tear gas the previous September 30 to the site of the outdoor graduation exercises. He wore a black gown and a black cap, with a white tassel.

His wife, son, parents and other relatives sat on folding chairs, with only a few empty seats separating them from the families of white graduates. The Reverend William Pennington of St. Andrew's Methodist Church in Oxford delivered the invocation. "We live in a difficult time when it is apparent that men do not love one another," he said. He prayed for "unity out of discord, love out of hate, hope out of despair."

The commencement address was delivered by John A. Hunter, president of Louisiana State University. He did not refer directly to racial matters, but said the South was experiencing a wave of changing events. "In spite of current problems, and in part because of them, there exist opportunities for the State of Mississippi which never existed before," he said.

Meredith, who marched to the ceremony in a double file that placed him next to a white graduate, was one of the first to receive his degree. When his name was called, he walked across a platform, took his degree from Chancellor Williams with his left hand, shook hands with the chancellor and walked off the platform.

So ended an historic chapter in the history of this country's race relations.

Meredith left the campus with his family that day and drove home. Later, he would devote most of his time to the scholarship fund he had organized for Negro students. Still later, he would announce plans to continue his studies at Ibadan University in Nigeria.

He left behind him at Ole Miss young Cleve McDowell, for whom the way seemingly would be easier than it had been for Meredith.

But it did not work out that way.

In midsummer, conditions at Ole Miss seemed sufficiently calm so that the federal troops and marshals were withdrawn from Oxford. McDowell continued his studies, apparently under far less pressure than that during Meredith's time on campus.

There was still, however, open resentment of any Negro's presence at the university. McDowell, without the protection of marshals and troops, could not stand up under the pressure. In September, he sought permission from campus police to obtain a pistol permit. The permission was denied. Nonetheless, McDowell bought a .22-caliber pistol for $9.98. He carried it with him secretly while on campus.

On September 23, hurrying to a class, he dropped his sunglasses. When he bent down to pick them up, the pistol fell out of his pocket to the ground. It was seen by three white students before he could pick it up. The students reported the incident to Sheriff J. W. Ford. A short time later, Ford went to the law school and questioned McDowell, who admitted having the pistol. Ford arrested him on a charge of carrying a concealed weapon. McDowell surrendered the gun to the sheriff.

Immediately after his arrest, the university suspended McDowell. University officials insisted they were treating his case in routine fashion. Yet they had not suspended any of the dozens of white students from whom guns were confiscated by federal authorities during and after the riots.

Governor Barnett and other officials had been waiting for just such an excuse to have McDowell expelled. Barnett swiftly issued a statement saying: "Carrying a concealed weapon is a plain violation of Mississippi law, and I feel that any student who violates the law, especially with reference to carrying a concealed pistol—that's loaded—should be expelled immediately."

On September 24, just one day after his arrest and suspension, McDowell was expelled. He left the campus immediately. Ole Miss—and indeed all of Mississippi's public schools—were again totally segregated. On September 28, McDowell was tried on the weapons charge, convicted and fined $100. That penalty was light, compared to the deprivation of his right to attend the best law school in the state.

There is a temptation to make excuses for McDowell. He was, after all, under pressure. He said he feared for his life. But he must have known that he could be expelled for the slightest infraction, much less a criminal charge of pistol-toting, and that there were many waiting anxiously for him to make a mistake. Under those circumstances, his action in getting the pistol was unwise in the extreme. Setting aside the belief that a white student probably would not have been dealt with so severely, it still seems that McDowell asked for what he got.

When McDowell was expelled, the first thought that came to my mind concerned the long talks I had with James Meredith at Ole Miss the previous May. Meredith's words came back to me:

A Negro should have the same right to fail as a white. I don't see that it makes any difference, for example, whether I pass or fail. What's important is that I—and other Negroes—have the right to go to the best school in the state.

McDowell and Meredith had been given the chance. McDowell had failed; but Meredith had passed. And though no Negroes were admitted to Ole Miss immediately following McDowell's expulsion, it seemed inevitable that other Negroes eventually would be given the chance—to fail or to pass.

9 Tuscaloosa

1

Tuscaloosa, Alabama, was a pleasant surprise for me. During my numerous trips around the South, I had never even passed through Tuscaloosa. I was expecting another sleepy college town like Oxford, Mississippi. Instead, I found a bustling city of 63,370, with unionized labor, fairly large industry—a paper mill and a rubber plant, for example—air-conditioned hotels and motels, shopping centers, even nightclubs and all-night restaurants. The Stafford Hotel, where I had made a sight-unseen reservation, turned out to be a modern establishment with a large swimming pool, good service and good food.

When John Mashek and I arrived at the Stafford the night of Thursday, June 6, my first reaction was: "Man, if I've gotta cover a race riot, I'd a helluva lot rather do it here than in Oxford. Maybe we can cover this one from the Stafford swimming pool."

It was not to be that easy.

Despite its outward appearance—almost cosmopolitan in comparison with Oxford—Tuscaloosa was still Deep South in philosophy. The crisis growing at the University of Alabama would not pass without attempts by extremists to capitalize on it. Tuscaloosa was the home of Robert M. Shelton, Imperial Wizard of the United Klans of America, Inc., and the nearest thing anyone will find to a national leader of the diverse organizations that make up the Ku Klux Klan.

Even more than at Oxford during Cleve McDowell's enrollment, the gathering at Tuscaloosa represented a re-union of the whimsical organization, Southern Correspondents on Racial Equality Wars (SCREW). Claude Sitton, of course, was there, with his cohort from the *Times,* Hedrick (Rick) Smith as were Charlie Whiteford of the *Baltimore Sun,* Tom Yarbrough of the *St. Louis Post-Dispatch,* Warren Rogers of Hearst Headline Service, Joe Cumming and Karl Fleming of *Newsweek,* Dudley Morris of *Time,* Jack Steele of Scripps-Howard Newspaper Alliance, Ray Coffey of the *Chicago Daily News,* Relman (Pat) Morin of Associated Press, Charlie Portis of *The New York Herald-Tribune,* Paul Hope of the *Washington Star,* Bob Baker of the *Washington Post,* and some of the best of Alabama's newsmen.

Joe Cumming and I set about trying to recruit new members and bring additional stature to the organization. We tried to find a printer who could turn out some membership cards for us, but all were jammed with work. So we put that project off for another time. We also discussed plans for getting lapel pins made. They would be gold in the form of tiny screws. But this, too, proved too complicated a task to handle in Tuscaloosa, so we postponed it.

The University of Alabama assignment looked, at least on the surface, as though it would be a lot simpler than some of the others. The university had made elaborate preparations for the arrival of the expected hundreds of newsmen. There were ample press facilities, plenty of phones, typewriters and other supplies. A large building, just across a parking lot from the Stafford, was set up as a press headquarters, with special Western Union printers and teletype operators working virtually around the clock.

What would make the coverage more difficult than it seemed would be the impossibility of knowing in advance how the story would develop. It had been developing in a most unorthodox fashion for more than a month.

While I had been in Birmingham during the racial demonstrations, the court fight leading to the impending crisis at the university was taking place in the city's federal court. The fight had begun on April 15. At that time, three Negroes—Vivian J. Malone, Sandy English and Jimmy Hood—had filed suit for an injunction ordering the University of Alabama to admit them. They contended that the university was still bound to admit Negroes under a federal court order that had led to the enrollment of Autherine J. Lucy in February, 1956.

Miss Lucy, the first Negro to attend a state-supported school with whites in Alabama, had not lasted long at the university. During her first day of classes, a mob of 1,000 students had marched to the university president's home, chanting "Keep 'Bama white" and "To hell with Autherine." Two days later, there had been a riot. Students had thrown eggs and rocks at Miss Lucy as she had been driven to class. Her car had been pursued to a classroom building by the mob and she had been forced to wait inside, listening to the roar of the mob, until rescued by state police. A short time later, she had left the university for her home in Birmingham, and, after accusing university officials of sharing in the responsibility for the riot, she had been expelled. And for seven years not another Negro had entered the university—or any other white school in Alabama. Thus, Alabama in 1963 represented the only state with no desegregated schools at any level.

The three Negroes seeking admission to the University of Alabama in 1963 were represented by Mrs. Constance Baker Motley, the NAACP attorney who had won similar cases for James Meredith and Cleve McDowell in Mississippi. Mrs. Motley contended in the Birmingham court that the university was obliged, under the order issued in the Lucy case seven years earlier, to admit all qualified Negro applicants. She asked for an order directing the students' admission and penalizing university officials with contempt proceedings if they failed to enroll the students.

U. S. District Court Judge Seybourn Lynne, who was to play a major role in the crisis both publicly and behind the scenes, ordered the new students' cases consolidated with the Lucy case on May 16. He thus upheld Mrs. Motley's position. He also made it clear that university officials would face contempt proceedings if they barred qualified Negro students whose admission was ordered by the courts.

University officials then made it clear that they were ready to comply with Lynne's orders and accept qualified Negroes. But not so Governor George C. Wallace, who was an ex officio member of the university's board of trustees. During his campaign for governor the previous year, Wallace had pledged to "stand in the schoolhouse door" if necessary to maintain segregation. In his inaugural address, he had cried: "I draw the line in the dust and toss the gauntlet before the feet of tyranny, and I say segregation now, segregation tomorrow, segregation forever. . . . We intend to carry our fight for freedom across this nation, wielding the balance of power we know we possess in the Southland."

During the legal maneuvering following Judge Lynne's ruling that the university must admit the Negroes, Wallace had made it plain that he was fully willing to risk jail in his battle to keep the state's schools segregated. It was not the first time that Wallace had taken such a position. He had initially won statewide attention while a circuit court judge by defying a federal court ruling to turn over voter-registration records to federal authorities. For this grandstand play, he had been threatened with jail for contempt of the federal court and had come perilously close to being put behind bars.

Now, in 1963, Wallace was even more adamant. Repeatedly he iterated his pledge to "stand in the schoolhouse door"—even if it meant jail. Repeatedly he accused President Kennedy of maintaining a "military dictatorship." Repeatedly he vowed that he would not back down. He was going to stand in every schoolhouse door in the state, if necessary, he said. He did not pledge that Alabama schools would remain segregated. But he did pledge that they would be integrated only after someone had moved him out of the doorway.

By the time I reached Tuscaloosa, it seemed obvious that the federal government was just as determined as Wallace. The federal court orders would be obeyed, even if it meant calling out troops or having Wallace arrested. But the President and Attorney General Kennedy were hoping to avoid the necessity of jailing Wallace or even having federal authorities lay hands on him. For one thing, they felt jailing or shoving Wallace around would tend to make him a martyr. For another, they realized that it would pour salt into the already open wounds in the South.

As the showdown approached, it became increasingly apparent that the cards were stacked hopelessly against

Wallace. The Negro students who wanted to enter the university—their ranks swelled to five with the addition of two more applicants—had the federal courts and the federal government in their corner. They also had the university officials, who wanted the inevitable desegregation to come about with as little tumult as possible. Moreover, the Negro students had the backing of Alabama's most influential newspapers. And some of the state's leading citizens, including numerous University of Alabama graduates, began putting pressure on Wallace to back down.

Wallace could not back down. He had made his reputation as "the Barbour Battler"—a former amateur bantamweight boxer in Barbour County. He had vowed he was going to stand in that school house door, no matter what odds were stacked against him. And the odds were constantly growing.

Judge Lynne, becoming impatient with Wallace's repeated threats to defy the court orders, issued a new ruling specifically barring Wallace—by name—from trying to obstruct the Negro students' admission. Still, Wallace shouted his defiance. Lynne privately sent Wallace word that, if he disobeyed the judge's rulings, he would be sent to federal prison for two years. Wallace's advisers began researching the law. They found that if he served such a prison term inside Alabama, he could remain governor. If he were sent to a federal prison in another state, he would have to give up the governorship.

And who had the power to determine where Wallace would serve his time, if jailed? Why, who else but Attorney General Kennedy!

The Attorney General and some of his close aides drew great amusement from contemplating the possibilities. Not only could they decide whether to put Wallace in a prison inside or outside Alabama—thus determining whether he would remain governor—they also could consider, mostly in jest, the possibility of having Wallace sent to the federal prison in Atlanta—which had the largest concentration of Black Muslims in the country, inside or outside of prison. Jest or not, word reached Wallace's associates in Alabama of this possibility. What effect it had on the Governor's plans no one will say. But, despite even this possibility,

Wallace continued pledging to defy the court orders.

On Friday, June 7, four days before the showdown, the federal and state governments were massing their forces. Only three of the five Negro applicants were involved in the showdown, since they were the only ones accepted for the summer term. The three were Vivian Malone, a business student from Mobile; Jimmy Hood, a psychology student from Gadsden; and Dave Mack McGlathery, a graduate student from Huntsville. Miss Malone and Hood were scheduled to enroll at the main campus in Tuscaloosa on Tuesday, June 11. McGlathery, a mathematician at the federal government's George C. Marshall Space Flight Center in Huntsville, was scheduled to enroll in the university's Huntsville branch two days later. The crisis was expected to come Tuesday in Tuscaloosa.

By Friday, Colonel Al Lingo, gruff and sarcastic as ever, had moved into Tuscaloosa with the advance elements of his force of state troopers, conservation and liquor officers, and sheriff's deputies. Eventually, this force would number about 825. Lingo had rolled his headquarters-communications tractor trailer truck, familiar to those of us who had covered the Birmingham demonstrations, onto the smooth lawn in front of one of the campus buildings. Taped to the door of the truck was a cartoon showing Burke Marshall telling a group of Negroes: "The NAACP sent me down here to desegregate you trash."

It would be three days before key federal officials arrived. But they had already spent weeks making detailed preparations for the showdown. Air force reconnaissance planes had taken aerial photos of the University of Alabama campus and the surrounding area. Maps had been prepared. Assignments had been made. Tentative decisions had been reached on how to react to various alternatives, all depending on exactly what George Wallace did when he stood in the doorway.

As Attorney General Kennedy had told me in our conversation in New York on May 24, the decision had already been made not to try to use large numbers of federal marshals at Tuscaloosa, as at Ole Miss. If a small force of hand-picked marshals could not accomplish the mission, then troops would be employed. At the time of the interview with Kennedy, no decision had been made on whether these troops would be from the army or the Alabama National Guard.

In subsequent weeks it had been decided to use National Guard troops, unless such violence erupted that army troops were needed. It was also decided that, if at all possible, only Guard troops from the immediate vicinity of Tuscaloosa would be used. This, it was thought, would tend to undercut any argument by Wallace and other segregationists that federal troops made up of "outsiders" were being used to desegregate the university. Instead, the desegregating would be done by men from the Tuscaloosa area, wearing uniforms of the Alabama National Guard.

As the time for the showdown approached, 7,000 National Guardsmen from Alabama and Mississippi were involved in training exercises. The Defense Department insisted that the exercises, annual events, came simultaneously with the integration attempt only by coincidence. But it did seem convenient that these National Guard troops, including several thousand at Fort McClellan, Alabama, were so handy.

Brigadier General Henry Graham, assistant commander of the famed Dixie Division of the Alabama-Mississippi National Guard, was among those on hand at Fort McClellan. Graham had earned wide respect in 1961 when, as Alabama's adjutant general under then-Governor John Patterson, he had commanded the National Guard troops called out during the Freedom Ride crisis. Federal officials had chosen Graham to command the Alabama Guard troops to be used, if needed, in the new crisis. He had been alerted to be ready to move to Tuscaloosa on short notice.

Other military precautions were being taken. About 2,000 riot-control specialists of the Second Infantry Division, normally stationed at Fort Benning, Georgia, were on standby-alert status at Fort McClellan. In addition, Signal Corps units of about 50 men each, from Fort Gordon, Georgia, were setting up communications facilities at Fort McClellan, Huntsville and other nearby military installations. Marine Corps helicopters, in undisclosed numbers, were flown from New River, North Carolina, to Dobbins Air Force Base near Marietta, Georgia, to be available for carrying troops to Tuscaloosa if they were needed.

Among the first federal officials to arrive in Tuscaloosa was Major General Creighton Abrams, the army's assistant deputy chief of staff. Abrams was well known to those of us on the racial beat. He had been on the scene at Ole Miss and at Birmingham, serving as liaison between field commanders and Army Chief of Staff General Earle Wheeler.

Shortly after I arrived at the Stafford Hotel, Abrams walked in with several aides. All of them were in civilian clothes. I greeted Abrams as quietly as possible and said: "I take it you'd rather nobody knew you were here."

"You take it right," Abrams said.

"OK. I won't spread it around, provided I can talk to you when you get settled."

"That's fine," Abrams said.

"Is Gordon Hill coming?" I asked. Lieutenant Colonel Lucius Gordon Hill had served as Abrams' press officer during previous racial assignments.

"Yes, he'll be here," Abrams said. "You can check with him."

When Gordon arrived, he was wearing a University of Alabama press badge that identified him as a reporter for the newspaper *Army Times*. Actually, he never filed a story from Tuscaloosa. He was there in his capacity as Abrams' public information officer. But wearing a press badge, he had a freedom of movement that would never have been possible if he had been in uniform. In short, he was to some extent a "spook"—a spy for the federals.

He was far from alone as a "spook." A number of federal marshals who wouldn't know a typewriter from a teletype machine soon were parading around with press badges. So were a number of undercover agents, male and female, for various Alabama law enforcement agencies. It got so a press badge meant little. Unless you knew the person wearing one, you told him nothing. There was so much "spooking" going on that on several occasions in the Stafford Hotel lobby federal and state "spooks" outnumbered bona fide newsmen.

(During Cleve McDowell's enrollment at Ole Miss, one federal "spook"—Deputy Marshal Ed Bartholomew of

Richmond, Virginia—had an embarrassing time. He had been walking around for several days with an Ole Miss press badge identifying him as "Ed Bartholomew, *Richmond Times-Dispatch*." On the day of McDowell's enrollment, an Ole Miss student nudged him in the ribs with an elbow and asked: "Hey, Marshal, when did you get fired by the government?" The student, who had a good memory, had been arrested by Bartholomew during the riots the previous September.)

In addition to "spooking," there was much suspicion of tapping of telephones and bugging of hotel rooms. There were so many communications trucks from radio and television stations parked outside the Stafford, with their cables strung through the swimming pool area to electrical outlets in the hotel, that one wag was moved to remark: "All we need is one short circuit and this whole hotel will go up in a wisp of smoke." With so much electrical equipment being used, the possibilities for someone to slip a wiretap instrument or some other recording device into the hotel seemed limitless.

Thus, although Tuscaloosa seemed outwardly calm on Friday, there was much behind-the-scenes maneuvering already taking place. During the day I dropped by the FBI office in the post office building, got acquainted with the local agents and made arrangements to check with them later for any information they were able to release. Otherwise, Friday was a rather uneventful day.

At sundown, however, the tempo of events began to quicken. Al Lingo's blue-helmeted state troopers sealed off the campus. Only those with business at the university were permitted past police roadblocks.

At 8 P.M., I rode out to the suburban community of Holt with several other reporters. The local Citizens Council had organized a rally, with Birmingham's Bull Connor as chief speaker, to mobilize support for Wallace's segregation stand. When we arrived, there were about 250 persons in the auditorium of Holt High School. Most of them looked like typical red-necks, hooting and applauding at appropriate times, waving Confederate flags and unleashing rebel yells when the spirit moved them.

The thermometer inside the school read 106 degrees. It

was smoky, steamy and sweaty in the auditorium. But the spectators would not have left for the world. They were all set to hear a call to arms from that authentic Alabama folk hero, Ole Bull, as he was fond of calling himself.

At the front door, Citizens Council officials were selling Confederate flags, racist literature and other paraphernalia. Someone was handing out leaflets calling attention to a Ku Klux Klan rally the following night. "Klans cross burning and public speaking," the leaflets said. "If you are WHITE, you should attend this MEETING! Klansmen in robes will show you the way to the meeting. Public invited." The leaflets bore a picture of a hooded horseman, carrying a burning cross. "Yesterday, today and forever," it concluded. Such an invitation was hard to resist. I didn't resist it. I attended the rally. But at that moment I was fascinated by Bull Connor's talk.

It was not the kind of speech everyone had anticipated. This was no call to arms. It was an appeal for law and order, which Connor said he was delivering at Wallace's request. To do justice to Ole Bull's remarkable talk, it is necessary to recount it in the dialect in which it was delivered. Bull postured on the stage, hands on hips, shirt sleeves rolled up above the elbows. Occasionally, he would run his meaty hands through his hair. It all looked like a scene from a stereotyped movie about a Southern politician. He said:

Of all the guvnahs we've had, ah don't know of any bettah than that lil feller, George Wallace. [Tumultuous applause filled the hall.] Ah'v known that li'l feller since ah was in the Legislature, and he came in with short pants—with patches in 'em—to get a job as a page. And ah'v watched him evah since. Now, ah had a talk yestuhday with George, and he said he knew ah was comin' up heah tonight to talk to this Citizens Council rally.

And that li'l feller said to me, "Now, Bull, would ya do me a favor?" And ah said, "George, ah'll do ya two. What do ya want?" And he said, "Tell those people up theah to let me and the law enforcement people handle this thing at the university Tuesday. Tell them to stay off the campus and let me stand up theah for them to handle those nigras."

Now, ah want ya to do it. Don't go aroun' the university. That's what ya'v got law enforcement agencies for. Leave it alone. They goin' to handle it. That li'l ole Bobby Sox and his brothah, the President, would give anythin' in the world to see ya start some trouble.

Here was Ole Bull, symbol of defiance for more than 40 years, asking for responsible action on the part of local segregationists. The request could have come from no better source, other than George Wallace himself. But would it succeed in preventing trouble? Who could tell?

Bull's talk was not all sweetness and light—far from it. While he asked for maintenance of law and order in Tuscaloosa, he also sounded a call for renewed opposition to desegregation by nonviolent means. In short, he urged adoption of the same techniques that Dr. Martin Luther King had used in Birmingham. He conceded that he had been "whupped" by King. And he said the only way to start winning the segregation fight was to beat the Negroes at their own game—economic pressure:

Now, these nigras in Birmin'ham—why, every night at one or the other of their 70 churches in Birmin'ham they're takin' up a collection and gettin' anywheah from a thousan' to 25 thousan' dollahs. You couldn't get a thousan' dollahs in all of Tuscaloosa tonight to fight for the white race. We've gotta beat them at theah own game.

Weah not goin' to whup them with brickbats, sticks or guns. And weah not goin' to whup them in court as long as that crowd on the Suuu-preem Court is theah. The only way to whup them is with economics. Do what Mar-tin Lu-ther Keeng's doin'. Boycott the devil outa them.

Now, ah don't read those lyin' Birmin'ham newspapers, excep' ovah somebody's shoulder. They ain't goin' to get mah money. If ah turn on the radio and heah somethin' ah don't like, ah turn it off real quick—befoah ah can heah any commercials.

Let's don't let the nigras be smarter than we are. Copy from them. We goin' blackball ouah enemies—the white businessmen who've sold us out for the almighty dollah.

Foah yeahs ago, ah tol' ya those niggers had us on the one-yard line and they had de ball. Now, they're on the half-yard line and they've still got de ball. We've got to get de ball back. And the only way ah know is through de almighty dollah!

In the back of the hall, an infant in his mother's arms

bawled. But his cries were drowned out by the whoops from the red-necks.

Encouraged, Bull shouted: "Weah comin' back! Weah comin' back!"

More whoops, rebel yells and applause filled the auditorium. As the crowd shuffled toward the doors, a speaker reminded them of the big doings the following night at the Ku Klux Klan rally.

At 9 o'clock Saturday morning Rick Smith of *The New York Times* and I walked from the Stafford to Imperial Wizard Bobby Shelton's office at the Austin Building in downtown Tuscaloosa. A genial Negro elevator operator dropped us off on the fourth floor and pointed the way to the Klan office, Room 409.

Rick and I had a twofold purpose in going to see Shelton. First, we wanted an interview. Second, we wanted to make arrangements for safe conduct for ourselves and other reporters interested in covering the rally that night. In the past, the Klan had been noticeably belligerent about having its meetings attended by newsmen.

We were to learn quickly from Shelton that he was embarked on a new course—trying to give the Ku Klux Klan, if you will, a Madison Avenue image. Not only would he guarantee us safe conduct to and from the rally, but he had already taken the trouble to have press cards printed. The idea of issuing press cards may not seem radical to some, but to those of us who had taken part in even minor dealings with the Klan in the past, it seemed revolutionary. The Citizens Council's issuing press cards might not have been hard to visualize. But the Ku Klux Klan? It was almost too absurd to believe.

Shelton gave me press card number four. He told me it would be good not only for the Saturday night rally, but for any future stories involving the Klan in Tuscaloosa or anywhere else. I have treasured that press card ever since, both for its intrinsic and its curiosity value.

Shelton is a slender, stern-faced man with a crew cut. He has been a Klan leader for a good part of his life. Now in his 30s, he formerly worked as a rubber plant worker. He currently devotes almost full time to Klan activities, although he claims to spend some time as a salesman. He will not discuss what he sells, for he says he has been victimized economically in the past for his Klan activities.

When Rick and I interviewed him, Shelton was sitting behind a medium-sized desk in a back room of the office. He wore a short-sleeved plaid sport shirt. His bare arms bore several tattoos, which he said he had acquired while in the air force. The office looked much like any business or fraternal headquarters, except for a two-way radio near Shelton's desk. He said he and other Klan members have two-way radios in their cars, for which they have acquired Federal Communications Commission licenses. He said the radios were used for normal communications purposes among friends, and denied any intention to monitor police or FBI messages. It is no secret to Shelton that he and other "kluxers" are under constant scrutiny by the FBI and other investigative agencies at the federal, state and local levels.

"Mr. Shelton, what do you think's going to happen at the university Tuesday?" I asked him after the amenities of getting acquainted had been completed.

"We're hopin' the federal government arrests Governor Wallace and puts him in jail," Shelton replied. "That would rally other Southern states to our cause."

I had been told that Shelton and Wallace were close political allies, that Shelton had brought Wallace a sizable bloc of votes in the gubernatorial campaign. I asked Shelton about that. He refused to discuss his relationship with Wallace. I then asked him whether he had discussed the impending crisis at the university with Wallace.

"I'm not gonna say I've ever even talked to the Governor," Shelton said, "but I'll say this much: George Wallace is a man of his word. He's said he's gonna stand in the schoolhouse door, and I'm sure he's gonna do it. You're gonna see the peelin' come off the peach by Tuesday."

"What do you mean by that?" I asked.

"The fuzz is gonna be removed," Shelton said.

We got down to discussing Shelton's notion of revamping the Klan to give it a better image. "We don't go in for floggin', hangin' or lynchin' any more," Shelton said. "We try to work out solutions without violence. We'd rather have 25 good, dedicated men than 1,000 rabble-rousers. During the Reconstruction Era, there was nigger, carpet-bagger and scalawag law. The only way the Klan had to protect its members' families, homes and farms was floggin' and lynchin'. But we have laws now. We don't have to use those methods today."

I asked: "Does that mean you think you can win your fight for segregation without violence?"

Shelton shook his head. "Violence is not goin' to be avoided forever," he said.

"What do you mean by that?"

"If the present trend of enroachment [Shelton frequently mispronounces words] of the nigger and the federal government on states' rights continues, there's gonna be war. It won't be a war between the North and the South. It'll be between the blacks and the whites."

"What do you propose to do about it?"

"I'd just as soon have the war right now as later."

"Who would you fight—the Black Muslims?"

"They'd probably be on the other side, all right."

"But don't they really want the same thing as you do— separation of the races?"

"They say they do. But they also preach about the whites bein' devils."

Returning to his "new image" theme, Shelton said: "You know, there's a lotta mumbo jumbo bein' passed around about the Klan. Actually, we're just a semireligious fraternal organization. Sure, we have some secrets, but so do all fraternal organizations. Hell, we don't have nothin' to hide. That's why we're invitin' all the press medias [sic] out to the rally."

Shelton said the Klan, after years on the decline, was on the rise again. "We've had inquiries from people interested in organizing Klans in Africa—places like South Rhodesia and South Africa. We have people doin' organizational work in California, the State of Washington, Oregon, Maryland, Virginia, Pennsylvania, New Jersey and even New York City."

"How do these people go about organizing up North?" I asked.

"They work undercover," Shelton said. "They work through social gatherings and meetings of other organizations."

"What kind of organizations?"

"Oh, all kinds. The John Birch Society, organizations like that."

"Mr. Shelton, it seems pretty obvious that the FBI and other law enforcement agencies must have infiltrated the Klan—either with agents or informers. Does this bother you?"

"No, I know we have these people. I don't mind them. I enjoy their company. I'm glad to have them. They pay their dues. They increase our membership. As I said before, we have nothin' to hide."

"Do you have any informers of your own in the FBI?"

"We've had some people in various law enforcement agencies. I won't say which ones."

"You say you don't have anything to hide. If that's so, how do you explain the restraining order the Justice Department got against you during the Freedom Rides, accusing you and other Klan leaders of participating in the bus bombings and beatings of the Freedom Riders?"

"There wasn't anythin' to all that. They didn't have anythin' on us."

(The Justice Department suit seeking the restraining order had been extremely specific. It had spelled out in detail dates, places and names of those—including Shelton and other Klan leaders—the government accused of bombing buses, beating Freedom Riders and otherwise trying to block desegregation of bus terminal facilities.)

Shelton then launched into the familiar racist harangue about mongrelization and depurification of the white man's blood. He seemed obsessed with the notion that all Negro men were preoccupied with the idea of trying to bed down white women.

"Mr. Shelton, if that bothers you so much," I asked, "why doesn't the Klan embark on a program to impregnate all the Negro women you can find? That way, you'd eventually turn their children's bloodstreams back to white."

"Shit, man," Shelton rasped, virtually exploding out of

his chair. "What are you, one of these guys who wants to have a purple race?"

End of interview—abrupt end.

About 8 that night, I rode out to the rally with Joe Cumming and several other reporters. The scene was a muddy pasture off busy U. S. Highway 11. It was all just the way the movies had pictured it: men in white, red and blue robes and women in blue and white were gathered in the pasture. All wore those absurd pointed hoods, looking for all the world like medieval wizards. Some wore masks. Several thousand spectators stood before a floodlit platform erected on an old flatbed truck, with almost bald tires.

There was a carnival atmosphere. Hawkers sold hot dogs and cold drinks. Lovers stood with arms around one another. Young couples, some with babies in their arms or perched on their shoulders, faced the platform. A beautiful red-haired girl wearing a green cocktail dress, but no shoes, stood holding hands with a clean-cut young man. A boy, about 4 years of age, played with a wooden glider at their feet. A boy of about 7, wearing a T-shirt bearing a map of Florida, played nearby. Elderly men and women in shabby clothing looked toward the platform as if it were Mecca.

Robed Klansmen had led all newsmen to a point just in front of the platform. We had been advised to stay together and not mingle with the crowd. Shelton explained that a number of Klan security agents had been assigned to keep an eye on us, for our own protection, and that it would be easier to protect us if we were together than scattered throughout the crowd. This was all very well, but I didn't particularly cotton to the idea of turning my back to the crowd. Neither did some of the others. So, for a good part of the rally, we stood facing the crowd, with our backs to the platform.

Scattered among the spectators, and the press corps, was a sizable number of "spooks." We knew they were not reporters. They obviously were either federal, local or state investigators. Some wore press badges. In the spot on the badges where their news media were supposed to be named, they had typed merely: "Stafford Hotel." Someone cracked: "That must be a helluva paper, that Stafford Hotel. It's got the biggest staff out here."

Off to the right of the platform, as the spectators faced it, was a wooden cross about 50 feet high. It was wrapped in oil-soaked burlap.

A man in civilian clothes—clean-cut, good-looking, well-dressed—stepped to the microphone. This man, who refused to identify himself to us, served as master of ceremonies throughout the rally. He introduced first a tall man in a red robe, with mask and hood. The master of ceremonies identified him as the pastor of an Atlanta church, but did not give his name. A wag in the press corps cracked: "I've met a lot of preachers who would have liked to hide their faces. But this is the first one I've ever seen actually do it."

The Atlanta minister opened the rally with a prayer. "Dear Heavenly Father," he said, "we as Klansmen acknowledge our dependence on Thee. We have grateful hearts. Grant Thy people Thy blessing. Bless each speaker. Give them words to edify Thee as we look to Jesus Christ, in whose name we pray. Amen."

All the floodlights were turned off. A Klansman put a torch to the wooden cross. The flame began rising into the air, doubled back toward the ground and spread from center to right and left simultaneously. From the loudspeaker blared the hymn "The Old Rugged Cross."

So there it was, the century-old ritual of the Klan, the cross-burning, being carried out in a carnival atmosphere in a university town in 1963.

After the cross-burning, the master of ceremonies introduced a number of the dignitaries, if that is the word, on the platform. These included Calvin Craig, the Klan's Grand Dragon in Georgia and a sometime political enemy of Bobby Shelton in the Klan's internecine warfare; the unidentified Grand Dragon of Tennessee; a grandmotherly woman in a blue robe and hood, identified as a leader in what can only be described as the ladies' auxiliary of the Klan; and an enormously obese man, who looked like Big Daddy in Tennessee Williams' *Cat on a Hot Tin Roof*, identified only as the Grand Dragon of Mississippi.

Most of the "dignitaries" merely stood up and acknowledged applause, much like former boxers raising their arms to the crowd when introduced before a championship fight. But Craig, perhaps self-conscious about reports of a split between Shelton and himself, felt obliged to deliver a few minutes' worth of invective for the occasion. After paying tribute to "that great man, Governor George Wallace" and receiving the expected hoorays, Craig cried into the night: "The niggers are creating a revolution in Alabama today. It's up to us—the white people—to protect the integrity of the white race. Some people think we've surrendered up in Georgia. We haven't surrendered whatsoever. That pipsqueak, Ivan Allen [Atlanta's mayor], may have surrendered—but we haven't."

Now came the big moment. That responsible Madison Avenue version of the Klansman, circa 1963, Bobby Shelton, took over the microphone. Shelton, unlike most of the others, was in street clothes. He was quite a different man on the platform from the one we had interviewed that morning in his office. Gone was the respectable facade. Gone was the "we try to work out solutions without violence" fairy tale. This was Bobby Shelton, "kluxer," racist, demagogue, activist. He paid lip service to the same kind of appeal Bull Connor had made the previous night, urging the crowd to stay away from the university campus and "let George [Wallace] do it" during the showdown with the federals.

But no sooner were the words out of his mouth than Shelton began a tirade, which seemed to last interminably, that could only be designed to inflame the populace. There is little sense repeating much of what he said. It was a combination of racist slurs, John Birch Society dogma ("This isn't a democracy; it's really a republic") and anti-Kennedy, anti-United Nations, anti-Jew, anti-Catholic hogwash. Much of it had as much to do with the integration crisis at the university as it did with the ideological struggle between Moscow and Peking.

Shelton rambled on and on and on. The danger did not seem to be so much whether Shelton would incite the listeners to violence as whether he would bore hundreds of them to death. While he talked and talked and talked, the hat was passed. Hundreds of dollar bills were stuffed inside. I wondered where that money would go, who would be responsible for it, what taxes would be paid on it. I never found out.

Two incidents during Shelton's monologue titillated me. One occurred when a large green insect—it looked like a praying mantis—perched on the microphone into which the Imperial Wizard was speaking. Shelton seemed oblivious to the intruder. The insect stared up at Shelton, but Shelton kept right on talking. Someone in the press corps cracked: "Well, Bobby's got at least one listener."

The other incident came during a portion of Shelton's talk in which he tore into Dr. Martin Luther King and his followers as lawless revolutionaries. He pointed to restraining orders against King and his organization, seeking to bar them from conducting peaceful demonstrations in Birmingham. And he deplored King's policy of refusing to abide by such court orders. What Shelton did not mention was that he, himself, was under such a restraining order—the one dating back to the Freedom Rides. And it did not bar him from any act so innocent as conducting a picket march. It barred him from bombing buses, beating bus riders and otherwise conspiring to commit violence.

It would not have mattered much if Shelton had referred to the restraining order. Hardly anyone was listening, anyway. By the time he finished his talk, it was past 10:30. Of the several thousand persons who had crowded the pasture earlier, perhaps only half were still there. And as ridiculous as the rally had seemed, it still made abundantly clear that there were several thousand persons in Tuscaloosa sufficiently upset about the pending integration attempt at the university to turn out for the festivities.

Three days remained before the confrontation between Governor Wallace and federal officials in the doorway of the university's registration building. Would these several thousand persons rise up to stand at Wallace's side, or would they obey his request that they remain away from the campus? What about armed outsiders invading Tuscaloosa, as they had Oxford during the Ole Miss crisis? What about Bobby Shelton's "kluxers," some of whom had been carrying pistols at the rally?

Some of these questions would have to await the showdown Tuesday. But one of them began to be answered shortly after the rally. Tuscaloosa police (who, incidentally, gave an excellent account of themselves throughout the crisis) began arresting gun-toters in the vicinity of the rally. They continued these arrests Sunday. A number of those arrested came from other cities and states. They reportedly had Klan affiliations. In any event, their bail was posted by that noted champion of the nonviolent approach to race relations, Bobby Shelton.

Sunday was relatively calm and uneventful. It gave many of us a chance to relax at the Stafford swimming pool. I filed a story on the rally and then wrote a brief biography of each of the three Negro students scheduled to be enrolled.

Following are excerpts from these biographies:

Vivian Juanita Malone, 20, tall and attractive, is the one [student] whom the segregationist diehards want most to keep out of the University of Alabama. She is seen by some as another Autherine Lucy, the first Negro to enter the school. . . .

Miss Malone has attended Alabama A&M College [for Negroes] for two years, majoring in business education, and she will enroll at the University of Alabama's School of Commerce. She has said that she does not want to be a martyr; she just wants to get an education. "I feel I'll be able to go through with it," she said. "I'm not really worried, but you might say I'm a little concerned. I'm going to get an education."

Jimmy A. Hood, outwardly calm, says: "This is just another semester of school for me." [As later events would show, Hood was not nearly so calm as he seemed.] He plans to "act natural" in the face of opposition. The son of a tractor driver who did not finish high school, Hood will enter the Alabama College of Arts and Sciences with a major in psychology.

Born in Alabama, he was co-captain of his high school football and track teams. He was his high school class president and was elected student council president. "I pray," he says, "that Governor Wallace will change his mind about barring me and Miss Malone from entering the school."

Dave Mack McGlathery will be the only Negro at Alabama's Huntsville campus when he enters this week as a postgraduate student. Born in Huntsville, he is 27. Since last October, he has worked as a mathematician at the federal government's George C. Marshall Space Flight Center in Huntsville—a major source of jobs in Alabama. Previously, he worked as a mathematician at a navy weapons laboratory. He is a graduate of Alabama A&M, where he majored in math and minored in several sciences. He holds an Alabama teaching certificate and is a veteran of the navy.

Hood and Miss Malone spent the weekend in New York City where they conferred with Jack Greenberg, chief counsel for the NAACP Legal Defense and Educational Fund, and other attorneys. It was a chance for the young Negroes to get away from the tension in Alabama and relax as much as possible. McGlathery stayed on his job at Huntsville.

2

As the time for the confrontation grew closer, the tempo of events quickened. In Tuscaloosa, security arrangements on the campus were tightened drastically. University officials put students under a 10 P.M. to 6 A.M. curfew for the duration of the crisis. Well remembering the use rioters had made of pop bottles at Ole Miss, officials had all soft drink machines dispensing bottles removed from the campus. They were replaced with machines dispensing cups. Also remembering the use made of bricks from a construction site at Ole Miss, the University of Alabama authorities directed contractors doing work on the campus to truck away all bricks. The campus was carefully scouted by police and university employes for any object that could be used as a weapon.

Security at the police roadblocks was increased. No vehicles except police cars were permitted past the roadblocks. Only persons with university credentials or press passes could enter the campus. Nonetheless, outside troublemakers continued to arrive in town and try to invade the campus. One, a member of the American Nazi Party, sought permission to make a speech. Tuscaloosa Police Chief W. M. Marable, an amiable but businesslike lawman, promptly ordered the Nazi to leave town. He did.

By Sunday afternoon, 15 persons had been arrested on

charges of carrying concealed weapons. Bobby Shelton had posted bond for all of them.

During the afternoon, Dr. Frank A. Rose, president of the university, conducted a press conference in the news center near the Stafford Hotel. He said he hoped troops would not be needed to enforce the court's integration orders. But he did not criticize Wallace for his planned defiance of the court. He said the Governor evidently felt obliged to carry out his campaign pledge to "stand in the schoolhouse door." Rose referred to "great tensions and anxiety," "critical hours" and "this crisis" in a prepared statement delivered at the press conference.

Under questioning, Rose said: "My feeling is that it is necessary for the Governor to be here with the highway patrol. The Governor has assumed the responsibility for security and we are now operating the university under strict police control."

I asked what sort of liaison university officials had with both Wallace and federal officials. This, it seemed to me, was the crucial question in determining what would happen Tuesday. In other words, was there any communication among federal, state and university officials, any attempt at a meeting of the minds? "We are funneling everything through the federal judge," Rose said. "The judge has asked staff members to meet with him."

This was highly significant to me. It meant that Judge Lynne was playing an active behind-the-scenes-role in the crisis. It seemed to me that Lynne, perhaps even more than Wallace or President Kennedy, was the man with the real power in the crisis. Wallace had his state troopers and, until or unless they were federalized, the National Guard troops. Kennedy had the armed forces, clearly superior to Wallace's forces and able to compel the integration of the university. But Lynne was the man who could send George Wallace to prison, and had already notified Wallace that a two-year stretch faced him if he insisted on disobeying the injunction against him.

On Sunday afternoon, an involved game of throat-cutting poker for table stakes moved into full swing. Wallace called the National Guard into active service and ordered units moved to Tuscaloosa for possible use in the crisis. By midafternoon, about 500 Guardsmen had arrived and taken up positions at an armory. Wallace made it clear the Guardsmen would not be used to try to block the Negro students, but only to maintain order. He planned to take care of the student-blocking assignment himself. The Guardsmen were to support the force of state troopers, local police and deputized game wardens and liquor agents —numbering about 825—under the command of Al Lingo.

On Sunday night, Wallace went on a statewide television network to call for peace at the university and pledge to keep his promise to try to block the Negroes. Citing the state motto, "We Dare Defend Our Rights," Wallace said his stand in the doorway Tuesday would point up the states' rights issue and dramatize "this omnipotent march of centralized government." He said the Justice Department was preparing "to send a loyal Southern governor to jail." He did not, of course, mention that the option of staying out of jail remained with him.

"In my opinion, this is military dictatorship," Wallace said. But he pledged to prevent violence at the university. "We will not tolerate any harm or desecration of this great University of Alabama on Tuesday or any day thereafter. I'm going to stand up for you at the University of Alabama. You can stand up for Alabama [this had been his campaign slogan] and stand up for me by standing up at your home or workbench on that day. I have kept the faith: you keep the peace."

Now, the same basic team of federal troubleshooters that had handled the Ole Miss crisis began moving into Alabama. General Abrams was already on the scene. From Washington and other cities came such men as Nick Katzenbach, who had been in charge at Ole Miss and would also be in charge at Tuscaloosa; John Doar; John Nolan, the attorney general's administrative assistant; Ed Guthman, who would handle press relations and help draft policy; Dean Markham, all-around White House troubleshooter, who had been a football-playing buddy of the Attorney General and a key man at Ole Miss; Joe Dolan, Nick Katzenbach's chief assistant; Jim McShane, the embattled chief marshal; Jack Cameron, Jim's top aide; and John Martin, the civil rights lawyer I had first met during Cleve McDowell's enrollment at Ole Miss.

Along with the lawyers and strategists came the muscle of the Justice Department team—the hand-picked group of marshals and deputized Border Patrolmen who had served with valor and distinction at Ole Miss and now would be charged with protecting the Negro students at the University of Alabama. These included such men as Cecil Miller, the huge judo expert who had been James Meredith's personal bodyguard at Ole Miss; Al Butler, the marshals' group leader; and Charles Chamblee, the Border Patrolman who had time after time brought supplies of tear gas into the Ole Miss campus.

By Sunday night, all these men either were in Alabama or on their way. They would make their headquarters at the Army Reserve Training Center at 2627 10th Avenue in Tuscaloosa—a different armory from the one being used by the National Guard. Most of them would stay at the Town House, a motel a block from the Stafford. Thus the Stafford—which would be occupied by Wallace and most of the state officials involved in the crisis—would become a sort of temporary state command post in Tuscaloosa. The Town House and the Army Reserve Training Center would become the federal command posts.

The federals, of course, were in constant communication with the President and the Attorney General in Washington. Precise logs of all communications and actions involved in the crisis were kept at the federal headquarters at the armory and at the Justice Department and White House in Washington. Though these logs are marked "confidential," I have been given access to them. The remainder of this chapter draws heavily on heretofore unpublished material contained in the logs, as well as on my own experiences, of course.

In addition to manpower sent to Tuscaloosa by the government, considerable equipment was dispatched. There were, for example, six Border patrol radio cars, one radio truck, several walkie-talkies, a shortwave radio set to serve at the headquarters communications center, several Border Patrol planes, army helicopters and even an army engineers' boat (to be used in patrol work on the Black Warrior River, adjacent to the campus).

On Sunday afternoon, I got word from Washington that Nick Katzenbach, Ed Guthman, John Doar and other federal officials were en route to Alabama. I called Ed's home and was told by his family that he was due on a commercial flight about 8 P.M. I went out to the airport to meet him, figuring I could get a fill-in on the government's latest strategy.

While I was waiting for the plane, Bobby Shelton furtively walked into the airport lobby, carrying an attaché case. He tried to slip around a corner without talking to me, but I headed him off. "Where you goin', Mr. Shelton?" I asked.

"Gotta get outa town in a hurry," he said.

"How come?" I asked. He did not reply.

Shelton walked off to board a light plane piloted by Alvin S. Sisk, who often flew the Klan leader on secret missions. Two months later, Sisk would be killed and Shelton injured in a crash of Sisk's plane near Seneca, South Carolina. They had been on their way to observe civil rights groups' March on Washington.) After watching Sisk and Shelton take off from Tuscaloosa, I checked with the Federal Aviation Agency controller on their listed destination. The controller said Sisk had checked his plane out only for a local area flight, meaning, presumably, that Shelton would return shortly.

Sure enough, several hours later, I found Shelton in the lobby of the Stafford, talking with some cronies. He spent most of the Tuscaloosa crisis making himself conspicuous in places like the Stafford, evidently so that nobody could accuse him of complicity if any violence erupted. At the Stafford, Shelton refused to say where he had flown. The assumption made at the time, which I find no reason to doubt now, was that he had gone to some secret Klan rendezvous either to plot strategy or pick up new supplies of cash to be used in bailing out jailed "kluxers."

As it turned out, my wait at the airport for the federal officials proved fruitless. They had caught a plane due in Alabama about 8, all right. But they had flown to Birmingham, not Tuscaloosa. There, they had conferred with other officials, including Judge Lynne. Ed Guthman and Dean Markham had driven from Birmingham to Tuscaloosa Sunday night. Nick Katzenbach had remained overnight in Birmingham, with some of the others, for further conferences Monday.

Late Sunday night, while strolling through downtown Tuscaloosa, I saw a familiar figure walking briskly in the opposite direction. I walked closer, realized it was Dean Markham and called out to him. We renewed acquaintances. I told him I had been waiting at the airport for him, Ed and the others to arrive. That's when I learned that they had flown to Birmingham, and driven the remainder of the way. Dean told me he and Ed were sharing a room at the Town House, that Ed had already gone to bed, and that they would see me in the morning. He gave me their room number and told me to come over early.

Later that night, I got a tip that was to play an important role in the remainder of my coverage of the crisis, and even more important, was to play a role in the crisis itself. I was talking to a news source, who must remain nameless, about the possibility of a deal between Governor Wallace and the federal officials, the same kind of deal Mississippi's Ross Barnett had made, only to renege later. In past discussions with this source and other members of both the state and federal camps, I had been told that Wallace was adamant in insisting that he would not even consider negotiations with the President. Now, my source said, Wallace was giving indications of wavering on this point.

"How come?" I asked.

"Wallace has a history of mental troubles," he said. "He wound up in a hospital in the service with combat fatigue. He got a medical discharge, with a ten-percent mental disability allowance. He's been getting federal disability checks ever since. A few years ago—to continue being eligible for the payments—he got himself reexamined by a psychiatrist. He was certified as still ten-percent mentally disabled. He's still getting the checks today."

I shook my head.

The implications were staggering. It was no disgrace to

be mentally disabled, particularly when your disability came while serving your country in wartime, as Wallace had. But for a governor, particularly one whose actions in such a crisis could be considered irrational by some, this information could be dynamite. It could ruin him politically.

About 7 A.M. Monday, I walked over to the Town House to see Ed Guthman and Dean Markham. Ed was shaving when I arrived. We began talking about the crisis, and the subject of Wallace's mental history came up. Ed conceded knowing about it, confirmed in general the combat fatigue story and the fact that Wallace was still collecting ten-percent mental disability checks, but said it would be almost impossible to obtain further data.

Ed was not very encouraging about the prospects for my getting the story firm enough to print it. But he did confirm that Wallace had been wavering slightly about negotiating with the President. Ed made it clear that no deal had been made, but that someone—evidently acting as an intermediary—had indicated that Wallace might be more willing to horse-trade than he had been in the past.

I tried to reach Wallace and his press secretary, Bill Jones, to ask them about the mental-history story. But both were described as too busy to talk. So I phoned Grover Hall, editor of the Montgomery newspapers and a close confidant of Wallace. I asked Hall to see if he could learn from Wallace whether there was any truth to the report that he had suffered mental difficulties while in service and was still receiving disability checks. Hall said he was sure there was nothing to the report, but would check with Wallace and call me back.

When Hall phoned back, he reviewed for me Wallace's entire military history. He told how Wallace had been sent to the Marianna Islands as the flight engineer on a B-29. He said Wallace had authorized him to tell me: "He (Wallace) saw a number of fellows crash. He was grounded in the Pacific for 'flight fatigue, anxiety state.' He has been getting 10-percent disability checks."

"What does that 10-percent disability mean?" I asked.

"All I know is that it means he's 10-percent disabled," Hall replied.

I informed my editors of the conversation with Hall.

They indicated they felt we could not use a story without knowing more about Wallace's precise mental problems. I set about trying to round up additional information.

While I had been working on the Wallace story, much had been happening in Tuscaloosa, Birmingham, Montgomery and Washington.

In Tuscaloosa, all deputy federal marshals and deputized Border Patrolmen assigned to protect the Negro students had been ordered to report to the Army Reserve Training Center by noon for briefings on the government's strategy and individual assignments.

Jack Cameron, in command until Jim McShane arrived, ordered four marshals to maintain security at the headquarters. John Nolan arranged a 1 P.M. meeting with Alabama Public Safety Director Al Lingo to discuss mutual problems. Nolan was to meet Lingo at the state troopers' mobile unit on the campus.

At 10:30 A.M., a secret strategy conference began in the federal headquarters. Attending were Jeff Bennett, assistant to University of Alabama President Frank Rose; General Abrams; Dean Markham; John Nolan; United States Attorney Macon Weaver of Birmingham; Ed Guthman; and Nick Katzenbach. Neither the press nor the public knew of this meeting at the time. In fact, no one knew Nick Katzenbach had even reached Tuscaloosa. He was believed to be still in Birmingham.

It was agreed at this meeting that Luther Callahan, university controller, would serve as the university's liaison man with the federal authorities. He was to come to the reserve center that afternoon and make himself available during the remainder of the crisis.

Bennett reported to the federal officials that registration would begin the following day at 8 A.M. The campus and Foster Auditorium, site of the registration, would be sealed off at 10 A.M. Bennett said that students residing in the Mary Burke Hall had been told the previous night that Vivan Malone would be staying there. Students at the Palmer Dormitory had been told Jimmy Hood would be staying with them. There had been good acceptance of the news by the students, Bennett reported.

Nick Katzenbach raised hell with Bennett over the fact

that the university had permitted—even directed—the painting of white semicircles outside three doors to Foster Auditorium, thus creating much speculation among newsmen, students and others about which doorway Wallace would stand in. Nick felt the confrontation was going to be a stage-managed spectacle under any circumstances and that the semicircles would only add to the theatrics. He was genuinely upset. But, as he later conceded to me, he poured on his displeasure a bit thick because he wanted three things from Bennett.

First, he wanted the keys to the dormitories to be used by the Negro students, and he wanted the dormitories searched and secured in advance. Second, he wanted permission to place men inside Foster Auditorium during the confrontation. Third, he wanted the floor plan of the dormitories.

Nick got everything he wanted. Bennett provided the federal men with detailed information on the plans for the confrontation. He said Wallace would have an office provided for him in the lobby of Foster Auditorium. He would also have a public address system. The two doors adjacent to "the door" Wallace planned to stand in would be locked. Two other doors, in addition to "the door" would be left unlocked, but there would be 15 to 20 highway patrolmen inside the lobby to secure the area.

All this information would prove invaluable if the federal authorities were forced into arresting Wallace. They needed to know what kind of resistance they would be likely to encounter.

After the meeting broke up, Nick assigned John Nolan to establish liaison with Tuscaloosa Police Chief W. M. Marable and handle all relations with him during the crisis. The federals had already formed a healthy respect for Marable. (A note in the log kept by the marshals read: "Marable, police chief, good man.")

At 1:33 P.M., Wallace took off from Montgomery for Tuscaloosa in a red and beige Cessna. The light plane set down at the Tuscaloosa airport about 45 minutes later. With the Governor were two of his brothers, Jack, a circuit court judge on the same bench the Governor had previously occupied, and Gerald, a Montgomery attorney.

Four state troopers on motorcycles escorted the Wallace party to the Stafford. A mob scene was waiting there. More than 100 newsmen, plus a number of Tuscaloosa citizens, were gathered in front of the hotel. When the Wallace party arrived, the Governor stepped out of a car jauntily. He was dapper, as always, in a black suit, white shirt and red-and-black striped tie.

"Nice to see you all here," he said, smiling broadly. He shook hands with several reporters. Then, as the newsmen swarmed around him, he laughed and said: "Let's don't have any mob violence here!"

Wallace made a chamber-of-commerce-style welcoming talk to the out-of-state newsmen. "When you go back home, I hope you'll have a better view and attitude about the people of Alabama," he said. "We're not going to have any violence. We're going to test the law in a peaceful atmosphere. Desegregation is not the law of the land. I'm the governor of this state, on the platform I ran on. I am going to test the illegal procedures being used by the federal government."

I shook hands with Wallace and introduced myself. Upon hearing who I was, he glared directly into my eyes. It was evident he recognized the name and realized I was the reporter inquiring into his mental history. I asked: "Governor, can you tell us whether you have any contact, either directly or through intermediaries, with the President and whether there are any negotiations going on."

The question seemed to surprise and anger Wallace. He pointed his finger at me and snapped: "Nobody contacts anybody in my behalf. I've decided what I'm going to do, and I'm going to do it. Nobody speaks for me."

Evidently, I had touched a sensitive nerve. Wallace must have heard the reports that he was believed to be wavering and receptive to a deal with the President.

He reiterated: "There's not going to be any mob violence in Alabama. We haven't had any race riots in this state. Race was not involved in Birmingham, as you know." (To an extent, this was true. White and Negro citizens, except for isolated instances, had not clashed in Birmingham. The violence had involved Negro citizens and white peace officers.)

A short time later, Wallace went to the National Guard armory and watched the 500 Guardsmen on duty run through riot-control drills under the blazing sun. One platoon would rush another, heaving pine cones and shouting: "Yankee, go home!" The defending platoon would push the mock rioters back with bayonets and M-1 rifles.

"You're doing a great job for the state," Wallace told the Guardsmen. "We're not going to have any violence in Tuscaloosa, but we did call you out, out of an abundance of caution."

Later Wallace inspected the state law enforcement agencies' deployment on the campus. He joked with the troopers. Some students came along and shook hands with him.

"I'm from Clayton," said one student from Wallace's home town. "We're behind you."

Another said: "We appreciate you keeping your promise, Governor."

Wallace basked in the adulation.

Meanwhile, Nick Katzenbach was briefing marshals on their duties. The marshals spent their spare time studying maps of the campus and surrounding area and floor plans of the buildings to which they would be assigned.

During the afternoon, John Nolan held his scheduled meeting with Al Lingo on the campus. Also present were Jack Cameron and Charlie Chamblee, who would play key roles in leading the small contingent of marshals. The meeting was cordial.

Lingo told the federal men: "All of our men have instructions to pass federal men with the proper credentials at all the checkpoints."

Nolan told Lingo: "We won't have sufficient force tomorrow to undertake any type of internal security. We'll have only 20 or 30 people. They'll arrive in six automobiles. I thought also I could give you the phone number where I could be reached. It would be a good idea for our people to take a look at what you have set up."

The federal and state officials then toured the campus, including Foster Auditorium. Cooperation, thus far, seemed smooth among the various law enforcement agencies. I recalled that at a comparable point at Ole Miss, the cooperation had seemed equally smooth. Only when rioting erupted did the cooperation break down. It was impossible to tell whether the smooth going would last.

In Birmingham, John Doar was attending to details involved in getting the Negro students safely to Tuscaloosa. A small force of marshals was in Birmingham, to rendezvous with the students the following morning and escort them to the university.

In Washington, the President and the Attorney General were in constant consultation. During the day, the President sent a telegram to Wallace, urging him to stay away from the campus the next day. Kennedy said Wallace's plan to stand in the doorway was "the only announced threat to orderly compliance with the law." He said Wallace's plan to try to block the Negroes' enrollment would be "in defiance of the order of the Alabama federal district court and in violation of accepted standards of public conduct."

The telegram continued: "State, city and university officials have reported that, if you were to stay away from the campus, thus fulfilling your legal duty, there is little danger of any disorder being incited which the local town and campus authorities could not adequately handle. This would make unnecessary the outside intervention of any troops, either state or federal. I therefore urgently ask you to consider the consequence to your state and its fine university if you persist in setting an example of defiant conduct and urge you instead to leave these matters in the courts of law, where they belong."

Wallace sent off an answering telegram almost immediately. "My presence here guarantees peace," he said. "This is the opinion of all here familiar with the facts, including the Legislature of Alabama and the president of the University of Alabama."

At 10:30 that night, Wallace would get support on this point from the university trustees. They passed a declaration that an abnormal situation existed. "The presence of Governor Wallace, with the state law enforcement agencies, is desirable to preserve the peace and order because of the Governor's appeals to the public to stay away from the campus and the apparent willingness of unauthorized persons to abide by his requests," the declaration said.

In other words, the trustees felt that extremists, in lieu of rioting the way they had at Ole Miss, seemed willing to let the little fighter from Barbour County stand in that doorway and "stand up for Alabama" for them. The trustees' declaration was signed by Gessner T. McCorvey, the board's president pro tem, and attested to by J. Rufus Black, a trustee.

Later, as Bobby Shelton would grudgingly concede, the extremists were to be somewhat disappointed with the way the battler from Barbour stood up for them, just as Bill Simmons and the Mississippi segregation bloc had been taken aback by Ross Barnett's decision the previous week not to stand in the doorway and block Cleve McDowell.

Wallace's problems were multiplying with each hour. He had kept preaching that there would be no violence. Yet he had brought the National Guard troops into Tuscaloosa. How, then, would he be able to justify his charge of military dictatorship if President Kennedy, by a stroke of the pen, made these Guardsmen federal, rather than state, soldiers?

If he did not move out of the doorway, he faced the possibility of two years in federal prison and loss of the governorship.

If he did move out of the doorway, he faced loss of prestige. He had vowed to go to jail, if necessary, to make his case in the court of public opinion.

If he forced the federals to arrest him, what then? Knowing from my inquiries that the secret of his past mental problem was a secret no longer, he could perhaps contemplate what the federals had done with General Walker after arresting him at Ole Miss. Win or lose on the confrontation, he could not win if he were shipped off to a federal prison hospital for psychiatric observation.

Monday night just before dinner time, I was at the press center, taking care of the dull, but essential, job of protecting my interests for the following day. By that, I mean I was seeing to it that I exercised all the options open to me in the University of Alabama's modified version of the original "Joe Sherman plan" for pool coverage.

With matters arranged, I was about to go back to the

Stafford and eat dinner when Ed Guthman approached. Ed had a few details of his own to handle at the press center. When he had finished, he said to me: "Let's take a little walk."

Guthman and I began walking casually back toward the Town House, where he and most of the other federal men were staying. When we reached the Town House, he opened the door of one of the rooms—not his own. I caught a glimpse of Dean Markham and John Nolan. A figure moved abruptly away from the door to a corner where he could not be seen from outside. Ed took me inside, and there, much to my surprise, I found that the quick-moving figure belonged to Nick Katzenbach. As far as the press corps was concerned, Nick was supposed to be in Birmingham.

Guthman abruptly left the room. "I'm gonna take a swim," he said.

I was astonished. Ed had never done anything like this with me before, except in getting me interviews with the Attorney General and other officials. I had asked for no interview. He had walked me over to the motel, put me in a room with the men every reporter in town would give his eyeteeth to see at this juncture and then walked out.

Nick sat in a chair in the corner across from me. Before I could ask a question, he asked me: "Well, what do you think we ought to do tomorrow?"

I shook my head in puzzlement. "Nick, this situation is straight out of *Alice in Wonderland*. You're asking *me* what to do? I was about to ask you the same question."

In the next minute or two, it became clear that Ed Guthman, with his usual tight-lipped approach, had said nothing to anyone about our discussion of Wallace's mental history. I gave Nick and the others a fill-in on what I knew.

"What are you doing about it?" Nick asked.

"Nick, I don't know. My editors haven't gotten very excited. I understood Wallace might be ready to horse-trade," I continued. "What about it?"

"Nothing solid," Nick said. "We just don't know what he's gonna do."

"It's not like Mississippi, then? There's no deal on?"

"Hell, no. He won't even talk to us. We hear one thing, then another. But there's no deal."

I walked slowly back to the Stafford and ate my first decent meal of the day. After dinner, I talked privately with some of the "old pro" charter members of SCREW, told them about the Wallace mental-history story, got a pledge they would not try to take the story out from under me, sought their advice and batted the whole matter back and forth with them.

Claude Sitton's initial reaction was: "It's a great story, but you can have it. *The Times* wouldn't touch it with a ten-foot pole. We have too many libel suits pending against us in Alabama right now." He was referring to a series of suits filed against *The Times* by Alabama state and municipal officials, some stemming from an ad placed on behalf of Dr. Martin Luther King's legal defense fund (he had been arrested shortly before the ad appeared) and others stemming from a series of news stories (not by Sitton). The Supreme Court has now thrown these suits out of court in an important decision broadening the press' right to criticize public officials.

After checking with other SCREW buddies, and feeling virtually certain that *Newsday* would not use the story— at least that night—I went to bed. So, apparently, did most of the others concerned with the crisis. Two federal marshals manned the telephones and shortwave radios at the army reserve center through the night. State and local police kept a sharp eye out for trouble. Several more outside troublemakers with weapons were arrested, only to go free on bail posted by Bobby Shelton.

At 11:30 P.M., Charlie Chamblee was given instructions to pick up Chief Marshal McShane and Joe Dolan at the Tuscaloosa airport at 5:30 A.M. Jim and Joe had gone to Huntsville to make preparations for Dave McGlathery's scheduled Thursday enrollment. Chamblee also was instructed to set up radio contact by 5:30 A.M. with the pilot of a Border Patrol plane who would be in the air to look for possible trouble.

3

It was up early in the morning for all of us. I got up at 6.

By 6:20, General Abrams advised Dean Markham that, if it were necessary to move Wallace out of the doorway with troops, he recommended using one company of local guerrilla-warfare experts. They could be marched to the campus from the Guard armory, where Wallace had inspected them on Monday. Abrams had talked with Attorney General Kennedy, who concurred in the plan.

At 6:30, Kennedy called Nick to discuss the matter further. At 6:50, Burke Marshall called Nick. What did Nick think of the latest plan and what were the alternatives? Nick told Marshall and the Attorney General: "The only basis for federalizing the Guard would be for contempt proceedings." Thus far, there were no such proceedings. Wallace would have to block the students physically before making himself subject to contempt.

Nick outlined three plans, later referred to by the federals in code as "Number One," "Number Two" and "Number Three."

Number One: No federal troops, regular army or National Guard, would appear at the confrontation.

Number Two: Use federalized Guardsmen, after first giving Wallace a chance to permit the troops to enter.

Number Three: Forget about the doorway. Have the students simply begin attending classes. See to it that state troopers block off class entryways.

At this point, no decision had been made. At 7 A.M., Jim McShane and Joe Dolan arrived at the reserve center to help direct operations at the federal base for the day. Minutes later, General Abrams reported that General Graham, the National Guard commander, "will be at Foster Auditorium with two [guerilla-warfare] men—ready to move the Governor from the doorway quickly." Abrams' report to Nick said that Graham, still with his "Dixie Division" troops on maneuvers, would enter Tuscaloosa by helicopter and "land in front of the armory."

Nick advised Abrams: "We'll have to set up a rendezvous point for me to meet Graham. If the Guardsmen remove Wallace from the door, they should take him into the lobby and his office in the auditorium—not away from the building on the outside! Joe Dolan thinks this would qualify as being under arrest."

At about 7, I walked over to the Town House. I found a note tacked to Nick's door. It said: "Katzenbach: call the Attorney General." Nick was not inside. I found Jack Cameron and gave him the message—to be passed on to Nick. I settled down to breakfast with Jack and some of the other marshals.

The waitresses were really giving the federals the business. If one of us ordered bacon and eggs, we would get waffles. If we sent it back, we would get wheat cakes. If we sent it back again, we would get cold eggs, scrambled instead of fried. We sat chuckling about the pettiness of some people, and eating each other's breakfasts until we had what we had ordered.

Butler and several of the others were veterans of one of the best highway patrols in the country, Maryland's. We talked about the sad state of the Mississippi patrol. "You know, Lingo has some damned good men working with him," I said. "They did a helluva job for Floyd Mann, Lingo's predecessor, during the Freedom Rides. But, with Lingo, they're under all kinds of political pressure."

The marshals had to leave to take up their assignments. I walked back over to the Stafford. Who should spot me and invite me to breakfast but Al Lingo? I did not mention that I had just eaten with the opposition. I figured maybe Lingo had something to tell me.

My relations with Lingo had been cordial. I did not like him or respect him, but he had been civil to me. I had tried to be civil to him.

As usual, Lingo had several of his top aides with him. Some had admitted privately to me that they were distressed over Lingo's tactics, and much preferred those used by Floyd Mann. Rumors had found their way into the Alabama press that Lingo might be replaced. Among those named as a possible successor was Bull Connor. I knew Lingo was touchy about it. I thought I'd needle him a little, to get his reaction. But first we joked back and forth for awhile. He kept calling me a "Yankee." I pointed out that I had lived and worked in the South, that my wife was from the South and one daughter had been born in Texas.

Lingo called to our waitress, "Bring this man some grits. He's doin' all this talkin' about not really bein' a full-fledged Yankee. Let's see how he does on some grits."

"Colonel," I said. "I'll eat those damned grits. I don't like them very much, but I can keep them down. Now, mustard greens, that's another matter entirely."

Lingo went on about how he wasn't going to permit any trouble at the doorway. "I've got to go fishin' in a couple of days," he said. "I'm not goin' to stand for any trouble."

"What will you do if the students are admitted?" I asked. "Will you give them protection?"

"Hell, no," he roared. "Why should we? We're not baby-sitters."

This was to become a major point. I would ask Lingo the question again later.

When we finished eating, Lingo would not let me pick up my check. It was all very puzzling. I wondered why he was being so nice to me. Later I was to conclude he had called me over to his table to be sure all his key men could recognize that damn Yankee who was trying to prove George Wallace was "nuts."

At 7:22 A.M., Nick Katzenbach, replying to the message I had left for him, phoned Washington. He said he would appear at the confrontation with U. S. Attorney Macon Weaver and U. S. Marshal Peyton Norville. The Negro students would remain in a car parked in front of the auditorium. They would be guarded by marshals. Katzenbach would ask Wallace what he intended to do. There would be no federal troops present. There would thus not be any direct confrontation between Wallace and the students.

This was a major decision. It gave Wallace a possible out. He could spare himself from contempt proceedings. But would he be keeping his campaign pledge? That was his problem.

General Abrams advised Nick that it would take two hours for General Graham to get into operation after the

Guard had been federalized, if it were necessary. It would take an hour to fly to Tuscaloosa by helicopter and another hour to be briefed.

At 7:35, the Attorney General approved these plans. He said he would check with Army Secretary Vance to see if they met with his approval. Abrams confirmed that any Guardsmen used would be local boys.

At 8 A.M., Jeff Bennett of the university staff phoned Ed Guthman to check on security precautions at the students' dormitories. He was told that Nick would dispatch three marshals at 10:30 A.M. to establish security in the dormitories. Nick, about this time, got confidential word that Wallace was not planning to come outside the auditorium any farther than the doorway. (This later proved untrue.)

At 8:15, Jack Cameron briefed Nick, Ed, Dean Markham, Joe Dolan, Jim McShane, John Nolan, Charlie Chamblee and General Abrams at the reserve center on security arrangements. Five minutes later, a state trooper captain phoned to ask for identification information on the federal autos that would enter the campus. He was told they would be unmarked, except for visor cards, and would bear Louisiana license plates. (New Orleans is a Border Patrol center, and most of the drivers were Border Patrolmen.) Checkpoints for the cars' entry were arranged.

At 8:35, Macon Weaver and Peyton Norville—local men —reported that they had been told Wallace would stand aside at the doorway. But under what circumstances, no one could say. And who could tell whether the report were true?

In Washington, it was now 10:45. President Kennedy, awake almost three hours, had conferred with his brother and other officials. He was told that it looked as though there might be trouble in Tuscaloosa. Troops might be needed. If so, Kennedy felt compelled to go on television and explain why they had been used. He was in the midst of helping aides draft a civil rights bill. That very morning, in the White House, the congressional leaders had gathered for their weekly breakfast meeting in the Red Room, with civil rights as the chief topic.

At 10:55, the President phoned Andy Hatcher, associate

press secretary and a Negro, and told him he was signing a proclamation on the Tuscaloosa crisis. The proclamation, following the usual "whereas" form, cited various legal provisions and accused Wallace of entering with others into an "unlawful obstruction and combination" to defy the federal courts. It read in part:

This . . . will, if carried out as threatened, make it impracticable to enforce the laws of the United States in the State of Alabama by the ordinary course of judicial proceedings. . . . [It] opposes the execution of the laws of the United States and threatens to impede the course of justice under those laws.
Now, therefore, I, John F. Kennedy, President of the United States of America, . . . do command the governor of the State of Alabama and all other persons engaged or who may engage in unlawful obstructions of justice, assemblies, combinations, conspiracies or domestic violence in that state to cease and desist therefrom. . . .

This proclamation, in itself, was not expected to accomplish anything. It merely laid the predicate, as lawyers put it, for what would come later. But it was indicative that there had been no "deal" during the night. The federals were still playing it by ear, although they had a plan for each expected contingency.

In Tuscaloosa it was 9:01. Nick Katzenbach, taking into cognizance that FBI agents in the South often are "buddy-buddy" with local officers, instructed: "Make sure the FBI doesn't let our plan leak to the local law enforcement." The local FBI men, whom I had met, seemed dedicated men who would not let such a leak occur, but Nick was tagging all the bases.

At 9:11, General Abrams changed the route for entry to the campus by the cars that would carry the Negro students from Birmingham. They had flown to Birmingham from New York. Abrams, too, was tagging all the bases.

At the same time, a single checkpoint was designated for the entry to the campus of the cars carrying the students.

About this time, I crossed through one of the checkpoints, flashing both my university press badge and my pool badge. I was not about to wear the badges until so instructed. Just such badges had been red flags to the rioters at Ole Miss. I stopped on the way to the auditorium and bought all the soft drinks I could carry. I was not going to be caught without food, drink, cigarets or pipe tobacco, as I had been at Ole Miss. If I had to cover a riot, at least I would be comfortable this time. I scouted the area for phone booths, marking down their locations. Then I carried my soft drinks to the area in front of the auditorium, where I distributed them to friends. Some had been sitting out in the sun for hours, waiting for they knew not what.

Equipped with a partial timetable, I knew a little more of what could be expected. It all looked more than a trifle absurd to me. The scene could have been a Hollywood sound stage. The white semicircles marked the boundaries beyond which we could not move without pool badges. Some pool members, afraid they might not be able to get inside the building later, were already inside the auditorium. Routine registration had been proceeding for a couple of hours. Now it came to a standstill. Faculty members and student employes sat at their desks, waiting for the two Negro students. It would be a long wait.

Rather than enter the building, I depended on a gentleman's agreement with Al Lingo to get me through the lines when I decided I wanted to go inside. State troopers already were lined up, as if in an honor guard, to await the arrival of their commander. A few, with guns, were on the roof of the columned, three-story building. The building, although called an "auditorium," is really a field house. Inside there are spectator benches at the upper levels.

Huge trailers carrying television and radio equipment were parked across the street. Platforms had been erected. Cameramen were at their places. Directors talked into headphones. If it were going to be a riot, it would be the best-covered riot there ever was.

But no riot seemed imminent. Later, perhaps. Now, hardly. I began pondering the possibilities. "If I lived in the Negro wards of this town," I said to one of my fellow correspondents, "I'd go visit relatives tonight. There's too much loose dynamite floating around in this state."

Afterwards, I was to recall this remark and regret its flippancy.

At 9:30, Bill Jones, the Governor's press secretary, arrived and entered the auditorium. Twenty minutes later, the star of the spectacular arrived. He walked through the rows of troopers like a general reviewing the troops. He was dapper, as always. He looked confident. He made another little chamber-of-commerce speech, saying how glad he was to have us in his fair state. Then he went inside to the office set aside for him. Now, if Bobby Shelton were correct, we would see the "peelin' come off the peach."

At the reserve armory, the wires crackled with messages. A rendezvous point still had not been chosen for Nick and General Graham.

At 9:40, Ed Guthman, John Nolan and Joe Dolan reached a campus checkpoint by car. They were cleared for entry, and proceeded on foot.

Precisely at 10, as if it were all worked out on a minute-by-minute basis, Justice Department lawyer John Martin came by me. I greeted him. Beside him was the mammoth marshal, Cecil Miller. A state trooper tried to stop them. Miller towered over the trooper. He just glared at him. John pulled out his credentials. They walked on into the auditorium. Martin phoned the reserve center, left a university extension number where he could be reached and gave an all-clear signal. There were about 15 troopers inside the lobby, he reported.

At 10:07, Harold Reis, the assistant attorney general who worked as Number Two man in the Justice Department Office of Legal Counsel, called the reserve center. He reported that President Kennedy's proclamation commanding Wallace to cease and desist had been released by the White House. Nick would carry a copy of the proclamation up to the doorway.

Ed Guthman, John Nolan and Joe Dolan had arrived at my vantage point now. Charlie Whiteford of the *Baltimore Sun* and I introduced Ed to some of the troopers we knew from the Freedom Rides. One of them, a major, shook hands, smiled ruefully and said: "You know, most of us are just interested in law enforcement."

Ed got the message. He talked cordially with the major. A few minutes later, Al Lingo came by. We introduced him to Lingo. They shook hands. So far, so good.

Jack Cameron appeared now. The preliminaries were being handled. Jack obviously was in direct command of the marshals on the scene. Jim McShane was calling the shots for them from the reserve center.

At 10:20, the lead car of the caravan bringing the students to Tuscaloosa checked out its two-way radio and equipment for taping all messages. Everything was OK. At 10:36, the Border Patrol driver radioed he was approaching the campus. At 10:40, Al Butler appeared. He talked with two state troopers in front of the auditorium. One of the troopers gave a message to his superiors by walkie-talkie.

It was now 10:44. The white lead car pulled in front of the auditorium. It was followed by a brown Ford carrying the students. John Doar sat on one side of Vivian Malone. Jimmy Hood sat on the other side.

Charlie Chamblee was outside one of the cars now, chattering into a walkie-talkie. But the students did not leave the car. They had been briefed: they would remain in the car. George Wallace might be "standing up for Alabama." But Nick was "standing up" for them.

A student with a small box camera suddenly rushed out of the group behind me and tried to take a picture. Troopers ran him off. John Doar, Vivian Malone and Jimmy Hood were smiling and talking in what appeared to be a relaxed manner. The Negro students were in Sunday best, a sharp contrast to the informal attire worn by most of the white students. Miss Malone, a beautiful girl, was chic in a black dress with her hair teased into a stylish hairdo. Hood wore a dark suit.

Nick, Macon Weaver and Peyton Norville climbed out of cars. They walked through the double row of blue-helmeted state troopers. Nick had a copy of the President's proclamation with him.

Wallace was surrounded by aides. Two of his brothers were there. Major General Albert N. Harrison, who had replaced General Graham as state adjutant general in the Wallace administration, walked hurriedly back and forth through the doorway, conferring with Lingo and others. Harrison obviously realized that he was not going to command any federalized troops this day. He was in civilian clothes. Seymore Trammell, state finance director and chief Wallace adviser on segregation and other issues, conferred with many of the others.

When Nick, Weaver and Norville approached, Wallace walked out and stood behind a lectern in front of the doorway. The lectern had been put in place by a state trooper. Wallace had a microphone draped around his neck, like a TV performer. It was connected to a public address system.

Nick approached, told Wallace he had a proclamation from the President, "commanding" the Governor to cease and desist from blocking the implementation of the court orders. But Wallace held up his hand, like a traffic cop, and cut Nick short. He said he had a statement and proclamation of his own.

Wallace then read his five page opus:

As governor and chief magistrate of the State of Alabama, I deem it to be my solemn obligation and duty to stand before you representing the rights and sovereignty of this state and its people. The unwelcome, unwanted, unwarranted and force-induced intrusion upon the campus of the University of Alabama today of the might of the Central Government offers frightful example of the oppression of the rights, privileges and sovereignty of this state by officers of the federal government. [At this point, the "might of the Central Government" was represented by about 25 men.] This intrusion results solely from force, or threat of force, undignified by any reasonable application of the principle of law, reason and justice. . . . [At this point, Wallace was the man commanding the troops on duty in Tuscaloosa.]

There has been no legislative action by Congress justifying this action. . . . [And, as the government had frequently pointed out, there would be no federal action if Wallace just permitted two of his state's citizens to enter a university that was ready to accept them.] There can be no submission to the theory that the Central Government is anything but a servant of the people. We are God-fearing people—not government-fearing people!

At this juncture, a roar went up behind the point where

I was standing. State troopers fanned out into the area to see where the noise had come from, but no incident developed.

I stand here today as governor of this sovereign state, and refuse to willingly submit to illegal usurpation of power by the Central Government. I claim today for all the people of the State of Alabama those rights reserved to them under the Constitution of the United States. Among those powers so reserved and claimed is the right of state authority in the operation of the public schools, colleges and universities. [This was, in the view of the executive branch, irrelevant. The government did not claim any authority to operate anybody's schools. It merely accepted as a duty the enforcement of court orders.]

My action does not constitute disobedience to legislative and constitutional provisions. It is not defiance for defiance['s] sake, but for the purpose of raising basic and fundamental constitutional questions. My action is a call for strict adherence to the Constitution of the United States as it was written—for a cessation of usurpation and abuses. My action seeks to avoid having state sovereignty sacrificed on the altar of political expediency. [The President had made no political pledge to integrate this university, but Wallace had pledged in a political campaign to stand in its doorway.]

Further . . . the illegal and unwarranted actions of the Central Government on this day, contrary to the laws, customs and traditions of this state is calculated to disturb the peace. [But Wallace had been saying that Alabamans were so law-abiding that there would be no threat of violence.]

I stand before you today in place of thousands of other Alabamans whose presence would have confronted you had I been derelict and neglected to fulfill the responsibilities of my office. . . . [Here, Wallace listed his "whereas" citations.] Now, therefore, I, George C. Wallace, as governor of the State of Alabama, have by my action raised issues between the Central Government and the Sovereign State of Alabama, which said issues should be adjudicated in the manner prescribed by the Constitution [the government contended they had been adjudicated and Wallace had lost]; and now being mindful of my duties and responsibilities under the Constitution of the United States, the Constitution of the State of Alabama, and seeking to preserve and maintain the peace and dignity of this state, and the individual freedoms of the citizens thereof, do hereby denounce and FORBID [capitalization by the author] this illegal and unwarranted action by the Central Government.

The statement and proclamation, when stripped of its verbiage, seemed to hang on the interpretation of that word "forbid." What was the fightin' little judge going to do about seeing to it that this "forbidden" act—carrying out a court's order—was prevented?

Nick said to him: "Governor Wallace, I take it from that statement that you are going to stand in the door and that you are not going to carry out the orders of the court, and that you are going to resist us from doing so. Is that correct?"

Wallace replied: "I stand according to my statement."

Nick scowled. "Governor, I am not interested in a show," he said. "I don't know what the purpose of this show is. I am interested in the orders of these courts being enforced. There is no choice for the federal government. I would ask you once again to responsibly stand aside. If you do not, I'm going to assure you that the orders of these courts will be enforced. From the outset, Governor, all of us have known that the final chapter of this history will be the admission of these students. These students will remain on this campus. They will register today. They will go to school tomorrow."

Nick made several more pleas in the same vein, forecasting the students' enrollment. He waited for the Governor to reply. It was his play now. But the Governor stood defiantly in the doorway, ever the fightin' little judge. His shoulders were thrown back. His carriage was military. His lips were a tight line.

At this point, Nick followed the prearranged plan. He, Norville, Weaver and others withdrew. Wallace had not blocked the students thus far. He had stood in the doorway to face two federal lawyers and one federal marshal.

Nick walked to the car containing John Doar and the students. Nick and Miss Malone, with Joe Dolan and Cecil Miller, walked toward Miss Malone's assigned dormitory, Mary Burke Hall. I fell in beside Nick. "So far, so good," I said. Nick just kept walking. "Are we [reporters] in or out of this building?" I asked.

"Out," Nick said firmly. I had seen him under a variety of stresses. But never had I seen him looking so furious, not even at Ole Miss.

Miss Malone entered the dormitory. A few reporters tried to shove their way in behind her. Since I was right next to Nick, I got caught in the jam. A house mother told all of us we would not be permitted to enter. Several marshals were there to back up her direction. Clearly, Miss Malone was now, in effect, a University of Alabama student. She was in a dormitory, with student status and federal protection. The fightin' little judge had done nothing to bar such a move. He, or his people, must have known it would be made.

So now all that remained was the charade of standing again in the doorway. But would Wallace "stand up for Alabama" again? Would he make the federals move him out of the doorway by force? On that, to informed persons, hung the question of whether Wallace was interested in a show, a true legal test of Alabama's constitutional rights or a mere gesture to pacify some of the less militant segregationists. The more militant ones were prepared to stand and fight for their rights if Wallace had the intestinal fortitude to stand up to the "KKK—Kennedy Koon Klan," as some segregationists were calling the federal force in Tuscaloosa.

While Miss Malone was being taken to her room, Hood was being driven to his dormitory in a car also containing "baby-sitter" John Doar. (It is perhaps appropriate here to point out that I have been using the term "baby-sitter" only to designate John by the term Al Lingo would have used. Lingo had said: "We won't baby-sit for them." John, as I have tried to make clear, is a man of great courage.)

During the maneuver to put the students in the dormitories, the federals had been proceeding with what they had designated in advance as "Option Use Plan B." This was an indication of the great care taken in preparing for the Alabama confrontation. Though such care also had been taken at Ole Miss, some of the possible options had not been figured out to the ultimate degree. The Justice Department was learning something with each new episode in its program to see that court orders were obeyed.

At 11:10, the Attorney General advised from Washington that the President was prepared to sign an executive order federalizing the Alabama National Guard, unless Nick had some objection. The President had, unlike the night of the Ole Miss riot, routinely been carrying on other business while keeping in touch with his brother. He had missed a live telecast of the first confrontation, but arranged to watch a taped rerun.

President Kennedy had been meeting during the day with Republican leaders to outline his plans for a sweeping civil rights bill, covering such subjects as public accommodations, school integration and voting rights. Typically, some thought, those two representatives of "the party of Lincoln"—Senate Minority Leader Everett Dirksen and House Minority Leader Charles Halleck—were described as skeptical. They wanted to study the proposal further.

But the President was determined to make his position clear. If he federalized the Alabama Guard, he felt obliged to go on national TV to explain his decision. He would use the occasion to deal with the whole area of civil rights. The President put speech writer Ted Sorensen to work on a draft covering both the Alabama confrontation and the broader theme of the need to respond to the worldwide yearning of black persons and other minorities for long-denied opportunities.

At 11:15, the Pentagon war room flashed the army personnel in Tuscaloosa to have Nick phone Bob Kennedy immediately. At 11:25, Nick phoned Washington from Miss Malone's dormitory.

"The students were never stopped," he told the Attorney General. "They were never confronted. Abrams will have to be thinking of a schedule for the pickup and delivery of students [by military personnel or with military supervision] to the auditorium with proper security."

Just as at Ole Miss, the federals had been forced to turn over a relatively simple task to the military. There would be later cries of "military dictatorship," but the federals had no choice.

At 11:35, Harold Reis advised for purposes of the marshals' log: "Executive order 11111 has been signed by the President and is being released at the White House now. The [accompanying] presidential proclamation is Number 3542."

At 11:40, General Abrams, apparently for security purposes related to possible wire-tapping, closed down a radio-telephone line to the Pentagon war room. A radio line was kept open.

John Doar and Nick Katzenbach left their young charges in the hands of federal marshals, dormitory personnel and university officials and students. Significantly, a number of white students came by the Negroes' rooms and wished them well, even as their elders were acting out the last chapters in the stage-managed TV spectacular.

Precisely at noon, the Attorney General sent word that Ed Guthman was to notify the press that Wallace had not blocked the students. FBI agents were assigned to find Ed and give him that message. Ed spread the word. But so many newsmen were in Tuscaloosa that hours later some foreign newsmen, who really didn't understand the entire problem beyond the black-and-white of Wallace *versus* Kennedy, were astonished to learn that Wallace would not be going to jail.

For 90 minutes, both sides huddled. Advisers were called in. Newsmen who did not have pool badges sweltered in the sun. Now I decided it was time to enter the auditorium, using my pool badge. Inside there was nothing to do but wait. Only Wallace's favored newsmen were permitted anywhere near the office he was using. Al Lingo, after keeping his word to permit me inside the auditorium, shouted "Clear the halls" every time he saw me near the Wallace office. Unlike those outside, we were fed, given cigarets and soft drinks, along with the "captive" university employes working on the registration.

Ed Ball, the Florida newspaper editor called in as a consultant by the university, was sitting upstairs in the gallery with some of the reporters. I had been downstairs most of the time. I had confided in Ball and sought his advice on the Wallace mental-history story. Now I asked him what Wallace was doing inside his office. "He's raising all kinds of hell," Ball said.

At 1:30, Nick Katzenbach advised General Abrams: "The Attorney General suggests that two to four Guardsmen move the lectern away from the door while Wallace speaks, so he will have to move away from the door."

Charlie Chamblee suggested the federals use walkie-talkies to maintain contacts with the National Guard.

At 1:45, the following plan was formulated: Registration of the Negro students would take place at 3:30 Tuscaloosa time. Nick, Miss Malone, Macon Weaver and Peyton Norville would rendezvous at Miss Malone's dormitory. Nick and General Graham of the Alabama National Guard would rendezvous at Elm and Sixth Streets at 3:25. John Doar, Charlie Chamblee and Hood would be in the lead car of a caravan accompanied by Guard troops.

While all this had been going on, Graham had been piloting a small reconnaissance plane over Fort McClellan. He was watching Dixie Division troops run through maneuvers. While cruising at 3,000 feet, he received a radio message instructing him to land. He was ordered to rush to Tuscaloosa by helicopter and take command of the federalized Guard troops.

When Graham had taken off, his commander had been George Wallace. Now, through General Abrams, his commander was John F. Kennedy.

At 2:29, Graham had landed and been briefed after the helicopter flight to Tuscaloosa. Abrams advised Dean Markham that Graham had been briefed by an adviser to Wallace. I quote here from the marshals' log:

Both [Graham and Wallace's advisers are] aghast at the possibility of moving Wallace bodily away from the door. [They are] sanguine that he will step aside when Graham confronts him, but wants 45 seconds for a statement. . . .

Guardsmen don't want the regular Army in. This will motivate local Guardsmen to do a good job. [Abrams] wants to know what he can tell.

Dean consulted Nick and was told: "Tell Abrams OK. We will not move the lectern and will give Wallace the chance for a brief statement."

At 3:15, the FBI reported to the reserve center that four truckloads of Guardsmen had been observed and were being escorted to the campus by Jefferson County (Birmingham) and Montgomery County motor police.

At 3:16, three truckloads of Guardsmen arrived at Miss

Malone's dormitory. The motorcycles and a jeep following the trucks screeched to a halt. Infantrymen, in green fatigues and armed with M-1 rifles, jumped down. Others appeared before the auditorium. And still others arrived with General Graham, who was in an unmarked green command car. Graham, a Birmingham real estate man in civilian life, was clearly in command of the situation now. A lanky, genial man with graying hair, he looked the picture of what he was—an airborne general still in fighting trim. He wore paratrooper's jump boots, fatigues and a billed cap.

Graham's troops, swiftly and authoritatively, took up positions in front of the auditorium and around it. Colonel Al Lingo walked over. He saluted Graham, who returned the salute. They shook hands.

Nick and other federal officials conferred briefly with Graham. At 3:31, a minute behind schedule, the Negro students left their dormitories with escorts.

Graham and four special-forces (guerrilla-warfare) Guardsmen, all sergeants, now strode determinedly toward "the door." Seymore Trammel, Wallace's finance director and key segregation adviser, turned toward the entrance— still inside "the door"—and put on his straw hat. At this signal, an aide straightened George Wallace's tie. The fightin' little judge walked out the door to meet the commander of his own Guard troops.

Graham walked to within a few yards of the Governor. He snapped to attention. Then, leaning forward so Wallace could hear him, he said in a grim voice: "It is my sad duty to ask you to step aside. . . ." His voice sank so low after "sad duty" that the public address system did not pick up the end of the sentence.

Wallace pulled a rumpled piece of paper from his pocket. "I wish to make a statement," he told Graham. "But for the unwarranted federalization of the National Guard, I would be your commander-in-chief. In fact, I am your commander-in-chief. I know this is a bitter pill for you."

If Graham were bitter, he did not show it then or later. He did say later that he had used the words "sad duty" because Wallace had been his commander. Now, though Graham did not place blame on anyone, the President was his commander.

Wallace continued:

"I am grateful to the people of Alabama for the restraint which they have shown. I ask the people of Alabama to remain calm, to help us in this fight. We must have no violence. . . . The Guardsmen are our brothers. The trend toward military dictatorship continues. But this is a constitutional fight, and we are winning. God bless all the people of this state, white and black."

Wallace snapped to attention himself, gave Graham a salute and received one in return. He stepped out of the doorway—not to regular army troops, not to the Negro students, not to a lawyer from Washington, not to Cecil Miller and other rugged marshals, not to Attorney General Kennedy, not to the President, but to his own National Guard commander and four local Guardsmen.

The federals not only had won this power play, they also had made Wallace look bad in the doing. And they had forced him to choose between pleasing Bobby Shelton and other extremists, and various other options—including going to jail and being shoved aside.

Inside the auditorium, the atmosphere changed almost instantly. Most of us had been killing time by lounging on chairs and tables, talking, joking and speculating on what Wallace might do. Now, after watching him walk away from the door, we knew the Negro students would arrive shortly. We took our places, according to the pool arrangement. Actually, at my suggestion, a local newspaper reporter had been chosen to be the one newspaper representative on the floor of the auditorium during the registration. I had figured he would be better able to identify local residents than any of us from outside the state.

Since his paper was shuttling men in and out of the building, university officials had permitted me to stay on the ground floor as a backstop for the local man. As I waited for the students to appear, I looked up. Several birds had flown inside through open windows and were trying to find their way out. "Looks like we haven't been the only captive audience for this extravaganza," I said to one of the TV network men.

One of Al Lingo's state troopers, who had been giving some of us a hard time all day, came along at that point and told several of us to clear the floor. "We have a right to be here," I said. "We have pool badges." He thought otherwise, and started to move us out. Just then I spotted John Doar, who had entered the auditorium with the two students. "Well, there's the Justice Department," I said to the trooper. "Still want to argue about it?"

The trooper conferred with a superior, then came back and apologized. It was clear that Al Lingo no longer was in the saddle.

I had determined in advance which desk the two students would approach first. Since most segregationists' resentment against the students was centered on Miss Malone—because she was considered to be "taking the place of" Autherine Lucy—I had decided to stick with her. I was waiting as she was ushered to the first registration desk. A kindly, middle-aged university employee, sitting behind the desk, said to her with a smile: "Hi, there. We've been waiting for you."

Miss Malone, looking elegant in a pink dress (she had changed from a black one since the morning confrontation), smiled. She had seemed tight as a knot at first. Now, with TV and movie cameras grinding and still cameras clicking, she appeared more relaxed. Her poise, for a girl her age, was remarkable. After filling out some cards and handing them to the employe, she said gratefully: "Thank you." No flourish. No "Thanks ever so much." Just a simple prim "Thank you."

State troopers, as they had been doing throughout the crisis, were taking still and motion pictures of their own —presumably for identification and intelligence purposes. While Miss Malone was registering for a math class, an incident occurred that gave many of us a taste of sweet revenge. Some of the troopers had been ordering us around. Now, a newsreel cameraman on the upper level shouted to two of the picture-shooting troopers: "Hey, move out of my way!" The troopers scurried.

Jimmy Hood was registering at different tables from

Miss Malone, since he was taking different courses. Other students now began drifting in to register. The university, the Justice Department and the military personnel had wanted to avoid as much disruption of routine as possible once Wallace had left the doorway. They were well aware that one of the incidents that had led to the Autherine Lucy rioting had centered on university officials' decision to register her ahead of many other students who had been waiting at the end of long lines. There would be no favored treatment this day, other than what was necessary for security reasons.

After completing the registration process, the students were directed by John Doar and university officials to the bursar's office. There they paid their tuition with scholarship checks issued by the same group of New York public utility executives who had paid Cleve McDowell's way into Ole Miss.

Each check was for $500. Hood paid first, and took $220 in change. Miss Malone took only $205.20 in change, since she was registering for more course credits. She and Hood seemed relatively composed. But the student employe handing out the change was all thumbs. A portly old man working behind the counter said gently to Miss Malone: "You'd better count it. He's pretty nervous."

During this period, except for telling the students to relax, that they were doing fine, none of us covering the registration had tried to interview them. We had been told they would say something to us later. Now, with their fees paid, Miss Malone and Hood officially were University of Alabama students.

John Doar told them that several hundred newsmen were waiting outside to hear what they had to say. In a touching gesture, Hood took Miss Malone's arm, like an older brother, and led her toward what they undoubtedly considered the latest in a series of difficult duties.

Outside they stood before the microphones set up by the electronic media. Hood spoke for both of them. "This is our first and final news conference," he said. "We are very happy our registration has taken place without incident. We hope to get down to our purpose—study." As they started to walk away, with an escort, someone asked Miss

Malone if she had anything to add. "Not right now," she said, smiling.

It was 3:45. The students were taken to their dormitories. The difference between the acceptance of these two students and the two who had enrolled at Ole Miss was startling. Miss Malone shortly was engaged in a gabfest with other coeds. She was invited to play bridge, after she got settled, by other girls. "She's very attractive," one coed said later. "I don't think we'll have any trouble with her. She was calm. She wasn't nervous or close-mouthed. She acted very mature."

Another girl said she had been anxious to meet Miss Malone. "We enjoyed meeting her and talking to her. I'm glad she's on our hall," this girl said. Still another was cool, but not belligerent. "She has a right to be here, but no one can be forced to accept her," she said.

Hood spent most of the day in his room. He was greeted by dormitory supervisors and had lunch in a student dining hall. His reception was perhaps not so warm as Miss Malone's, but no one was unpleasant.

Few harsh remarks were heard. Undoubtedly there were some resentful, even outraged, white students. Pamphlets issued by a "rebel underground"—similar to the rabid group at Ole Miss—had been circulated. But most responsible student leaders had performed admirably. The student body as a whole was in a much better frame of mind than had been the one at Ole Miss. Perhaps it had been the Ole Miss rioting that had sobered the students. Perhaps it was the memory of the Autherine Lucy rioting. At any rate, the faculty, student body and local community had reacted with much more realistic attitudes than had those at Oxford.

Now, with Hedrick Smith of *The New York Times*, I drove back to the Stafford. Smith had not been at Ole Miss, but had been in Birmingham when I was there. "Quite a difference," I said, as we left the parking space just off campus. I gave him a quick fill-in on what he had missed because he had not been in a pool. Later, I would do the same for other out-of-state newspapermen.

About two blocks from the Stafford, a teen-ager tossed a rock at our car. It could have been just an isolated prank, but it also could have been an indication of future trouble. Again I made the remark: "I don't think I'd like to live in a Negro ward anywhere in Alabama tonight."

At the Stafford, the first thing I did, after phoning my office, was to take a swim. It had been an arduous three days for me. Now, barring another grandstand play by Wallace when the third Negro student appeared two days later for enrollment at the university's Huntsville branch, I would be going home. I very much needed a rest.

In the pool, I was astounded to find that a number of foreign reporters, whose deadlines were hours away because of time-zone differences, were under the impression that Wallace would be going to jail.

"He never blocked those students," I said. "He just blocked a few Justice Department people. He didn't do enough to be cited for contempt, the way the judge's order was drawn. What I'll be interested to see is how the 'kluxers' react, and what kind of protection Al Lingo gives the Negro students."

In the lobby of the hotel about ten minutes later, I encountered Lingo, leading Wallace out to a car that would take him to the airport. Wallace looked grim. When I tried to ask him something, Lingo pulled him aside and whispered something in his ear. Wallace said he had nothing to say to me.

"Colonel, what are you going to do about protecting those students?" I asked.

"We're going to maintain law and order here and everywhere in the state," Lingo replied.

"But you're still not going to 'baby-sit' with the students, is that it?"

"Why the hell should we?" Lingo rasped.

He and Wallace walked outside. They went to the airport, where the Governor boarded his small plane and flew back to Montgomery. Waiting to meet him were about 200 well-wishers, including his mother, Mrs. Mozelle Wallace. "I think we are helping to wake the country up," Wallace said. (He would repeat this theme many times later in his effort to win national support for his candidacy for President on a ticket that he hoped would be a coalition of Northern and Southern States' righters.)

A reporter asked whether he planned to go to Huntsville on Thursday to carry out his pledge to stand in every schoolhouse doorway, if necessary. "I don't want to make any further statement on that," he replied.

It was not necessary. The fightin' little judge had played with the big boys and had been not only outmanned and outgunned, but outfinessed. For all his shrewdness, George Wallace did not have the class of a John F. Kennedy or a Nick Katzenbach.

Wallace would not appear at Huntsville. Dave McGlathery would be registered without incident and with only a feeble protest from the Governor.

But in Tuscaloosa, the activity was still somewhat hectic. At the precise moment that Vivian Malone and Jimmy Hood had been facing the press in front of Foster Auditorium, General Abrams had been making arrangements for a meeting at the National Guard armory of all the chief security officers. Among those attending were Generals Graham and Abrams, Nick Katzenbach, a major in the state police, John Nolan, and Jack Cameron.

At 3:48, Katzenbach had ordered that the National Guardsmen providing security for the Negro students should be removed and that state highway patrolmen should replace them, until Lingo pulled his men out of town. Katzenbach clearly wanted Lingo to assume responsibility for maintaining law and order as long as possible. He wanted as few troops as necessary in evidence.

The patrol boat that had cruised the Black Warrior River during the crisis was now docked. Arrangements were made for marshals, state police and local police to take over security for the campus and surrounding area.

By 4:40, John Doar was leaving for Huntsville and, later, Washington. Joe Dolan, Jim McShane and Dean Markham were en route to Huntsville. The federal "takeover," if that is what Wallace chose to call it, had lasted five hours. Most of the federal men were leaving, although some marshals would remain briefly.

After dinner, Ed Bounds, head of the university news bureau, made a moving, if slightly corny, announcement to the press at the downtown news center. "It is my responsibility and pleasure to announce the closing of this news center," he said. "We hope that, a year from now, some of you will return for roundups on the university's additional honors and reports on how we have handled ourselves with dignity. You've been of much assistance."

I made a mental note at the time: I'll bet dollars to doughnuts not 20 of these several hundred newsmen will come back, but I'm going to try.

4

With Vivian Malone and Jimmy Hood enrolled at the University of Alabama, token desegregation had at last been accomplished in all 50 states. Despite the implications of the word "token," this accomplishment was no minor victory in the civil rights revolution. For it meant that, by mediation or by might, the federal courts and the executive branch had determined —100 years after the Civil War—that no state ever again would seriously challenge the supreme authority of the United States government. The doctrine of interposition might not have died at Appomattox, but it surely died 100 years later in Oxford, Mississippi, and Tuscaloosa, Alabama.

The night of Tuesday, June 12, only hours after George Wallace had stepped out of the University of Alabama "door," President Kennedy went on television to explain his decision to federalize the Alabama National Guard. But, more important than this was his use of the occasion to sound what may, in retrospect, be considered a second Emancipation Proclamation.

Kennedy, ever since taking office, had been under severe criticism from militant Negro leaders, as well as militant segregationists. He had campaigned in 1960 on a strong civil rights platform, saying that racial and religious discrimination in federally financed housing and some other fields could be eliminated by "the stroke of a pen" (the incumbent President Eisenhower's). He had also played a leading role in getting Dr. Martin Luther King released from a Southern jail during the 1960 campaign.

Negroes and other civil rights advocates had expected the Kennedy administration to come up with bold new approaches to solving 20th-century problems of minority groups. Instead, it found a sincere effort—far superior to that in the Eisenhower years—but all too often a tendency to surrender to political expediency.

Burke Marshall, John Doar and a well-chosen group of civil rights lawyers in the Justice Department had done a magnificent job of establishing liaison with responsible white and Negro leaders in the North and South. They had established a rapport with such leaders that permitted them to accomplish with a few phone calls what previously had taken protracted legal battles, battles that the Eisenhower administration had undertaken only reluctantly. Jim McShane and his force of "riot squad" marshals and Border Patrolmen had shown great courage in trying to enforce orders of federal courts. But too frequently Kennedy appointees on the federal district court benches in the South were segregationists who had to be dragged, kicking and screaming, into the 1960s. They had lived too long under the Southern "way of life." Only after they had been reprimanded in decisions by higher courts had they recognized that this "way of life" could not endure forever.

In the legislative field, the Kennedy administration had been notably gun-shy. The President was having enough problems with his legislative program to cause him to be wary of antagonizing Southern congressmen and senators, whose votes he badly needed for his New Frontier legislation.

With Negroes carrying their struggle for "freedom now" into the streets of scores of communities in the North and South, Kennedy decided it was time to make his long-delayed big push for civil rights legislation. He would put his prestige and political future on the line for what he considered the major moral issue of his time.

Ted Sorensen had completed the text of the television address. The President took a few minutes out for a swim in the White House pool. Shortly before air time, he strode into his office. He had made a few hand-scrawled improvements of his own on the Sorensen text.

"The monitor is all right," Kennedy said, looking at the TV set that serves as a test vehicle. "But the camera ought to be brought up." He was a veteran of such encounters with the all-seeing video eye and knew by now what devices he needed to come across best on the home screen. Technicians adjusted their equipment. "Three minutes," one of them said.

The President sat gently, favoring his always-sensitive back, on the pillow of his chair.

"Thirty seconds."

Everyone in the room fell silent. The President's fingers played absently with the sheets of paper from which he would read.

"Stand by, Mr. President."

Now began what must be considered one of the most stirring of all of John F. Kennedy's eloquent speeches, one that well may, in the year 2060, be remembered as the most significant of his all-too-brief career:

Good evening, my fellow citizens. This afternoon, following a series of threats and defiant statements, the presence of Alabama Guardsmen was required to carry out the final and unequivocal order of the United States District Court of the Northern District of Alabama. That order called for the admission of two clearly qualified young Alabama residents who happened to have been born Negro.

That they were admitted peacefully on the campus is due in good measure to the conduct of the students of the University of Alabama, who met their responsibilities in a constructive way. I hope that every American, regardless of where he lives, will stop and examine his conscience about this and other related incidents. This nation was founded by men of many nations and backgrounds. It was founded on the principle that all men are created equal, and that the rights of every man are diminished when the rights of one man are threatened.

Today, we are committed to a worldwide struggle to promote and protect all of those who wish to be free, and when Americans are sent to Vietnam or West Berlin we do not ask for whites only. It ought to be possible, therefore, for American students of any color to attend any public institution they select without having to be backed up by troops. It ought to be possible for American consumers of any color to receive equal service in places of public accommodation, such as hotels and restaurants and theaters and retail stores, without being forced to resort to demonstrations in the street, and it ought to be possible for American citizens of any color to register and vote in a free election without interference or fear of reprisal.

It ought to be possible, in short, for every American to enjoy the privilege of being American without regard to his race or his color. In short, every American ought to have the right to be treated as he would wish to be treated, as one would wish his children to be treated. But this is not the case.

The Negro baby born in America today, regardless of the section or the state in which he is born, has about one-half as much chance of completing high school as a white baby born in the same place on the same day, one-third as much chance of completing college, one-third as much chance of becoming a professional man, twice as much chance of becoming unemployed, about one-seventh as much chance of earning $10,000 a year, a life expectancy which is seven years shorter and the prospects of earning only half as much.

This is not a sectional issue. Difficulties over segregation and discrimination exist in every city, in every state of the Union, producing in many cities a rising tide of discontent that threatens the public safety. Nor is this a partisan issue in a time of domestic crisis. Men of goodwill and generosity should be able to unite regardless of party or politics. This is not even a legal or legislative issue alone. It is better to settle these matters in the courts than in the streets, and new laws are needed at every level, but law alone cannot make men see right.

We are confronted primarily with a moral issue. It is as old as the Scriptures and as clear as the American Constitution. The heart of the question is whether all Americans are to be afforded equal rights and equal opportunities, whether we are going to treat our fellow Americans as we want to be treated.

If an American, because his skin is dark, cannot eat lunch in a restaurant open to the public, if he cannot send his children to the best public school available, if he cannot vote for the public officials who represent him, if, in short, he cannot enjoy the full and free life which all of us want, then who among us would be content to have the color of his skin changed and stand in his place? Who among us would then be content with the counsels of patience and delay?

One hundred years of delay have passed since President Lincoln freed the slaves; yet their heirs, their grandsons, are not fully free. They are not yet fully freed from the bonds of injustice. They are not yet freed from social and economic oppression, and this nation, for all its hopes and all its boasts, will not be fully free until all its citizens are free. . . .

The events in Birmingham and elsewhere have so increased the desires for equality that no city or state or legislative body can prudently choose to ignore them. The fires of frustration and discord are burning in every city, North and South, where legal remedies are not at hand. Redress is sought in the streets, in demonstrations, parades and protests which create tensions and threaten violence and threaten lives.

We face, therefore, a moral crisis as a country and as a people. It cannot be met by repressive police action. It cannot be left to increased demonstrations in the streets. It cannot be quieted by token moves or tort. It is a time to act in the Congress, in your state and local legislative body and, above all, in all of our daily lives.

It is not enough to pin the blame on others, to say this is a problem of one section of the country or another, or deplore it. The fact that we face a great change is at hand and our task, our obligation, is to make that revolution, that change, peaceful and constructive for all. Those who do nothing are inviting shame, as well as violence. Those who act boldly are recognizing right, as well as reality.

Next week, I shall ask the Congress of the United States to act, to make a commitment it has not fully made in this century to the proposition that race has no place in American life or law. The federal judiciary has upheld that proposition in a series of forthright cases. The executive branch has adopted that proposition in the conduct of its affairs, including the employment of federal personnel, the use of federal facilities and the sale of federally financed housing.

But there are other necessary measures which only the Congress can provide, and they must be provided at this session. The old code of equity law under which we live demands for every wrong a remedy, but in too many communities, in too many parts of the country, wrongs are inflicted on Negro citizens and there are no remedies at law. Unless the Congress acts, their only remedy is the street.

I am, therefore, asking the Congress to enact legislation giving all Americans the right to be served in facilities which are open to the public—hotels, restaurants, theaters, retail stores and similar establishments. This seems to me to be an elementary right. Its denial is an arbitrary indignity that no American in 1963 should have to endure, but many do. . . .

I am also asking Congress to authorize the federal government to participate more fully in law suits designed to end segregation in public education. We have succeeded in persuading many districts to desegregate voluntarily. Dozens have admitted Negroes without violence. Today, a Negro is attending a state-supported institution in every one of our 50 states, but the pace is very slow. Too many Negro children entering segregated grade schools at the time of the Supreme Court's decision nine years ago will enter segregated high schools this fall, having suffered a loss which can never be restored. The lack of an adequate education denies the Negro a chance to get a decent job.

The implementation of the Supreme Court decision, therefore, cannot be left solely to those who may not have the economic resources to carry the legal action or who may be subject to harassment. Other features will also be requested, including greater protection for the right to vote. But legislation, I repeat, cannot solve this problem alone. It must be solved in the homes of every American in every community across our country. . . .

We have a right to expect the Negro community will be responsible, will uphold the law, but they have a right to expect that the law will be fair; that the Constitution will be color-blind, as Justice Harlan said at the turn of the century. This is what we are talking about and this is a matter which concerns this country and what it stands for, and in meeting it I ask the support of all of our citizens.

Thank you very much.

The President's address was greeted warmly by civil rights advocates. Dr. Martin Luther King called it "one of the most eloquent, profound and unequivocal pleas for justice and the freedom of all men ever made by any President." In a telegram to Kennedy from Birmingham, King said: "I am sure that your encouraging words will bring a new sense of hope to the millions of disinherited people of our country."

In New York, NAACP Executive Secretary Roy Wilkins said the address "gave forthright support to, and encouraged, Americans who wanted to eliminate racial discrimination." Wilkins and other Negro leaders expressed some disappointment that the address came so late in the Negro revolution. Southern leaders assailed the proposed legislation, as anticipated.

It was clear that, just as the Birmingham crisis had served as a catalyst for Negroes determined to carry their struggle into the streets, Kennedy's speech would mark the beginning of a long, bitter, but bipartisan drive to give the American Negro his long-denied freedoms.

Ahead lay the March on Washington, acrimonious congressional hearings, but eventually passage of a bill encompassing the aims set forth by the President.

The night of the President's speech, the contingent of national reporters that segregationists liked to call "the nigger junket" was breaking up again—until the next time. We sat around the Stafford Hotel restaurant, saying our goodbyes, making our travel plans, joking about the facts that at least our eyes were not running from tear gas this time.

As I walked through the Stafford lobby to an elevator, I spotted Ku Klux Klan Imperial Wizard Bobby Shelton sitting in an armchair. As usual, he was jawing with some of his cronies. Curious to get his reaction to Wallace's capitulation in the "doorway," I approached him and asked: "Well, Mr. Shelton, what did you think of the big doin's today?" He mumbled something under his breath.

I asked whether he had been satisfied that Wallace had "stood up for Alabama." He snapped: "What the hell do you think?"

I couldn't resist the temptation. "Well," I said, "we sure saw the peelin' come off the peach."

One of his companions rushed at me, shouting: "Why don't you leave this man alone? You're gonna be sorry if you don't keep away from him."

My jaws clenched. I had not meant to start a ruckus, just to apply a gentle needle to see how Shelton reacted. Now, there was the danger of an ugly scene in the middle of the lobby. But a young bellhop, bigger than either of us, stepped between us and asked us to break it up. Otherwise, he said, he would have to ask us to leave the lobby. The bellhop, who had always been very pleasant to me, later came to my room and apologized. He said the hotel could not prevent Shelton from sitting in the lobby, but did not want any trouble.

After phoning my story on the confrontation to New York, I went downstairs again to get some coffee. John Mashek was arranging plane reservations for the two of us. He planned to leave the next morning for his base in Washington. I would fly with him that far, then either remain in Washington for a day or go directly home.

Mashek would catch that plane; I would not. A long, anguished night lay ahead.

I had decided that, in view of developments in other racial crises, it would be wise to stay up rather late at night. If racists were running true to form, there would be violence this night—if not in Tuscaloosa, then somewhere else. It had happened in Birmingham several times. Let the Negroes win some small measure of equality and some white trash, usually bolstered by a few belts of distilled spirits, would go "nigger-hunting." In the South, where firearms laws are lenient and dynamite is readily accessible, it was almost inevitable.

By midnight, all appeared calm in Tuscaloosa. I had checked several times with local and state police and with National Guard officers. The city and campus seemed secure. It would be fruitless, it seemed, to stay up any longer. My office could always phone me if news of some new violence moved across the press association wires.

As I was headed for the elevator to go to my room, National Guard General Graham walked out. Karl Fleming and Pete Goldman, both of *Newsweek,* also were in the lobby. The three of us stopped to talk with Graham. A couple of other reporters joined in. Some of us, who had known Graham during the Freedom Ride crisis, renewed acquaintances. He assured us that, from his reports, all was serene. He was on his way to a meeting. If anything happened to change the situation, he said, we would hear about it.

Some of the reporters went to bed. A few of us decided to have a last cup of coffee. After that cup, everyone else drifted up to bed. I decided to phone my office one more time before going to bed. I made the call from a phone booth in the lobby. All was clear. I would catch my plane in the morning and be home the next afternoon, unless I decided to stay over in Washington.

As I again headed for the elevator, a longtime news source of mine hurried out. He will remain nameless, for his superiors would not like it if it were known he was a tipster.

"What's the rush? Where you goin'?" I asked.

"Medgar Evers just got shot in Jackson," he said. "I've got to get over there as soon as I can."

"Good Lord," I said. "I was afraid something like this would happen. But why Medgar?"

I rushed back to the phone and called my office. Roy Hanson, *Newsday*'s assistant chief copy editor, answered at the city desk. "Have the wires got anything on Medgar Evers being shot in Jackson, Mississippi?" I asked.

"Wait a minute, I'll check," he said.

A few moments later, he came back. "It's just moving now," Roy said. "Wait a minute, Dick Estrin wants to talk to you." Estrin is night news editor, the man who puts the paper's main section together.

"What have the wires got?" I asked.

"They just moved a couple of grafs [paragraphs]. It's very sketchy."

"Is Medgar dead?"

"They don't know yet. He's been taken to a hospital."

"Damn, I hope he's not dead. He's a good man. I hope to hell he's not dead." I kept saying this again and again, unable to believe that Medgar, whom I had seen and talked with numerous times only a week earlier, might be dead.

I was physically, mentally and emotionally drained. This was the last straw. I had gone three days on a total of five hours of sleep. Had I known what was good for me, I would have left the story to the wire services and gone to sleep. But something inside compelled me to offer: "Do you want me to see what I can find out from here by phone, Dick? I know Medgar pretty well. And some of the federal guys are still in town. They should be hearing something pretty soon."

Estrin said that, if I didn't mind, such help would be welcomed, since the wire services thus far had only meager information. The upshot was that I never did get to sleep that night. It was not until close to noon the next day that I finally got to bed.

When I arrived home two days later, I was exhausted. I had lost 12 pounds in a week. I took some time off to get myself back in one piece again, then went back to work.

My first day back in a reporting job (I worked an editor's shift for a few days, replacing a man on vacation), I was thrown right into the racial crisis again. But this time it was not in the South. It was in New York City, where militant civil rights groups were demonstrating on behalf of Negroes and Puerto Ricans seeking equal opportunities in construction industry labor unions.

The problem facing the Negroes and Puerto Ricans in New York was not unlike the one that had initially faced Jim Meredith at Ole Miss. Meredith ostensibly had been denied admission to the university not because he was a Negro, but because he could not produce recommendations from a half-dozen Ole Miss graduates, all of them, naturally, whites. The Negroes and Puerto Ricans in New York ostensibly had been unable to join some construction industry unions not because they were Negroes and Puerto Ricans, but because they could not produce recommendations from union members, most of them whites.

There were differences, of course. Ole Miss is a state university. Unions, although under public control, are private organizations. But these unions were doing work on projects financed by the city, state and federal governments. It was at these projects that civil rights groups swarmed on picket lines, blocked trucks from delivering cargoes, tussled with police and sang fervently the songs of the Southern Negro protest movement.

If anything had been needed to drive home President Kennedy's message that the civil rights revolution of the 1960s was not confined to one region, the demonstrations I covered in New York provided ample corroboration. At this writing, such demonstrations are still in progress all over the country.

Kennedy, like Medgar Evers, lies dead from an assassin's bullet. Both men were victims of systematic campaigns of hate-mongering by extremists of all political colorations. And still demagogues try to capitalize on the by-products of such hate-mongering. A George Wallace, while asking God to bless all Alabamans black and white, makes an ambitious effort to run for President on what can only be described as a racist platform. A Malcolm X withdraws from the Muslim sect to try to make political capital out of his own brand of racism.

It is this kind of hypocrisy, from all sides, that helps prevent reasonable men from working out reasonable solutions to difficult problems. Instead of counseling together, whites and Negroes draw apart. They stoop to name-calling, invective, claim and counterclaim. The segregationists charge integration is all a Communist plot. The militant integrationists charge some of their more reasonable supporters with being "Uncle Toms." The politicians balance the Negro vote against the segregationist–states' rights vote.

In such an atmosphere, it was inevitable that George Wallace's history of mental troubles finally would come to the public's attention. A politician of Wallace's ilk, with a positive talent for arousing the ire of those with conflicting views, was bound to butt heads one day with someone whose shrewdness and daring exceeded his own.

The someone was that abrasive gentleman from Oregon, Senator Wayne Morse. In early September, 1963, less than three months after the "doorway" episode, Morse and Wallace became involved in a running exchange of insults between Washington and Alabama. It was a childish affair, unbecoming the purported dignity of the United States Senate or the Alabama State Capitol.

On September 4, Morse denounced Wallace as a "punk." In reply, Wallace suggested that Morse "needs his head examined." This was a reckless choice of words, for it gave Morse an opportunity to go into the long-secret story of Wallace's own head examinations, if that is not a flippant term.

On September 5, Morse took the floor of the Senate and announced that Wallace was receiving disability payments for psychoneurosis incurred during the war. Referring to what he said was a Veterans' Administration report, Morse told his fellow senators:

We [he and Wallace] have a mutuality of disrespect. Khrushchev does not have a more effective ally in the United States than the governor of Alabama.

Morse then noted that Wallace "has raised some questions as to the psychiatric soundness of the senator from Oregon." He proceeded to read what he said were official records of Wallace's military service, disability and psychiatric examinations. "Since he has not been examined since November, 1956, it would seem to be appropriate for him to volunteer to be examined at this time," Morse said.

From his libel-proof sanctuary on the Senate floor, Morse read into the record five points from Wallace's VA file:

1. Governor Wallace entered active military service October 20, 1942, and was honorably discharged December 8, 1945, with the grade of sergeant in the Army Air Corps. His military specialty was that of flight engineer, with nine combat missions completed in B-29s. He participated in the offensive against Japan and earned the air medal, plus area and good-conduct medals.

2. During service, he was hospitalized from April 1, 1943, to June 3, 1943, for acute cerebral spinal meningitis. He was also hospitalized in September, 1945, for severe anxiety state, chronic, manifested by tension states, anxiety attacks, anorexia [author's note: lack of appetite] and loss of weight. It does not appear that he was disciplined for any infractions while in service.

3. He filed claim for compensation in June, 1946, and in December, 1946, was granted service connection for psychoneurosis, for which an evaluation of 10 percent was assigned.

4. He was last examined by the VA in November, 1956, when he gave his age as 37, married, three children, and was occupied as a circuit judge. He was tense, restless and ill at ease, frequently drummed the desk with his fingers, changed position frequently, sighed occasionally, showed a tendency to stammer, resulting in the diagnosis of anxiety reaction. The 10-percent rating was continued.

5. His accredited representative is the American Legion.

So now it was out in the open. Newspapers across the country carried lengthy accounts of Wallace's mental troubles. Wire services, which had spurned the story at the height of a crisis that gave it relevance, now moved stories slugged "urgent" at a time when the relevance was partly diminished. *Newsday,* I must concede, was among the papers that did not touch the story until it came over the wires, with the libel-free label of the U. S. Senate stamped on it. But, as I had said at the outset, we "honchos" only got the news; we did not decide what to do with it after we had it.

Wallace was not long in replying to Morse. No longer could he duck the issue. Now he had to stand up for himself, along with Alabama, and put his statements on the record.

Wallace issued a statement from Montgomery:

I receive 10-percent disability for a nervous condition caused by being shot at by Japanese airplanes and antiaircraft guns in combat missions during World War II. To what does Senator Morse attribute his condition?

Later in the day, Wallace issued an expanded statement:

Yes, like many other veterans who saw combat, I am nervous, like many thousands who saw combat and were shot at while in combat in Japan during World War II. I wonder if Senator Morse was shot at by enemies of this country. If not, I wonder what causes his nervousness. Maybe, as Mrs. Clare Booth Luce once said while testifying before a congressional committee, he was kicked in the head by a horse.

Severe criticism was leveled at Morse and the VA as a result of the exchange of insults. Alabama's Representative George Huddleston, Jr., demanded that the House Veterans' Affairs Committee investigate the matter. The American Medical Association newspaper accused Morse and the VA of violating Wallace's private rights.

The VA, throughout, had refused to release Wallace's records to the press. Now a VA spokesman said information about a veteran's disability could be given to a doctor, the veteran's family, legal agencies or an investigating member of Congress—but, even then, only in confidence. The VA said Morse had not requested Wallace's records and that it had not provided the records to Morse. The Senator's office would not say where he had obtained the records, but that they had not been obtained from the VA.

Wallace was not the only participant in the Alabama crisis who would suffer from attacks of anxiety and nervousness. Jimmy Hood, struggling with his conscience and his newfound role as a symbol of Negro triumph in the Deep South, was troubled by what he considered his misunderstood sentiments on racial problems.

On June 27, less than two weeks after his admission to the University of Alabama with Vivian Malone, Hood said in an article in the campus newspaper that Negroes would be better off in classrooms, instead of on picket lines. He stated:

> The protest movement should be centered around educational objectives, rather than immediate social and economic objectives such as sit-ins, lie-ins and swim-ins. I have taken a careful look at race relations and have concluded that the protest movements have resulted in, literally, a big unnecessary mess. In order for one to be accepted in a certain society, he must meet certain standards in accordance with that society in which he is seeking a position. . . . It is my firm belief that, through the process of education, the sit-ins and swim-ins will be unnecessary. There must be more time spent in the classroom and less time wasted on picket lines.

Hood meant well. He spoke from deep conviction. But his words were misunderstood by those whose esteem he valued, the civil rights workers in the militant protest movement in his hometown of Gadsden. In July, in an effort to make his position clear, he went home to Gadsden to address a meeting of protest workers. Two "spooks" from the state police subversive unit, with tape recorders, sat in the audience.

In the talk, Hood asserted that university officials were engaged in a conspiracy to drive him out of the university. The "spooks" turned over their tape recordings to Wallace's office. The Governor gave them to university offical. Proceedings aimed at expelling Hood were begun.

Sad and disillusioned, Hood withdrew from the university, giving health as the cause. He said he was physically and mentally exhausted from the ordeal that followed the "doorway" confrontation.

He, like Wallace, had been tested under stress. He, like Wallace, had faltered.

Again, Jim Meredith's words came back to me: "A Negro should have the same right to fail as a white."

Epilogue

In the late summer of 1963, I made the last Southern trip necessary for researching this book. I went to Washington, saw Attorney General Kennedy, Nick Katzenbach, Burke Marshall, Jim McShane, Ed Guthman and a number of army officers involved in various racial crises.

The North and South were still gripped by daily tension and violence. While I was in Washington, only the Attorney General's intervention in negotiations had put a halt to bloody rioting in Cambridge, Maryland.

From Washington, I headed into Virginia, the state where my wife's family had resided for generations and where we had been married. I had made many trips to Lynchburg, my wife's hometown, and thought I knew the area's people pretty well. On this trip, I found I had been mistaken.

I went to Danville, a city I had visited numerous times with my wife's father when he had been a traveling salesman. The serenity of Danville was gone. In its place was the kind of venomous hatred I had last seen in Alabama and Mississippi. Dr. Martin Luther King had brought his crusade for equality to Danville, and the white citizenry was reacting with as much initial resistance as its Birmingham counterpart. I met King, by prearrangement, at a Negro church. We talked about Birmingham, Danville and what lay ahead.

"Danville is the most critical city in the country at the moment," King said. "The potential for violence is the worst here. Sixty-nine Negroes have already been hospitalized—not from the work of the hoodlum elements, but from the brutality of the local police." He said Danville would be the site of the next big push by his organization.

Over the long haul, King saw greater problems north of the Mason-Dixon line than south of it. "The problem will be much more difficult in the North," he said. "There, the resistance will be much more sophisticated and more difficult to overcome."

At the Negro church, as FBI agents watched from outside, I heard again the stirring sound of a multitude of Negroes singing with determination: "Black and white together, we shall overcome, someday!"

Two days later, I was in another Negro church, in Farmville, seat of Prince Edward County. This was the county whose Negro children had been deprived of schooling for four years when the public schools were closed because of a bitter court wrangle over desegregation. In Farmville, I met Bonnie Angelo, then a member of *Newsday*'s Washington bureau (who joined the Newhouse newspaper a few weeks later). Bonnie, a Southerner, had won the Paul Tobenkin award—given for outstanding reporting on civil-liberties problems—for a penetrating series of articles on Prince Edward County.

We spent two days watching a group of teachers and prospective teachers from New York who had come voluntarily to Virginia on their summer vacations, trying to give the county's Negro children a cram course that would prepare them for the opening of a private academy. The New Yorkers, whites and Negroes, had a difficult time. They quarreled over everything from teaching techniques to whether it was proper for young women to wear shorts on the streets of Farmville. But in the end they accomplished their mission. In the fall, a private biracial academy sponsored by an out-of-state foundation—and formed with the unofficial cooperation of the Justice Department—opened its doors in Prince Edward County. Negroes who had been denied admission to the tax-supported private academies set up previously for white students were back in school once more.

On my way to Lynchburg from Prince Edward County, I made a stop at Appomattox Court House, where, almost 100 years earlier, the War Between the States had ended and 100 years of disappointment and frustration for Negroes had begun. I tramped the fields of the national historical park at Appomattox for hours. A guide from the National Park Service took a number of visitors, including me, on a tour. He explained what had happened at various historic spots.

We entered the McLean House, the two-story home where General Robert E. Lee had surrendered to General Ulysses S. Grant on April 9, 1865. The guide gave us each a pamphlet to help us grasp his account. I became intrigued with the pamphlet and lagged behind the others, reading. The pamphlet stated:

Grant climbed the steps of the McLean House. Two years earlier, Wilmer McLean had left Manassas to escape the war; now the war was to end in his parlor. Inside, Lee rose to meet the man whose armies he had fended off for nearly a year. . . .

The two men sat in McLean's parlor, talking of the Mexican War and old Army days. Grant's staff officers, who had entered with him, remained at a respectful distance, lining the walls of the room. After a time, Lee turned the conversation to the business at hand. Grant, with quiet humility, offered surrender terms generous in every way. Officers could keep their sidearms and horses. Men in the rank and file who owned horses or mules could keep them, Grant said, "to work their little farms."

"This will have the best possible effect upon the men," replied Lee. "It will be very gratifying and will do much toward conciliating our people."

The terms of surrender were drafted in final form, and Lee and Grant signed them. . . . Afterward, waiting for an orderly to bring his horse, Lee stood on the porch—gazing eastward. He seemed lost in reverie and unconscious of the yard full of Union officers. . . . Manassas, Chancellorsville, Gettysburg, the Wilderness—all had but led to this. Sergeant Tucker brought up Traveler, the big iron-gray horse. Rousing himself suddenly, Lee swung into the saddle. . . .

Grant, just leaving the house, stopped abruptly and raised his hat. The other federal officers standing about followed his example. Lee returned the salute and rode from the yard, back eastward, through the village and over the river to his waiting men. . . .

My thoughts raced to Oxford, Mississippi, and the Mary Buie Museum. There I had seen Mississippians lavish near-adoration on a twist of hair from the tail of Lee's horse. I had seen some of these same Mississippians mount an armed insurrection against the United States government.

I thought of the respect shown by two old soldiers, Grant and Lee, for each other and for their divergent beliefs. Then I thought of two other former military men, George Wallace and John F. Kennedy. What respect had Wallace shown for his commander in chief? What respect had he shown for his President's beliefs? Was he really upholding the "Southern way of life" for which Lee and so many other soldiers of the Confederacy had fought so valiantly? Of was he merely trying to capitalize on this "way of life" for his own political ends?

The other members of the guided tour came downstairs. I stayed behind after they had left. Curious about one point, I asked the guide to answer another question: "Have you had any integration problems around this county?"

"It's funny," the guide replied. "You might have thought we would have—this being the place where the war ended. But, awhile back, about a half-dozen colored folks walked into the drugstore downtown. They sat down at the counter. Nobody batted an eye. The waitress asked them what they'd have. They ordered some coffee. And that was all there was to it. Nobody paid any attention or thought it was anything to get excited about."

I had my answer.

Acknowledgments

A book such as this is the product of many hours of legwork, reading, interviews and evaluations. Much of it is a distillation of the recollections of persons with differing motives and memories. Making no attempt to differentiate between those who wished me well or ill, I would like particularly to thank the following persons for being good enough to spare me the time to discuss their roles in the civil rights struggle of the 1960s:

Attorney General Robert F. Kennedy; his capable aides, Nick Katzenbach, Burke Marshall, Jim McShane, Ed Guthman, John Doar, John Nolan and Joe Dolan; Dean Markham of the White House staff; James H. Meredith; former Governor Ross Barnett; Mississippi National Guard Captain Murry C. Falkner; Bill Simmons of the Citizens Councils; Lieutenant Colonel Lucius Gordon Hill of the Department of the Army's headquarters information staff; the Reverend Dr. Martin Luther King and his aides, the Reverend Wyatt Walker, the Reverend Ralph Abernathy and the Reverend Fred Shuttlesworth; that gracious and courageous lady, Mrs. Constance Baker Motley of the NAACP Legal Defense and Educational Fund; and Bobby Shelton, Imperial Wizard of the Knights of the Ku Klux Klan.

To William Bradford Huie I am indebted for advice and encouragement. To Miss Elizabeth Otis, Richard Kennedy and Ross Claiborne, my thanks for faith, patience and advice.

To my wife, Jeanne, and daughters, Pamela and Patricia, my gratitude for not disowning me during a year of absences from the family circle.

It would be impossible to list all the law enforcement

officers to whom I am indebted for information—not to say protection. It would also be impossible to enumerate the reporters who have provided bits and pieces of information for this book.

I would like, however, to name a few of the members of Southern Correspondents on Racial Equality Wars (SCREW), who have been both good friends and staunch allies: Claude Sitton and Hedrick Smith of *The New York Times;* Fred Powledge, formerly of the *Atlanta Journal,* now on the *Times;* Charlie Whiteford of the *Baltimore Sun;* Ray Coffey of the *Chicago Daily News;* Joe Cumming and Karl Fleming of *Newsweek;* Tom Yarbrough of the *St. Louis Post-Dispatch;* Warren Rogers of Hearst Headline Service; Jack Steele of Scripps-Howard Newspaper Alliance; Stan Opotowsky of the *New York Post;* and one honorary member, to whom I am deeply indebted for a purely personal favor, Red Holland of the *Birmingham News.*

It goes without saying that this book would have been impossible if *Newsday*'s editors had not seen the wisdom of covering the civil rights revolution in such detail.

Many persons with divergent motives, from a skeptical Ross Barnett to a helpful Ed Guthman, have offered to read the manuscript in advance to guard against errors of fact or interpretation. I have politely refused all such offers, on the theory that the interpretations—for better or worse—should be mine. I accept responsibility for any errors. I do, however, reassert that I have tried to be objective on a subjective topic.